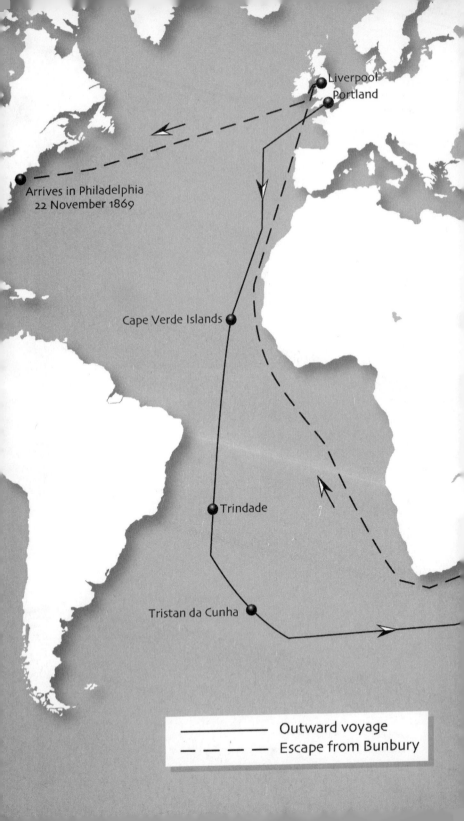

Liverpool
Portland

Arrives in Philadelphia
22 November 1869

Cape Verde Islands

Trindade

Tristan da Cunha

Outward voyage
Escape from Bunbury

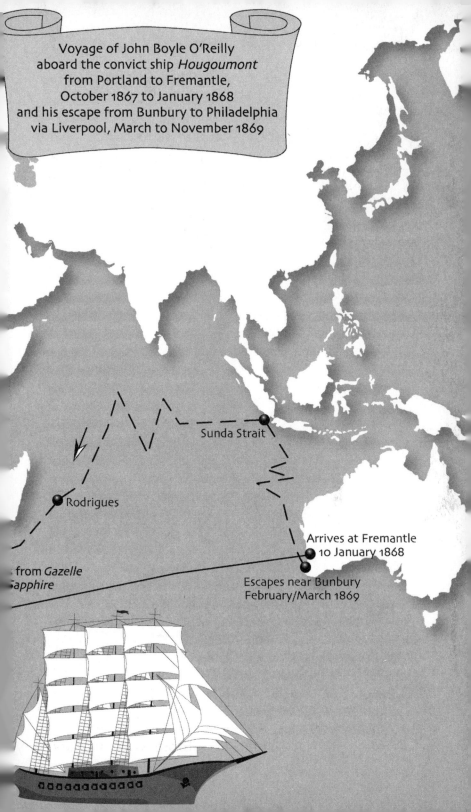

Voyage of John Boyle O'Reilly
aboard the convict ship *Hougoumont*
from Portland to Fremantle,
October 1867 to January 1868
and his escape from Bunbury to Philadelphia
via Liverpool, March to November 1869

Sunda Strait

Rodrigues

Arrives at Fremantle
10 January 1868

from *Gazelle*
Sapphire

Escapes near Bunbury
February/March 1869

FROM
THE EARTH,
A CRY

IAN KENNEALLY, from County Limerick, studied at University College Cork where he completed an MPhil in History. He is currently researching a PhD at NUI Galway. He combines his love of travel and history in his writing. *The Paper Wall* and *Courage & Conflict* are his previous books.

www.iankenneally.com

For Fiona

FROM THE EARTH, A CRY

The Story of John Boyle O'Reilly

IAN KENNEALLY

The Collins Press

First published in Ireland in 2011 by
The Collins Press
West Link Park
Doughcloyne
Wilton
Cork

British Library Cataloguing in Publication data
Kenneally, Ian.
1. O'Reilly, John Boyle, 1844-1890. 2. Journalists—
Ireland—Biography. 3. Fenians—Biography. 4. Political
prisoners—Ireland—Biography. 5. Ireland—History—
1837–1901—Biography. 6. Newspaper editors—United
States—Biography. 7. Irish—Massachusetts—Boston—
Biography. 8. Poets, Irish—19th century—Biography.

I. Title
941.5'081'092-dc22

ISBN-13: 9781848891319

Typesetting by Red Barn Publishing
Typeset in ArnoPro 10.5/13.5
Printed in Sweden by ScandBook AB

Cover photographs
Front (main) and spine: John Boyle O'Reilly photographed in Mountjoy Prison during 1866
(New York Public Library).
Bottom panel (l–r): lithograph of the Battle of Ridgeway, 1866 (US Library of Congress, LC-
DIG-pga-01485); the *Catalpa* (US Library of Congress, LC-USZ62-12755); John Boyle
O'Reilly in Father Teeling's summer house, *c.* 1888 (Donahoe's Magazine, September 1893).

MIX
Paper from
responsible sources
FSC
www.fsc.org   FSC® C007584

Contents

Acknowledgements

The life of John Boyle O'Reilly was lived on an epic canvas and he has left traces of his story in Ireland, England, Australia and the United States. I would like to take this opportunity to thank all the many people who have helped in the production of this book. First, I would like to thank everyone at The Collins Press and my editor Cathy Thompson. Once again, I owe a debt of gratitude to staff in many libraries and archives. I would like to thank the staff at John J. Burns Library of Boston College, Boston Public Library, New York Public Library, J.S. Battye Library of Western Australian History in Perth, James Hardiman Library of NUI Galway, National Library of Ireland, National Archives of Ireland and the National Archives of the United Kingdom. I would also like to thank the staff in the Special Collections section of the Boole Library at University College, Cork. The fact that the Boole Library holds a complete collection of *The Pilot* newspaper was of immense value to my research.

I would like to thank my brother, Enda, who again acted as a research assistant and who did vital work in the United States. Both he and my wife, Fiona, read the manuscript and provided their thoughts. Billy Phillips and Dr Gerald Naughton also read sections of the manuscript and offered their advice. Thanks also to Dr Michael Curran for offering me his insights into O'Reilly's medical history. I must also thank the archivist Gillian O'Mara. She took time to answer my queries on O'Reilly's time in Australia. Of course the usual proviso applies that any errors, omissions or misinterpretations are my fault.

I would like to thank my parents, my sister and all my family, in Limerick, Westmeath and Cork, for their love and support. Finally, I would like to thank my beloved Fiona.

1

Early Life

In June 1963 the President of the United States, John F. Kennedy, visited Ireland, the country of his ancestors. While there, he addressed a joint session of the Oireachtas, the Republic of Ireland's national parliament. Kennedy, in a brilliant speech, spoke of the historical links between the United States and Ireland and he invoked the names of Thomas Francis Meagher, James Hoban, Daniel O'Connell, Robert Emmet, John Barry and Charles Stewart Parnell as proof of this shared heritage. But Ireland was only a starting point for Kennedy's oratory and he then described the common bonds of humanity that transcended race, politics, religion and geography: 'And no nation, large or small, can be indifferent to the fate of others, near or far. Modern economics, weaponry and communications have made us all realise more than ever that we are one human family and this one planet is our home.' To underline his point the US President quoted a once famous Irish poet: '"The world is large," wrote John Boyle O'Reilly. "The world is large when its weary leagues two loving hearts divide. But the world is small when your enemy is loose on the other side."' Kennedy continued, 'The world is even smaller today, though the enemy of John Boyle O'Reilly is no longer a hostile power . . . The supreme reality of our time is our indivisibility as children of God and our common vulnerability on this planet.'[1] Whether Kennedy had a deep knowledge of O'Reilly's work is unclear but the President's use of an O'Reilly poem to stress 'our common vulnerability' suggests an understanding of the Irishman's life. O'Reilly was a particularly apt choice with which to explore the themes of equality and humanitarianism.

He was remembered in the United States not only as a poet but as an opponent of oppression and a dedicated proponent of black civil rights. For over twenty years in the late nineteenth century the County Meath-born newspaper editor had used the Boston newspaper, *The Pilot*, as a means by which to attack the hypocrisy and injustice of racism. In Ireland O'Reilly was similarly remembered as a poet but he was celebrated more for his actions as a Fenian and his involvement in such legendary escapades as the *Catalpa* rescue. He was a man whose life story seemed to fulfil all the requirements for a hero of Irish nationalist mythology. Yet O'Reilly had a long and torturous relationship with the Fenians. His membership of that organisation had a profound effect on his life. It resulted in him being convicted as a rebel, after which he spent time in a variety of English jails from Millbank to Dartmoor. He was later transported as a convict to the penal colony of Western Australia aboard one of the most famous of all convict ships, the *Hougoumont*. The voyage of the *Hougoumont* has, understandably, drawn the attention of many writers over the years but fact and fiction have often been freely intermingled. This book will follow O'Reilly aboard the ship and examine his life as an Australian convict. The best-known aspect of O'Reilly's convict years is his truly remarkable escape from that continent. However, on its own, it is a feat that would not have merited the fame that later followed the Irishman in the United States. O'Reilly was a public figure throughout his life in that country and he played an important role in the political, economic, religious and literary circles of Boston in the second half of the nineteenth century. His work as a newspaper editor and writer brought him into contact with a range of renowned American personalities such as Walt Whitman, Wendell Phillips and Frederick Douglass. O'Reilly's continued commitment to Ireland meant that he was a friend and colleague of John Devoy, Michael Davitt and Charles Stewart Parnell, among many others.

O'Reilly was a prolific writer during his career: over twenty years of editorials in *The Pilot*; four books of poetry; one novel; one collaborative novel; and a host of speeches and articles. All his writing is available in various archives and forms the bulk of any study of O'Reilly's life. With this information we can assess the man and the career, as well as the personal beliefs, influences and events that formed his character. In the course of this book O'Reilly's voice will be heard through the use of his journalism, his poetry and his fiction. His poems, for example, made O'Reilly a beloved figure to many and he received a string of important commissions in the United States. O'Reilly's poetry has rarely been addressed in anything other than perfunctory, sometimes patronising, terms but that poetry is of consequence because, through it, the author explained how he saw the world. An examination of his literary endeavours also helps to reveal some aspects of O'Reilly's life and character that were not always apparent in his other work. Despite this voluminous amount of material, a constraining factor in any study of his life is the relative paucity of personal papers. There are few surviving letters and there is no diary or memoir that we can consult. This issue will be addressed, as it arises, throughout the book but the lack of personal records means that there will be times when no answers can be provided to the questions raised by O'Reilly's story. However, the book will attempt to tease out possible explanations in such cases where the evidence is partial or, as in some cases, completely lacking. Also, surprisingly, little has been written on O'Reilly since his death. Nevertheless, there have been works of great quality that have addressed different aspects of his life. Those historians and writers who have examined the career of O'Reilly since 1890 and whose work I have built upon will receive due mention throughout the text.

O'Reilly lived a life of extraordinary vitality whose details, such as his transportation and later escape, could easily be skewed to tell a tale comprised only of derring-do and romanticism. Those aspects of his life are vital to any understanding of O'Reilly but they are merely parts of the story. He was a complex man whose character can sometimes be elusive and whose work is often riven with contradiction. It will, at times, be necessary to depart from the narrative and to engage in a more thematic approach to O'Reilly's life. Different paths will be followed throughout the book: the soldier; the Fenian; the convict; the newspaper editor; the novelist; the poet; the family man; the civil rights activist; the immigrant; and many more facets of the personality that so enthralled those who knew him. This book will attempt to unify these diverse elements and so tell his story.

Very little is known about O'Reilly's childhood and teenage years. What glimpses we can have of this time are found in papers at Boston College's John J. Burn's Library, the National Archives of Ireland and in the pages of James Jeffrey Roche's biography of O'Reilly, which was published in 1891. Roche was a colleague and close friend of O'Reilly during his time in Boston and he knew many of O'Reilly's family and friends. His well-written biography is often hagiographical but it is still a vital resource, containing many documents from O'Reilly's life. Even so, much of the information on O'Reilly's youth is anecdotal although an outline can be pieced together. O'Reilly's parents were Eliza Boyle and William David O'Reilly. They were both Catholics and married in Dublin sometime during the 1830s before moving to County Meath.[2] Their destination was Dowth, a village set in a bend of the river Boyne between the village of Slane and the town of Drogheda in neighbouring County Louth. It is uncertain when they made this move. It may have been in 1836 but definitely no later than the birth of their first child, Margaret, in January 1841. A second child, William, followed in August 1842. John, the third of eight children, joined the family on 28 June 1844.[3] William David had wanted to name the new arrival after Daniel O'Connell, perhaps inspired by 'The Liberator's' repeal rally at the nearby Hill of Tara during 1843.[4] However, Eliza insisted that the child be named after the men in her family line and so the boy was christened John Boyle O'Reilly on 18 July 1844. The family, at this time, resided in Dowth Castle, a short distance from the village, although their existence was not as salubrious as the address may suggest. The castle and the surrounding lands had been owned by the Netterville family for centuries. However, in 1780 the sixth Viscount Netterville abandoned the castle in favour of Dowth Hall, a new domestic residence. By the early nineteenth century the castle, a square three-storey structure, was in disrepair but on his death in 1826 the Viscount left funds for the building to be renovated as a charitable institute for destitute widows and orphans. Eliza Boyle, after her arrival in Dowth, became the manager of the orphanage. Roche described her as 'a woman of rare intellectual gifts, combined with a generous, hospitable, kindly heart, which made her beloved by the beneficiaries of the Institution.'[5] She was also adored by her children and the young John seems to have been far closer to his mother than his father. The castle, now operating under the name of the Netterville Institute, was host to a local national school from 1836. A board of Commissioners for National Education had been established by the British government in 1831 and they directed funds towards such schools and the provision of teachers. William David O'Reilly was one of these and was appointed the schoolmaster of the Dowth Castle national school, which had been set up in the castle's old chapel. He was paid an annual salary of £15 but the elder O'Reilly was not a successful teacher. In 1855 a school inspector rebuked him over his pupils' poor performance in 'arithmetic and penmanship'. The next year the schoolmaster was fined £1 for his continuing poor performance. However, the Dubliner was a successful disciplinarian. In 1857, the Assistant Commissioner of the National School Board visited Dowth and was probably not surprised to find that the pupils were underperforming, bemoaning the fact that 'None of them can parse a sentence'. The Assistant Commissioner did find some solace in his observation that the children were orderly and 'well regulated'.[6]

He may not have been an effective teacher but William David's salary, allied to that of his wife, had helped to insulate the family from the misery which the Great Famine inflicted upon Ireland. The experience of the O'Reilly family appears to have been replicated across the country, in that public servants with a steady income were far better equipped to survive the turmoil of the times. The well-documented early history of John Phillip Holland, who would later become famous in the United States through his work on submarines, provides a parallel to that of John Boyle O'Reilly. Holland had been born during 1841 in Clare, a county which suffered very badly during the Famine. However, his father had likewise been a public servant, although in his case it was with the coastal service rather than as a teacher. The Holland family, while not unscathed by the Famine, were able to maintain a standard of life that was unavailable to many of those around them.[7] So it was with the O'Reillys. Their situation was further helped by their location in a part of the country that was not as badly affected by the Famine as the more distressed areas of the west and south. Yet County Meath did suffer the effects of crop failure and disease. Geraldine Stout, who has written on the Boyne Valley region of the county, shows that famine-related illnesses were prevalent in the area. Rossnaree, a few miles from Dowth, was hit by an epidemic of cholera in the 1840s, while the population of east Meath fell by 14 per cent over the decade 1841–1851.[8]

Not only were the O'Reilly family relatively safe but John was probably too young to remember the worst of the Famine. Nor would he have remembered Europe's 'year of revolutions' and the failed Young Ireland rebellion of 1848. In later years O'Reilly described his childhood to Roche. While his account may have been tinged with nostalgia, it does seem to have been a happy childhood and one that O'Reilly recalled fondly. His recollections betray little in the way of hardship but include events such as the time a friend presented the nine-year-old O'Reilly with 'a brown, broad-backed, thick-legged, round-bodied, spaniel puppy, about a month old . . . that could not walk through the meadow, but had to jump over every tangled spot, and miss five times out of six, and fall and roll over when at last he succeeded.'[9] 'Its possession', he remembered, 'was one of the delicious incidents, and is now one of the delicious memories of my life.' Roche wrote that O'Reilly was lucky to have a 'good constitution' and throughout his youth 'was passionately devoted to out-door sports'.[10] This was a characteristic that would remain constant through his entire life. He had a large circle of friends and was the family favourite. O'Reilly's older sister Margaret later recalled that: 'His smile was irresistible but I think his greatest charm was in his manner. From earliest childhood he was a favorite with everybody, and yet the wildest boy in Dowth. If any mischievous act was committed in the neighborhood, John was blamed, yet everybody loved him and would hide him from my father when in disgrace.'[11]

O'Reilly, as he later said of his childhood, 'was born among books' and was devoted to the works of William Shakespeare.[12] From his early days he had a deep curiosity about the past. Such was his enthusiasm that he would often read historical tales to his friends. One childhood friend remembered that O'Reilly would read aloud books about Theobald Wolfe Tone and the United Irishmen Rebellion of 1798. Another friend of O'Reilly remembered how John would call to her family's house to hear her father tell stories from Irish history: 'He never tired listenin' to talk about Robert Emmet an' when my father'd stop talking the question'd often be, 'Will there ever be a rising' again . . . ?' 'Maybe there would, avic, maybe there would', is what my father'd always say to him.'[13] O'Reilly was also aware of current affairs. His earliest known poem was written when he was eleven years old and lamented the death, in 1855, of Frederick Lucas, founder of the Catholic journal *Tablet*. Lucas was a leader of the Irish Tenant League, which sought fair rent, fixity of tenure and free sale for Irish tenants:

> He is gone, he is gone, to a world more serene
> Than the one in which our most true friend has been.
> He is pale as the swan, he is cold as the wave,
> And his honored head lies low in the deep, hollow grave.

His death has caused sorrow throughout our green isle,
For now he is gone, he'll no more on us smile.
And now is his poor brow as cold as the lead,
Because our beloved Frederick Lucas is dead.[14]

John would leave the national school in Dowth that same year after his older brother William contracted tuberculosis. The illness meant that William had to give up his position as an apprentice with the *Drogheda Argus* newspaper. This was a potential disaster for the family as they stood to lose the £50 they had paid to the newspaper to cover the cost of William's apprenticeship. John volunteered to take his brother's place, an offer to which the newspaper owner agreed.[15]

He worked as a 'printer's devil', a job that involved fetching type and ink for the printers. It was not physically demanding work but the hours were long: 6 a.m. to 9 a.m., then breakfast; 10 a.m. to 2 p.m., then dinner; and 3 p.m. to 7 p.m. (sometimes later), then supper.[16] His salary for this was 2s. 6d. a week. In taking this job, the young O'Reilly was setting a pattern that would remain in place throughout his life. Not only would he later return to journalism but he always remained a prodigiously hard worker. Even as an eleven-year-old this trait of O'Reilly's was evident and he had soon doubled his salary. O'Reilly enjoyed his time as an apprentice and, bearing in mind his lament for Frederick Lucas, his developing political awareness must have found a welcome home on the paper. The *Drogheda Argus* was a weekly that had supported the Irish Tenant League throughout the 1850s, as well as the short-lived Independent Irish Party, a grouping of Irish members of parliament who had agreed to vote together on issues such as tenants' rights. The Drogheda paper, according to Roche, was the first to publish an O'Reilly poem (although, as the poems in the paper are unsigned, it is impossible to judge which poem or poems were written by the apprentice). This work came to an end during 1859 when the owner of the *Argus* died and O'Reilly found himself released from his apprenticeship. The fifteen-year-old returned to the family home in Dowth but his period of unemployment was to be brief. In August of that year the O'Reillys received a visit from James Watkinson. An English ship's captain from Preston in Lancashire, Watkinson was John's uncle, having married Eliza Boyle's sister Christiana (Crissy). He was a merchant sailor whose ship, the *Caledonian*, was then carrying a cargo of barley from Ireland to England. Watkinson invited John to accompany him back to England. With no other prospects in sight, John accepted the invitation and in late August or early September 1859 set sail for Preston.

The town of Preston, at that time, was thriving economically. Its population had expanded to around 80,000, having numbered only about 10,000 people at the beginning of the century. This rise in population was a direct result of the continual influx of immigrants seeking work in Lancashire's cotton mills. The emigrants poured in from the surrounding countryside and also Ireland, especially in the years after the Famine. Consequently, the town had a strong Irish community. Initially there was not enough housing for these new arrivals and there was 'a rash of unregulated building based not on providing a solid roof over people's heads in so much as to get as much rent out of as many people as possible.'[17] This overcrowding was worsened by a lack of clean water or proper sanitation and meant that much of the city's population lived in squalor. Yet O'Reilly would be spared the fate that awaited most Irish and English migrants to Preston. The Watkinsons were not rich but had a relatively secure lifestyle in their house at 81 Barton Terrace, Deepdale Road, not too far from the town centre.[18]

O'Reilly became a lodger in their home and within a few weeks the young Irishman had obtained a position with one of the town's newspapers, the *Preston Guardian*. Over time he would graduate from being a printer to a reporter, learning shorthand in the process. It was primarily a trade and agricultural paper that also carried items of local interest and O'Reilly quickly established himself as a fixture in the community. Sometime in the summer of 1860 the journalist joined Company 2 of the local militia, the 11th Lancashire Rifle Volunteers. He was an enthusiastic part-time soldier and over the next few years would become a non-commissioned officer.[19] The 11th Lancashire Rifle Volunteers had been set up only in 1859 and O'Reilly's involvement provided an interesting hint as to his success in Preston. Each member of the militia had to pay a yearly subscription of one guinea, while officers had to pay five guineas. Ostensibly this subscription was to pay for uniforms and equipment but it had a second aim in that the subscription helped to exclude 'the working-class element'.[20]

Apart from the drilling and field excursions undertaken with the 11th Rifles, O'Reilly regularly attended Sunday Mass at St Ignatius' Church as well as involving himself with an amateur theatrical group. Each Christmas he turned a room of the *Guardian's* office into a little theatre where he helped produce plays for the children of friends and colleagues.[21] Other than these snippets not much else is known of O'Reilly's years in Preston but he loved his time in the Lancashire town. Writing to a friend in 1881, he reminisced:

> It is pleasant to be remembered kindly through nearly twenty years of absence. To me every impression of Preston has kept its sharp outline. Yet I have been very busy and very unsettled during that time ... But all the years and events fade when I think of dear old Preston – and I find myself on the Ribble in an outrigger, striking away under Walton heights, or pulling a race with Mr P. between the bridges. Do you remember the day we went to Ribchester, and then walked up along the river to Stonyhurst? Somehow that day stands out as one of the happiest and brightest in my life. I remember every incident as if it were yesterday. Though I lived only a few years in Preston, I love it and the friends I made there better than any I have since known. In worldly way I have prospered; and in literary repute I stand well in this country. I am busy from morning till night. But under all the changed appearances and surroundings the stream of my old friendships and pleasures flows steadily along.[22]

This happy time would end in March 1863 when O'Reilly resigned from the *Preston Guardian* and the 11th Rifles and returned to Ireland. Why he left Preston is not clear although Roche claimed that O'Reilly's father summoned his son back to Ireland.[23]

It seems that William David O'Reilly then told John to find himself a job in an Irish newspaper. Whether the son ignored this request by his father or was unable to find any work in a newspaper office is unknown, but around two months later John Boyle O'Reilly travelled to Dundalk and enlisted in the British army.[24] He joined the 10th Hussars, a cavalry regiment, more popularly known as 'The Prince of Wales' Own' due to the presence of the future King Edward VII among its officers (although he was not in Ireland while O'Reilly was with the regiment). The regiment had most recently seen action during the Crimean War of 1853–1856 but was now stationed in various barracks around Ireland. O'Reilly may have spent some time after his enlistment in Dundalk and was certainly stationed in Cahir, County Tipperary, for around nine months, although the dates of his deployment there are uncertain.[25] Finally he was moved to Dublin, where he was stationed in Islandbridge Barracks, on the south bank of the river Liffey (it would later be known as Clancy Barracks). His first two years in the 10th, from 1863 to 1865, were relatively quiet: a life of parading, guard duty and training manoeuvres. O'Reilly loved the pageantry of life in a cavalry regiment, especially the blue uniform. He later admitted that, while carrying communiqués and orders from one barracks to another, he often made sure to ride by large shop windows so as to admire his reflection.[26]

Years later, a manuscript was found among O'Reilly's papers that contained a scene from his army life. Called 'The Picket of the Dragoons' the document described a 'bright March morning' on the quay by the River Liffey.[27] A mounted picket of dragoons were on their way to Dublin Castle. The picket, comprised of twelve regular troops, a sergeant and a corporal, rode in a leisurely manner until they saw a lady on the footpath a little distance away:

> Oh! the subtle influence of the sex. Every man in the picket sat a little straighter, and even the horses seemed to curve their necks until their lips kissed the brazen boss of the breastplate. It was a sweet moment for the sergeant. He leaned forward, taking the reins in his right hand a moment to pat the horse's neck with his left white-gauntleted hand, which was next the sidewalk. Then he sat easily back, right hand on thigh again, and blandly turned to beam on the admiring divinity. Rare moment! Only he who has worn war-paint knows the meaning of it. The foam-fleck on the bit, the shining color of the chain on the horse's neck, the reminding touch of the hilt against the thigh, – all these common, daily things are felt anew, with a fresh significance known to the recruit, when they are mirrored in the admiring, ignorant eyes of womanhood.[28]

There is no hint in such light-hearted reminiscences that the 10th Hussars were stationed in a country that was simmering with discontent. Nor is there any indication that O'Reilly was following political developments in Ireland or was in any way perturbed by the state of the country. To his officers it appeared that O'Reilly was a model soldier who would progress well in his military career. Yet, in 1865, a young revolutionary named John Devoy would enter O'Reilly's life and play a role in sending the soldier on a dangerous new path.

2

Soldier

While O'Reilly had been earning his living as a journalist and then as a soldier in the British army, a new revolutionary organisation had, slowly at first but then more steadily, expanded its presence in Ireland. This was the Irish Republican Brotherhood (IRB) and it was an organisation that would have a profound impact on O'Reilly's life. The Brotherhood had been formed in 1858 out of the debris left by the Young Ireland movement's defeat in July 1848. The new organisation's main architects were two veterans of that defeat: James Stephens and John O'Mahony. Stephens, from Kilkenny, had been an apprentice railway engineer before 1848 but fled to Paris after the rising. O'Mahony from County Limerick was from a wealthier background and owned a large farm near Carrick-on-Suir in County Waterford. By 1848, however, he was penniless, having transferred ownership of the land to his sister before fleeing Ireland after the rising. O'Mahony followed Stephens to Paris in the winter of 1848, where they both lived for the next few years. There is much speculation as to the extent to which the two men involved themselves in the myriad revolutionary groups then active in the French capital. It seems likely that they were never more than low-level operatives in any group they may have joined but their time in Paris afforded both men ample opportunity to 'immerse themselves in the ethos of radicalism and revolution that had already reached out to them in Ireland and which was redolent of oath-taking, conspiracy and secret fraternity.'[1]

O'Mahony moved to the United States in 1853 where he, along with another Young Irelander, Michael Doheny, established the Emmet Monument Association (EMA), named after the revolutionary Robert

Emmet. The two men were still motivated by Young Ireland ideals. During 1847 and 1848 leading Young Irelanders Fintan Lalor and John Mitchel had argued that the Famine had exposed the nature of British rule in Ireland. Mitchel wrote that the government was unaccountable to the people and 'above law', that trial by jury in Ireland was a 'fraud' and that all British professions of impartial government in Ireland were 'false'.[2] Thus, the British government had no moral or legal claim to rule Ireland. Mitchel called for complete independence through revolution while Lalor wrote that Dublin Castle and the British government 'may be lawfully, and ought to be, resisted by any and every means of force whatsoever.'[3] Consequently, the goal of the EMA was to foster an uprising in Ireland that would result in independence from Britain.

However the EMA met with little success among the Irish in the United States and by 1855 was practically defunct. Both O'Mahony and Doheny realised that there was little point in having an Irish revolutionary organisation in America unless a counterpart existed in Ireland. O'Mahony contacted Stephens about the possibility of a similar group to the EMA being founded in Ireland and over the next three years there were regular interactions between the two men. Stephens returned to Ireland from Paris in 1856 and, throughout that year and 1857, he toured the country with another former Young Irelander, Thomas Clarke Luby. During the tour Stephens met with other veterans of 1848 and tried to garner support for a new organisation. The year 1857 seemed a propitious moment to advance these plans. The Indian rebellion of that year suggested that the British Empire was vulnerable. This impression was strengthened by the struggles of the British army to contain the violence and the vicious manner in which it ultimately defeated the rebellion. There was a chance, Stephens believed, that a transatlantic Irish revolutionary organisation could succeed in providing enough men, weapons and money to defeat the British army in Ireland. During his journey around the country Stephens had found potential recruits and his tour gave momentum to the idea of a new revolutionary body. By the beginning of 1858 he and O'Mahony had almost completed their negotiations on how this group would be organised.

The result of these manoeuvres was a secret society launched in Dublin on St Patrick's Day 1858. Although at this stage it had no established name, the society would become known as the Irish Republican Brotherhood. It was a military organisation but more than that it also sought to be a fraternal society that hoped to instil in Irish people an ability to think 'as befits citizens of a nation that is determined to be free'.[4] Luby later described the birth of this new society:

> on Patrick's Day, 1858 . . . the I.R.B. (Irish Revolutionary or Republican Brotherhood) movement was formally commenced. I drew up the form of oath, under Stephens' correction . . . This first text had clauses of secrecy, and of obedience to all commands of superior officers not immoral. I swore Stephens in and he swore me[5]

The Brotherhood that the paper represented was organised on a system of 'circles'. The head of each circle was a 'centre' known as A. This figure corresponded to the rank of colonel. The A chose nine captains, known as Bs. These captains, in turn, chose nine sergeants each. These sergeants, called Cs, then chose nine men each. These men, the Ds, were the lowest level of the movement. Each circle should therefore have corresponded to 820 men although, in practice, the size varied. Sitting in the middle of this web was James Stephens as the Brotherhood's 'Head Centre'. Another facet of the circle system was that the lower ranks of the organisation would not know the identity of members of other circles. In theory, if a circle member was captured or was an informer they were limited in the damage they could cause to the organisation. All members were tied to the organisation by an oath of allegiance. The IRB, at least at this time in their history, did not conceive of themselves as a guerrilla organisation. Their military strategy was to build a secret army and then engage the British army in conventional warfare. When the leadership judged that the time was right, it would launch a surprise uprising against the British army in Ireland, take control of the country and establish a revolutionary government.

Over the summer of 1858 Stephens and Luby began another tour of the country, through which they inducted new recruits into the Brotherhood, mostly in towns and villages. The most important of these early admissions was probably Jeremiah O'Donovan Rossa, who merged his Phoenix National and Literary Society into the IRB. More recruits followed O'Donovan Rossa over the summer but Stephens realised that continued American help and finances were vital to the success of the IRB. He travelled to the US in the autumn of 1858, arriving in New York on 13 October. Soon after, in early 1859, the American wing of the organisation was founded with John O'Mahony as its Head Centre, although he was ultimately subordinate to Stephens. That spring Stephens travelled to Paris and remained outside Ireland for most of the next two years. The Brotherhood was barely visible in Ireland during this time but it would gain a new vitality from the arrival of O'Mahony and then Stephens in the country during 1861. During that year Stephens and Luby toured Ireland gathering new recruits, making particular progress among Dublin-based artisans. Also, from March 1861, the IRB began to involve itself in public demonstrations in both Ireland and the United States. The funeral of Terence Bellew McManus was one such event. McManus was a veteran of the 1848 rising who had died in the United States. His body was transferred from San Francisco to New York before being brought to Ireland. The IRB in the States had arranged well-attended gatherings as the body was taken across the country. The huge public funeral of McManus in Dublin, although only partly organised by the IRB, gave further momentum to the growth of the Brotherhood in Ireland. Stephen's goal was now to make use of the 'massive public sympathy for the spirit of Young Ireland'.[6] This public sympathy was demonstrated again at the end of 1861 during the 'Trent Affair', in which the IRB organised a large public demonstration in protest against the British government.[7] Through such efforts the organisation grew rapidly over the next two years with figures of future importance such as John Devoy joining the Brotherhood.

However, when it was recruiting and organising so many new members the IRB could hardly remain a secret body. Nor could it remain a relatively small vanguard of oath-bound comrades since it was now, potentially, an army. That was the crux of the dilemma facing the IRB leadership. To maintain the discipline and coherence of the movement it was necessary to have some means by which the tens of thousands of members could be made to feel a part of a united body. Stephens decided that a newspaper would be the best tool for speaking to the Brotherhood and for making further inroads into what he sensed was a latent public support for revolution. O'Mahony opposed this decision, preferring that the Brotherhood remain a secret organisation, but despite these internal divisions Stephens won this particular battle. The decision to found the *Irish People* was made in the summer of 1863, around the same time that John Boyle O'Reilly enlisted with the 10th Hussars. Once the requisite finances and structure were in place, the *Irish People* began publishing in

November 1863 with John O'Leary as editor. The paper, whose offices on Parliament Street in Dublin now became the unofficial headquarters of the Brotherhood, openly proclaimed its motives: 'the one great end – National independence, and the one great means – armed resistance.'[8] The *Irish People* was, as R. V. Comerford has written, 'largely responsible for transforming Stephens' movement into a major phenomenon in Irish public life in the mid-1860s.' It was a fact lamented by a British official a few years later: 'The lower orders read nothing but these treasonable effusions . . . Few are too poor to buy those penny papers, which are passed from hand to hand.'[9] The *Irish People* equalled this success across the Irish Sea. Alexander Martin Sullivan, editor of the *Nation,* moaned that this rival newspaper swept 'all before it amongst the Irish in England and Scotland.'[10] It also found an audience across the Atlantic amid the ranks of Irish soldiers in the Union army, a reservoir of potential recruits that the IRB hoped to tap.

The paper had arrived at the right moment to capitalise on the growing reputation of the Brotherhood both within and outside Ireland. In October 1863 the *New York Mercury* newspaper published a detailed feature on what it called the 'Fenian Brotherhood'; this feature was then carried by Irish papers.[11] This development was followed soon after by the first Fenian Brotherhood convention in Chicago. To many outsiders, and probably much of the rank and file of the IRB, the Brotherhood had the appearance of a powerful, transatlantic organisation that would soon have the ability to free Ireland of British rule. This was the time when the term 'Fenian' became the epithet of the Irish Republican Brotherhood. Although the term had originated with John O'Mahony in 1859 ('Fenian' was supposed to recall the Fianna of Irish legend), it was not until 1863 that it became a part of popular parlance. From now on the IRB was invariably termed the Fenian Brotherhood in newspapers across Ireland and Britain.

In March 1864 Stephens made another trip to America, at a time when the former United States was embroiled in its great Civil War. There he found 10,000 Fenians whom he informed that the time for action would be 1865, although O'Mahony was dubious that such a promise could be kept.[12] Stephens returned to Ireland in August 1864 to begin preparations for the rebellion that was to take place the following year. Although he had received less money from the US than he had expected, Stephens was confident that he could take advantage of the fact that there were hundreds of thousands of trained Irish soldiers currently serving in various armies. There were tens of thousands of Irish soldiers in the British army, while many more could be found across the Atlantic as a result of the American Civil War. In that conflict there had been 150,000 Irish-born soldiers in the Union army and 20,000 or more in the Confederate army. Many had reached high ranks and nearly all of them would have been disciplined, well-trained and battle-hardened soldiers. Also, from early 1865, O'Mahony had begun sending experienced soldiers to Ireland who would act as the officer corps of the Fenian army.

By the summer of 1865 the IRB's planning for the rising was well advanced. However, it is hard to judge how many men the organisation could call upon at this time. What is certain is that the Fenians were operating in a climate of Irish discontent with British rule. The poor rural and urban classes were a part of this, as were substantial sections of the middle classes. Shopkeepers, artisans, civil engineers, small farmers and some of the clergy were all sympathetic to Fenianism. Yet the organisation did have powerful enemies within Irish nationalism. A. M. Sullivan's *Nation* was a consistent opponent of the Fenians, as was the Roman Catholic hierarchy. After the *Irish People* began publication, bringing increased support for the Brotherhood, 'priests began requesting that parishioners inform the police of any secret societies in their parish.'[13] This directive was aimed at the Fenians and members of the organisation were threatened with excommunication, a threat which was also directed at people who merely read the *Irish People*.[14] Church opposition was not based on any real support for the British government but rather fear of the consequences for their societal position of any revolution in Ireland. At a local level Fenian leaders were starting to take on the role of 'a rival community leader to the parish priest'.[15] Despite the Church's attack on the Brotherhood, the Fenians continued to take advantage of the opportunities provided to them by the Irish population's disquiet; a mood which had been further fuelled by an agricultural crisis that persisted from 1860 to 1863. The general atmosphere across the country over this decade was pithily expressed by Field Marshall Hugh Henry Rose, Commander-in-Chief of the British forces in Ireland, in a memo to the British government. Across Ireland, he believed, there was: 'A dangerous feeling of aversion to British rule, which can be called nothing other than disloyalty.'[16]

Throughout 1865 the Royal Irish Constabulary and Dublin Metropolitan Police extended their intelligence gathering on the Fenians. What they found made disturbing reading for the government. The Chief Secretary was informed in 1865 that there were 15,000 sworn Fenians in the British army and militia in Ireland, 100 in the Royal Irish Constabulary, 80 in the Dublin Metropolitan Police, and hundreds of sympathisers in both organisations.[17] How accurate these figures are is a matter of conjecture and they may have been overstated. However, if the scale of Fenianism in the Crown forces was at, or anywhere near that level, it threatened the whole system of British rule in Ireland. Government disquiet was worsened that autumn by intelligence suggesting that a rising was imminent. On 8 September 1865 Stephens had written a bellicose letter to a Fenian circle in Clonmel: 'There is no time to be lost. This year – and let there be no mistake about it – must be the year of action. I speak with a knowledge and authority to which no other man could pretend and I repeat, the flag of Ireland – of the Irish Republic – must this year be raised.'[18]

This letter was passed to the police by Pierce Nagle, an informer within the Fenians. It led to intense discussions among officials in Dublin Castle who authorised widespread police raids on the night of 15 September. Thomas Clarke Luby, John O'Leary and Jeremiah O'Donovan Rossa, all key staff on the *Irish People*, were captured, although Stephens avoided arrest and went into hiding. Perhaps a worse blow to the Fenians was the discovery by the police of hundreds of documents at the *Irish People*'s offices, which contained details on the whole movement. The police also raided Luby's bank account and seized much of the money available to the movement. It was these arrests that would create an opportunity for O'Reilly within the Fenians. Although many of the leaders had been arrested, others were quick to fill their places. John Devoy, from County Kildare, was one of these. He was amongst the most talented Fenians then operating and had spent about a year in the French Foreign Legion.[19] Following the arrests Stephens had written to Devoy from one of his safe-houses with news that the Kildare man was to be given a promotion. Years later Devoy explained his new role: 'I had some acquaintance with the army, through living near the Curragh camp, and, when all the "organizers" for the army had been arrested or forced to remain "on their keeping", James Stephens, the chief executive of the Irish republic that was to be, appointed me "chief organizer" for the British army.'[20]

In taking on this role Devoy was following after Patrick 'Pagan' O'Leary and William Roantree. They had infiltrated the army over the previous two years and had recruited many soldiers into the Brotherhood but, not unexpectedly given the nature of their work, both had been discovered and arrested. Despite the risks, Devoy, according to his own memoir, succeeded in recruiting many soldiers across all the regiments of the Dublin garrison.[21] The exception was O'Reilly's 10th Hussars. The Hussars were mainly English but there were around 100 Irish soldiers. Devoy had enrolled a few of these soldiers into the Fenians but he was not impressed by their abilities, describing them as 'not of much account'.[22] However, in October 1865 an opportunity for further infiltration into the ranks presented itself through a veterinary surgeon named Harry Byrne. This man told Devoy about 'a young fellow of his acquaintance in the Tenth who would just fill the bill'.[23] This 'young fellow' was O'Reilly and Byrne offered to bring Devoy to Islandbridge Barracks where he could introduce the Fenian to the soldier. Byrne, perhaps because he provided his veterinary services to the British army, was well known to the troops and his request to enter the barracks with Devoy raised no concerns among the guards. In the barracks square the two men were met by a sergeant major; 'a hearty Englishman of the best type'.[24] He told them that O'Reilly was currently at the Royal Barracks a short distance away (after independence the Barracks became Collins Barracks and is now part of the National Museum), but that they were welcome to wait for his return. The sergeant major offered them some tea in the canteen and during their chat he was full of praise for O'Reilly. 'The best young soldier in the regiment', he told them, 'I shouldn't wonder if in five or six years that young fellow'd be a troop sawjent majah.'[25]

They remained with the sergeant major for some time, but with no sign of O'Reilly the two men made their excuses and departed across the river to the Royal Barracks. They found the soldier just as he was about to leave on an errand:

O'Reilly was in the stable tightening his saddle girths and getting ready to mount and start off to the vice-regal lodge with a dispatch for the lord lieutenant from Sir Hugh Rose, the commander of the forces in Ireland. Byrne had just time to introduce us, and O'Reilly and I to make an appointment for the next evening, when he brought out his horse, sprang into the saddle, and was off. O'Reilly was then a handsome, lithely built young fellow . . .with the down of a future black moustache on his lip. He had pair of beautiful dark eyes, that changed in expression with his varying emotions. He wore the full-dress dark blue hussar uniform, with its mass of braiding across the breast, and the busby with its tossing plume, was set jauntily on the head and held by a linked brass strap, catching under the lower lip.[26]

The meeting of the two men on the following night was O'Reilly's introduction into the Fenian conspiracy to infiltrate the British army. In a practical sense that was the night that O'Reilly became a Fenian, although it would emerge in his later court martial (see chapter 3) that O'Reilly had actually joined the Brotherhood in 1863. O'Reilly may have joined the group while he was stationed at Cahir with the Hussars but he had not been in any way an active member of the Brotherhood. Nor does his membership seem to have made any difference to his daily life as a soldier. This is confirmed by John Devoy's statement that O'Reilly 'was more than two years in the service before he did any work for the movement.'[27] Whether O'Reilly retook the Fenian oath in the presence of Devoy is unclear but the soldier was now evidently willing to work towards the ideals expressed in that oath. Differing forms of this oath are in existence but the version most likely taken by O'Reilly would have been:

I, John Boyle O'Reilly, in the presence of Almighty God do solemnly swear allegiance to the Irish Republic now virtually established; and that I will do my very utmost, at every risk while life lasts, to defend its independence and integrity; and finally that I will yield implicit obedience in all things, not contrary to the laws of God, to the commands of my superior officer, so help me God.[28]

Why did O'Reilly take this decision in September 1865? It seems unlikely that his earlier reasons for joining the Brotherhood in 1863 were militaristic. He may well have had sympathy with the goals of the Fenians but his actions over the following two years do not display any urgency in this regard. It is clear from his court martial that between 1863 and 1865 O'Reilly was an excellent soldier whom senior officers held in high regard. Also, John Devoy dismissed claims made by James Jeffrey Roche that

O'Reilly had joined the army so as to spread Fenianism among its ranks. Devoy had little doubt that O'Reilly had enlisted for the sole reason that 'like many other Irishmen, he liked soldiering'.[29]

R. V. Comerford, in his study of the Fenians, has shown that aside from political motives there was a noticeable social aspect for many of the men who joined the group, especially among the artisans, tradesmen, shop assistants, teachers and young educated urban dwellers who comprised the bulk of the membership. Many of these found the Fenians 'a mechanism for autonomous self-assertion and the defiance of social restraints',[30] whether those restraints were the police, clergy or landowners. The public demonstrations and the constant drilling of Fenian recruits effectively became a pastime for many members. In some ways the Fenians were similar to the militia that O'Reilly had been a member of in Preston and, although already a member of the army, the Brotherhood may have appealed to this side of his character. He may well have joined simply because it was a fashionable thing for young Irish men to do at the time. If he had become a Fenian in 1863, O'Reilly would have joined the Brotherhood at a time, after the Terence Bellew McManus funeral, when the organisation was gaining in popularity and recruits by the day.

Yet, between 1863 and 1865, O'Reilly had changed. Perhaps the journalism of the *Irish People*, the increasing radicalisation of the country, the ongoing expectation of a rising, the arrests of leading Fenians, or a growing sense of nationality had played a role in crystallising his thoughts on Ireland and the Fenians. Also, there is the fact that his older brother William was a Fenian and it may be that support for the group was widespread through the O'Reilly family. Whatever the reason, by October 1865 O'Reilly was ready and willing to commit himself fully to the Brotherhood. From now on he would be charting a more dangerous course. It was one thing to be secretly a member of a revolutionary organisation waiting for a call to action but in actively trying to recruit fellow soldiers to the Fenians he was committing treason and would greatly increase his chances of being exposed as an enemy agent. Despite the risks and his army duties (one of which was being a guard at the trial of O'Donovan Rossa), O'Reilly was extraordinarily active for the Fenians during the next four months. Devoy recalled that over the winter of 1865/66, as Ireland was transfixed by the newspaper accounts of the trials of arrested leaders, he met with O'Reilly 'almost every day'.[31]

Whenever O'Reilly was off duty he spent a 'good deal of time' with Devoy discussing plans 'while walking along unfrequented streets'.[32] They also used a soldier named William Curry as an intermediary. He was a corporal in the 87th Foot Regiment and was then on a period of leave from the army. Curry 'could go in and out of the barracks' across the city and O'Reilly often used him to pass on militarily sensitive information to Devoy.[33] This included the key to a barracks' gate (presumably Island-bridge Barracks). In his role as a Fenian recruiter O'Reilly succeeded brilliantly and his fine reputation across the regiment seems to have helped to shield his covert activities from his superiors. Of the 100 or so Irish soldiers in the 10th Hussars, men who had proved impervious to Devoy's efforts, O'Reilly recruited eighty into the Fenian ranks. He introduced every one of the eighty men to Devoy who administered the oath to each new Fenian. O'Reilly divided these recruits 'into two prospective troops', which he would lead into battle when the signal was given for the rebellion to begin.[34]

That signal never arrived. Stephens was located by the police and arrested on 11 November 1865. He was taken to Richmond Prison but his incarceration was to be brief. On 23 November a Fenian rescue party, led by John Breslin and aided by supporters in the prison service, spirited Stephens out of Richmond and into hiding. The escape thrilled the newspapers and mortified the government. The Lord Lieutenant, John Wodehouse, wrote to a colleague: 'I feel like a general who has let his camp be surprised in the night and lost half his army'.[35] With Stephens free, it seemed to Fenians across the country and to the Irish-American officers in Dublin that the last obstacle had been cleared and that a rising was now inevitable. Yet Stephens dithered and persuaded the Fenian's military council that the rising must be postponed. There was, he argued, no prospect of outside help from the United States other than the Irish-American veterans already in the country and the correct moment was not yet at hand. He was also uncertain as to how many of the Fenians within the British army would actually join a rebellion. Stephens may have lost his nerve, as was later claimed by his detractors, but it is far from certain that a Fenian rising at the end of 1865 would have been successful. Over the previous seven years Stephens 'had made no systematic efforts to arm his followers'[36] and the thousands of Fenians were armed only with pikes and perhaps a thousand, mostly obsolete, rifles. Without external support these

Fenians would have had little hope of victory against the British army. Despite Stephens' assurances that the rising had only been postponed, the year ended with a whimper and with his prestige in the Brotherhood rapidly diminishing.

In February 1866 the British government decided to finish the job it had started during the previous September and began to arrest known or suspected Fenians in the British army. Since so many of the soldiers in Ireland were sworn Fenians, any attempt to identify and punish these men risked antagonising the bulk of the common soldiers. Therefore it was vital to locate the Fenian recruiters such as O'Reilly. If the government could remove those recruiters they would excise the most committed of the army's Fenians. The government could also make an example of these Fenians that would resonate throughout the rest of the army. Once this series of arrests began it was inevitable that O'Reilly's name would come to the attention of the police. The Fenian circle system devised by Stephens was supposed to limit the damage that could be caused by informers but the Brotherhood was so riddled with spies that, in J. J. Lee's memorable line, 'the organisation could no more hold its secrets than a sieve could hold water.'[37] O'Reilly knew as much but could do little other than wait. On 12 February he saw one of his fellow conspirators being taken away by the police and two days later he was arrested at Islandbridge Barracks. As the prisoner was being removed by the police one of his commanding officers, Colonel Valentine Baker, shouted after him: 'Damn you, O'Reilly! You have ruined the finest regiment in Her Majesty's service.'[38] O'Reilly was held in police custody for the next few weeks and may have heard news of John Devoy's arrest on 21 February. On 6 March he was returned to Islandbridge Barracks and placed in the guardroom. By that time the British Parliament had rushed through a bill permitting the indefinite detention of anyone in Ireland by order of the Lord Lieutenant. O'Reilly remained in Islandbridge until 1 April, at which point he was transferred to Arbour Hill, a small military prison very near to the Royal Barracks on Dublin's north side.

O'Reilly does not seem to have been mistreated while in Arbour Hill even though the prison guards and army officers made regular attempts to gain his testimony against other Fenians. One guard warned him that: 'It will be better for you to save your own neck, my boy.'[39] O'Reilly dismissed all these demands although he was mindful that other arrested

Fenians had gained immunity by testifying against their comrades. Devoy later wrote that an officer named Captain Whelan (who would serve as the prosecutor in O'Reilly's court martial) 'went from cell to cell in Arbour Hill Military Prison . . . telling each man that the others had turned informer and that I [Devoy] had supplied to the Castle a list of all the men I had sworn in.' Whelan also told each man that O'Reilly 'had informed on them all'.[40] O'Reilly, in a letter to his parents, expressed his disdain for those soldiers who had offered to testify against other Fenians:

> They told those poor cowardly hounds who <u>did</u> [underlined in original] turn, that Chambers [Thomas Chambers, a fellow Fenian and a member of the 61st Regiment who would later be imprisoned with O'Reilly] & I were going to give evidence against them – so as to frighten them into giving evidence against us. They have been done by officers & gentlemen. We are 10,000 times happier than any of such hounds can ever be. When we go to our prisons & all suspense will be over we will be quite happy. Never fear for me whatever I get. Please God in a few years I will be released and even if prevented from coming to Ireland, we'll be happy yet and if not God's holy will be done. Pray for me & for us all.[41]

In the same letter he told his family of the camaraderie between the prisoners and of the cathartic effect that the arrests had had upon some of the Fenians:

> It would please you to hear the poor fellows here talking. At night they knock on the wall as a signal to each other to pray together for their country's freedom. Men who a few months ago were careless thoughtless soldiers, are now changed into true fierce patriots, however humble. They never speak on any other subject and all are happy to suffer for old Ireland or as the greater number of them call the 'ould country'.

The last line about the 'ould country' suggests that O'Reilly was incarcerated with some of the many Irish-American soldiers who had been arrested during the February raids. He is known to have shared his cell with at least one Irish American, Captain James Murphy, a veteran of the American Civil War.[42]

Little else is known about O'Reilly's time in Arbour Hill other than that he was able to get a few letters smuggled out of the prison, either through the empathy or avarice of individual guards. One of these letters assured his parents that all was well:

> They all like me here, and if I sent you all the notes I get thrown to me for 'dear J. B.' or 'J. B. O.', you would be amused. There's a fine young fellow here, a Preston Irishman, named Kelly. He begged even a button from me for a keepsake. I gave him the ring of my plume, and he's as happy as possible.[43]

The imprisoned soldier was sure that a rising was still in the offing: 'Perhaps you think there will be none, but you'll see, either this or next month, please God. Even in here we get assurances of not being forgotten, and that the work goes on better than ever.' He promised his parents that, whatever happened, he would pray for them and he urged them not to worry: 'Never grieve for me, I beg you. God knows I'd be only too happy to die for the cause of my country. Pray for us all; we are all brothers who are suffering.'

To fill the empty hours of imprisonment O'Reilly composed some poems, including 'The Old School Clock'. The poem, which became one of his best-known during his lifetime, has a maudlin nostalgia that seems strange for a man in his early twenties to have expressed. It is, however, typical of what remains of O'Reilly's very early work. The background to the poem's story is a visit O'Reilly had made to his old school in Dowth while serving with the Hussars. He was saddened to see that a beloved old clock, which had once hung on the wall of his classroom, had been replaced by a newer model. The third stanza is especially sentimental:

> Well, years had passed, and my mind was filled
> with the world, its cares and ways,
> When again I stood in that little school
> where I passed my boyhood days.
> My old friend was gone! And there hung a thing
> that my sorrow seemed to mock,

> As I gazed with a tear and a softened heart
> at a new-fashioned Yankee clock.[44]

O'Reilly also made reference to writing poems of a more political nature, but it is not certain which poems they were or if they even survived his time in prison.[45] When O'Reilly was eventually moved from Arbour Hill he left 'The Old School Clock' and others with Murphy, who hid them in the ventilator of the cell. (Remarkably, these poems were discovered years later and returned to him.[46]) However, his days of waiting were nearing an end. By the summer of 1866 the army had begun the courts martial of the Fenians in the British army. O'Reilly had one last letter to his parents smuggled out of the prison:

> I wrote these slips before I knew my fate, and I have nothing more to say, only God's holy will be done! If I only knew that you would not grieve for me I'd be perfectly happy and content. My own dear ones, you will not be ashamed of me at any rate; you all love the cause I suffer for as well as I, and when you pray for me, pray also for the brave, true-hearted Irishmen who are with me. Men who do not understand our motives may call us foolish or mad, but every true Irish heart knows our feelings and will not forget us. Don't come here to bid me goodbye through the gate. I could never forget that. I'll bid you all goodbye in a letter.
>
> God bless you![47]

On the morning of Wednesday 27 June 1866, the day before his twenty-second birthday, John Boyle O'Reilly was taken under guard to the Royal Barracks. Here, the prisoner would face his court martial.

3

Fenian

O'Reilly was facing a general court martial, a category reserved for the most serious cases, and it consisted of at least thirteen officers. A full transcript was made of the evidence and, before its findings were promulgated, the record of the trial was submitted to the Judge Advocate General who checked the legal propriety of the court proceedings.[1] It is the proceedings of this court martial that give us the best account of O'Reilly's activities as a Fenian agent in the British army. The court was held in the mess room of the 85th Regiment at the Royal Barracks. O'Reilly was charged with 'Having at Dublin, in January, 1866, come to the knowledge of an intended mutiny in Her Majesty's Forces in Ireland, and not giving information of said intended mutiny to his commanding officer.' O'Reilly replied to this charge, through his Counsel, and pleaded 'not guilty'. Standing alongside him in the dock were Colour Sergeant Charles Henry McCarthy, Privates Patrick Keating, Michael Harrington, Thomas Darragh, and Captain James Murphy.[2]

The court martial was constituted with Colonel Sawyer of the 6th Dragoon Guards as president of the court. The prosecutor was the same Captain Whelan of the 8th Regiment who had sought to obtain the testimony of the prisoners in Arbour Hill. He was assisted by Mr Landy QC, while O'Reilly was defended by Mr O'Loughlen, advised by Mr John Lawless, solicitor.[3] The Deputy Judge Advocate General was a Mr Johnson. Captain Whelan opened the prosecution case by telling the court:

> The enormity of the offence with which the prisoner is charged is
> such that it is difficult to find language by which to describe it. It

strikes at the root of all military discipline, and, if allowed to escape the punishment which it entails, would render her Majesty's forces, who ought to be the guardians of our lives and liberty, and the bulwark and protection of the constitution under which we live, a source of danger to the state and all its loyal citizens and subjects, and her Majesty's faithful subjects would become the prey and victims of military despotism, licentiousness, and violence. Our standing army would then be a terror to the throne, and a curse, not a blessing, to the community; but at the same time, as is the gravity of the offence, so in proportion should the evidence by which such a charge is to be sustained, be carefully and sedulously weighed. It will be for you, gentlemen, to say whether the evidence which will be adduced before you, leaves upon your mind any reasonable doubt of the prisoner's guilt.[4]

He assured the court that the required evidence would be forthcoming throughout the trial and so the prosecution opened its case. O'Reilly's Fenian connections were established with the first witness. This witness was Lance Corporal Fitzgerald of the 10th Hussars and he testified that he had seen O'Reilly in the company of John Devoy: 'I know the prisoner [O'Reilly]. I know Hoey's public house in Bridgeport Street. I was in it in the month of November, 1865, with the prisoner. He brought me there. I was introduced by the prisoner to a man named Devoy.'[5] Fitzgerald continued:

The prisoner introduced me to Devoy and said: 'This is Corporal Fitzgerald,' and I spoke to him. Devoy said O'Reilly had spoken to him several times about me, and said he should like to get me. We three sat down together and I asked Devoy who was carrying on this affair. He said [James] Stephens. I asked, were there any arms or ammunition. He said there was, and they were getting lots every day from America. I asked who were to be their officers. He said there would be plenty of officers. He said it was so carried on that privates did not know their non-commissioned officers, nor they their officers. Devoy then left the room and the prisoner went after him. After a few minutes prisoner came and told me that Devoy wanted to speak to me. I went down to the yard and found Devoy there. He said, 'I suppose O'Reilly has told you what I want with you.

O'Reilly's counsel interjected: 'I respectfully object, sir. What the witness now states to have taken place, was not in my presence.' However, the judge ruled that an answer should be given and ordered Fitzgerald to continue: "I said that I did not know. He said that it was for the purpose of joining them he wanted me, and that there was an oath necessary to be taken. I said I would not take the oath, and he then said that he would not trust any man that did not take the oath. We then returned upstairs. Nothing further took place." '[6]

The president of the court then asked what purpose lay behind all these meetings and the oath. Fitzgerald's reply was damning for O'Reilly. 'I meant the Fenian conspiracy'. He went on:

When I went upstairs I saw the prisoner, who bade me good-night. The next time I saw him was one evening I met him in town coming from the barracks. Some arrests took place that day, and I said, 'This business is getting serious.' He said it was, and that my name had been mentioned at a meeting a few nights before. I asked what meeting, and he said a military meeting. I asked him who mentioned my name, and he said he did not know exactly, but that it was a man of the Fifth Dragoon Guards. He added, 'If you come home to-night I will take you to a similar meeting.' I gave him no decided answer. I afterwards met him in the barracks. This all occurred before the meeting at Hoey's, of which I stated. When I met him in the barracks he asked me was I going out. I replied that I was. He said, 'Will you meet me at the sign of the Two Soldiers?' I said yes, and went there and waited until O'Reilly came in. He called for some drink, and after we drank we left the house, but came back again to get my gloves, and he said, 'I want to introduce you to a person.' I said that I had no time and should go, but he said, 'I shall not detain you a minute.' I then went with him to Hoey's public house. It was on that occasion that I had the interview with Devoy of which I have given evidence.[7]

After a short adjournment, Fitzgerald returned to his testimony:

The conversation of which I have last spoken took place either toward the end of November or the beginning of December, 1865.

Prisoner never told me the object of the military meetings of which he spoke. I know Pilsworth's public house, James's Street. I met prisoner in that house on the 13th of January, 1866. There were with him Denny, Mullarchy, Hood, Loftus, Crosby, and Sinclair, all Tenth Hussars, and two deserters from Fifth Dragoon Guards. They were in civilian clothes. There was a man named Williams present, and also Devoy. On that occasion I had no conversation with O'Reilly, nor with any other person in his hearing. I never had any further conversation with the prisoner about Fenianism. Prisoner never asked me the result of my conversation with Devoy.[8]

Fitzgerald concluded by saying that he never made any of his commanding officers aware of his conversation with Devoy which was, in itself, a punishable offence but he repeated on a few occasions that he had never taken the Fenian oath and had no involvement in any planning for a mutiny. With that, Fitzgerald's testimony was complete and he was followed by another member of the 10th Hussars, Private McDonald. His testimony was far less useful to the prosecution case than that of Fitzgerald, much to the annoyance of the president of the court, Colonel Sawyer. McDonald began by discussing another meeting at Pilsworth's public house:

I know Pilsworth's house. I was there about Christmas last with the prisoner. I went with him to the house. There were other persons there but I cannot say who they were. There were some civilians, but I did not know their names. Since then I heard that Devoy was one of them. The prisoner did not introduce me to any one on that occasion. Any drink the soldiers had they paid for themselves. There was no conversation relating to Fenianism in the presence of the prisoner.[9]

Here again the president of the court interjected: 'Remember that you are on your oath.' McDonald replied: 'I had some conversation with O'Reilly while he was sitting by me. I cannot now tell what it was about, but it was not about Fenianism.'[10] In the course of a testimony that lasted through the rest of the day and into the next morning, McDonald's testimony proceeded in the same manner, with the president of the court becoming more and more exasperated. McDonald recalled seeing O'Reilly at various public houses. On some of these occasions John Devoy was also present but McDonald recalled nothing of a seditious nature having occurred. One typical back and forth provided the court with some moments of light relief:

> *McDonald*: I afterwards, in the same month [December 1865], went with prisoner to Bergin's, James's Street; remained there from half-past eight to quarter-past nine; did not know any persons present, they were all strangers; there were four infantry soldiers, one of them, I think, of the Fifty-third. Prisoner was there the whole time; there was no conversation between prisoner and those present. There was singing.
> *President*: No conversation!
> *McDonald*: None.
> *President*: Public houses must be mortal slow places according to your account.[11]

McDonald's testimony continued along these lines although he did describe a conversation with O'Reilly in April 1865. During this conversation O'Reilly apparently told McDonald that he had 'belonged to the Fenian brother-hood in Cahir'[12] while the 10th Hussars was stationed there. This statement was actually of little use to the prosecution. This case was not about whether O'Reilly was a Fenian. That was taken for granted by the court since thousands of soldiers within the British army, at this time, were Fenians. The government could not try all of these men, nor was it willing to do so. This court martial was concerned with whether O'Reilly knew of the intended mutiny and whether he failed to pass on any such knowledge to his commanders. McDonald was dismissed from the witness stand in the afternoon, without adding anything of importance to the court martial.

He was followed by Private Dennis Denny, also of the 10th Hussars. Denny's testimony was far more damaging to O'Reilly's defence:

> I remember the evening of the 1st January, last. I was in the 'Two Soldiers' public house with the prisoner. He told me that if I went to Hoey's with him he would show me the finest set of Irishmen I ever

saw in my life. We went there and found a number of civilians assembled. The prisoner, after some time, took me out of the room and told me that the Fenians were going to beat the English army and make this country their own. He asked me to take an oath to join the Fenians. I answered that I had already taken an oath to serve my queen and country and that was enough for me. I then came down and went into the yard and he again asked me to be a Fenian. I told him no.[13]

Denny had not told any of this to his superior officers at the time. He was arrested in early March and only then had he made a statement regarding O'Reilly.

The next witness was Private John Smith of the 10th Hussars who likewise testified that O'Reilly was a member of the Fenians. Smith claimed O'Reilly told him that he was in the habit of meeting at Hoey's pub 'Fenian agents, and men from America'.[14] There was a brief change of tone with the next witnesses, Colonel Baker and Colonel Hass of the 10th Hussars, both commanding officers of O'Reilly. They each spent only a few minutes on the stand. Baker was the officer who had shouted at O'Reilly following his arrest that he had 'ruined the regiment'. However, both he and Hass testified to the good character of O'Reilly. They were both called to the stand as part of the prosecution's attempt to prove one of the charges against O'Reilly: that he had never passed any information regarding the mutiny to his superiors. The two officers duly informed the court that O'Reilly had never passed them any information regarding the intended mutiny.[15] Next on the stand was Head Constable Talbot, a member of the Royal Irish Constabulary who had infiltrated the Fenians under the name of John Kelly. He was one of the police's most successful agents and had been a witness in a number of Fenian trials. Here, he testified that O'Reilly was a recruiter for the Fenians whose role 'was the enlistment of agents in the various branches of the British service'.[16] The ultimate aim of this enlistment, Talbot told the court martial, was to use soldiers of the British army in a Fenian attempt to overthrow British rule in Ireland.

He was followed by Private Mullarchy and then Private Rorreson of the 10th Hussars, both of whom testified to O'Reilly's links to Fenianism although this was via his association with other known Fenians in the army rather than any direct statements by O'Reilly. Counsel for O'Reilly objected to such testimony but the Deputy Judge Advocate, whose role was to oversee the legality of the trial, overruled the objection, saying: 'I submit that the acts or conversations of co-conspirators are admissible as evidence against each other, even though one of them on his trial [O'Reilly] was not present at these acts or conversations.'[17]

Next up was Private Patrick Foley of the 5th Dragoon Guards who had taken the Fenian oath but who had been acting as an informer for a period of perhaps a few months before the arrests. He told the court: 'I kept no memoranda of the meetings I attended, as I reported them all to my commanding officer in the mornings after they took place.'[18] These reports consisted of verbal exchanges between Foley and his commanding officer. Foley admitted that he 'never took down the names' of those he met at Fenian gatherings. In making these reports to his superiors, Devoy suggests, probably correctly, that Foley was the first person to implicate O'Reilly as a Fenian recruiter.[19] However, Foley gave a rambling account of his meetings with O'Reilly and Devoy with much vague testimony such as: 'I frequently met Devoy in company with O'Reilly. I have heard Devoy speak in presence of the prisoner about Fenianism, but I cannot remember that he said anything about what was to be done in connection with it.'[20] This evidence was of little help to the prosecution but Captain Whelan tried to extract some useful testimony by asking Foley, 'Was there at any of these meetings of which you spoke and at which the prisoner was present, any conversation of an intended outbreak or mutiny?' O'Reilly's defence counsel objected to this question arguing that 'The prosecutor had no right to lead the witness, and put into his mouth the very words of the charge.' This was overruled and Foley answered, 'There was a conversation of an intended mutiny that was to take place in January or the latter end of February. The prisoner could have heard the conversation that took place in Hoey's, in January, and in Barclay's, in February. I reported to my colonel in February the subject of the conversation.'[21] After that testimony the court adjourned and did not resume until 5 July. Foley continued with his testimony but offered little of value to the prosecution case.

Foley was followed to the stand by Private Meara of the 8th Regiment who declared that he had joined the Fenians and taken the oath.[22] His testimony was particularly detrimental to O'Reilly. He claimed that he had seen the prisoner at a meeting in Hoey's public house in January 1866,

where he was in the company of Devoy. On that occasion he said he had
seen a sketch of Islandbridge Barracks in O'Reilly's hand. O'Reilly was
discussing this map with Devoy. Meara then told the court how Devoy
picked certain soldiers as Fenian ringleaders for the mutiny: 'Devoy said he
wanted a few men out of the Hussars to give them instruction what to do,
and he wanted about ten men out of each regiment in Dublin.'[23] Meara
then spoke about O'Reilly's part in the meeting:

> The prisoner spoke of cutting the hamstrings of the horses in the
> stables in case of any emergency. The conversation then turned on a
> rising in the army and how the men would act. I said the Irishmen in
> the army saw no prospect before them, and they would be great fools
> to commit themselves. Devoy said they would not be asked until a
> force came from America.

Meara was excoriated in Roche's biography of O'Reilly as a 'ruffian' and a
'malicious knave'.[24] Meara's testimony was certainly self-serving. He
portrayed himself as an undercover agent who had joined the Fenians 'out
of curiosity' but then became determined to spy on the organisation so as
to prevent any rebellion. He had decided to undertake this mission without
informing any of his superior officers. If any armed uprising was planned,
he said, he would 'have known it days before and then given information'.[25]

Meara's testimony stretched credulity, weaving a tale of supposed hidden
heroism and containing incidents where he debated and defeated John
Devoy. Far from acting as an undercover agent, Meara had only informed
his commanders after the Fenian arrests during February and March, when
it is likely that he was implicated by others who had been arrested. He then
informed on his fellow Fenians. Meara, rather than playing the secret hero,
had looked out for himself and played both sides until he could pick a
winner. His appearance at the court was most likely as a result of a deal with
his commanding officers; the testimony was given to avoid punishment.
Indeed it seems that Meara had testified in a previous trial of one of the
civilian Fenians and on that occasion his testimony had been dismissed. Yet,
despite his double-dealing, Meara's testimony regarding O'Reilly was, most
likely, accurate. Devoy had met with O'Reilly during the time period
mentioned by Meara and had been in receipt of military information from
the hussar over the following months. Furthermore, Devoy liked O'Reilly,

not only because of the hussar's good nature but also because of his keen and proactive mind. Devoy described O'Reilly as having 'a good military head . . . his ideas about the capture of Dublin, and the way to get out of the city with our forces intact, in case we failed, were all practical. Mere boy that he was [Devoy was only two years older], he believed the blow should be struck in Dublin, where our organisation was the strongest and our membership of the British army was largest.'[26]

Based on Devoy's account, it is not hard to imagine O'Reilly giving the Fenian recruiter a map of Islandbridge Barracks or planning to hamstring the barrack's horses.

Meara's testimony closed the case for the prosecution. That case involved three points: that there was an intended Fenian mutiny; that O'Reilly knew of, and was complicit in, the intended mutiny; and that, having knowledge of the mutiny, O'Reilly had failed to inform his commanding officers of this fact. The court was satisfied by Talbot's evidence that there was indeed an intended mutiny, leaving them to decide whether O'Reilly knew of it and had then failed to pass this information to his commanders. O'Reilly's defence began stating their case on 7 July. His counsel argued that the court had to prove each of these allegations before it could find O'Reilly guilty and also asked the court to bear in mind O'Reilly's good reputation in the regiment while considering the evidence. The defence then pointed out that even if the evidence provided by the prosecution witnesses was true, 'it would not bring home to him one fact to bear out the charge.'[27]

This was true, in that the prosecution had no direct evidence that O'Reilly was involved in any conspiracy. The evidence was entirely based on verbal reports of supposed conversations between O'Reilly and the various witnesses or between Devoy and the witnesses while in the presence of O'Reilly. Some of the evidence was based on meetings and conversations at which O'Reilly was not even present. The defence also questioned the integrity and motives of the two most damaging witnesses against O'Reilly, Foley and Meara:

> In the whole evidence, which, in the cases of Foley and Meara was that of informers, there was much to which the addition or omission of a word would give a very different colour to what it had got. What was the amount of credit to be given to those men, when it was

remembered that they both took the Fenian oath, the one as he said, through curiosity, the other with the deliberate design at informing?[28]

The defence called on the court to reject their testimony and rely upon that of the officers who had given evidence of O'Reilly's good character as a soldier. One final witness was called to stand as a character witness for O'Reilly. He was Captain Barthorp of the 10th Hussars, who was also a member of the court. Barthorp accordingly told the court that he had known O'Reilly for nearly three years and that his character was good. Overall, the defence case was weakly put. It had sought to cast doubt on the integrity and motives of the witnesses for the prosecution but this was not done in any concerted manner. Why the defence was so poorly constructed is a matter of speculation. John Devoy wrote that, by this time, the Fenian Brotherhood was so short of funds that it 'had no money to pay counsel to defend the men'.[29] Perhaps this meant that O'Reilly was burdened with an incompetent barrister as his defence. Perhaps O'Reilly's counsel felt that the case was already lost. We do not know the answer to those questions but the defence case was concluded within a few hours whereas the prosecution had put their case to the court over a period of three days.

There was still time for the prosecutor, Captain Whelan, to launch a rebuttal of the defence before the Deputy Judge Advocate General summed up the whole case for the benefit of the court. He reminded them that:

if the court has no rational doubt of the prisoner's guilt, then it is bound, without favour, partiality, or affection, to find their verdict accordingly. Remember, though, that although you may feel very great suspicion of the prisoner's guilt, yet if you are not satisfied that the charge is proved home to him beyond rational doubt, no amount of suspicion will justify conviction.[30]

At the conclusion of the Deputy Judge Advocate's address, the court retired to consider their findings. We know that O'Reilly was indeed guilty but, if we can forget that fact for a moment, it could hardly be said that the case against O'Reilly had been proved 'beyond rational doubt'. The evidence was merely a collection of comments reported second hand and these reports were often vague. Nevertheless, when the court reconvened on 9 July 1866 they found O'Reilly guilty. That afternoon a sentence of death was passed upon all the military prisoners. That sentence was only a formality by which the court could show its leniency. Later that day it was commuted to life imprisonment in the cases of O'Reilly, Darragh, Keating, Harrington and McCarthy. Another soldier, Thomas Chambers, who had been tried separately, was given a similar sentence. O'Reilly's sentence was shortly afterwards commuted to twenty years' penal servitude, seemingly as a result of an officer in the 10th Hussars, Adjutant Russell, who asked to speak before the court and who testified to O'Reilly's good character.[31]

Remarkably, O'Reilly was not informed of the verdict. As the cruel tradition demanded in such cases, the prisoner would have to wait until the day he was drummed out of the army to hear his sentence. He was taken from the court to Mountjoy Prison, in the Phibsborough region of north Dublin. Here O'Reilly would have faced the usual processing routine. He was stripped and searched and then his head was shaved. He was given the standard convict uniform of grey woollen tunic and trousers and placed in a cell on his own. O'Reilly languished in Mountjoy for nearly two months before he was removed from the prison on 3 September 1866 and taken back to the scene of his trial, the Royal Barracks. He was, for the final time, dressed in his full military uniform and marched to the middle of the barracks' Royal Square. O'Reilly stood in front of his regiment and also the 5th Dragoon Guards, 2nd Battalion, 3rd Regiment, 75th Regiment, 92nd Highlanders and 85th Light Infantry, some several thousand troops.[32]

As an officer read out the charges that had been made against the prisoner, O'Reilly would have seen many of his former comrades and friends in the throng of troops. This officer affirmed O'Reilly's guilt and then read aloud the sentence that had been handed down. This was the first time that O'Reilly had heard his fate and learned that twenty years of penal servitude lay ahead of him. Then, to the accompaniment of a slow drumbeat, O'Reilly was stripped of his military uniform and dressed again in the uniform of a convict. He was shackled in chains and taken back to Mountjoy Prison. Officially and symbolically his career as a soldier had been taken away forever. O'Reilly remained proud of his role with the Fenians and maintained his belief in the rightness of his actions. This was a man who, just over six weeks earlier, had scraped into the wall of his cell in Mountjoy: 'Written on the wall of my cell with a nail, July 17th 1866. Once an Irish soldier, now an English Felon, and proud of the exchange.'[33] Even with his defiant attitude, the drumming out must have been a humiliating experience for him and it may be significant that James Jeffrey Roche skipped over the incident in a few lines. Roche rarely missed an opportunity to highlight O'Reilly's sufferings but he did, as we shall see later, leave out incidents that were embarrassing or uncomfortable for his friend. Whatever O'Reilly felt that day as he was ritually shamed before thousands of soldiers, he would not have long to dwell on the event. The military Fenians (those Fenians, like O'Reilly, who had been part of the British army) were to be treated more harshly than the civilian Fenians. Once the military Fenians were drummed out of the army they were classed as ordinary criminal convicts meaning that, unlike the civilian Fenians, they were not exempt from punishments such as flogging. Also, none of the military Fenians was to be allowed serve his sentence in Ireland. Within twenty-four hours O'Reilly would be taken from Mountjoy Prison and transferred to England.

4

Convict

On 4 September 1866 John Boyle O'Reilly, chained to two other ex-soldiers, Charles McCarthy and Thomas Chambers, was marched under guard through the streets of Dublin from Mountjoy Jail to the port. Here they were herded onto a ship which carried them to Portsmouth, from where they travelled overland to London. The destination of the three convicts was Pentonville Prison in the north of the city. On arrival, O'Reilly was placed in solitary confinement in a cell 13.5 feet long, 7.5 feet wide and 9 feet high. The former soldier would have to spend twenty-three hours a day in his new cell, his only luxury being a hammock hung across two iron rings protruding from the back wall.[1] The other hour was devoted to exercise but this, such as it was, consisted of walking back and forth in a large room. His stay in Pentonville, however, was to be mercifully short and within a week, he, Chambers and McCarthy were on the move again to what was their next assigned place of incarceration, Millbank Prison.

Opened in 1816, Millbank had become, in the decades before John Boyle O'Reilly's arrival, a prison holding those likely to be transported to the colonies. Not far from Westminster Abbey the prison, which was demolished in the late nineteenth century, sat on the site now occupied by the Tate Britain art gallery. A contemporary observer described Millbank's exterior as O'Reilly would have seen it:

> the enormous mass of brickwork to which the first attention is directed is low, dark, beetling, and full of depressing influences from its regular irregularity. The exterior entrance is far from imposing . . . as it consists of a lodge door and a great pair of yard gates, supplied

with a very obvious and noisy bell . . . The building itself as seen from the roadway, not towering, but huddling, above the outer wall, has been aptly described . . . as 'one of the most successful realisations, on a large scale, of the ugly in architecture, being an ungainly combination of the madhouse with the fortress style of building.' It may be considered, however, that this immense structure is sufficiently elegant for its purpose, and that even the small embrasures containing the long lines of barred windows are quite suggestive of the use for which it was designed[2]

It was the interior of the vast prison that would have been of more concern to O'Reilly and it was indeed a gloomy place. Millbank's initial design had been based on the utilitarian philosopher Jeremy's Bentham's 'Panopticon', a system through which the prisoners could be under constant observation by warders. This design was heavily modified in the early stages of planning although the basis of Bentham's design remained in the prison's layout. From the air it would have looked like a giant wheel with six pentagonal cell blocks arrayed in a circle around the 'governor's house', an administrative building which was the hub of the prison.[3] Although considered a progressive prison when first built, it had been erected on marshy ground and respiratory problems afflicted many inmates. An investigation of conditions within the prison compiled a few years before O'Reilly's arrival was highly critical of the conditions within Millbank: 'All the cells are well ventilated, and the prison generally is kept scrupulously clean, but the site of the building is low and marshy, and although enormous sums have been spent in draining and improving the soil, its dampness still renders it very unhealthy.'[4] According to prison records Millbank had illness rates and deaths among the convicts far higher than in similar prisons such as Pentonville.[5] Thomas Archer, a journalist who visited the prison in 1865, wrote that: 'The amount of sickness at Millbank is sometimes very considerable.'[6]

In some ways, Millbank was a collection of prisons rather than a single entity, with each of the six pentagons separated from each other and holding a different designation of convict. Pentagon 3, for example, held women inmates, while Pentagon 5 held males in individual cells. O'Reilly's new home was within this pentagon where he was placed in Cell 32. The cell, 12 feet long and 7 feet wide, offered no view onto the outside world; the small window which provided light was set high on the back wall near the ceiling. The cell's entrance was fitted with an iron-barred door and outside that stood a second door made of wood. Upon this door there hung a small white card bearing the inscription: 'John Boyle O'Reilly, 20 years'.[7] Above the door was another card bearing the letters 'RC'. All cells within Millbank that contained Roman Catholics were marked as such and most Catholic prisoners were kept in Pentagons 4 and 5. These cells were generally of the same type and were described in a report from the 1860s:

> The furniture of the cells consists of a tub for washing . . . a large earthenware pan, and a small deal table-flap, upon which may be seen, beside the tin pint mugs for cocoa and gruel, the salt-cellar, plate, and wooden spoon, the Bible and Prayer-book, some school books, a slate and pencil, and probably some volume which each prisoner is allowed to receive once a fortnight from the prison library. The bedding and hammock are neatly folded into a square package, which looks like a large knapsack, and is placed in a particular corner of the cell; a comb and towel, and a broom for sweeping the floor.[8]

The Fenian convicts did not have the same access to reading material as the regular criminal convicts. The reason for this was not the prison authorities but the prison's Catholic clergy. They intervened to prevent Catholic prisoners receiving books from the prison library which they deemed as unsuitable.[9] The relative paucity of reading matter was a privation keenly felt by the Fenians and a source of constant complaint. Four years later, in 1870, Michael Davitt, the great social reformer and future friend of O'Reilly (see chapter 13), would spend ten months in Millbank as a convicted Fenian. Davitt, whose experiences of the prison were very similar to those of O'Reilly, described how the priests, whom he reckoned were antagonistic to the Fenian prisoners, refused his requests for new reading material. 'The class of book', he wrote, 'supplied to Catholic prisoners were as such as may be suitable to children, or people ignorant of the truths of the Catholic faith.'[10] It is not known if O'Reilly was involved in any such confrontations with the priests but he was allowed to read Thomas à Kempis' spiritual work, *The Imitation of Christ*, a strangely appropriate book, as we shall see below, given its focus on silent contemplation and monasticism.[11]

O'Reilly's little cell was to comprise the physical limits of his world for at least the next six months. All new prisoners at Millbank underwent the 'Separate Confinement System', a standard form of punishment in British prisons at the time.[12] The separate system was officially defined by the Surveyor-General of Prisons in Britain as a mode of penal discipline 'in which each individual prisoner is confined in a cell, which becomes his workshop by day and his bed-room by night, so as to be effectually prevented from holding communication with, or even being seen sufficiently to be recognized by a fellow-prisoner.'[13] This incarceration was not only to be punitive but would also have, supposedly, a rehabilitative aspect. Speaking in the 1860s a journalist named Henry Mayhew who had investigated conditions at Millbank explained the reasoning behind the separate system:

> The object of this discipline is stated to be twofold. It is enforced, not only to prevent the prisoner having intercourse with his fellow-prisoners, but to compel him to hold communion with himself. He is excluded from the society of the other criminal inmates of the prison, because experience has shown that such society is injurious, and he is urged to make his conduct the subject of his own reflections, because it is almost universally found that such self-communion is the precursor of moral amendment.[14]

The prisoners would live and work in isolation, alone with their thoughts. However, by the time O'Reilly arrived at Millbank, its convicts were encumbered by yet another method of control. He would suffer an innovation in British prisons that had been introduced in the Prison Act of 1865, the 'silent system'.[15]

Under this system prisoners had to live their lives in total silence and were not allowed to communicate with other inmates by word, sign, or gesture. It was an extension of the 'separate system' and was designed to prevent prisoners from talking to one another and through conversation spreading their criminal tendencies. Davitt, for example, wrote that during ten months in Millbank his collective conversations with warders and fellow inmates amounted to less than a total of twenty minutes.[16] The Prison Act of 1865 had been the government's response to the English public's fears over rising crime, especially street violence and muggings, and its passage into law signified the introduction of stricter rules and tougher punishments in British prisons. These new rules were pithily summarised by the Assistant Director of Prisons at the time, Sir Edmund du Cane, as 'Hard Labour, Hard Fare and Hard Board'.[17] Prisoners were punished severely for any contravention of the rules, as a contemporary commentator explained:

> All that can be said is that it [making noise or talking] is not allowed, and that when a prisoner is detected in a breach of this rule it leads to punishment; either to a renewal of separate confinement, or, if he be refractory, to the dark cell and bread and water diet. Of other punishments at Millbank, handcuffs, and even whipping, have not been entirely abolished; and it is not unwise to retain them, since they are both found useful in cases of exceptional violence and brutality.[18]

The 'dark cells' were another common penalty for breaking the rules and combined solitary confinement, total silence and total darkness. They were considered, even at the time, to be a brutal form of punishment.[19]

O'Reilly would have had little scope to offend the warders since he spent most of his time locked in his cell. Each day for O'Reilly was an almost exact repeat of the day before. The day's work began at 6 a.m. when the prisoners swept and cleaned the cells and wards. On certain days they also 'holystoned' the corridors, which involved scouring the floor with a piece of sandstone. That work lasted until breakfast at 7.30 a.m., after which most prisoners attended chapel for thirty minutes. O'Reilly, though, and the other inmates in separate confinement would have remained in their cells during these services. Dinner was served at 1.00 p.m. and supper at about 5.30 p.m.[20] Each meal lasted thirty minutes and the Millbank menu of the time was as follows:

> breakfast, ¾ of a pint of cocoa made from ½ oz. of cocoa nibs, sweetened with ½ oz. of molasses, and containing 2 oz. of milk; 8 oz. of bread. Dinner, 5 oz. of beef without bone, and weighed after boiling; 1 lb. of potatoes (or occasionally ½ lb. of potatoes and ½ lb. of parsnips or other vegetables); ¼ pint of meat liquor; 6 oz. of

bread. Supper, 1 pint of gruel made with 2 oz. of oatmeal or flour, sweetened with ½ oz. of molasses; 8 oz. of bread.[21]

O'Reilly got an hour's exercise each day, which consisted, in his words, of 'walking in single file, with long distances between the prisoners, around the exercise yard, and then turning an immense crank, which pumps water into the corridors.'[22]

O'Reilly was not idle while in his cell. All Millbank's inmates were employed in some form of work, mostly either 'tailoring' or 'picking'.[23] The tailoring consisted of sewing mail bags and simple garments while the 'picking' consisted of picking apart old ropes, called oakum. This oakum was old tarred ropes that were cut into pieces measuring around 2 feet long, and which the prisoners were then required to pull apart until they were left with strands as fine as silk. It was an extremely dirty process and after a few hours the picker's hands would have been black with tar; a situation aggravated by the prison policy of providing baths to male convicts only every fortnight. Those engaged in this work were required to reach a daily quota of picked oakum (around 2 lb a day seems to have been the standard).[24] As was the practice in Millbank, O'Reilly was not allowed move around his cell while picking, being forced to sit on his tub, which when turned upside down doubled as a stool. The painstaking nature of the work was described by Henry Mayhew:

> The prisoner takes up a length of junk and untwists it, and when he has separated it into so many corkscrew strands, he further unrolls them by sliding them backwards and forwards on his knee with the palm of his hand, until the meshes are loosened. Then the strand is further unraveled by placing it in the bend of a hook fastened to the knees, and sawing it smartly to and fro, which soon removes the tar and grates the fibres apart. In this condition, all that remains to be done is to loosen the hemp by pulling it out like cotton wool, when the process is completed.[25]

When not picking oakum O'Reilly was involved in the less dirty but no less meticulous work of picking coir; a process which involved picking apart untarred coir ropes and mats into individual threads. Most of these newly freed oakum and coir fibres were re-spun into ropes, which were sold by

Millbank to shipbuilders, fishermen and the government. For the prison it was literally 'new money for old rope'.

O'Reilly hated Millbank and he scorned what he saw as the hypocrisy inherent in the imagined rehabilitative aspects of the convict's life. In *Moondyne*, a novel O'Reilly would publish in 1878 and which we will encounter again in later chapters, he wrote of Millbank: 'Better the old dungeon, with its gloom; better for the sake of humanity. The new prison is a cage – a hideous hive of order and commonplace severity, where the flooding sunlight is a derision, and the barred door only a securer means of confinement.'[26] On both sides of that barred door, silence reigned, cloaking the jailed and the jailer alike. The psychological impact of this inescapable hush was described by Michael Davitt:

> The vagrant sunbeam that finds its way to the lonely occupant of a prison cell, but speaks of the liberty which others enjoy, of the happiness that falls to the lot of those whom misfortune has not dragged from the pleasures of life; the cries, the noise, and uproar of London which penetrate the silent corridors, and re-echo in the cheerless cells of Millbank, are so many mocking voices that come to laugh at the misery their walls inclose, and arouse the recollection of happier days to probe the wounds of present sorrow.[27]

After around six months O'Reilly's separate confinement came to an end. In later years the Fenian convict wrote an account of how he was reintroduced to the company of other people:

> I was brought 'cheek by jowl' with the regular criminals. I confess I had a fear of the first plunge into the sea of villainous association; but my army experience rendered the immersion easier for me than for many others who had been dragged to confinement from the purity of a happy home.[28]

That morning O'Reilly was taken along with other prisoners to one of the exercise yards, a large gravelled court. Here they were ordered to work on the 'crank'. This was a pump on which, normally, sixteen men were placed, four at each large handle with two on one side of the handle and two on the other:

The men stood at this crank facing each other, and the man facing me was a perfect type of the brutal English jail-bird. I had noticed the fellow in the chapel for three mornings previously, but this was the first day I had taken the regular exercise. He was a man about thirty-five years of age, with a yellowish-white, corpse-like face, one of those faces on which whiskers never grow, and only a few long hairs in place of a mustache. Of course he was closely shaven, but I felt that that was the nature of his whiskers when 'outside'. I had noticed, sitting behind this man as I did in chapel, almost directly in the rear of him, that I could see his eyes. He had a narrow, straight face, and there was a deep scoop, as it were, taken out of each bone where the forehead joined the cheek, and through this scoop I saw the eye from behind even more clearly than when standing in front of the man, for his brows overhung in a most forbidding way.

We had marched, Indian file, from our cells on my first morning's exercise, and had taken about three circuits of the yard when the officer shouted in a harsh, unfriendly tone, the prison order – 'Halt! Pile on to crank, No. 1.' No. 1 turned toward the center of the yard, where ran the series of cranks arranged with one handle for two men facing each other. When I got to my place I was face to face with the Corpse-man, and when he turned his head sideways, I saw his left eye through the scoop in his cheekbone. The officers stood behind me. There were three of them to the gang of twenty men, and their duty was to watch so that no communication took place between the prisoners. I felt that the corpse-man wanted to talk to me, but he kept his hidden eyes on the officers behind me and turned the crank without the movement of a muscle of his face. Presently, I heard a whisper, 'Mate', and I knew it must be he who spoke, although still not a muscle seemed to move him. I looked at him and waited. He said again in the same mysterious manner: 'Mate, what's your sentence?'[29]

O'Reilly would have little time to get to know other inmates in Millbank. At the end of March or early April 1867, O'Reilly, Chambers and McCarthy were on the move again, to Chatham Prison in Kent. By this time the three men may have heard the news from Ireland that a Fenian uprising had failed.

The Fenians in Ireland had undergone many changes since the time of O'Reilly's arrest in February 1866. James Stephens had left his hideout in Ireland amid the February arrests and made his way to the United States, via Scotland, England, France and then by passenger ship across the Atlantic. He found the Fenians there to be divided into two main factions (see chapter 9) and Stephens would spend the remainder of 1866 trying to unite these groups in support of a rising in Ireland. However, as the year drew to a conclusion Stephens again counselled that a rising was premature. Many Fenians discerned the same pattern of indecision that had characterised Stephens' actions in 1865 and by the end of the year he had been forced from his position as leader. Stephens' place was taken by his former protégé, Thomas Kelly, a long-standing Fenian and a Union soldier during the American Civil War. In January 1867 Kelly sailed to Europe with the goal of fomenting rebellion in Ireland. He brought with him a cadre of veterans of the Civil War, mostly former Union soldiers but also at least one former Confederate, County Limerick-born Godfrey Massey. This man would later give evidence against his Fenian comrades and may have been an informer even at this stage. Another noteworthy companion was Gustave Paul Cluseret, a 43-year-old French soldier. Cluseret had been a soldier most of his adult life, having seen action in Algeria and the Crimea. He had served with Garibaldi in Sicily and, for a short period, had been a brigadier general in the Union army during the Civil War. Cluseret was Kelly's choice as commander of the Fenian army in Ireland.

Kelly, though, would not travel to Ireland. Habeas corpus had been suspended during February 1866 and many of the Irish-American soldiers already in the country had fled to England as a result. Ireland remained in a state of emergency and the police had further ruptured the command structure of the Fenians with a series of arrests in December 1866. Kelly judged that he would be more easily able to avoid police detection by basing himself in London. His decision, although understandable, would add an extra layer of confusion to the planning of the rising. Cluseret also remained in England and control of the Fenian army was handed to Massey. It was Cluseret's intention that the early stage of the rising would consist of raids for arms and small-scale guerilla attacks, which would allow the Fenians to gain experience and weaponry while stretching the resources of the police and army. Cluseret would then travel to Ireland to lead the Fenians in larger engagements with the Crown forces. This plan was ripped asunder by the arrest of Massey on 4 March, thereby wrecking the high command of the Fenian army.

Nevertheless, the rising took place over 5 and 6 March. Although Fenians went into action in many places around the country, most heavily in Tallaght, their efforts were utterly undermined by a lack of adequate weaponry. There were a few minor successes: some police barracks captured near Dublin and in Ballyknockane on the border of Cork and Waterford; a coastguard station and all its arms captured in Cork. Even such successes were rendered useless by the fact that there was no overall Fenian strategy or a commander who could direct events. Elsewhere, the police were able to scatter large groups of Fenians who had congregated in Dublin, Drogheda, County Limerick and other locations. The Fenians were further hampered by cold and stormy weather on the night of 5 March and when the military, including O'Reilly's former regiment, went into action on 6 March they dispersed any groups of Fenians that remained intact throughout the west and south of the country. That marked the end of the rising although there would be occasional outbursts of violence over the rest of the month.

It seems unlikely that the rising in Ireland had any bearing on the decision to move O'Reilly from Millbank. He had finished his period of separate confinement and the next stage in his sentence was hard labour. When O'Reilly and his comrades arrived at Chatham they were put to work in the British Royal Navy's huge complex on the river Medway. Chatham had been the site of a major prison riot in 1861 and conditions seem not to have greatly improved by the time O'Reilly arrived. The numbing boredom and loneliness of separate confinement was now replaced by the brutality of hard labour as the three men, along with hundreds of other convicts, became involved in the building of a naval dockyard. At Chatham, O'Reilly and two other inmates (perhaps Chambers and McCarthy) made an attempt to escape. The details of this attempt are unknown but the three men were apprehended and were put in solitary confinement for a month and further punished with a diet of bread and water.[30] On his release from solitary O'Reilly was sent to Portsmouth, as were Chambers and McCarthy. Once more they were involved in heavy labour and again O'Reilly made an attempt to escape. Unfortunately for the Irishman this was merely a replay of his earlier escape at Chatham. Capture, solitary confinement and a diet of bread and water were the end results.[31] It was June 1867 before O'Reilly was back in the company of his fellow convicts and, in what was becoming a tour of the English penal system, the trio of O'Reilly, Chambers and McCarthy were dispatched to another jail. They were moved to what would be O'Reilly's final place of incarceration within England, the legendary and feared prison of Dartmoor.

Historical records for Dartmoor Prison are more sparse in number than those for other prisons such as Millbank. This is mainly due to the destruction wrought by a huge riot at Dartmoor in 1932. There is no doubt, however, that Dartmoor was a harsh and disgusting environment. The cells were tiny: 7 feet long, 4 feet wide, and 7 feet high. The prison was also damp, a condition greatly worsened by the poor ventilation and its position on the cold and wet moors.[32] Michael Davitt was unfortunate enough to spend over six years in Dartmoor from 1871 to 1877. He often had to kneel by the opening at the bottom of his cell door to suck in some air. The food was much worse that at Millbank: insufficiently nutritious and regularly spiced with insects, horsehair, bits of bones and even pieces of coal. Perhaps fortunately, O'Reilly would spend far less time in his cell at Dartmoor than he had done at Millbank, as each day the convicts were corralled into groups and sent to work on the moor. O'Reilly had remained relatively strong despite his captivity over the previous sixteen months and he was able to withstand this hard labour. Yet the work undertaken by convicts at Dartmoor was far more strenuous than anything O'Reilly or his comrades had experienced in the other prisons and he later described the destructive effects that it had upon Chambers and McCarthy:

> Here they were set to work on the marsh, digging deep drains, and carrying the wet peat in their arms, stacking it near the roadways for removal. For months they toiled in the drains, which were only two feet wide, and sunk ten feet in the morass. It was a labor too hard for brutes, the half-starved men, weakened by long confinement, standing in water from a foot to two feet deep, and spading the heavy peat out of the narrow cutting over their heads. Here it was that Chambers and McCarthy contracted the rheumatic and heart diseases which followed them to the end.[33]

Dartmoor's prisoners were engaged in various forms of hard labour such as stone-breaking, bone-breaking and digging drains. It was the last activity that was O'Reilly's most commonly allotted method of punishment and he spent many days burrowing through the landscape.[34] Scattered among these convicts were the prison warders, usually stationed atop high points on the moor. These warders had to keep a lookout on two fronts: for runaway prisoners and approaching fog.

Situated on the peninsula that juts out from the south-west coast of England, Dartmoor is regularly shrouded in a blanket of fog, the legendary Dartmoor mists. These are the result of an airflow that predominantly comes from the south-west and is laden with moisture picked up from the warm currents of the North Atlantic Drift. Once the air current hits the high plateau of Dartmoor it is cooled by the lower temperatures and creates cloudy conditions, usually in the form of rain or thick mists. These mists can quickly shroud the whole landscape, reduce visibility to a few feet and leave even locals unsure as to their whereabouts. As such, part of each warder's duties was to get the work parties back to the prison before any incoming fog settled. This could be a rushed affair and amid the disorder convicts often took their chance and absconded. It is likely that O'Reilly was witness to some of these escapes and they may have inspired him to make his own bid for freedom. Of course, escape from Dartmoor was not simply a matter of scurrying into the mist. The often cold and damp environment would be unforgiving to an escapee clad only in his simple convict garb. O'Reilly, though, was nothing if not resourceful and he fashioned a rough suit of clothes from one of the coarse bed sheets supplied to each prisoner.[35]

He made his escape around September 1867. O'Reilly was engaged in digging a drain when another fog rolled in over the moor. As the warders signalled for the convicts to return to the prison the Fenian hid himself in a drain. His absence was not noted until the warders conducted a headcount on their arrival behind the prison walls.[36] The shortfall in this count was the signal for the guards to launch a huge search operation. O'Reilly, his self-made suit adding an extra layer of warmth under his convict clothes, had managed to gain a brief head start on his pursuers but a fugitive on his own in the wilds of Dartmoor had little hope of success. Nevertheless, O'Reilly remained free for two days. On the first day he was forced to climb onto the roof of an old house and hide behind the chimney as guards marched by the building. On the second day he hid in a dyke that ran into a nearby river. All the while his pursuers moved back and forth along the dyke but the escapee remained unseen. He planned to wait for nightfall and then move to the river and from there make his way to the coast. It was not to be. O'Reilly was undone by the sharp eyes of a warder who, surveying the dyke with field glasses, spotted some ripples in the water. The guard notified his comrades and minutes later O'Reilly was recaptured. The reward for the escapee's initiative was the standard penalty of a month in solitary with a diet of bread and water.[37]

In later years O'Reilly would speak of his time at Dartmoor with genuine revulsion and there is no doubt it left the usually ebullient and optimistic young Fenian on the verge of despair. With his capture he knew that there could be no escape from Dartmoor and he later described his feelings of hopelessness: 'The excitement was dead. There was nought left now but patience and submission. I have said that the excitement, even of failure, was dead.'[38] Yet, at the beginning of October when he thought himself without a future, a murmur of hope began to echo through the prison:

> A rumor went through the prison – in the weirdly mysterious way in which rumors do go through a prison. However it came is a mystery, but there did come a rumor to the prison, even to the dark cells, of a ship sailing for Australia! Australia! the ship! Another chance for the old dreams; and the wild thought was wilder than ever, and not half so stealthy.[39]

The time between rumour and action was bewilderingly short and O'Reilly was to be plucked from his cell to be sent onwards to yet another prison: 'Down the corridor came the footsteps again. The keys rattled, doors opened, and in five minutes we had double irons on our arms, and were chained together by a bright, strong chain. We did not look into each other's faces; we had learned to know what the others were thinking of without speaking.'[40] The reach of the British Empire was a long one and the fantastic rumours sweeping through the cells of Dartmoor were indeed true. John Boyle O'Reilly's next prison was going to be at the other end of the world. Like so many Irish and British convicts before him, he was to be transported to Australia.

5

The *Hougoumont*

It was the British government of Edward Stanley, the Earl of Derby, which had decided to send the Fenians to Western Australia. The government had been mulling over the idea of transportation since the summer of 1867 but the final impetus for this decision may have been the rescue of Fenian leaders Thomas Kelly and Timothy Deasy in Manchester on 18 September. The two Fenians were being moved from a court hearing to a local prison when a group of about thirty Fenians ambushed the police transport. The ambushers succeeded in freeing the prisoners and making their getaway. One of the police, Sergeant Charles Brett, was shot dead in the skirmish. English newspapers and the public, already unnerved by the reputation of the Fenians, were shocked by the incident. Amid the ensuing hysteria, the government responded with a series of armed raids across the city and eventually twenty-eight of the ambushing party were captured.[1] The ambush seems to have convinced the government that it would be prudent to remove imprisoned Fenians from England to Australia lest they be a focus for further Fenian rescue attempts.

The day that John Boyle O'Reilly was informed of his impending transportation to Australia (in the first few days of October 1867) was also the point where his path diverged from that of Thomas Chambers and Charles McCarthy. The two men would spend another twelve years in prison, most of it in Dartmoor, and through this their health was destroyed.[2] Later that same day O'Reilly was part of a group of six prisoners, including three Fenians, taken by prison officers to the local train station. Here the group was put on a train to Dorset, their next destination being Portland Prison. O'Reilly later described what happened on their arrival:

It was late at night when we arrived there, and got out of harness. The ceremony of receiving convicts from another prison is amusing and 'racy of the soil'. To give an idea of it, it is enough to say that every article of clothing which a prisoner wears must at once go back to the prison whence he came. It may be an hour, or two, or more, before a single article is drawn from the stores of the receiving prison – during which time the felon is supremely primitive. To the prison officials this seems highly amusing; but to me, looking at it with the convict's eye and feelings, the point of the joke was rather obscure.[3]

After their long wait to receive clothes the convicts dressed themselves and were allowed some sleep. On the next day they were sent to the exercise yard where they met with a party of twenty other Fenians, who had arrived in Portland two days earlier. As O'Reilly wrote, 'They had come from Ireland – had only been in prison for a few months.'[4] They brought with them news from home. One of them told O'Reilly that he had met O'Reilly's brother William who was imprisoned and awaiting trial as a Fenian (William would die in prison sometime during the next twelve months)[5]. Many of the other Fenians were given similar news. They remained in Portland Prison for around a week, all the time being joined by prisoners from other jails across England.

The prisoners had their first view of their transport ship, the *Hougoumont*, on 6 October. Unknown to O'Reilly and his comrades, the *Hougoumont* had already been to London, where it had taken on board prisoners from Millbank. One of these was the 27-year-old civilian Fenian Denis Cashman from Waterford, who would keep a diary of the journey to Australia. Cashman would become a friend of O'Reilly's while aboard the transport ship and they would have a long association that continued in the United States.[6] Another of the civilian Fenians, John Sarsfield Casey from County Cork, likewise kept a diary.[7] Both Cashman and Casey are among our main sources for what happened on the voyage. There is also the diary of yet another civilian Fenian, Thomas McCarthy Fennell from County Clare. His account, however, was written years later in the United States and is not a daily record comparable to those of Cashman or Casey.[8] As was the case with O'Reilly, none of the Fenians aboard the *Hougoumont* expected to be sent to Australia. The news had been a moment of hope for O'Reilly but to the ten Fenians with wives and children the thought of transportation was heartbreaking. Cashman, who had heard the news a week before O'Reilly, was one of the married men and he confided to his diary:

> On Tuesday 24th of September, whilst very busily employed at the (to me) very disagreeable occupation of picking 'coir', I heard steps approaching along the corridor, and halt opposite my cell door; instantly, the Iron gates, and the massive wooden door of my cell were flung open, and the order 'stand at ye gate' given. I was glad of anything that would even for a moment thwart the monotony, or break the wretched grave-like silence of the place, immediately came to 'attention' at the door; and found my visitors to be Head Warden 'Handy' and some warders of lower grade. Then for the first time I learned that I was to be sent to Australia. I received the news with a very bad grace, and protested in the strongest terms against being sent – but recollecting that I had no voice in the matter, and that go I should, I strove to make the most of it, and drown the bitter feelings which filled my breast, by fiercely working at or rather tearing the tough coir – I really felt wretched – the thought of being sent 14,000 miles away from my dear wife and children – from all that I loved on earth; with the fact staring me in the face, that I should not again for years see them, caused me to feel an acute agony, that I never before felt, and plunged my whole being into the deepest melancholy.[9]

Over the next few days the convicts were loaded onto the ship. The Fenians went aboard on either 7 or 8 October. They were in the exercise yard when the order was given to assemble. O'Reilly, in an article he wrote years later, described the moment:

> Then came the old routine – old to us, but new and terrible to the men from Ireland – double irons and chains. This time there were twenty men on each chain, the political prisoners separate from the criminals. 'Forward there!' and we dragged each other to the esplanade of the prison. It was a gala day – a grand parade of the convicts. They were drawn up in line – a horrible and insulting libel on an army – and the governor, and the doctors of the prison and ship reviewed them. There were two or three lounging in the prison

yard that day, who, I remember well, looked strangely out of place there. They had honest, bronzed faces and careless sailor's dress – the mates and boatswain of the *Hougoumont*, who had come ashore to superintend the embarkation.[10]

The last of the prisoners were about to walk up the gangway to the ship when there was an incident that left a lasting impression on those who saw it:

> The review was over. The troops – Heaven forgive me! – formed in columns of chains, and marched to the steamer which was waiting to convey them to the transport. Our chain was in the extreme rear. Just as we reached the gangway to go on board, a woman's piercing shriek rose up from the crowd on the wharf; a young girl rushed wildly out, and threw herself, weeping and sobbing, on the breast of a man in our chain, poor Thomas Dunne. She was his sister [Bridget]. She had come from Dublin to see him before he sailed away. They would not let her see him in prison, so she had come there to see him in his chains. Oh! may God keep me from ever seeing another scene like that which we all stood still to gaze at; even the merciless officials for a moment hesitated to interfere. Poor Dunne could only stoop his head and kiss his sister – his arms were chained; and that loving, heart-broken girl, worn out by grief, clung to his arms and his chains, as they dragged her away; and when she saw him pushed rudely to the gangway, she raised her voice in a wild cry: 'Oh, God! Oh, God!' as if reproaching Him who willed such things to pass. From the steamer's deck we saw her still watching tirelessly, and we tried to say words of comfort to that brother – her brother and ours. He knew she was alone, and had no friends in wide England.[11]

As Bridget Dunne looked on powerlessly the last of the convicts were marched aboard the ship. O'Reilly described the fearful moment:

> Our chains were knocked off on the soldier-lined decks, and we were ordered to go below. The sides of the main hatchway were composed of massive iron bars, and, as we went down, the prisoners within clutched the bars and looked eagerly through, hoping, perhaps, to

see a familiar face. As I stood in that hatchway, looking at the wretches glaring out, I realized more than ever before the terrible truth that a convict ship is a floating hell. The forward hold was dark, save the yellow light of a few ship's lamps . . . There swelled up a hideous diapason from that crowd of wretches: the usual prison restraint was removed, and the reaction was at its fiercest pitch. Such a din of diabolical sounds no man ever heard. We hesitated before entering the low-barred door to the hold, unwilling to plunge into the seething den.[12]

O'Reilly stood uncertainly at the door and watched as a tall gaunt man pushed his way through the crowd. This man beckoned to O'Reilly, 'Come, we are waiting for you.'[13] O'Reilly did not recognise the face but he immediately knew the voice. It was a fellow comrade from the British army, Patrick Keating, who had been tried alongside O'Reilly in 1866. The gaunt features that made the 41-year-old unrecognisable to O'Reilly were a consequence of the constant illnesses that had afflicted Keating during his time in prison. O'Reilly followed his friend through the throng to a door leading amidships away from the criminal part of the ship. As O'Reilly remembered, 'this door was opened by another gaunt man within, and we entered. Then the door was closed and we were with our friends – our brothers. Great God! What a scene that was, and how vividly it arises to my mind now!'[14] For the next three months, the *Hougoumont* was to be their shared prison.

The *Hougoumont*, built in 1852, was a frigate of 875 tons and had seen service as a troop carrier during the Crimean war. The ship had also made the journey from England to Australia on at least one occasion in the 1860s before it was chartered as a convict ship by the British government in 1867. In his novel *Moondyne*, O'Reilly wrote in great detail about the journey of the *Hougoumont*. However, while there are many elements of O'Reilly's life scattered through the narrative of that book, it is a work of fiction. The ship's voyage as described in *Moondyne* is a composite of reports from many convict transports and the novel serves as an indictment of British penal practices, especially the policy of transportation. Therefore, while much of *Moondyne*'s tale of the convict ship took place only in its author's mind, there is still much of value as a historical source. His description of the ship's layout is one example:

She was fitted in the usual way of convict ships. Her main deck and her lower deck were divided into separate compartments, the dividing walls below being heavy and strong bulkheads, while those on deck were wooden barriers about nine feet high, with side doors, for the passage of the sailors while working the ship. At each of these doors, during the entire voyage, stood two soldiers, with fixed bayonets on their loaded rifles. The hatch coverings opening to the lower deck, where the convicts were confined, were removed, and around each hatchway, reaching from the upper deck, or roof of the convict's room, to the lower deck or floor, was one immense grating, formed of strong iron bars. This arrangement gave plenty of air and a good deal of light, the only obstruction being the bars. Seen from below, on the convicts' deck, every hatchway stood in the centre of the ship like a great iron cage, with a door by which the warders entered, and a ladder to reach the upper deck. The convicts below never tired of looking upwards through the bars, though they could see nothing above but the swaying ropes and sails, and at night the beautiful sky and the stars. In the forward and smallest compartment of the ship between decks lived the crew, who went up and down by their own hatchway.[15]

O'Reilly continued to describe the sections of the ship within which the convicts were held. *Moondyne* describes compartments for male and female convicts but since Western Australia did not receive female convicts there were none aboard the *Hougoumont*. However, the Fenians were kept in a separate compartment from the criminal convicts so if we replace 'Fenian' for 'female' we can get an accurate picture of how the ship was divided:

In the next, and largest compartment, lived the male convicts . . . The central compartment was the hospital, and next to this the compartment for the female convicts. The after compartment between decks was occupied by the sixty soldiers who kept guard on the ship. The main, or upper deck, was divided as follows: the after part, under the poop deck, was occupied by the staterooms for officers and passengers, and the richly-furnished cabin dining room. Forward of this, beginning at the front of the poop, was a division of the deck to which the female convicts were allowed at certain hours of the day. The next section was the deck where the male convicts were allowed to exercise, one hundred at a time, throughout the day. The fore part of the main deck, running out to the bowsprit like a ^ was roofed in, the angular section taking in the bowsprit. The front of this section, running across the deck, was composed of enormous bars, thicker than a man's arm, like those around the hatches, and within these bars, in sight of the male convicts on deck, were confined the malefactors, or rule-breakers. This triangular section was the punishment cell of the ship.[16]

Apart from the punishment cell there was the flogging triangle attached to the foremast where troublesome prisoners could be tied and whipped. For the more serious examples of indiscipline aboard the ship, such as mutiny, the punishment was death by hanging. A rope was kept ready at the foremast for such occasions.

All told, there were 431 people aboard the ship. The convicts comprised 280 of the ship's population and of these 62 were Fenians. Strange as it may seem, there were 34 children on the *Hougoumont*. At least one of these was a baby, a boy named James McLewin who was baptised at sea. These were the children of some of the warders and the 50 pensioner guards, retired soldiers who were accompanying the convicts as extra security and who had decided to settle in Western Australia. Overseeing the transport of all these individuals was Captain William Cozens but he was not the sole authority aboard the ship. Supervising all important decisions with regard to the convicts including their diet, exercise and clothing was the ship's Surgeon Superintendant, Dr William Smith. Religious guidance would be proffered to the convicts through Father Bernard Delany and Reverend M. Williams. Delany had volunteered to accompany the Fenians on their transportation and would actually settle in Western Australia where he worked with the colony's convicts.[17]

The Fenian prisoners assigned to the *Hougoumont* were a combination of civilian members of the Brotherhood and former soldiers. The trials at which these men had been convicted took place over two discrete time periods: December 1865 until August 1866 and February to August 1867. In this second period, trials were held not only in Dublin and Cork but also in Limerick, Kerry, Clare, Tipperary and Louth. Some of the prisoners, such as O'Reilly, were already experienced convicts. However, over half of the Fenians transported on the *Hougoumont* were convicted in the later series of trials and had only been imprisoned for a few months. John Goulding of Tralee, for example, had been convicted in August.[18] Twelve of the Fenians had been sentenced to life imprisonment, O'Reilly and one other man had received sentences of twenty years, two of fifteen years, and ten had been given a sentence of ten years. The remaining thirty-six had been given sentences of between five and seven years.[19] Including O'Reilly, seventeen of the men had been members of the British army.[20]

The prison records described the trades and careers that the Fenians were involved in before their incarceration. There were eleven labourers, eight clerks, seven farmers, five carpenters, three bakers, three shoemakers and one each of schoolmaster, building contractor, weaver, plasterer, tailor, gardener, fitter, horse trainer, mill master, shipsmith, builder, cooper, coachman, coachman's groom. Two of the men were compositors. One of these was O'Reilly and he was also classed as a reporter.[21] The rest were probably career soldiers. Many of these men were important figures in the Fenians. Michael Moore had made weapons for the Brotherhood. Thomas Duggan and John Kenneally had been the chief Fenian recruiters in Cork city and county. Kenneally had also been a confidant of James Stephens. Another important figure was Hugh Brophy, who was involved with the publication of the *Irish People* newspaper. John Flood had helped plan James Stephens' escape from Richmond Bridewell. He was also heavily involved in a later Fenian plot to seize weapons from Chester Castle in England. Edward Kelly from Cork had been a high-profile member of the rising in March 1867.

Although the military Fenians such as O'Reilly were supposed to have been kept separate from the civilian Fenians, this stricture was never put into practice. However, as Denis Cashman described, the Fenians were kept apart from the criminal convicts:

We had a separate compartment in the convict portion of the ship. We were very glad of this as the majority of the convicts were the greatest ruffians, and the most notorious robbers in England. Of course we did not associate or scarcely speak to the unfortunates, although I believe a portion of them had been very respectable and well educated – A good many of them had a great respect for our men and endeavored to show it by several acts of good nature – &

being most respectful in their deportment. Some of them were very notorious characters – viz the Scuttlers of the ship 'Severn' – The owner appeared a gentlemanly sort of fellow – The great jewel robbers – The boy that stabbed his fellow-apprentice – a cool murderer – A fellow who killed his mother. In fact they were all an extremely proficient class at their business.[22]

Cashman's description of the criminal convicts is borne out by the surviving records. Most of them were house burglars, thieves and pickpockets but a high percentage had been convicted of more serious crimes, including twenty-two who were convicted of rape, twelve of murder, twelve of manslaughter, ten of grievous bodily harm, eight of arson and four of attempted murder.[23] The criminal convicts had come from the prisons at Portland, Millbank, Chatham, Portsmouth, Pentonville, Woking and Dartmoor. None of these convicts had been given sentences of less than seven years, while ninety-two of them had received sentences from twelve years to life imprisonment.[24]

With all its prisoners and passengers aboard, the *Hougoumont* weighed anchor at 2.55 p.m. on Saturday 12 October 1867 and began its journey southwards. Its destination was the Western Australian town of Fremantle. The ship was not alone, being accompanied by a gunboat named the *Earnest*. This vessel was tasked with the protection of the *Hougoumont* from any Fenian-controlled ship that might bid to rescue the prisoners. With a favourable breeze the *Hougoumont* made swift progress away from the Dorset coast and, seeing no sign of any rescue ship, the *Earnest* soon returned to port. On the following morning the Fenians were given a breakfast of biscuit and tea. This would be the standard morning fare for the rest of the journey although they would occasionally be given some chocolate at breakfast. Dinner consisted of pea soup, beef, mixed vegetables and preserved potatoes. On some days the pea soup was replaced by plum duff (a pudding with raisins or currants). Every afternoon at 2 p.m. each prisoner was given a glass of wine and at 4 p.m. a pot of gruel.[25] Lime juice was administered regularly to each prisoner as a protection against scurvy. Occasionally the convicts received tobacco and from seven to fourteen pints of water daily. Father Delany was also able to obtain on behalf of the Fenians some extra tobacco and other luxuries from the ship's stores over the voyage.

The serving of meals was the timetable by which the men lived over the following weeks. Their days consisted of sitting upon deck chatting while their nights were spent below decks, talking some more. For those, like O'Reilly and Cashman, who had endured separate confinement and the silent system this freedom to talk and laugh had already made the prison ship less of a punishment than the prisons they had left behind. The Fenians may have been on a convict ship, living in cramped conditions and constantly watched over by the armed guards but their journey was not to be the perilous and brutal experience that many of them had expected nor the 'floating hell' that O'Reilly had feared on first boarding the ship. They were allowed to celebrate Mass most mornings and they mingled freely during the day. However, after almost two weeks of doing nothing but sitting and talking, boredom had set in by 24 October. They had had enough of chatting and watching distant coastlines from the deck. Denis Cashman wrote in his diary about the mood on board:

> We had a debate today as to the best means of killing time and amusing ourselves during the voyage – I proposed theatricals; it was agreed to but in consequence of not having sufficient room for a stage we abandoned the project, to substitute which I drew up a programme for a concert which I expect will come off with éclat at 6 o.c. this evg. – Jack O'Reilly and I preparing to recite 'Brutus & Cassius', but I believe the beggar doesn't take much interest in it.[26]

Throughout all the following day the Fenians prepared and rehearsed a programme for their first concert. O'Reilly did not play a starring role in that night's show but he was involved in its preparation and that first concert was much enjoyed by the Fenians.

The ship's captain was doubtlessly happy to let the Fenians concentrate their enthusiasm and active minds upon the concerts but while the revolutionaries sought to alleviate their boredom through song and poetry, the criminal convicts resorted to fighting among themselves. On the following day O'Reilly and his comrades witnessed one of the criminals receive forty-eight lashes for some offence committed during the night. At the last strike of the whip, the criminal convicts let out a cheer. To counter what seemed a burgeoning mood of defiance from the criminal convicts, the captain had them all placed in irons. Some of these men were kept in irons for the rest of the journey. Cashman later wrote that it was 'awful to hear the unfortunates – with the chains clanking everywhere they went – there were so many of them in the chains that the clank was continuous on deck and below – they had to bring them to bed with them – as they did not get them off till ship came to anchor.'[27] The Fenians kept themselves out of trouble and held more concerts on the following nights. They endured a serious squall through the night of 27 October while about 30 miles off the coast of the Portuguese island of Madeira. This was the second storm that the ship had encountered and it left all aboard, according to Cashman, badly shaken. O'Reilly made his first concert appearance on the evening of 29 October and performed his own composition, 'The Old School Clock', written while awaiting trial in Arbour Hill Prison.[28]

The journey continued in a similar manner over the next week; long periods of boredom punctuated with nightly concerts, regular sightings of exotic marine life, some morning Masses and the occasional storm. The Fenians spent each day huddled together on deck and from all their talk emerged the idea that they should make an attempt to gain control of the ship. According to Cashman, O'Reilly was 'father to a scheme to capture the ship, guards, convicts and all.'[29] Over the end of October and beginning of November the Fenians discussed potential actions. This talk may have given the men a brief sense of hope but the reality of their situation impinged on any dreams of a heroic escape to America. Not only would the Fenians have to keep their plans secret but they would have to overcome and disarm over forty armed guards and the ship's crew. Even if they succeeded in taking the ship they would then have to control the ship's criminal convicts, who outnumbered the Fenians by almost four to one. Failure would result in further punishments, perhaps death and too many of the sixty-two Fenians were opposed to idea for it to have any chance of success. There were too many risks and imponderables and, probably reluctantly at first, O'Reilly and his more impetuous comrades agreed that the plan was too dangerous and too unlikely to succeed.[30]

Instead of risking all, the Fenians sought a new means of improving their daily lives. Their idea was a remarkable one, considering the fact that they were on a convict ship; they decided to start a newspaper. This was agreed on 5 November.[31] Two days later the newly formed newspaper group began to put together the first edition of their new journal, which would be published under the name of *The Wild Goose*. The new paper would be edited by John Flood with O'Reilly as sub-editor.[32] In his diary, Thomas McCarthy Fennell described how the paper was transcribed by the best 'pensmen' among the Fenians; there being no printing equipment on board.[33] He also stated that 'the discussion of politics was forbidden in its columns' by order of the captain.[34] In reality, the Fenians would slip the occasional political barb into the paper's poems and satirical pieces while its title, *The Wild Goose*, was a reference to Patrick Sarsfield and the Irish soldiers who had fled from Ireland in 1691. As O'Reilly and his fellow journalists compiled their newspaper, the *Hougoumont* passed within sight of the Cape Verde Islands, a few hundred miles off the coast of Senegal. The weather had become much warmer over the previous week causing the convicts much discomfort. Cashman reported that it was insufferably hot between decks and it must have been even worse for the criminal convicts.[35] To alleviate the situation the captain granted extra water rations to each person on board.

On 9 November the first edition of *The Wild Goose* was ready for its audience and that night O'Reilly read aloud its contents to his eager listeners. It was four sheets of white paper, provided by Father Delany, folded and bound at the middle to provide an eight-page newspaper. Its front page was decorated with an ornate masthead that carried the name of the paper in bold capitals and which was covered with shamrocks. Beneath the name of the paper was the subtitle 'A collection of ocean waifs'.[36] Much of the paper's content was in a light-hearted vein, with articles such as the latest news from 'the Markets', which contained items on the prices and demand for such commodities as plum duff. There was also Edward Kelly's 'guide' to Australia:

> This great continent of the south, having been discovered by some Dutch skipper and his crew, somewhere between the 1st and 19th centuries of the Christian era, was, in consequence, taken possession of by the government of Great Britain, in accordance with that just and equitable maxim, 'What's yours is mine; what's mine's my own'. That magnanimous government in the kindly exuberance of their feelings, have placed a large portion of that immense tract of country at our disposal, generously defraying all expenses incurred on our way to it, and providing retreats for us there from the inclemency of the seasons and the carnivorous propensities of the natives.

There were more serious pieces such as Kelly's 'Prison Thoughts', which he had composed while imprisoned at Millbank earlier in the year. O'Reilly also read his own composition, which he had written, he said, on the day that the *Hougoumont* left Portland. It was called 'Farewell' and it lamented the Fenian's enforced emigration. The last stanza read:

> Never more thy fair face am I destined to see;
> E'en the savage loves home, but 'tis crime to love thee.
> God bless thee, dear Erin, my loved one, my own!
> Oh! how hard 'tis these tendrils to break that have grown
> Round my heart – But 'tis over, and memory's spell
> Now steals o'er me sadly. Farewell! Oh, Farewell!

The Fenians were delighted with the newspaper and it served as a regular morale boost over the rest of the voyage, running to seven editions. Captain Cozens was also pleased with the enterprise and from early December onwards he provided the eight or so convicts involved in the paper's production with extra rations. They later responded by giving Cozens a special copy of the Christmas edition.[37]

The afternoon of 13 November saw an incident that greatly amused the whole population of the ship and serves to underline the generally relaxed atmosphere that now prevailed aboard the *Hougoumont*. Cashman described how a criminal convict was caught stealing supplies from the ship's stores. The Surgeon Superintendent ordered that the offender be tried by a 'Court Martial of Convicts'. After an entertaining trial, witnessed by most of the ship, the court martial found the convict guilty and sentenced him to be 'washed and scrubbed' as he was 'a slovenly fellow'.[38] Some of the prisoners even helped save the ship on 22 November when the *Hougoumont* was caught in a sudden and vicious storm while passing within sight of the island of Trindade, off the coast of Brazil. John Casey described how 'several huge waves crashed over the ship, almost capsizing her, and shaking every timber in her'.[39] Two sails had been simultaneously ripped to shreds and 'six or eight' convicts helped to get the mainsail down before the wind could tear it apart. The storm raged for most of the day before calm returned, leaving the ship battered but still floating.

The *Hougoumont* passed the Tropic of Capricorn on 23 November and enjoyed a relatively quiet week. The Fenians continued their routine of regular Masses, concerts and readings of the latest publications of *The Wild Goose*; their main irritations at this time were a horde of rats that seemed to grow in number each day[40] and the *Hougoumont's* failed attempt to dock at the island of Tristan da Cunha, over 1,700 miles west-southwest of the Cape of Good Hope on the southern tip of Africa's west coast. Stormy weather had convinced Captain Cozens that it was too dangerous to bring his vessel too close to land.[41] His ship had been making around 150 to 200 miles a day during the previous week but the weather became unsettled in early December and the *Hougoumont* passed through a particularly violent storm on seventh of the month. Apart from the occasional torn sail, the vessel made it through these gales and high seas unscathed and continued on its journey, keeping a wide distance from the southern tip of Africa. The conditions had had become much colder and Cozens supplied an extra blanket to each of the convicts.[42]

The miserable weather had a dampening effect on the morale of everyone aboard, a feeling that was compounded on 16 December. That evening saw a funeral at sea for one of the criminal convicts, Thomas Cochrane, who had died the previous night. Denis Cashman watched the melancholy ceremony:

> the convicts ranged themselves at either side of the starboard side of the ship – & on Forecastle deck – and after a few minutes – the procession began – A cross bearer leading – he was followed by two acolites followed by the officiating Priest in robes – and his clerk – next came the corpse covered with a Union Jack and borne by 6 convicts – when the procession reached the inside of the bulkhead door 'The Miserere' & 'Te Deum' were repeated – the body being placed in a slanting position projecting from a starboard port hole – at the conclusion of the prayers the body with a heavy weight tied to the feet, was gradually allowed to slip – A splash immediately intimated that it was consigned to its watery grave – the whole scene was very solemn and impressive – I hope he may requiescat in pace.[43]

Cochrane was the only person to die aboard the *Hougoumont* during its voyage to Western Australia. His funeral disheartened many of the Fenians. They had previously refused to let their circumstances drag them into despondency but the sight of Cochrane's lifeless body sinking between the waves was a stark reminder that any of them could die alone and exiled. Fennell ruminated on the loneliness of Cochrane's 'Saddest, cruellest, most disconsolate death.'[44] John Casey's diary entry for that day expressed a similar sentiment, which was doubtlessly shared by many of the convicts, both Fenian and criminal: 'Cannot think without emotion of dying in a far distant land away from friends, home and kindred without a single hand to sooth and comfort me in my last moments.'[45]

The weather remained bitterly cold over the following week but the blustery winds had the benefit of pushing the ship at a good speed towards Western Australia. The *Hougoumont* was now around two weeks from the town of Fremantle and life aboard ship was losing whatever lustre it may once have held for the Fenians: 'We are all wishing most anxiously for the termination of the voyage,' Denis Cashman noted in his diary on 22 December.[46] Christmas Day 1867 brought little relief for the convicts as the *Hougoumont* spent the day, as it had done on Christmas Eve, trying to stay afloat in the midst of another storm. The seas were too turbulent for there to be a Christmas Mass but everyone aboard joined in the singing of 'O Come all ye faithful'.[47] The prisoners were rewarded with a breakfast of 'sweet bread', which was much appreciated by the men. The ship was pitching about too much for anyone to remain on deck so the Fenians went below for their 'Christmas Goose' where they listened to O'Reilly as he read aloud the new edition of their newspaper.

These included two poems by O'Reilly, 'Christmas Night' and 'The Flying Dutchman'; the first poem told the tale of a prisoner in his cell one Christmas while the second was a story of the legendary ghost ship which portends doom to sailors. There was a final editorial from John Flood, which addressed the fast-nearing end to their journey and the inevitability of the group's break-up after their disembarkation in Australia: 'I know not what may be in store for you. I cannot pierce the inexorable veil of the future, drawn alike for me and for you; but bidding you a long farewell most likely, however we may wish it, never to meet again, I say to you – Courage, and trust in Providence.'[48] O'Reilly's reading of the newspaper gave solace to the prisoners. Cashman admitted to his diary that he felt cheerful for the first time in a while and like many of the others his thoughts turned to home. He continued his journal with the hope that his family were enjoying their Christmas Day and by sending his wife, Kathleen, '1000 kisses across the 1000s of miles which divide us.'[49] The performance was also watched and enjoyed by some of the crew. Captain Cozens had already received his complimentary copy and, once O'Reilly had finished reading, a few of the ship's mates asked if he would put together a copy for them. It was a request to which he happily assented.[50]

Their journey had entered it last stages but a string of gales continued to buffet the ship from the end of December and into the first days of 1868. New Year's Eve was the backdrop to a particularly dangerous storm. Amid the havoc of the night some of the criminal convicts broke into the ship's stores. One of them was caught and flogged on deck two days later. That was the second of only two such punishments during the whole journey. A week later, 9 January, Captain Cozens had brought his ship to the last leg of its voyage. That day the ship passed Rottnest Island a few miles off the coast of Fremantle and where the Fenians could see Aboriginal convicts working on the beach. The island was a penal colony for Aborigines, a telling indication of their marginalisation in Western Australian society. It was an unsettling sight for the Fenian prisoners and as their vessel carried them over the last hours of the voyage they pondered their situation and their future. Many of them passed notes of support and dedication to one another. O'Reilly devoted an untitled poem to Cashman, 'as testimony of our true and lasting friendship'. The first verse ended, 'Let your motto be "Honour", my brother / Your watchword and war-cry be "Hope"'.[51] The sixty-two Fenians had all served time in prisons across Britain and Ireland. They had travelled over 14,000 nautical miles to a new continent, which would be filled with exotic plants and animals, a new climate, new sights, sounds and smells. They had lived together for three months and formed friendships that would last a lifetime. Yet, despite all that they had experienced, their condition had not changed. They were still convicts and across the water lay their destination and their latest prison, the penal colony of Western Australia.

The Penal Colony of Western Australia

John Boyle O'Reilly was to serve the remainder of his prison sentence in the Colony of Western Australia, the precursor of the modern Australian state of the same name. As of the 1860s this colony had had a short and uninspiring history. Of course, long before there was any European colony, Australian Aborigines had been living in the landscape for tens of thousands of years. It was not until the seventeenth century that Europeans, in the form of Dutch sailors, began to explore and document the coast of Western Australia, reaching the area around what is now Perth in 1697. It was one of these Dutch explorers, Willem de Vlamingh, who first explored a waterway he named Swan River after seeing large flocks of black swans at its mouth.

Throughout the following century the British and French navies would both make voyages along the coast and traces of the French explorers still live on in place names such as Geographe Bay and the Leschenault Estuary, locations that would be a background for some of the important events in John Boyle O'Reilly's life in Australia. In 1801 the French were the first to produce detailed maps of the Swan River area and it was this increasing French interest in the south-west of Australia that forced the British to intervene. The British government had laid claim to the eastern half of Australia in the previous century and created their first Australian colony of New South Wales. They were now concerned about the possibility of a rival French colony being established on the coast of western Australia and so, in 1826, the governor of New South Wales, Ralph Darling, ordered Major Edmund Lockyer to establish a settlement at King George Sound on the south-western tip of Australia. This was the first British settlement in the west of Australia and it would be followed within a few years by the Swan River Colony.

It was now that Captain James Stirling, the man who is often titled 'father of modern Western Australia', entered the story. He explored the Swan River area during 1827 and was hugely impressed by the settlement potential he saw in the region. Once back in London, he lobbied politicians to create a 'free colony' in the area. A free colony would not, unlike already existing Australian colonies such as New South Wales, receive any transports of convicts but would be peopled by settlers willing to make a new life. The Colonial Office assented to the creation of a free colony and in 1828 the *Challenger* skippered by Captain Charles Fremantle was ordered to take possession of the territory and to hold it until a settler ship arrived. This ship, the *Parmelia*, captained by Stirling and containing sixty-seven settlers, arrived at the end of May 1829, four weeks after the *Challenger*.

As might be expected of people who had decided to leave behind all they had known and start a new life in a distant colony, the settlers did not lack for enthusiasm. By the end of the year the towns of Fremantle and Perth had been established. Fremantle and its port was to be the Colony's link with the rest of the world while Perth, about 13 miles up the Swan River, was to be the seat of government. The people who were to fill these towns arrived aboard another twenty ships that docked at Fremantle over the rest of 1829. This left the official population at 1,290.[1] Many more settler ships sailed to Fremantle over the next three years but the difficulties in clearing and farming land in the often unpredictable local climate quickly countered the enthusiasm of many of those original pioneers. The colony was renamed Western Australia in 1832 but this rebranding of the territory did nothing to improve the circumstances of those already there or to encourage new settlers. From 1833 to 1834, twelve ships carried 1,358 passengers away from Western Australia leaving its total population only slightly higher than it had been at the end of 1829.[2] The reports of hardship and misery from those who returned to Britain did much to discourage other potential settlers from heading to the colony. The rest of the 1830s and 1840s saw a continuation of the pattern of low economic growth and nineteen years later the colony's population had reached a mere 4,622 people.[3] The potential development of the settlement was further hampered by the lack of transport and administrative infrastructure, a situation exacerbated by the almost complete lack of workers needed to build these projects.

Western Australia was a settlement on the verge of failure and it was apparent to those living there that the colony required an infusion of new people. Since hardly anyone was willing to settle in the state any more that left one option: penal transportation of convicts. From the middle of the 1840s wealthy farmers in the Swan River region lobbied the state legislature to recast the free colony as a penal colony. The legislature in turn successfully lobbied the British government to make this change. In seeking to turn itself into a penal colony, Western Australia was acting counter to the other Australian colonies. When transportation had started in 1788, the hope of the authorities in Britain was that the continent of Australia would 'swallow a whole class', that of Britain and Ireland's criminals and destitute.[4] However, as the Australian colonies became more firmly established they were less willing to accept convicts. By 1850 all the penal colonies in Australia had either abandoned or were in the process of abandoning transportation. This was done in the midst of a fevered debate in Britain and Australia about the transportation of convicts and the damage they supposedly wrought to the moral and social order of a colony. However, Britain still needed somewhere to send its convicts and, as the historian A. G. L. Shaw puts it, 'Western Australians were willing to risk moral corruption for the economic advantages of transportation.'[5] So it was that on 1 May 1849 Western Australia was legally established as a penal colony with an order signed by Queen Victoria.[6]

The colony covered nearly one third of the entire continent but most of its landscape was harsh, uninhabitable desert. In John Boyle O'Reilly's time the population of this vast area was almost entirely concentrated in the south-west corner of the state. Even today this whole area of nearly 1 million square miles is populated by slightly more than than 2,000,000 people, with Perth alone comprising around three quarters of the state's total population. The history of the state has, in many ways, been an endless battle against the harshness of the vast deserts, with most life and farming concentrated into the narrow southern coastal strip. Today Western Australia is in the midst of an extraordinary mining boom and is a massive exporter of commodities such as petroleum, iron ore, gold, nickel and alumina, but in O'Reilly's time the economy of the state was entirely based on wheat, meat and wool.

By bringing convicts into the colony, a vast new source of cheap labour would be available for the building of public and private projects such as clearing land as well as building roads, harbours and public buildings. The muscle and sweat of convict labourers were to be the fuel that powered the future expansion of the colony. The move also tied Western Australia more securely to Britain since what was often a forgotten backwater would now be a part of the British penal system. This fact alone would bring the colony more clearly into the minds of British politicians and civil servants. The first convicts arrived on 1 June 1850 and between that year and 1868 a total of 9,718 convicts (including those on the *Hougoumont*) arrived at Fremantle.[7] All of these convicts were male as it was decided, when the state was made a penal colony, not to send female convicts to Western Australia. To prevent the population of the colony becoming more convict than free, the British government had encouraged the emigration of more settlers to Western Australia so that by 1868 the population had increased to a total of around 20,000 people, including 3,220 convicts.[8] Most of these people lived in and around Fremantle, Perth and Bunbury. Yet only slow progress had been made by the colony in clearing the land for roads and farming and one of O'Reilly's Fenian compatriots described the landscape around the three main towns as 'one mass of unbroken forest, except here and there, as the eye can reach, a patch of ground in tillage may be perceived'.[9]

By 1868 the colony was far more self-assured than it had been twenty years earlier and the convicts had played their allotted role in developing Western Australia's society. With settlers arriving in higher numbers every year, the colony was relying less on convict transports and the system was rapidly petering out; in fact, it had almost ended. Surprisingly, the convicts knew of the planned transportation before the Governor of Western Australia, John Hampton. Although the colony had been informed in mid-September that a convict transport would soon be despatched to Western Australia, the British government had made no reference to any Fenians being involved. The first official acknowledgement that Fenians would be a part of the transportation was a letter sent by mail ship to the Governor from Richard Temple-Grenville, the Duke of Buckingham and Chandos and Secretary of State for the Colonies. This was dated 17 October, five days after the *Hougoumont* had set sail for the colony. Temple-Grenville's letter tersely explained to Hampton the decision of the British government:

> Her Majesty's Government have decided that some of the Fenian Prisoners . . . should be included among the convicts on the *Hougoumont* . . . .the Fenians who have been selected to proceed in

the Vessel consist exclusively of men of humble position and . . . the
leaders of the party or others who were likely to prove troublesome
in the Colony have been carefully excluded . . . a picked Guard of
Pensioners amounting to 50 men will accompany the Vessel who
will serve to maintain order among the Prisoners on board and to
recruit the ranks of the Pensioner Force now stationed in the
Colony.[10]

The news was not welcomed by officials in Western Australia, although it
seems that Temple-Grenville had expected an angry reaction. His
assurance to the effect that the Fenians on the *Hougoumont* were men of
humble position within that organisation was not entirely accurate while
his claim that those 'who were like to prove troublesome in the Colony
have been carefully excluded' was patently false. The seventeen military
Fenians, of which O'Reilly was one, were sent from Britain for the very
reason that they were expected to be a source of trouble. The government
had concluded that the Fenians would probably attempt to rescue these
men. At the very least the continuing incarceration of the prisoners in
England would be a boon to Fenian propaganda. It was also thought that
these military Fenians would be potential ringleaders of future
revolutionary activity.

The Fenians impending arrival distressed many Western Australians.
The local newspapers had been providing regular reports on the latest
activities of the revolutionary group and, while the *Hougoumont* had been
voyaging to Western Australia, the colonists were reading stories of the
Manchester ambush and the policeman's death. Over the previous few
years the trials of arrested Fenians had been covered in the local press as
had the rescue of James Stephens and the failed risings of 1867. These
reports had combined to give the Fenians a fearsome reputation
throughout Western Australia and each day the press further stoked the
public's dread. On 21 December 1867 the *Fremantle Herald* published an
account from a journalist who had inspected the *Hougoumont* before its
departure from England. He painted a grisly picture:

I went to the East India Docks . . . to inspect the *Huguemont*, which
has just left with its criminal freight. The result of my observation is
that the entire arrangements are as bad and as inconsistent with

discipline, morality and order as ever. The whole 280 convicts are
packed on the main deck as close as they possibly can be in two rows,
eighteen inches by six feet being the measure of each man's berth and
seventy of them having to sleep in hammocks. The bulkheads may
be more strongly protected with iron and nails than was formerly the
case, and there are little arrangements in the way of carbine holes for
enabling the guard to fire freely on the convicts in case of need. Of
prison discipline, of profitable occupation, or of industry there was
not a sign or possibility. It will be a mercy if the *Huguemont* reaches
the Swan River without some frightful scene. But, at all events, the
highest aims of reformatory discipline are sacrificed by the
demoralizing arrangements of such a system of deportation.

The *Fremantle Herald* was a paper opposed to the policy of transportation
and this undoubtedly coloured the reporter's description of the ship. The
draconian hell that the reporter described was very different from the
reality of the *Hougoumont* as experienced by O'Reilly and most of the
prisoners. Yet it must have seemed to the *Fremantle Herald*'s readers that
the *Hougoumont* was carrying a plague of rebellion and criminality, far
more deadly than anything that they had encountered before.

A week after that report the *Fremantle Herald* published a letter from an
anxious colonist, William Burges, to a member of the colony's government,
Lionel Samson. Burges was one of many Western Australians visiting
London at the time of the *Hougoumont*'s departure and it was letters from
these people who would do much to cause so much anguish back in the
colony. Burges' letter was not short of hyperbole, predicting a Fenian attack
on Fremantle prison that would result in hundreds of crazed convicts
sweeping over the town. It does make clear, however, the fears and
rumours that were soon swirling through sections of the colony:

I write to you to inform you as a member of our Legislature, of the
very perilous position in which the Colony of Western Australia has
been placed by the Home Government sending out in the Convict
Ship, *Huguemont*, which sailed last week for Western Australia, a lot
of Fenian convicts. Such was the apprehension of an attack in the
channel, to rescue the Fenian prisoners, that a man-of-war was sent
by the Government to convey them out of the Channel. I have been

to the Colonial Office on the subject, the Colonial Authorities here were unaware of their being sent until the vessel had sailed, and it made a great row in *The Times* and other papers . . . Governor Hampton had been asked some time back if he would have some of these Fenians or 'Political' prisoners, he refused to have them as it would only draw upon the Colony an American raid to liberate them, and he had no means to resist it . . . they will surely attempt to rescue those men by bombarding Fremantle, knocking down the Prison walls, and letting six hundred ruffians loose to pillage and plunder the town and commit all sorts of atrocities. There is no attempt too daring or too vile for these Fenians[11]

The Australian historian Keith Amos has shown that many of the colony, especially its large Irish population, were unperturbed by the news of the Fenians' transportation. One prominent Western Australian citizen, a successful importer and an Irish immigrant named Joseph Thomas Reilly, later dismissed the whole frenzy as a product of newspaper gossip-mongering and anti-Irish sentiment among some colonists, which was 'as ridiculous as it was reprehensible'.[12] The *South Australian Chronicle* also criticised what it considered to be the rank hypocrisy of Western Australians:

Why our neighbours should regard the Fenians as exceptionally desperate and formidable characters, we do not perceive. They have had, at their own invitation, prisoners convicted of murder, rape, arson, burglary, and almost every other crime against society; and surely they are become suddenly fastidious, when they regard with such unprecedented horror, the introduction of a few disaffected Irishmen.[13]

However as the *Hougoumont* neared Fremantle, it was the attitude of those like Burges that had become dominant. The more newspaper ink that was spilled on the issue the more unrestrained became the debate on the Fenians' transportation; one letter to the *Fremantle Herald* breathlessly claimed that: 'a shipload of more daring reckless men never floated on the ocean'.[14]

The restive atmosphere within the colony had also unnerved the authorities, especially the commander of the Western Australian

Volunteers in Fremantle, Captain Charles Manning. In early December he warned the colony's senior military officer, Major Robert Crampton, that he had received 'hints' of a 'probable rising' by the convicts of Western Australia. He had no proof of any of this but apparently the convicts planned to seize the town and harbour of Fremantle and carry off 'what booty they could secure and such women as they might in their raid take a fancy to.' Manning also raised the idea that Irish-American Fenians would seek to gain control of the *Hougoumont* and then 'sail away with such of our wives and daughters they might please to select and three or four hundred convicts that assisted them in their enterprise.'[15] As we shall see in a later chapter, the fears that a US-based Fenian ship would sail to Western Australia and rescue Irish convicts were not unreasonable. However, the rest of Manning's 'warning' was the product of a hyperactive imagination, especially his obsession with convicts or Fenians overrunning Fremantle and sailing into the distance with the town's women.

Hampton did not take Manning's warning very seriously but he did have concerns that many of the military in Western Australia were Irish. Bearing in mind the recent Fenian infiltration of the British army in Ireland, it was sensible for him to wonder if all these could be counted upon to quell any supposed Fenian machinations. By the end of 1867 the ever more agitated state of the colony convinced the British government that it was necessary to enhance security measures in Western Australia. They ordered two companies of soldiers to be despatched from Tasmania to Western Australia while a gunboat, the *Brisk*, was dispatched from Sydney.[16] These decisions would turn out to be little more than a sop to public opinion. The *Brisk* would not arrive until after the *Hougoumont* had delivered the convicts and left Western Australian waters. The troops would not arrive for months. To further calm popular opinion Governor Hampton even transferred his family from Perth to Fremantle, publicly announcing 'my intention to remain there until the Fenians were disposed of; at the same time quietly endeavouring to allay the apprehension of the residents and, without attracting their attention, making every practicable arrangement which the means at my disposal would permit.'[17]

Hampton's decision was good politics although it is debatable whether it had any positive effect on the mood of the colony. The *Fremantle Herald* reported that, on the day of the *Hougoumont*'s arrival, the town was 'in a state of great excitement'.[18] Yet, for all the anxiety that had consumed

Western Australia, the arrival of the Fenians proved to be an anticlimax. As the convict ship neared Fremantle, local journalists sailed out to meet the ship and talk to those aboard. Reverend Williams, the Protestant clergyman who had travelled with the prisoners, said that they had been 'most civil, obedient and religious'.[19] Father Delany also spoke of the prisoners' good conduct and of his belief that they would have a peaceful future.[20] The press interviewed Captain Cozens as well. He rubbished the claim then widely circulating that the *Hougoumont* was a 'floating hell' and also sought to assure the people of Western Australia of the good conduct of all the prisoners, especially the Fenians:

> The fellow who wrote it ought to be kicked. He knows nothing about the discipline of a convict ship. We were supposed to have a very bad lot, and yet no attempt was made to take the ship, nor were prisoners kept below like a lot of wild beasts. On the contrary, they were on deck every day from daylight. . . . and gave not the slightest trouble. The Fenians conducted themselves in the most satisfactory manner, and only two of the other fellows had to be flogged; and I can only say that if convict ships be hells afloat, then let me long be the devil rather than skipper of an Australian emigrant ship.[21]

Cozens' strong defence of the Fenian convicts in tandem with the comments of the clergymen helped to allay the anxiety of the colonists temporarily. The newly arrived convicts would begin their sentences in Western Australia amid a relatively calm atmosphere.[22] The controversy over the *Hougoumont* shows how divisive the issue of transportation had become and was an indicator that the process was rapidly nearing its end. Yet nobody realised at the time that O'Reilly and his fellow prisoners would prove to be the last of over 160,000 men, women and children to be transported as convicts to the Australian continent. The system that had begun in 1788 and which had helped to colonise Australia had finally ended with the *Hougoumont*.

John Boyle O'Reilly had his first view of Fremantle on the morning of 9 January 1868, a moment he described in *Moondyne*:

> An hour later, the ship had approached within a mile of the pier at Fremantle. The surrounding sea and land were very strange and

beautiful. The green shoal-water, the soft air, with a yellowish warmth, the pure white sand of the beach, and the dark green of the unbroken forest beyond, made a scene almost like fairyland. But there was a stern reminder of reality in the little town of Fremantle that lay between the forest and the sea. It was built of wooden houses, running down a gentle hill, and in the center of the houses, spread out like a gigantic star-fish, was a vast stone prison. There was a moment of bustle and noise on the deck . . . the anchor plunged into the sea and the cable roared through the hawse-hole. Every soul on board took a long breath of relief at the end of the voyage.[23]

Today the port and town of Fremantle present a pretty and friendly face to visitors. The same was certainly not true of the town that O'Reilly would have seen. It was much smaller and the vista was dominated by the huge prison which stood on a slight rise behind the town. The town's regularly laid out streets contained a host of buildings that pointed to the reality that Fremantle was part of a penal colony. These included the old prison and what was called the 'Convict Establishment Fremantle Lunatic Asylum and Invalid Depot', with its austere Gothic façade. Built in 1864 it, like many of the public buildings in Fremantle and Perth, had been constructed by convict labour. The novelist Anthony Trollope passed through the town in the early 1870s and he was unimpressed with what he experienced. Fremantle was, he declared, 'a hot white, ugly town, with a very large prison, a lunatic asylum, and a hospital for ancient and worn out convicts'.[24]

At 3.30 a.m. on the morning of Friday 10 January 1868, the *Hougoumont*'s warders, accompanied by some members of the Fremantle police, roused the convicts from their sleep. It was time for their transfer to Fremantle's huge limestone prison, known to locals as 'The Establishment'. All 279 convicts were placed in chains and ferried to the dockside in Fremantle. Then they shuffled through the town to the prison entrance. Before them stood a stone gatehouse that, although built in the 1850s, had been designed to remind one of a medieval castle. The reasoning behind this design was, apparently, to make the townsfolk feel protected from the convicts on the inside.[25] Two octagonal towers flanked the outer iron gate, above which was a large round clock. Behind this was a courtyard leading to an inner iron gate, flanked by stone guardhouses. Convicts making their way through the gates (which at the time was the only way in or out of the prison) could not fail to notice that the guardhouses were manned to defend the gatehouse area against attack from both inside and outside the prison. Riflemen positioned at the slot windows could fire upon anyone trying to get through the gates. The walls of the guardhouses had rifle slits instead of windows so as to afford the guards maximum protection as they aimed their weapons.

Once through the gates the prisoners were met with a large open expanse of white sand, surrounded by a limestone wall, almost 16 feet tall. Behind this was the prison in all its utilitarian glory. Its original design was supposed to have been based on one of O'Reilly's former prisons, that of Pentonville in London. Such ambition had proved too expensive for the Colony of Western Australia so instead a vast limestone cell block was erected, four storeys high and 500 feet long. This cell block, which could hold around 1,000 inmates, was separated into two wings by a central building, which served as the administrative heart of the prison. All of this had been constructed by convict labourers. In this open area, the prisoners were paraded past the Governor of Western Australia, John Hampton, and the colony's Comptroller General of Convicts, Henry Wakeford. That done, the processing of each prisoner began. Each man was washed and had his hair cropped. He then went through a medical examination in which his height, weight, physical features and any ailments were noted. The convict then received his convict uniform, which consisted of a leather belt, two pairs of boots, four pairs of socks, four handkerchiefs, four cotton shirts and two flannel shirts. As it was the southern hemisphere summer, O'Reilly would have received one grey vest, two pairs of grey trousers and a felt hat (extra clothing was supplied in winter months).[26]

During processing, the prisoners were read a copy of the prison rules. These formed the new parameters of each convict's life and, if the prisoner was to develop a good reputation and avoid punishment, they would have to be followed exactly:

> No prisoner shall disobey the orders of the overseer or any other officer . . . or be guilty of swearing, or any indecent or immoral expression or conduct, or of any assault, quarrel, or abusive language, or smoking inside the ward, cell, privy cookhouse, washhouse, or workshops, or any talking or other noise during meal-hours, or after the silence-hours at night; leaving the square allotted as their

exercise ground on any pretence, except to the closet, or converse or hold intercourse with any other prisoner or tradesman employed about the yard, except as authorised by the prison rules, or cause annoyance or disturbance by singing, whistling, or making unnecessary noise, or pass or attempt to pass, without permission, out of his ward or beyond the bounds of the ward or other place to which he may belong, or when at work go without leave beyond the limits assigned for such work, or disfigure the walls or other parts of the prison by writing on them or otherwise, or deface, secrete, destroy, or pull down any paper or notice hung up by authority in or about any part of the prison, or wilfully injure any bedding or other articles, or commit any nuisance, or have in his bay or possession any articles not furnished by the establishment or allowed to be in the possession of a prisoner, or shall give or lend to or borrow from any other prisoner any food, book, or other articles without leave, or refuse or neglect to conform to the rules and regulation or orders of the prison, or otherwise offend.[27]

Punishments for breaking the rules ranged from flogging to solitary confinement or a combination of both. The prison had twelve special punishment cells and six windowless dark cells. Each of these dark cells had extra thick walls while the entrance was barred by inner and outer doors, meaning the cell was practically soundproof. The effect was to leave the prisoner utterly isolated from the outside world. Stays in dark cells were between one and six months and this punishment was particularly feared by the convicts. One contemporary commentator described how a dark cell inmate typically reacted to their incarceration. He 'whimpered and prayed for a little light . . . the dark cell made him as temporarily willing and obedient as a dog'.[28]

Once each prisoner had been processed they were taken to their cells. The Fenians were kept separate from the other prisoners so it is likely that O'Reilly was placed in one of the individual cells. Even compared to his time in English prisons his new home must have been a forbidding and depressing place, the cells being only 5 feet wide and 7 feet long. They were unfurnished, except for a bucket and a hammock slung from two iron hooks protruding from one of the walls.[29] The next day the new arrivals were incorporated into the prison's daily regime. This began at 4.30 a.m. each day and continued until supper in the cells at 6 p.m.[30] O'Reilly, luckily, had served his period of separate confinement and hard labour while in England and he would be freed from much of the daily prison routine. On his fourth day in the prison he was appointed orderly and librarian to the prison's Catholic chaplain, Father Thomas Lynch.[31] While most of the Fenians were dispersed to convict camps around the colony, O'Reilly was one of six Fenians from the *Hougoumont* who were retained at the prison. Two of these, Denis Cashman and John Flood, were appointed as clerks. Patrick Doran, David Joyce and Patrick Reardon were assigned to work in the prison storerooms.[32] In his role as orderly and librarian, O'Reilly acted as caretaker for the prison's Catholic chapel, sacristan and general dogsbody for Father Lynch. He also was responsible for the loan and issuing of books to prisoners. Although still incarcerated, this was a tolerable existence, especially relative to O'Reilly's experiences at Millbank and Dartmoor. This job, though, was to be his for only a few weeks. On 11 February the Superintendent of Fremantle Prison decided to send O'Reilly, whose prisoner number was 9843, to one of the convict depots scattered around Fremantle: 'John O'Reilly will be transferred hence to Bunbury for the party about to clear the new line of Road between Bunbury and the Vasse. The Accountant of Stores will make the necessary requisition for transport.'[33]

The reasons behind O'Reilly's relocation are unknown although his transfer to Bunbury fitted perfectly with the authorities' plan to scatter the military Fenians as individuals or small groups across Western Australia. The decision to move O'Reilly had come from Governor Hampton who explained that the 'risk of such men [Fenians] combining together for evil purposes, induced me to disperse them as widely as possible throughout the colony, not sending one or two of them to the same station.'[34] A further impetus may have been the news that had reached Western Australia of the deaths of the three 'Manchester Martyrs'. These Fenians, William Allen, Michael Larkin and Michael O'Brien, had been arrested following the Fenian ambush of the police in Manchester during September. They were tried, convicted and then publicly executed on 23 November 1867. It was widely believed that the death of the policeman during the ambush had been an accident and the executions were the subject of huge outcry among the Irish in Ireland and Britain. The authorities in England were so nervous of a Fenian response to the executions that on the day of the hangings the three men were guarded by 500 police, 2,000 special constables, 500 soldiers and two batteries of artillery.[35] When the news reached Fremantle Prison, via a newspaper smuggled into the prisoners, it deeply upset the Fenians. O'Reilly was moved to write 'The Dead Who Died for Ireland'. The third verse may have been as much a commentary on his current predicament as that of his homeland:

> The dead who died for Ireland,
> How hallowed are their graves!
> With all the memories fresh and green,
> Oh! How could we be slaves?
> How could we patient clang the chain?
> How could we fawn and bow?
> How could we crouch like mongrels
> 'neath the keeper's frowning brow?[36]

On 12 February O'Reilly was equipped with some new clothing and supplies including his prison Parchment Record, which was to accompany him to his new assignment. He was booked as a passenger, as was a prison warder, on a small transport vessel heading south. Denis Cashman later described his friend's hurried departure: 'We waved him an adieu as we were bustled through the gates. Our hearts were heavy; we could not speak . . . Flood, whom O'Reilly loved [John Flood and O'Reilly had become close friends while working as editors on *The Wild Goose*], never saw him again.'[37]

In being moved to a convict depot O'Reilly's experience would match that of the vast majority of the other *Hougoumont* Fenians. In the weeks after their arrival the group of sixty-two Fenians who had travelled on board the ship was broken apart. On 18 January twenty of the civilian Fenians were sent to a convict depot on the Clarence Road, south of Fremantle. They were under the control of one of the warders from the *Hougoumont*, William Howard. Two days later, another group of twenty civilian Fenians was sent to a convict depot at West Guildford, north-east of Fremantle (now Bassendean near Perth Airport). Another warder from the *Hougoumont*, Charles McGarry, was in charge of this group.[38] The other five civilian Fenians were the five who remained at Fremantle with O'Reilly. However, it was the military Fenians who caused the authorities most anxiety. One of these military Fenians, John Lynch, had preceded O'Reilly to Bunbury, although they would work in separate road parties.[39]

The other fifteen military Fenians were sent to the Mt Eliza convict depot in Perth, to the north of Fremantle. Over the following weeks this group would be further divided and the men sent as individuals or in small groups to widely separated convict depots throughout the colony.[40]

Prisoners were allowed to send letters home and although they were liable to censorship they often provide much detail on life in the colony. Throughout 1868 letters from Fenians incarcerated in Western Australia appeared in the Irish newspaper *The Irishman*. One of the Fenians, George Connolly, described the West Guildford camp in a letter to his wife:

> You may easily guess life here is a camp one, when I tell you that our hut is composed of a few withered sticks nailed together and covered with rushes. To lie upon we have each got a hammock, but neither sheets, beds or pillows, and at night our only visitors are fleas and mosquitoes . . . Our work is quarrying and blasting stones under almost a tropical sun, and in the open air we have to cook and eat our victuals.[41]

The mosquitoes were a constant irritation for the convicts and another of the Fenians, Patrick Walle, described similar experiences to Connolly. He had been sent to the Clarence Road site and he wrote to his parents about his and his fellow convicts' 'rude habitation', which consisted of 'four miserable twig huts and a tent':

> We are sure of nocturnal visits from mosquitoes, and a species of very small lively insect which takes the greatest delight in playing with you . . . We work pretty hard all day under a burning sun; the only comfort the place affords us is that we are near to the sea shore, where we bathe after our day's labour.[42]

There is no doubt that the convicts in these work parties endured harsh living conditions and were involved in often brutal hard labour. Yet, in a grim testimony to the harrowing environment of the prisons they had left behind – Dartmoor, Millbank, Pentonville and others – the letters that appeared in *The Irishman* plainly show that the Fenians found their new conditions preferable to prison life in England.

For the rest of 1868 O'Reilly would spend most of his time at a convict camp 15 miles south of Bunbury, between that town and an area called the Vasse. Because of the scarcity of records concerning O'Reilly's time in the convict depot, the type of work he was engaged in during his first month at the camp is unknown. However, his experience of camp life would not have differed from that of Fenians such as Connolly and Walle. From mid-March it is known that O'Reilly and the other convicts left camp each morning to work on the road-building project to link the town of Bunbury with the Vasse region.[43] During the next few months O'Reilly worked on the road, clearing scrub, digging ground, laying foundations and filling in the surface. The convicts routinely worked through the hottest hours of the day. Although March was the beginning of autumn, daytime temperatures still averaged around 30 degrees Celsius. While these average daily temperatures would have fallen twelve degrees by July, the first few months were exhausting for convicts used to the more temperate and wetter climate of Ireland and Britain. In *Moondyne* O'Reilly gave an evocative description of the road party at work:

> All free things were at rest; but the penetrating click of the axe, heard far through the bush, and now and again a harsh word of command, told that it was a land of bondmen. From daylight to dark, through the hot noon as steadily as in the cool evening, the convicts were at work on the roads – the weary work that has no wages, no promotion, no incitement, no variation for good or bad, except stripes for the laggard. Along the verge of the Koagulup Swamp [now known as Cokelup, O'Reilly's camp was located very near this swamp] one of the greatest and smallest of the wooded lakes of the country, its black water deep enough to float a man-of-war – a party of convicts were making a government road. They were cutting their patient way into a forest only traversed before by the Aborigine and the absconder. Before them in the bush, as in their lives, all was dark and unknown-tangled underbrush, gloomy shadows, and noxious things. Behind them, clear and open, lay the straight road they had made – leading to and from the prison.[44]

O'Reilly was one of around 100 convicts who were overseen by thirteen warders. Of this century of convicts O'Reilly would have recognised many of the faces, since thirty-eight of the *Hougoumont's* criminal convicts had been sent to Bunbury. James Jeffrey Roche left a colourful description of O'Reilly's campmates:

> Among the criminals with whom he was forced to associate were some of the most degraded of human kind – murderers, burglars, sinners of every grade and color of vice. They were the poison flower of civilization's corruption, more depraved than the savage, as they were able to misuse the advantages of superior knowledge. They were the overflow of society's cesspool, the irreclaimable victims of sin – too often the wretched fruits of heredity or environment. Happily for the young, generous, clean-minded rebel, who had been doomed to herd with this prison scum, God had given him the instincts of pure humanity; and ill-fortune, instead of blighting, had nourished their growth. He looked upon his fellow-sufferers with eyes of mercy, seeing how many of them were the victims, directly or indirectly, of cruel, selfish, social conditions.[45]

Roche's description of the criminal convicts may have been florid but, as was seen in the previous chapter, it was not inaccurate. However, there is no record of O'Reilly having any altercations or being in any way troubled by the criminal convicts. In fact he seems to have been on good terms with many of them. Neither is Roche's description of O'Reilly's humane reaction to the criminal convicts inaccurate as, in later life, the Fenian would be an unremitting critic of the prison system in England.

O'Reilly was to spend only a couple of months clearing roads with the criminal convicts. The same month that O'Reilly had arrived at the convict depot also saw the arrival of Henry Woodman as the camp's head warder. Woodman would have responsibility for every aspect of the convicts' lives as well as for the ongoing construction of the Bunbury to Vasse road. Flowing from these responsibilities was a river of paperwork that needed to be diverted to the convict depot's regional headquarters at Bunbury. Like most warders in rural areas Woodman required a clerk and in most instances this job was handed to a suitable prisoner. As Woodman got to know each of the convicts over those first few months he soon realised that in John Boyle O'Reilly he had an excellent candidate for the job and sometime during the middle of 1868 O'Reilly became the warder's assistant.

There has been some confusion in the past as to the exact role that O'Reilly was given by Woodman. It was stated by Roche that O'Reilly was made a convict constable.[46] These convict constables were prisoners who were judged by the warder to be trustworthy enough to be given a measure of power over their fellow convicts and they formed an extra layer of control over the wider convict population. However, Roche was in error and it was shown by Martin Carroll that O'Reilly remained a warder's assistant whose main role was clerical.[47] O'Reilly may now have been freed from the physical labour of the road camps but he would not be allowed forget that he was still a convict. On his trips to and from Bunbury he was ordered not to associate with anyone except penal officials and he was to travel to the town only via approved routes. His clothes would have marked him out as a convict and once at Bunbury he was obliged to walk in the centre of the street. He was forbidden to loiter or to speak to any civilians. If he was seen to be in contravention of any of these rules he would have been punished, at the very least losing his position as warder's assistant.

Although O'Reilly's life of administration and errand-running was far preferable to that of the convicts engaged in hard labour, he was still subject to the sometimes capricious whims of individual prison warders. This was cruelly demonstrated by one warder of the convict depot in Bunbury who, in the words of Roche, had taken 'a bitter dislike to the young O'Reilly'.[48] On one of his regular visits to Bunbury this warder accused O'Reilly of being late and reprimanded the Irishman. Days later, the same man called O'Reilly to his office and informed him that he had in his possession a letter from Ireland addressed to the convict. The warder then held up a black-bordered envelope, a sight which caused O'Reilly great anxiety. He was aware that his mother, Eliza, was gravely ill and he immediately surmised that she had died. However, the warder told O'Reilly that, as punishment for his supposed tardiness a few days earlier, he would withhold the letter for six months. When O'Reilly eventually received the letter it provided belated confirmation of his fears because it did indeed contain news of his mother's death.[49]

This is one of the few stories we have about O'Reilly at this time. One other story that has passed into legend is the tale of 'Boyle O'Reilly's tree'. There is no official documentation to support the truth or otherwise of this story but local tradition in Western Australia maintained that O'Reilly saved a huge eucalyptus tree, which stood on the proposed path of the Bunbury to Vasse road, from destruction. The tree, which O'Reilly described as 'a magnificent tree, a giant among its fellows, the growth of centuries towering aloft to the sky and spreading enormous arms on every side',[50] so impressed the Fenian that he appealed to Warder Woodman for its preservation. The warder provided a stay of execution while O'Reilly took his case to Bunbury convict depot. Here, he petitioned the Bunbury depot's commanding officer, Principal Warder Josiah Woodrow, to slightly change the planned course of the road and thus spare the tree. Apparently, Woodrow's wife interceded on O'Reilly's behalf with the result that the route was indeed changed and the tree preserved. It is a charming tale and one that may have happened. Martin Carroll, in his 1950s' exploration of O'Reilly's time in Australia, discovered that the story remained a living oral tradition in and around Bunbury. Tantalisingly, a very large and old eucalyptus stood by a kink in the old Bunbury to Vasse road until 1953. That year the tree, damaged by pollution from a nearby factory, was chopped down.[51]

It was while stationed at the convict depot that O'Reilly encountered the local Aboriginal population towards whom he developed a strong affinity. O'Reilly had a lifelong love of the outdoor life and he picked up bush skills from individual Aborigines with whom he became friendly. He would also have been witness to the discrimination they faced on a daily basis. As we shall see, when O'Reilly became an influential newspaper editor he would devote much of his energies to opposing discrimination and in the pursuit of social justice for the oppressed of American society. His experiences with Australian Aborigines may have played an important part in the development of this aspect of O'Reilly's thought. *Moondyne* displays an attitude towards the Aborigines that, while often condescending and marked by the racial assumptions of the time, is compassionate and Roche quoted O'Reilly as saying in later years:

I found that those creatures were men and women, just like the rest of us; the difference between those poor black boys and the men of the Somerset Club [a private gentleman's club that O'Reilly would join in Boston] was only external. I have good friends among those Australian savages, to-day, that I would be as glad to meet as any man I know.[52]

While O'Reilly's time as a convict in Western Australia is relatively poorly documented, it can be ascertained that the job as a warder's assistant lessened the amount of heavy labour in which he was involved. Although he still worked with the road party, he would spend much time travelling to and from Bunbury. His rapport with Woodman also spared him some of the harsh treatment to which other Fenian prisoners were subjected throughout 1868.

Throughout the first months of the year the Fenians, to the relief of the authorities, were model prisoners and individuals even won themselves the praise of Governor Hampton. In March James Wilson was one of a group of convicts who rescued a burning bridge from destruction, while in April two Fenians, Joseph Noonan and Daniel Bradley, saved the life of a prison schoolmaster who had been attacked by one of his convict pupils.[53] All three were rewarded with a short remission of their sentences: Wilson, two months; Noonan and Bradley, one month each. The Fenian prisoners and the authorities had, at this point, a relatively benign relationship but this began to change around March and April 1868 when news of the Clerkenwell explosion reached Western Australia. The explosion had been caused by a Fenian bombing of Clerkenwell Prison on 13 December 1867. By that stage the Fenians in England had split into two factions. The leader of one of these groups, Richard O'Sullivan Burke, had been arrested by the police and taken to Clerkenwell Prison. His supporters had planned to blow a hole in the prison's outer wall and thus free Burke. To achieve this they triggered a massive explosion using a barrel filled with gunpowder. The attempt failed but the explosion killed twelve people, injured over a hundred, and destroyed many buildings. The size of the bomb and the callous disregard for the lives of the locals living around the prison infuriated public opinion in Britain.

The reports of what had happened at Clerkenwell and the consequent heavy newspaper coverage of the Fenians led to a change of attitude among the authorities and many colonists of Western Australia. The new mood was intensified by the shocking news that arrived from Sydney at the end of March. The Duke of Edinburgh, Prince Alfred, had been on a visit to the city when he was shot and seriously wounded by a Fenian named Henry James O'Farrell. So ran the information that reached Western Australia but it was not entirely accurate. The Duke of Edinburgh had indeed been badly wounded (although he would make a full and speedy recovery) but the man who had pulled the trigger was not a Fenian. He was Irish, however. He had been released from a Sydney mental institution only days before the assassination attempt and had carried out the attack on his own. He was tried, found guilty and, despite a plea for mercy from the Duke of Edinburgh, hanged in Sydney on 21 April. That a royal plea for moderation was ignored by the authorities in Sydney gives some idea of the furious atmosphere within the Australian colonies after the attack. A series of 'indignation meetings' were held across the colonies over the following weeks in tandem with a steep rise in anti-Irish attacks and newspaper commentary. It was inevitable that this ill-feeling would reach Western Australia and the news reawakened the latent fear of the Fenians that seems to have been quenched back in January 1868.[54]

This manifested itself in some of the convict depots through increased antagonism from the warders towards their Fenian prisoners. Towards the end of April Martin Hogan, who was one of the military Fenians, fell into an altercation with a warder at the West Guildford convict depot. The warder had apparently made some anti-Irish remark to Hogan who responded in language deemed 'abusive and insubordinate'.[55] Hogan also refused to continue working at the depot. He was the first of the *Hougoumont* Fenians to be reported for misconduct in the colony. But when the case was brought before the resident magistrate at Guildford, the convict was sentenced to a six-month spell of solitary confinement in Fremantle Prison. The warder who was said to have insulted Hogan denied making any such comments and a magistrate was legally bound to take the word of a warder over that of a convict. Hogan, therefore, could not have escaped punishment but the excessive penalty given to him cannot be divorced from the wider furore instigated by the attempt on the Duke of Edinburgh's life. The Fenian would be in chains throughout the entire six months and would subsist on a diet of bread and water.[56] Once his prison sentence was over he was due to return to the same convict depot where he would again be under the control of the warder with whom he had had the altercation. The fickle nature of the convict system in Western Australia was a major problem for the prisoners. Their welfare was utterly dependent on the character of the prison guards under whom they served their time. O'Reilly was lucky to have a fair-minded man in Warder Woodman and this fact would play a vital part in his life in Australia.

O'Reilly would have been aware of all these developments and,

Woodman's decency notwithstanding, they confirmed to him the utter vulnerability of a convict's existence. He seems to have been contemplating escape throughout much of 1868 although he was aware of the enormity of the task facing him. Yet, in the second half of that year, he decided to try and make a break for freedom by disappearing into the Australian wilderness. At first he told no one of his plan but a chance encounter made him change his mind. One day, probably in September, he was at work with the convict road party when he met with the local Catholic priest, Cavan-born Father Patrick McCabe. The priest, who was visiting O'Reilly's camp, had spent three years in the Bunbury district and most of his parishioners were convicts and former convicts. Over the years he had developed a strong association with many of these men. 'He was', O'Reilly later wrote, 'the best influence; indeed, in my time, he was the only good influence, on the convicts in the whole district of Bunbury.'[57]

As the two men walked and talked, O'Reilly told McCabe of his plan to escape. This plan was not well conceived; it involved O'Reilly, much as he had done at Dartmoor, absconding into the wilderness. McCabe's response was blunt: 'It is an excellent way to commit suicide.'[58] McCabe refused to discuss the matter any further but as he mounted his horse to leave, he leaned from the saddle and told O'Reilly: 'Don't think of that again. Let me think out a plan for you. You'll hear from me before long.' McCabe's offer to help O'Reilly was a truly selfless act; if the escape failed it would ruin his reputation in Western Australia and expose him to possible prosecution as an abettor of Fenians. As to why he offered to help O'Reilly, we can guess that McCabe was sympathetic towards the Fenians and was more than willing to help another Irishman in defiance of the British Empire. Thomas Keneally, who included O'Reilly in his epic history of the Irish diaspora, *The Great Shame*, suggests that McCabe sensed the convict's growing desperation and so acted to save him.[59] It is an observation that may well be correct. O'Reilly's warm and open personality seems to have acted powerfully upon others in drawing them to his cause. The poet William Hovey who later befriended O'Reilly in Boston explained why the Irishman was loved by so many: 'He was governed, in his acts and in his opinions, by impulse, and it was because of this, and because his impulses were broad, generous, manly, and distinctly human, that his friends held him in such warm and affectionate esteem.'[60]

In undertaking to help O'Reilly escape from the colony, McCabe would be involving himself in a plot that, statistically, was almost certain to fail. Escape from Western Australia seemed virtually impossible. Any potential escapee would have faced a choice between the unforgiving, unmapped and mostly deserted Australian interior or to try escaping by sea. To head into the bush without supplies meant almost certain death, while any convict trying to escape by sea would need money to pay for passage aboard a ship. Even if they somehow were able to pay for passage, all ships that left Western Australian ports during periods when convicts were on the loose were routinely searched by the police. The port was especially well guarded by the authorities who were always attentive to the possibility that a convict might try to stow away on a ship. Despite these hurdles, it is estimated that around one third of convicts made escape attempts. Of this third, practically all were apprehended by the authorities.[61] The punishment for such convicts, designated as Absconders Class, offered a nightmarish conclusion to those dreaming of escape. During Governor Hampton's term of office (1862 to late 1868) the penalty most often imposed on captured absconders was 100 strokes of the lash, followed by six months in solitary confinement on a diet of bread and water and two years working in irons while all the time watched over by armed guards.[62]

The 100 strokes of the lash were administered via the 'cat o'nine tails', nine knotted strings of horse- or cowhide, designed to lacerate the skin with each strike. The recaptured absconder was placed against the 'flogging triangle' (three wooden poles set in the ground and meeting at the top in the form of a tripod). The prisoner's legs were tied to the base of the flogging post and their hands to the top. The person's back was then stripped bare and a leather kidney belt fastened around their waist to protect vital organs. A second collar was fastened around the neck to protect the major arteries.[63] With that done, the punishment began. Thomas McCarthy Fennell described one flogging that he had witnessed: 'With each lash the laceration seems to change from blue to intense black, the flesh tears apart, 'tis now red, and ghastly flow the purple fluid from the mangled pulp'.[64] The prison's surgeon acted as a witness at each flogging and sometimes intervened if it seemed that the prisoner's life was in danger. On other occasions the flogging was ended as a result of the victim fainting through pain or blood loss. If a flogging ended prematurely it was only a temporary respite for the victim. Once a convict's wounds had healed, the punishment was completed at a later date, starting at the point where the first whipping had ended. After the convict was taken down from the post his shredded and bleeding back was liberally rubbed with salt. This was done to prevent infection but left the convict in excruciating pain.

The placing of prisoners in irons was another cruel punishment. Leg irons were shackles placed around a prisoner's ankles and joined together by a chain to restrict movement. They varied in weight according to the severity of the punishment and prisoners in leg irons were assigned to hard labour, working ten hours a day. Reports in the prison's medical journal refer to this combination of hard labour and iron shackles resulting in severe groin pain, bruising of the skin, lesions and skin ruptures.[65] To encounter prisoners punished by being placed in irons was a regular occurrence around Fremantle. A woman named Mrs Millett left an eyewitness depiction of such a chain gang travelling to the town in the late 1860s:

> The fetters that they carried were of such size and weight that the first time I ever saw the gang I turned my head on its approach to look, as I supposed, at a jingling team of horses coming up behind us. I then perceived that the noise was caused by the irons on the legs and feet of fifty men who were walking, or rather shuffling along, in rank of four abreast, and dressed in parti-coloured clothes. Before the prisoners marched soldiers with mounted bayonets, and behind, bringing up the rear were other soldiers carrying revolvers on the full cock. The chain-gang was thus being escorted back to the 'Establishment' after working on the road and the sight was most painful.[66]

If these regularly employed punishments failed to deter prisoners from absconding there existed a complex system of control and vigilance which underpinned the success of the authorities in apprehending escapees. Prison warders were assigned to each prison and convict depot. They kept a constant watch over the prisoners and were assisted in the work by armed pensioner guards. If a prisoner did escape the warders or the guards, then the colonial police force would be called upon. This group of 147 men was always available to be scrambled into action. Of this number, forty were Aboriginal trackers whose ability to discern movement through the landscape resulted in the capture of many escapees. All these men were well paid and they had a network of police stations throughout the colony. Most of these stations were assigned two horses but a larger one such as Bunbury had four horses.[67] From these stations the police daily travelled to and from each convict depot and if anything untoward was noticed or reported, they could send one of their number to gain reinforcements in as short a time as possible.

However, the Colonial Police Force, no matter how skilled and well-equipped, would have been little use without support in the wider community. When it came to capture of an escaped convict the police and the government were very generous to those who proffered information. Big rewards were given to anyone who helped in the capture of a convict. As soon as it became known to the police that a convict had escaped they immediately took efforts to circulate the news through the colony. For example, until April 1868, if an escape occurred at Fremantle Prison, the whole town would be informed by firing of the prison guns and the hoisting of a red flag to the top of the prison's main flagstaff. This put the locals on notice that a fugitive was on the loose and it also let people know that a potential opportunity for financial gain was in the offing.[68] Ultimately, this cost the authorities very little as any captured convict would have to pay for the rewards out of any money he earned in future years. In 1868 alone a total of 171 constables, warders, police officers, colonists and Aborigines received rewards approaching £500 for their aid in recapturing 127 absconders (nineteen of these had been criminal convicts on the *Hougoumont*).[69] In the period that O'Reilly was in the camp near Bunbury, twenty-four convicts attempted to flee from that area. All were caught and punished in the standard manner of a flogging, solitary confinement and chains.[70]

Over time, and as failed escape followed failed escape, it became apparent to both the convicts and the authorities that there was only one viable but still unlikely means of escape from Western Australia: passage aboard an American whaling ship. A police report from the early 1860s detailed: 'During an existence of 12 years not a single prisoner of the Crown has made good his escape from custody; and of 5,896 men, only 42 have left the colony clandestinely, all of them being ticket-of-leave holders; and of these 21 at different times left the colony on board American whalers.'[71] Even then, many of those who left aboard American whaling ships were subsequently apprehended when those ships docked at ports in territory controlled by the British Empire. As the statistics demonstrate, there was one potential weak spot in the net that the authorities had cast around the convicts: the ticket-of-leave system.

A ticket-of-leave allowed a convict to work in the community and receive a wage before their sentence had expired. Although, legally, they were still convicts, ticket-of-leave men were allowed to marry. The system was designed to begin the integration of convicts into society and to make them more of an economic asset to the colony. Ticket-of leave convicts had to observe a strict set of conditions that, if contravened, would usually result in the loss of the ticket-of-leave. As one example, ticket-of-leave men were not allowed to drink alcohol. Convict depots were set up throughout the colony to serve as accommodation and employment depots for ticket-of-leave men. They had to report regularly to local magistrates and to present their ticket to anyone who asked. They were not allowed to leave the colony but they had a wide freedom of movement. Some of them used this autonomy to make their escape from Western Australia. As a warder's assistant O'Reilly did not have the same privileges as a ticket-of-leave prisoner but on his regular trips to and from Bunbury he experienced similar, albeit very brief, periods of independence. Although he was governed by strict regulations regarding his conduct on these trips he was often outside of the gaze of warders and police. O'Reilly would use this limited freedom to try and achieve the ultimate freedom of escape from Western Australia.

O'Reilly did not hear from McCabe over the following months and he had begun to worry that the priest had forgotten him. However, Father McCabe was at that time actively but carefully formulating a plan of escape. To this end, McCabe had enlisted an Irish emigrant named James Maguire, living in the town of Dardanup, 6 miles south-east of Bunbury. The town of Dardanup, as O'Reilly later described in *Moondyne*, was an excellent location for McCabe to seek help:

> There was a colony of Irish settlers at Dardanup, free men, who had emigrated there forty years before, when the Western Colony was free from the criminal taint. The families were all related to each other by intermarriage, and the men of the whole settlement, who had been born and reared in the bush, were famous throughout the colony for strength, horsemanship, good-fellowship, and hard fighting qualities.[72]

Maguire, who was thirty-seven years old, had left Ireland at the age of ten. He was now a farmer and a well-respected figure in the area.[73] Evidently he had the trust of McCabe and he was to prove a shrewd choice. Not only was Maguire happy to help a fellow countryman and a Fenian but his knowledge of the local landscape as well as his logistical skills were to be vital aids to O'Reilly. Maguire worked on his own land but also contracted for other employment and regularly criss-crossed the countryside around Dardanup and Bunbury. Therefore, it was not unusual to see him on the move and he would not arouse suspicion if he had to carry messages back and forth between McCabe and O'Reilly. By chance, at the end of 1868, he was involved in clearing land within a short distance of the road on which O'Reilly and other convicts were working.[74]

It was in December that Maguire first contacted O'Reilly. The convict was carrying Henry Woodman's weekly report to the Bunbury convict depot when he was approached by a stranger. This man greeted O'Reilly warmly and followed up by saying: 'My name is Maguire; I'm a friend of Father Mac's, and he's been speaking about you.'[75] O'Reilly was suspicious and did not acknowledge that he knew McCabe until Maguire took a card from his pocket on which the priest had written a short message for the convict. Once Maguire had established his authenticity he explained McCabe's plan to his now-eager listener. It was a far better plan than O'Reilly's previous idea of fleeing into the bush and it involved passage aboard an American whaling ship. O'Reilly's opportunity would come in February 1869 since every year American whalers arrived at the port during that month and the result was something of a festival for the inhabitants of the Bunbury as described by an inhabitant:

> This is a busy time with our tradespeople, who generally manage to drive a good trade with the whalers in tobacco, soap, candles, etc., which are sold in barter for potatoes, onions, and pumpkins . . . It is really amazing to witness the doings of the people. No sooner does a Yankee whaler drop anchor than the news is immediately telegraphed throughout the district. Then all are in bustle and confusion; dowager dames are anxious to go on board to see what can be got, while the younger ladies are equally eager to form fresh acquaintances. Visitors are always made welcome on board these

vessels, and pleasant parties are sometimes formed . . . The good people here return the compliment by making the officers and men welcome to their houses.[76]

It was during this period of bonhomie that McCabe would mastermind O'Reilly's escape. Once he had divulged the plan, Maguire left O'Reilly with the promise that 'You'll be a free man in February as sure as my name is Maguire'.[77]

O'Reilly had two months to wait but December 1868 was to be a strange, disturbing and almost fatal time for the 24-year-old Fenian. Over the previous few months O'Reilly had been involved in a clandestine love affair with the daughter of Warder Henry Woodman. Her name was Jessie Woodman. Almost all the details of this relationship are lost to history, although parts of O'Reilly's novel *Moondyne* may reflect their affair. O'Reilly never publicly spoke or wrote about what happened in later life. Indeed, the story of Jessie Woodman is entirely absent from James Jeffrey Roche's account of O'Reilly's life. O'Reilly's lifelong reticence to talk about his life in Australia can be seen in a letter he wrote to a friend years later. This friend had contacted O'Reilly about composing a life story but it is apparent that the, by then, former convict was uncomfortable about the idea:

> You grieve me about the biography. I am so tired of it, and it is such a hopelessly mixed biography, with every kind hand taking a whack at it. I read it in each new phase with a new sensation of horror and admiration. I will not send you any part of the Oriental story [his time in Western Australia] – and I lay upon you the Geasa (which is a spell from the remote darknesses held by all seers of the Gael) not to search for it elsewhere. And, as for your 'necessary dates', all such things are unnecessary. Dates are only fit for clerks, and facts are the opposite of truths. Facts are mere pebbles; unrelated accretions of the insignificant. If you want necessary truths – here, I am a man. I have written a poor little book of poems, and I have sent it out to be chopped into mince-meat. Seriously, I do not like the biographical notice. I know how kindly your thought was, but if you had to read so many 'stories of your life' that you yourself got mixed on the truth and the fabricated, you would hate it as I do.[78]

In 1890 he wrote to another journalist who was composing a story on O'Reilly. In this letter he wrote about his time as a convict:

> I was transferred to West Australia. You have no conception what a beautiful country it is. The air how balmy, the forest how magnificent, the plain so imposing. In West Australia I was treated with distinction. I was never expected to work. The other prisoners took off their caps to me whenever we met. I was a political prisoner. As they pursued their convict-labour I walked about and explored the country. So long as I came in to the time fixed, and kept regular hours, no questions were asked.[79]

This account of his time in Western Australia is obviously false. It could be suggested that it was an attempt to protect the identities of those who helped him during his escape attempt, but in 1881 a journalist named Alexander Young had published a long piece in the *Philadelphia Times* that named many of the protagonists in O'Reilly's Australian life.[80] Therefore, his reticence cannot be explained as an attempt to provide cover for his collaborators. O'Reilly would later get married in the United States and it may be that he was anxious to prevent his wife and family from learning of his relationship with Jessie Woodman. However, there were also darker reasons as to why O'Reilly may have wanted to hide or forget what had happened in Western Australia during those last few months.

The affair may never have become known to the wider public had it not been for Michael Davitt. He visited Western Australia in 1895 and while there he heard from locals about O'Reilly's time in the colony. He was the first to mention the relationship in print, writing in 1898, a few years after O'Reilly's death:

> He succeeded in winning the confidence of the warder in charge of the road-making gang at Bunbury, and was placed in a position of trust. He helped the officer write his reports, regulated the business of the convict stores, and was privileged to become the bearer of reports from one depot to another. In these journeys he attracted the ardent attention of a young girl, daughter of a warder, who conceived a strong attachment for the handsome young rebel, whose convict dress could not disfigure the fine physique and manly bearing of the prisoner.[81]

Davitt was not surprised to hear of the relationship, writing that 'No man or woman could resist the magnetic charms of O'Reilly's personality'.[82] Martin Carroll, an American historian, was the next person to examine this relationship in the early 1950s. Carroll interviewed descendants of Bunbury residents who knew O'Reilly in the 1860s. Especially important to him was the testimony of 83-year-old Anne Stokes, the only surviving child of James Maguire. She confirmed to Carroll that the relationship between Jessie Woodman and John Boyle O'Reilly had occurred and that Michael Davitt's version of events was at least partially correct.[83] Carroll's account of O'Reilly's time in Australia is an excellent work and historians of O'Reilly's life owe him a debt of gratitude but in the case of the Woodman and O'Reilly's affair he speculated freely on the basis of sparse evidence. Carroll had uncovered little of substance to add to Davitt's description of the love affair other than the testimony of Anne Stokes. Yet he described the pair spending illicit moments amid the wild flowers of a Western Australian spring: 'Passion and joy and peace were theirs – all the fierce promises and madness of first love.'[84]

Perhaps Carroll's version of their time together is correct. He was criticised by later writers who doubted the existence of any affair but the truth of a relationship was finally confirmed in 1989 by the Australian historian and archivist Gillian O'Mara. During that year a slim notebook, which had once been owned by Father McCabe, was given to the Battye Library in Perth. It was signed 'By John Boyle O'Reilly, 13 March sixty eight, in the bush near Bunbury'. Tests conducted by the library staff in the Battye Library confirmed the document's authenticity. O'Mara then deciphered the shorthand script in which O'Reilly had scrawled messages across the cover of the book.[85] It was a book that O'Reilly had kept from March onwards while in the convict depot. Unfortunately, it was not a diary and does not contain much personal information, being mostly poems composed by O'Reilly while he was aboard the *Hougoumont* and in Western Australia. Yet it does establish that O'Reilly was involved with a local girl named 'Jessi' and contains the admissions that: 'I am in love up to my ears' and 'It would take a saint to give her up'. That their relationship was physical was confirmed by his gripe that 'I wish she was not so fond of kissing'.[86]

However, that does not change the fact that we have no evidence at all of Jessie Woodman's part in the affair. There is not one document that describes her thoughts about the relationship or her feelings for O'Reilly.

There is little doubt that O'Reilly was in love with Jessie Woodman but did she feel the same way towards him? The few authors who have written about O'Reilly assume it was a passionate affair: a tale of mad and forbidden love between the handsome young convict and the warder's beautiful daughter. That may have been the case but by the end of the year their relationship was over. Could it also have been a tale of unrequited love? Did Jessie Woodman end their affair? There are two poems in the O'Reilly manuscript that are undated but seem to have been written at the end of 1868 and are reflections on the relationship. They both go under the title 'Night Thoughts' and one of these supports the view that Woodman scorned O'Reilly:

> Oh! no! I would not love again
> E'en had I still the power given;
> I would not risk its pain and fears
> E'en though its joys were taste of heaven.
> A breath may blight the heart we prize;
> A whisper weave deceit around it;
> And then our heart's most tender chord
> Is wounded by the chain that bound it.
> 'Tis hard to see death's chilling hand
> The life-strings of our treasure sever:
> But harder still when loving hearts
> Are rudely rent apart for ever.
> But ah! such griefs are naught to those
> That fill the heart where passion burned
> Till falsehood burst the mask and showed
> That love by heartless scorn returned.[87]

It is too easy to portray Jessie Woodman as the villain, capriciously scorning the young O'Reilly. Perhaps she did but if we need to maintain a sceptical eye in examining any historical document we need to be especially careful in a case such as this. This is O'Reilly's version of their failed affair and driven by pain he may have wanted to pass all the blame onto Woodman; his love and suffering was real, the poem seems to say, but hers only a façade. This could be true or it could be self-pity on O'Reilly's part.

The exact timing of events is also uncertain. Perhaps the end of the affair was what pushed O'Reilly to try and escape aboard a whaler. Perhaps his decision to try and escape from Australia caused a rupture between himself and Jessie. There were other complicating factors that we know almost nothing about. Hovering over the relationship is the spectre of George Pickersgill, a local famer. Jessie Woodman would marry this man only a few months later, in March 1869.[88] Why she married Pickersgill has raised many questions that remain without answers. It is usually assumed that Woodman was naïve, innocent and O'Reilly her first love. Maybe that is true but perhaps she was involved with Pickersgill the whole time? Perhaps she had been involved with other men? Perhaps her affair with O'Reilly, an actual rebel, was an act of rebellion against her parents? This love triangle, if that is what it was, may have been addressed obliquely by O'Reilly in *Moondyne*. In that novel the hero, Wyville (also known as Moondyne), is passionately in love with a woman named Alice Walmsley. Her affections, unfortunately for Wyville, are directed towards Will Sheridan, whom she has known since childhood and whom she eventually marries. The couple live happily ever after in a house that Wyville had once built with the intention that it would be a future home for him and Walmsley.

In the novel Sheridan is a kind and noble man whose goodness is outshone only by that of the saintly Wyville. As Sheridan and Walmsley make their life together, Wyville dies a hero in the Australian bush. The character of Wyville is clearly based, albeit loosely, on O'Reilly's own life. Could this tale of Wyville loving and losing be an idealised version of what O'Reilly experienced in Western Australia during 1868? Could Alice Walmsley be Jessie Woodward? Could Sheridan be Pickersgill? It could similarly be argued that the dashing Will Sheridan represents aspects of O'Reilly's character and that the novel's description of the 'deep and unutterable' love between the Catholic Sheridan and the Protestant Walmsley has elements of O'Reilly's and Woodman's relationship. Then again, in *Moondyne*, Alice initially spurns Sheridan, preferring another suitor, the caddish Sam Draper. The only man she never loves is Wyville, although she is aware of his affections for her.

All this serves as a warning that to treat *Moondyne* as evidence in studying their relationship is to risk running into an investigative dead end. One such dead end has been reached by a number of authors who have used *Moondyne* to suggest that Jessie Woodman became pregnant by O'Reilly and gave birth to a stillborn baby.[89] This argument is based on a misreading of the novel. Alice Walmsley does give birth to a child in the novel but it is a healthy baby, not stillborn. However, the baby is soon after murdered by an insane woman.[90] Alice is wrongly accused of the killing and transported to Australia after a few years as a convict in Millbank Prison. In *Moondyne* the horrific murder serves primarily as a plot contrivance by O'Reilly that allows him to examine and criticise the British penal system. To suggest that it reflects some aspect of his time with Jessie Woodman is, in this instance, to give a meaning to *Moondyne* that is simply not there.

Yet Jessie Woodman's marriage to Pickersgill does raise the question as to whether she had become pregnant by O'Reilly. If so, was she later married to Pickersgill to hide this fact and to prevent a birth outside of wedlock? Also, if she had been involved with Pickersgill, perhaps she became pregnant by him? Keith Amos and, before him, Martin Carroll, searched the relevant birth and death records for the years 1868 and 1869 but they reveal no babies named Woodman, O'Reilly or Pickersgill.[91] That does not preclude the fact that a baby may have been born or that Jessie Woodman miscarried or even underwent an abortion. However, there is no evidence for any of this. Martin Carroll wrote that local gossipmongers in early 1869 apparently had claimed that Jessie Woodman was pregnant but such rumours are worthless in themselves.[92] Also, in the 1950s Martin Carroll found no evidence of any local folklore that O'Reilly and Woodman had a child together. In the tight-knit communities of the time it seems unlikely that Jessie Woodman could have kept hidden a baby conceived outside of marriage.

O'Reilly's two poems in his 'Night Thoughts' do not suggest that the relationship ended because of a pregnancy and there is nothing in *Moondyne* to suggest Jessie had a child by him. If there can be found any hint of a child of his being born to a woman other than his future wife it is to be found in his poem 'The Statues in the Block', from his 1881 volume of poetry of the same name. The poem is an unsettling tale that contains a bleakness rarely seen in O'Reilly's verse. It describes four people in a sculptor's studio looking at a block of marble. Each person imagines a figure being fashioned from this block and each vision is markedly different from the other. One of them sees Ireland 'in the marble, bowed / Before thy tyrant, bound at foot and wrist'.[93] Another sees a woman emerge from the block:

Her hair was rippled and her eyes were deep,
He breasts and limbs were white and lily-curved,
But all the woman, soul and wondrous flesh,
Was poison-steeped and veined with vicious fire;
And I, blind fool, who trusted, was but one
Who swooned with love beside her.

It is the last vision that tells of 'The little hands still crossed – a child in death / My link with love – my dying gift from her'. Yet this vision speaks of two graves, those of a mother and a child. The child in this vision is a baby of at least a few months old. By the end of December 1868 O'Reilly and Woodman had been together for only a few months, six at the most. It seems more likely that the relationship was far shorter than this and that they may have only been a couple for a few weeks or months. If she had become pregnant and O'Reilly was the father, he would never have seen the child as he never saw Jessie again after that December. It could even be possible that Woodman became pregnant and that O'Reilly was unaware of the fact. This is all speculation and the stories of Jessie Woodman's pregnancy are based on little else other than hearsay and conjecture.

Ultimately, there remain only three acknowledged facts: there was a brief affair; it ended at the close of 1868; and in later years O'Reilly did not openly talk or write about what had happened. The evidence for this relationship is: the local tradition carried on by protagonists in the O'Reilly story such as James Maguire and his descendants; O'Reilly's notebook; and perhaps some references in *Moondyne*. That is all we have. Beneath those dry facts there was a whole world of emotion, perhaps a tale of romance, of love or unrequited love, of passion and tragic choices. Unless new evidence is found, our knowledge of the affair is so slender and so skewed towards O'Reilly as to prevent any real study of their relationship. This is not an attempt to minimise O'Reilly's emotional turmoil but to make clear that we know very little of what happened to him during those closing months of 1868. Whatever did transpire caused him immense distress. The results of the break-up were devastating for the 24-year-old and the other poem in 'Night Thoughts' gives a chilling view of his state of mind at this time:

Have I no future left me?
Is there no struggling ray

From the sun of my life outshining
Down on my darksome way?
Will there no gleam of sunshine
Cast o'er my path its light?
Will there no star of hope rise
Out of this gloom of night?
Have I 'gainst heaven's warnings
Sinfully, madly rushed?
Else why thus were my heart strings severed?
Why was my love-light crushed?
Oh! I have hopes and yearnings –
Hopes that I know are vain
And knowledge robs life of pleasure –
And death of its only pain.[94]

If anyone else had seen this poem they may well have recognised the warning signs flashing through the text. Nobody did and on the evening of Sunday 27 December John Boyle O'Reilly walked into the bush and slashed the veins in the wrist of his left arm. He was saved by another, unnamed, convict who found O'Reilly unconscious and bleeding. Proof that this occurred was a report by the sub-inspector of Bunbury Police Station, William Timperley who recorded in his diary that day:

> Started for the Vasse at 4 p.m. . . . overtook Dr Lovegrove trotting out of town – accompanied him as far as Woodman's camp where the probation constable named Riley [sic] one of the late head centres of Fenianism had attempted suicide by cutting the veins of his left arm and being accidently discovered prisoner when in a faint from a loss of blood.[95]

The discovery and prevention of O'Reilly's suicide raises the question as to why the incident was not reported to the Comptroller General for Convicts' office in Fremantle. If the suicide attempt had been reported then O'Reilly would certainly have been taken back to Fremantle to spend time under observation at the town's 'Lunatic Asylum'. That would have stymied his plans to escape via a whaling ship. It is likely that O'Reilly would have had to wait until the following February and, bearing in mind his mental anguish, it is doubtful that he could have lasted another twelve months as a convict. Once again, the reasons can only be guessed at. Woodman could have been attempting to prevent the news from spreading, thereby protecting his daughter's and his family's reputation. He could also have been trying to protect his own position as a head warder. If his superiors had gained knowledge of the affair they would surely have questioned Woodman's ability to perform his role successfully. If they judged that he had known of his daughter's romantic involvement with a convict, it would have been seen as an extraordinary dereliction of duty. On the other hand, if one of his convicts was shown to have been conducting an affair with his own daughter behind his back then Woodman would have been judged as incompetent. Woodman had more than enough reason to hide the facts of O'Reilly's attempted suicide.

It could have been a cover-up and it is possible that Warder Henry Woodman and O'Reilly had a special bond, perhaps as a result of O'Reilly's affair with the warder's daughter. The head warder in any convict depot was an isolated figure, both geographically and socially. Woodman was overseer of a convict depot deep in the Australian bush. Most of the people he encountered every day were convicts, many of them criminals guilty of vicious crimes. His only other opportunity for social interaction was his fellow officers but he was their superior and so had to maintain a professional distance from his men. He liked and trusted O'Reilly enough to make the Fenian his assistant. Could they have become friends? As we shall see, Woodman would, soon after the attempted suicide, help O'Reilly again. Throughout O'Reilly's life we can see in people's reaction to him the verification of what Michael Davitt once wrote: 'It would be impossible for O'Reilly to be anywhere on earth where human beings congregated without making friends'.[96] Did the warder take pity on O'Reilly? Did Woodman even give his blessing to his daughter's relationship with O'Reilly? Of course, it may be an assumption to believe that warders reported everything that happened under their control. At the very least what can be said with certainty is that he bore no ill will towards O'Reilly and his actions saved the convict from an incarceration that might have killed him.

However, that does not explain why William Timperley did not inform the Comptroller General's office, which oversaw the prison service. A. G. Evans, an English historian, has made the valid point that the police and the prison service were two different sections of the penal authority within Western Australia.[97] Timperley reported the event to his own superiors but it was not part of his remit to inform the prison service. It is no rare event for one section of the public service, in any country or time, to fail to pass information to another section of the public service. Within the prison service the news of O'Reilly's actions climbed no higher than Warder Woodman. Through the actions of Woodman, O'Reilly would be allowed rest and recover in the bush camp.

O'Reilly's physical recovery continued through the month of January but psychologically he remained a broken man. Maguire, who regularly checked on O'Reilly, could see that the convict was mired in misery during these weeks. In later years Maguire told his children that, during this time, 'Boyle, poor Boyle, cried and cried in desperation for help'.[98] O'Reilly and Maguire, though, could do little other than wait for February. Three whalers duly arrived at Bunbury in the first week of that month and this gave McCabe the chance to make an arrangement with the captain of one of the ships. He chose a ship called the *Vigilant* and met with its captain, Anthony Baker. How much money Baker was given is uncertain but £30 is the most frequently quoted sum.[99] Again, it is unknown whether McCabe paid Baker the whole amount but is more likely that he gave the captain a down payment. The rest of the money was probably given to Maguire for safe keeping until Baker had fulfilled his side of the agreement and rescued O'Reilly.

O'Reilly, despite his attempted suicide, had remained in his job as warder's assistant and by February, perhaps even January, he was back to his routine as messenger between the convict depot and Bunbury. On 14 February he was returning from the town where he found Maguire waiting for him at what is now the race track, south of Bunbury. Maguire was not a man to waste time and his first words were 'Are you ready?'[100] He then let O'Reilly know the details of the escape plan and told the convict to leave his hut at 8 p.m. on 17 February and head towards a former convict depot on the Bunbury to Vasse road, near a place called Picton Junction, a short distance east of Bunbury. From O'Reilly's convict depot this would take about three hours' walking. Once there, O'Reilly was to remain out of sight until his hiding spot was approached by someone who would whistle the tune to 'St Patrick's Day'. Maguire made O'Reilly repeat what he had been told so that there would be no confusion as to the plan of action. Before he departed Maguire gave O'Reilly a pair of civilian working boots since the standard convict boots were spiked and left a mark on the ground that could be easily discerned by any trackers in the Colonial Police.[101]

During the daylight hours of 17 February O'Reilly carried out his duties as normal although, while on a visit to Bunbury, he attempted to make contact with some of his fellow Fenians from the *Hougoumont*. The authorities at Fremantle Prison had recently moved a handful of Fenian prisoners to Bunbury and O'Reilly wanted to wish them goodbye before he made his escape. While O'Reilly's choice to contact his friends casts light on that aspect of his character and shows one of the reasons why he was so well liked by those who knew him, this decision also points to the reckless side of his personality. It was not a wise idea and he had been instructed by Maguire to let nobody know of his plans. Luckily, a prison guard refused O'Reilly permission to see the Fenians and so he left Bunbury to return to his convict depot.[102] While in the town he may have heard the unsettling news that two Bunbury convicts who had recently fled on a small sailing boat had been captured.[103] O'Reilly knew what it was like to break free of prison and be recaptured, having experienced this crushing disappointment at Dartmoor, Portsmouth and Chatham. The capture of these two convicts was more evidence, although he hardly needed it, that his escape was more likely to lead him to a solitary confinement cell than freedom.

Later that evening of 17 February O'Reilly wrote a letter to his father about his intended escape, a task he completed around 7 p.m.[104] A short time later he was visited by one of the warders who was making his customary inspection of the convict depot. The warder merely glanced into the hut and moved on.[105] The by now very anxious convict had a second visitor a few minutes later: a fellow prisoner who had come looking for some tobacco and a chat. O'Reilly, desperate not to be seen acting suspiciously, conversed with the man for the best part of an hour. A late departure could have thrown all his plans into disarray but fortunately for O'Reilly the other convict left before 8 p.m.[106] As soon as he had gone O'Reilly changed into his civilian boots, put out the candle by his bed and moved to the door of his hut. There he could see that it was a clear night. When he believed that there was no one around O'Reilly stepped into the open and walked towards the nearby woods. His great escape had begun.

Fugitive

John Boyle O'Reilly's exit from the Vasse convict depot did not go unnoticed. As he walked into the woods he heard a ticket-of-leave prisoner, Thomas Kelly, call after him, 'Are you off, Boyle?' O'Reilly turned to see Kelly walking towards him. It seemed as if his plans had been dashed. Kelly further frightened O'Reilly when he continued: 'I knew you meant it. I saw you talking to Maguire a month ago, and I knew it all.' O'Reilly had been caught utterly by surprise and he stood looking at Kelly, unsure what to do next. He later recalled that he thought Kelly was going to raise the alarm. Instead, Kelly held out his hand to O'Reilly and told the aspiring escapee, 'God speed you. I'll put them on the wrong scent to-morrow.' O'Reilly, unable to speak, shook Kelly's hand, turned and headed into the bush. He walked for three hours, crossing two rivers until he reached the location where he was to meet his contacts. This was near the junction on the Bunbury–Dardanup road, close to Picton on the eastern outskirts of Bunbury. At shortly after 11 p.m. O'Reilly lay down beneath a giant gum tree at the roadside and waited.[1]

While O'Reilly had been making his way to the Bunbury–Dardanup road, James Maguire and a friend of his, Thomas Milligan, were moving on horseback from Dardanup to the meeting spot. They arrived at the assigned location around 11.30 p.m. The convict, now a fugitive, heard the horses approaching but remained hidden until he heard one of the men whistle the tune to 'St Patrick's Day'.[2] On hearing those welcome notes O'Reilly emerged from his hiding spot to see that the duo had brought an extra horse. There was no time for talk. O'Reilly mounted his horse and followed his new companions, in a northerly direction, towards the Collie

River Bridge, to the north-east of Bunbury. This bridge they reached after an hour's riding. It was now early morning. As the three men dismounted Maguire gave a series of whistles into the darkness. He was answered by a whistle. Seconds later another three men appeared, all of whom remain unnamed in the accounts of the escape. One of these men, whom local tradition claims was Father McCabe, gave O'Reilly 'a warm shake of the hand, expressive of his good wishes'.[3] He then took the horses belonging to O'Reilly, Milligan and Maguire and galloped off. The other two, both cousins of Maguire, remained and led the group towards a spot on the coastline about a mile distant.[4]

All the time, they marched in single file so that any pursuers who happened upon the trail, especially the police's Aboriginal trackers, would be unsure how many people were in the group. To bury the evidence of their passage through the sand further Maguire had also arranged for a family member to drive a herd of Maguire's cattle through the area later that morning.[5] They walked for about an hour to get to the coastline. Here the group stopped again. While O'Reilly remained with Milligan the other three went off in search of the rowing boat that was to take O'Reilly out to sea. O'Reilly had thirty minutes of an anxious wait before a series of lights in the distance signalled that it was safe to proceed. O'Reilly and Milligan headed towards the lights, which proved to be about half a mile away. When they reached the other three men they could see that the vessel was ready. It contained two men, including the boat's owner, an English ex-convict named Joseph Buswell.[6] This man was now living as a fisherman and he was the key figure to the next leg of the journey, being the only person in the party with local knowledge of the waters of the Leschenault Inlet. As the tide was out, both O'Reilly and Maguire had to wade knee-deep through the mud to reach the water. Milligan refused to follow them, claiming, 'No, I promised my wife not to go in the boat.' His refusal resulted in an angry exchange between some of the men until one of them told Milligan, 'All right, go home to your wife.'[7]

This next section of their journey was potentially the most perilous. There was a real chance of being discovered by the harbour police or some random craft plying its trade along the coast. The four men had to row as quietly as possible down the inlet, into Koombana Bay and the port of Bunbury. If they could get through the port unnoticed they would then head out into the Indian Ocean. Fortune favoured the four men and they

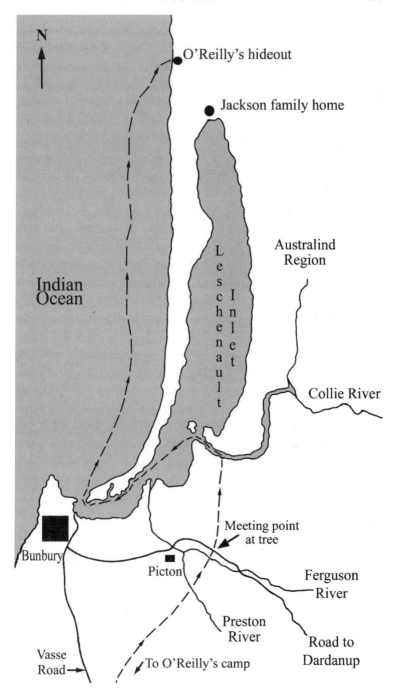

remained unseen and unheard as they stealthily guided their boat through the port. By sunrise, they had passed the town and were almost out of sight of land. Now they turned north, their new target being a deserted stretch of beach about 12 miles up the coast of the Leschenault Inlet. The men rowed at a brisk pace until they were near the location selected for their hideout, a deserted portion of a beach a few miles beyond the northern tip of the inlet. It was then around noon and they were tired from their overnight exertions. Above them, a cloudless sky offered no protection from the heat of the midday sun. During February the daytime temperature in this part of Western Australia can often climb above the daily average of 33 degrees Celsius. This situation would have been uncomfortable but tolerable except for the fact that nobody aboard the boat had brought water or food.[8] This was a surprising oversight, especially as Maguire had, so far, planned the escape brilliantly. It meant that the group faced a possible wait of over a day before the *Vigilant* arrived with fresh supplies.

Shortly after noon they beached the boat. While hauling their craft onto the sand the men were cooled by the waves but the the lack of drinking water was becoming unbearable. O'Reilly was the most badly affected and seemed on the verge of collapse.[9] Maguire decided that the group should make a search for water among the mostly dry swamps that littered the coastline. The four men wandered through the swamps for hours but their efforts met with no success. By now O'Reilly had been further weakened by what he described as a severe burning pain in his chest. Yet, having expended so much energy in the pursuit of water, the group was not willing to head back to the boat unsatisfied. As dusk settled they found what appeared to be their reward when they happened upon a cattle track. It was a tantalising and ultimately exasperating discovery. The tracks took them to a shallow muddy pool in which the water was too foul to drink.[10] Maguire, however, was not out of options. He recognised this landscape and realised that their long trek through the bush had brought them within a thirty-minute walk of a local farmer's cabin, a man whom Maguire knew. This dwelling was home to an Englishman named Jackson, his wife and son.[11] Jackson was a former convict who now ran a farm along this stretch of coast. It would be a risk to bring a stranger into their plans but, as Jackson's log cabin was the only habitation within 40 miles, they had little choice. Maguire decided that it was best if O'Reilly remained hidden while the three others walked to Jackson's cabin in search of sustenance. If all went well, one of the men would then bring some food and water to O'Reilly.

Back in Bunbury the authorities had begun a manhunt for O'Reilly. This search had been initiated around 10 p.m., only two hours after the Fenian had left camp and far sooner than he would have hoped. A woman passing through Bunbury shortly before 10 p.m. had seen a convict walking through the town. This woman was the wife of the principal warder of Bunbury convict depot and she informed her husband, Principal Warder Josiah Woodrow (not to be confused with the warder in charge of O'Reilly's convict camp, Warder Henry Woodman), that there was an escaped convict in the town.[12] O'Reilly was not the only absconder that night as two criminal convicts, one called Thompson and the other George Corton, had fled from separate camps.[13] Mrs Woodrow may have seen one of these men and once she brought the news to her husband the police immediately began to search the locality. Police riders were sent to all convict depots with news of the escapes and through this action O'Reilly's absence was discovered by the wardens at his convict depot. The police searched through Bunbury until approximately 3 a.m. but no sign of the convicts was found. At 8 a.m. the search, led by Sub-Inspector William Timperley, moved to the harbour area where a police party boarded and searched a whaling ship that was due to set sail that morning. This was the *Vigilant*, O'Reilly's hope of escape. In making their deal, Captain Baker and Father McCabe had acted wisely in agreeing that the ship would meet with O'Reilly further up the coast. The police thoroughly searched the vessel, especially the hold, but there was no convict to discover. Satisfied that the *Vigilant* was not in breach of the law, Timperley gave Baker permission to take his ship out of the port.[14] Almost as soon as the police had left the ship, the *Vigilant* began its journey north towards its rendezvous with O'Reilly.

Once back on shore, Timperley reported his lack of results to Woodrow. The authorities were now aware that three men were missing and that O'Reilly was one of these. It was then that the escaping Irishman was the beneficiary of some extraordinary good luck. Once she heard the name of O'Reilly, Mrs Woodrow insisted that he was the convict she had seen in the town around 10 p.m.[15] O'Reilly had been in regular contact with her husband over the past six months as he brought reports to and from the Vasse convict depot. She would have seen O'Reilly on many occasions.

Indeed, if the story of O'Reilly's quest to save the giant eucalyptus tree earlier in the year is accurate, she would have actually have spoken with O'Reilly and known him relatively well. It was her insistence that he was the man she had seen in Bunbury on the previous night that was to put the police on the wrong trail. Warder Woodrow completely trusted his wife's evidence and was certain that O'Reilly had made his way onto the *Vigilant*. Timperley assured Woodrow that the ship had been searched and contained no convicts. To Timperley this left one conclusion; that O'Reilly had failed to make it aboard the whaler and was hidden somewhere in the locality of Bunbury. He now ordered his men to concentrate their search on the sand dunes and bush around the town. Their efforts were destined to fail. At that time their quarry was rowing along the coast with Maguire and the others.

The police search was further hampered by the testimony of Warder Henry Woodman. O'Reilly had left the convict depot at 8 p.m. but, on the following day (18 February), Woodman told Timperley that he had spoken briefly with O'Reilly at about 10.30 p.m. the previous night.[16] Why had Woodman said this? There are two options: either he deliberately misled his colleagues to aid O'Reilly's escape, or he was attempting to cover any accusations of negligence that might, in any future enquiry, be made against him. As we have seen, Woodman and O'Reilly may have been friends and he may have wanted to help O'Reilly. It is also possible that he was keen to get O'Reilly out of Western Australia so as to keep the Fenian and his daughter apart. Whatever his reasons, Woodman's statement further compounded Timperley's confusion. He had two witnesses, both ostensibly respectable individuals in Western Australian society: a warder and a warder's wife. Both of these witnesses claimed to have seen O'Reilly between 10.00 and 10.30 p.m. at widely separated locations. Of the two statements, Timperley was more suspicious of Woodman's but he had no proof that the warder was lying. (It may be an unrelated fact, but Woodman was transferred from O'Reilly's camp to the West Guildford convict depot shortly after this incident.) For the moment all Timperley could do was to continue the search and he publicly offered a £5 reward for information on O'Reilly's whereabouts.[17]

Further up the coast and with his companions gone to Jackson's farm, O'Reilly was left alone in the sand dunes. He was scared, hungry and parched with thirst. Exacerbating his misery was the constant 'terrible

John Boyle O'Reilly photographed in Mountjoy Prison during 1866 (New York Public Library).

Left. A Roman Catholic prisoner in a Millbank cell, c. 1862 (from Mayhew, Henry and Binny, John, The Criminal Prisons of London and Scenes of Prison Life. *London, Griffin, Bohn & Co., 1862). Right. Fenian leader James Stephens in 1866 (US Library of Congress, LC-USZ62-48597).*

Equipment regularly used in the punishment of Australian convicts, including a ball and chain, iron manacles and a cat-o'-nine tails (US Library of Congress, LC-USZ62-82955).

John Boyle O'Reilly in March 1871, before he became editor of Boston newspaper The Pilot *(US Library of Congress, LC-USZ62-38163).*

A contemporary, albeit romanticised, lithograph of the Battle of Ridgeway, 1866 (US Library of Congress, LC-DIG-pga-01485).

The 1871 New York riot as portrayed in the press (US Library of Congress, LC-USZ62-120337).

Contemporary sketch of the destruction caused by the Great Boston Fire of 1872. The black arrow in the centre of the photograph marks Franklin Street, the site of The Pilot's head office. (US Library of Congress, LC-DIG-pga-03933).

Contemporary sketch of the army charging a crowd of railroad workers during the great strike of 1877 (US Library of Congress, LC-USZ62-53839).

Patrick Ford, O'Reilly's great contemporary and sometime rival, c. 1910 (US Library of Congress, LC-B2-1311-14).

The 'Cuba Five' in 1871. Standing on the left is John Devoy and seated on the right is Jeremiah O'Donovan Rossa. (US Library of Congress, LC-USZ62-72818).

blistering pain' in his chest, which was at its worst when he lay down.[18] To alleviate the pain, he walked about the sand dunes for a large portion of the following day, stopping now and then to peer into the hinterland in the hope of seeing one of his comrades. It was nightfall before Maguire returned. He brought with him some food and a bottle of water but remained for only a few minutes before heading back to Jackson's cabin.[19] Fed and watered, O'Reilly had a relatively comfortable night under the stars. The area in which he was hiding was heavily populated with peppermint trees and he fashioned a sweet-smelling bed of branches. He slept well until dawn when he was awoken by Maguire and the other two men. It was time to head back to the beach and the rowing boat.

From O'Reilly's hiding spot they had to walk through an area thick with peppermint trees until they reached the white sand dunes that ran parallel to the coast. It was 9 a.m. on 19 February when they reached these dunes.[20] From the summit of one they could see the waves of the Indian Ocean crash upon the shoreline. The pristine white beaches stretched for miles but the men could be forgiven for ignoring the natural beauty all around them. The hours ahead would be a time of nervous anticipation. Maguire had brought a telescope and he sent one of his companions to the top of the highest sand dune in the area to keep watch for the *Vigilant*. O'Reilly and the others could do nothing now but wait. It was 1 p.m. when the lookout spotted the ship in the distance, sails unfurled and heading north, directly towards the rendezvous point. Any residual tiredness or anxiety among the four men was forgotten in the hectic few minutes that followed. They dragged the boat into the water, climbed aboard and rowed as hard as they could out to sea. Part of the plan was that they would make contact with the *Vigilant* about 3 miles off the coast, outside Australian waters.

They had the benefit of a calm sea and rowed for the next two hours. All the while they could see the *Vigilant* and since it now appeared to be heading directly towards them they stopped rowing and waited. It seemed inevitable that O'Reilly would soon be climbing aboard his means of escape and would be on the way to America and freedom. Whatever thoughts of his past or his potential future were running through the fugitive's mind were rudely displaced by a shout from one of his comrades. The *Vigilant* had come within 2 miles but it had changed course and had begun to move away from the rowing boat. The four men were confused.

The confusion turned to anxiety as every moment confirmed that the ship was indeed sailing away from them. Maguire turned to O'Reilly and said more than once that 'Captain Baker had pledged his word to take them on board, and he could not believe him mean enough to break it.'[21] The *Vigilant*, though, kept to its new course.

At first the men had judged that the crew of the *Vigilant* were not as keen observers as the name of their ship might suggest. They may not have seen the boat. As time passed, this hope was dispelled as it became clear that the *Vigilant* was navigating around the smaller vessel in a wide arc. The ship was purposefully avoiding the boat. Why Captain Baker made this decision is not known. Perhaps he had always planned to betray McCabe and merely saw the deal as a means to make some easy money. Perhaps he had taken fright the previous day when his ship had been searched by Timperley and the police. When the distance between the two craft had increased to around 3 miles, Maguire took a white shirt and fixing it to an oar made a last despairing effort to attract the attention of the crew of the *Vigilant*.[22] The whaling ship sailed onwards, taking O'Reilly's hopes with it, and continued until it had disappeared from sight. This was a disaster, not only for O'Reilly but for all those who had helped him. If the Irishman had made it to freedom aboard the *Vigilant*, it would have been a perfectly executed plan, leaving the authorities with no means to discover how O'Reilly had fled and who had helped him. Now, with no idea what to do next and with the police likely to use every one of their considerable resources to catch the fugitive, it appeared that O'Reilly's recapture was a certainty. If that happened all of O'Reilly's benefactors could be implicated and punished.

It was James Maguire who devised a new strategy. Maguire realised that O'Reilly would have to remain hidden back at the spot where he had spent the previous night. This was in the midst of an isolated wilderness and would minimise the chances of O'Reilly being spotted by the police or any watchful civilian. The minimisation of the risk was countered by the fact that to leave O'Reilly hidden in the sand dunes would necessitate involving Jackson, the local farmer, in the plot. Maguire's plan was agreed upon by the four men as they rowed back to shore, a destination they reached in the evening. Here O'Reilly would have to wait, now a prisoner of events. Maguire explained to him that he would inform Jackson of what had happened and make arrangements with the farmer to bring O'Reilly provisions. While the fugitive remained concealed, Maguire would travel to meet with Father McCabe, assess the situation in Bunbury and see if they could arrange passage for O'Reilly on another whaling ship. O'Reilly at least had the consolation of knowing that if anyone could cobble together a new plan it was likely to be the Dardanup farmer and the Bunbury priest. With this agreed, the three men got ready to leave O'Reilly. Before they departed Maguire made a last effort to raise O'Reilly's spirits. He also implored him to stay at this location and remain hidden. Martin Carroll visited the area in the 1950s and described it as an excellent hiding place for the Fenian:

It is heavily wooded and the underbrush is thick and profuse. In many places the trees and bushes have very short trunks from one to four feet in height and these are topped by thick branches and foliage which, umbrella-like, reach almost to the ground. The place is called Molly's Thicket and from the estuary is approached through a swampy sandy region swarming with mosquitoes ... Should anyone unexpectedly traverse the swampy area between Jackson's place and the Thicket it was possible for O'Reilly effectively to conceal himself in hundreds of places. No one could have been more secure.[23]

That night O'Reilly received confirmation that the first part of Maguire's new plan had worked when he was visited by Thomas Jackson. The farmer brought food and water and promises of more to come. On the second night, 20 February, it was Jackson's son, Mathew, who brought supplies to the fugitive. O'Reilly never wrote in any detail about this period of his life but there can be little doubt that he was in emotional turmoil. He could not have been otherwise, considering the bitter disappointment he had just suffered, his attempted suicide, the end of his affair with Jessie Woodman and the years of imprisonment. His fragile mental state may have been a partial explanation for what he did next. By the third day of waiting O'Reilly had convinced himself that the episode with the *Vigilant* had been a misunderstanding. Captain Baker had not broken his agreement with Father McCabe. The simple fact, O'Reilly now believed, was that the ship's crew had not seen the rowing boat. Following this line of reasoning he further convinced himself that the *Vigilant* was at that moment sailing up and down the coast looking for him. The logical conclusion to this argument was that he could not be found if he was hidden in the Australian bush. In fact, he needed to get himself out to sea.

To this end, O'Reilly tried to drag Buswell's boat off the beach but it was far too heavy for one man. Frustrated, he waited until he was visited by Mathew Jackson. The lad arrived near nightfall bringing further provisions. O'Reilly enquired of Jackson whether he knew of any small vessels in the locality. The younger Jackson told him of a rowing boat half-buried in the sand further up the coast. There was no guarantee that it was seaworthy but O'Reilly was in no state to be diverted by such a possibility. This boat would carry him to freedom and he was so animated by the thought that he hardly paused to eat the food he had received. He walked for 6 or 7 miles before he found the boat and its oars. It was a cloudless night and the craft's dark hull was visible amidst the white sand. The boat was old and warped but O'Reilly plugged some small gaps in the hull with strips taken from local paperbark trees. He was satisfied that his new vessel was seaworthy but he realised that he had left all his food and waters back at his hideout, so he made the return journey that same night.

The next morning, 22 February, O'Reilly prepared to begin his reckless voyage. He had already stockpiled a supply of meat since, over the previous few days, he had alleviated his boredom by catching and killing possums.[24] This meat he brought with him as he went back to the boat. Once there it took a little effort to drag the craft into the water. To keep his stockpile of meat cool, he fastened it to the boat's stern using a short rope that he had made from some paperbark. All set, he started rowing in a northerly direction before turning west. He rowed for a few hours until he was a couple of miles off the coast and remained at sea all that day and through the night. The next morning, the Western Australian mainland was visible only as a thin white line on his eastern horizon. O'Reilly had hoped to spot the *Vigilant* or at least find himself within shouting distance of another whaling ship plying its trade along the Australian coastline. Instead he was alone, in a rickety old boat and with no protection from the sun. Not only did the heat cause him great discomfort but the dazzling reflection of the sun's rays off the water's surface left him practically blind. He could not even assuage his hunger as most of his meat had been 'taken by sharks' during the night. What little meat remained had gone putrid.[25]

Yet, about noon, while O'Reilly drifted hopelessly upon the water, he spotted a whaling ship in the distance. What was more, it was heading towards him. This ship, O'Reilly later claimed, was the *Vigilant*, still hunting whales in the area. He described the moment in an 1879 interview with the *Boston Daily Globe*: 'I saw a sail – it was the Vigilant. There was no other vessel there. She drew near to me – So near to me that I heard voices on deck. I saw the men aloft on the lookout.'[26] O'Reilly waved and shouted but, like a ghost ship, the *Vigilant* drifted blithely by the frantic fugitive, its crew seemingly divorced from what was happening in their immediate vicinity. He watched as the ship slowly receded into the distance. Or so he claimed. Amid all the drama of O'Reilly's life and his attempts to escape from Australia this incident, the supposed second near miss with the *Vigilant*, could be an embellishment. Perhaps that is harsh and it did happen but the sheer improbability of this encounter, as described by O'Reilly, makes it seem as if it was a later fiction invented by him to rationalise his foolhardy voyage. Michael Davitt, who later wrote of O'Reilly's escape, may have been more correct than he realised when he described the incident as 'a phantom vision of [O'Reilly's] "dream" of liberation.'[27] Whatever happened that day, the one indisputable fact was that O'Reilly had not been rescued. Without food and short of water, he did not have the energy to remain at sea for a second night and so he turned his boat for the coast. It took him until noon of the next day to reach land. He returned the boat to where he had found it and then trudged back to his hideout. It was now 23 February and O'Reilly was almost broken by exhaustion. The fugitive spent nearly all of the next five days sleeping.[28]

In Bunbury, Timperley was shocked by the lack of evidence on O'Reilly's escape. On 20 February, less than seventy-two hours after O'Reilly had gone missing, he had reported to the Superintendent of Police in Western Australia, Gustavus Hare:

> I have made this report somewhat lengthy, but regarding the escape of this man as involving more mystery than any other that has ever come under my notice, I simply wish to point out that I have constantly and carefully considered the matter and acted under the circumstances to the best of my ability with the means at my disposal.[29]

Timperley, as can be guessed from the above, was preparing his superiors for failure. He wanted them to know that he had done his best, everything that would normally be done in the case of an escaped convict. Despite that, he had no clue how O'Reilly had evaded detection. His letter drew a strong rebuke from Superintendant Hare who threatened to replace Timperley as head of the investigation.[30]

So motivated, Timperley decided to widen the search. He sent Aboriginal trackers through the landscape around O'Reilly's former camp south of Bunbury. The police also visited houses throughout the area. They carried out house searches at Dardanup, probably due to town's large Irish population. There, also, they found nothing. Maguire was absent, visiting O'Reilly or Father McCabe when the police called to his house, but Maguire's wife convinced the officers that her husband was on official business in the town of Pinjarra, about 60 miles north of Dardanup.[31] Since Maguire was on the local road board and a respected figure in the area, the police readily accepted her explanation and did not follow up on the matter. While the search for O'Reilly floundered, the police did have success in their hunt for the other absconders, Thompson and Corton. Both of these had been caught by the Aboriginal trackers within days of their escape.[32] As O'Reilly waited amid the sand dunes near the Jackson homestead both men were sentenced to three months' solitary confinement, followed by hard labour. All that time they would be kept in irons. Each man had started his punishment with three dozen lashes. This would be O'Reilly's fate should he be captured.

While O'Reilly spent the days recovering from his solo voyage, the police continued to scour the area around Bunbury, Dardanup and the Vasse. More than a week had passed since the escape but the police had made no progress and were left without further leads. The police trackers had no tracks to follow, the £5 reward had elicited no information from the population, and house-to-house searches had turned up nothing. Timperley had also ordered his men to enquire with locals about missing horses in case O'Reilly had stolen an animal and ridden away from the colony. If O'Reilly had escaped in this manner he would have left ample proof of his exit through the horse's hooves. Yet there were no tracks, so O'Reilly could not have escaped by horse. Anyway, where could he have ridden to? Outside the settled areas there was nothing but wilderness. Could the fugitive have swum from the shore to meet a whaler? Perhaps, but there was no evidence of footsteps on the beach or clothes left behind. Then there was the testimony of Mrs Woodrow, the head warder's wife.

She continued to insist that she had seen O'Reilly in Bunbury the night of the escape. In this claim she was fully supported by her husband and her 'evidence' seems to have taken on the status of urban legend in Bunbury. Many other people in the town repeated the opinion that O'Reilly had made his way aboard the *Vigilant* and was long gone.

All this brought Timperley to make the deduction, one which most of his colleagues had already made, that O'Reilly had indeed escaped aboard the *Vigilant*. It was a conclusion that he arrived at haltingly but it seemed to be an inescapable endpoint to the evidence; somehow, O'Reilly had been so well hidden aboard the *Vigilant* that he had escaped the attention of his officers when they had searched the ship on the morning of 18 February. Timperley was doubly frustrated by the lack of information regarding O'Reilly's escape. It was bad enough that a convict had evaded his grasp, his failure was aggravated by the fact that more than a few members of the local population, supposedly law-abiding citizens, had aided and abetted a fugitive. Timperley was certain that the Fenian had benefited from having a wide network of supporters. A few days after O'Reilly's escape the police officer had reported to a superior 'That O'Reilly has friends I can have no doubts, having had constant and frequent opportunity of communicating with different persons while travelling about . . . and I am equally certain that many would help a Fenian who would not offer hand or foot for an ordinary prisoner of the Crown.'[33] O'Reilly was lucky to have such resourceful companions. McCabe and Maguire's plan to get the fugitive aboard the *Vigilant* may have gone awry but they had managed to keep the number of people involved in the escape confined to a small number of trustworthy individuals. Maguire had also done a remarkable job in covering O'Reilly's tracks, literally in some cases. Most importantly, once McCabe and Maguire's first plan had failed they began to formulate an alternative.

After O'Reilly returned from his solo voyage he, perhaps chastened by the episode, remained in his hideout. His recovery was helped by the Jacksons who each night brought him more provisions. James Maguire also made at least one trip to check on O'Reilly during this time. How he would have been affected had he heard the latest news of Jessie Woodman we can only guess but on 1 March she married George Pickersgill in the Congregational Church of Bunbury.[34] Whatever the truth of the affair between O'Reilly and Woodman, there was nothing to hold him in

Western Australia now. On the night of 2 March O'Reilly was cheered by the arrival of Maguire, Milligan and a third man. They brought him welcome news from Father McCabe (there is no indication that Maguire told the still volatile O'Reilly of Jessie's marriage). The priest had arranged O'Reilly's passage on another whaling ship.[35] This time O'Reilly would depart Australia aboard the whaling ship *Gazelle*, an American vessel under the command of Captain David Gifford. The *Gazelle* would then carry O'Reilly as far as the island of Java, at that time a Dutch possession and outside the British Empire. McCabe had paid Gifford £10 (it is not certain if this was a down payment or the whole sum) and, in return, had been assured by the captain that he would not break his agreement. Gifford was told of O'Reilly's location and the captain agreed to meet with O'Reilly around 3 miles off the coast on 3 March.[36]

The one, potentially disastrous, hurdle to this plan came in the form of the third member of the group that now stood before O'Reilly. This man was 38-year-old Thomas Henderson, better known by his alias Martin Bowman (or sometimes Beaumont). Bowman had been transported from England as a criminal convict in 1856. He had been convicted of attempted murder in England and his prison record in Millbank and aboard the prison transport that brought him to Australia was classified as 'very bad'.[37] Yet, after a period of hard labour, he had been granted ticket-of-leave in 1860. While going about his daily business, Bowman had chanced upon the fact that Maguire was aiding an escaped convict. He approached Maguire and demanded that he be allowed to escape with O'Reilly aboard the whaler. If Maguire refused, Bowman told him that he would go straight to the police.[38] Maguire and McCabe had no choice but to accede to the convict's demand. He was not a welcome addition to the party. O'Reilly later made a character called Isaac Bowman one of the chief villains in his novel *Moondyne*. In the book he described Bowman as 'all evil, envious and cruel; detested by the basest, yet self-contained, full of jibe and derision, satisfied with his own depravity, and convinced that everybody was just as vile as he.'[39]

Despite O'Reilly's distrust of his new companion, the fates of the two men were inextricably linked. The whole group slept under the stars that night with 'someone always keeping an eye on Bowman'.[40] At dawn they dragged Buswell's rowing boat into the water. Also helping the four men were Thomas and Mathew Jackson. They had come to shore, as had Jackson's wife, to wish good luck to O'Reilly. He would not have survived the previous two weeks without their aid. The Jackson family had no ties to O'Reilly and it was merely chance that had brought him into their lives but they had risked serious punishment to help him. Mathew Jackson later explained why they helped the escapee: 'He was possessed of considerable Irish charm, and so was able to command the sympathy and practical help of folks who, had they been known to help in the escape, would have been sent to prison and would probably have lost their respected positions in the small community of those days.'[41] O'Reilly would never forget their extraordinary generosity.

Once the boat was afloat, O'Reilly, Bowman, Maguire and Milligan, who by this time seems to have overcome or ignored his wife's objections to sea travel, headed away from the beach. Around noon, two whaling ships came into view and over the next few hours the distance between these ships and the rowing boat diminished until the smaller craft was within earshot of the ships. This time there was no confusion and no disappointment. The four men were hailed by the leading ship, the *Gazelle*, one of whose crew shouted out: 'Boyle O'Reilly, come on board.'[42] The rowing boat pulled alongside the whaler and O'Reilly was helped aboard by Henry Hathaway, the third mate. Once on deck, he was cordially welcomed to the ship by Captain Gifford. As the boat pulled away from the *Gazelle*, Milligan also shouted a farewell while Maguire stood up and cried, 'God bless you; don't forget us, and don't mention our names till you know it's all over.'[43] O'Reilly, in tears, could only wave farewell to his saviours.

By coincidence, on the same morning as the *Gazelle* sailed to its meeting with O'Reilly, the fugitive's would-be nemesis, William Timperley, had officially declared the results of his investigation. In a letter to a superior officer he wrote:

> In conclusion I beg to state that I have kept up a strict enquiry into this subject and in addition to the most positive information that O'Reilly has gone, the facts and circumstances that I have collected leaves me the most certain conviction that O'Reilly is at this time sailing in the Barque [a vessel with three or more masts] 'Vigilant'. I will continue to make every possible enquiry.[44]

O'Reilly had finally broken away from the Colony of Western Australia in which he remained a wanted man. His name would be added to the list of absconders who were on the run from the police and shortly after O'Reilly's escape the following appeared in the *Police Gazette* of Western Australia:

> ABSCONDERS: John B. O'Reilly, registered No. 9843, imperial convict; arrived in the colony per convict ship *Hougoumont* in 1868; sentenced to twenty years, 9th July, 1866. Description – Healthy appearance; present age 25 years; 5 feet 7 inches high, black hair, brown eyes, oval visage, dark complexion: an Irishman. Absconded from Convict Road Party, Bunbury, on the 18th of February, 1869.[45]

This succinct account was largely a result of continued ignorance among the police as to the details of O'Reilly's escape. Some years later, in 1876, a friend of O'Reilly would show him a copy of the above notice in the *Police Gazette*. As we shall see, O'Reilly was at that time a successful newspaper editor of the Boston newspaper *The Pilot*. Using headed notepaper from his newspaper's office, O'Reilly composed a helpful, if sarcastic, note for the police of Western Australia:

> Dear Sir,
> I have just seen a copy of the Police Gazette of Western Australia, in which under the head 'Absconders' I have found my name and description. Should you desire any information regarding my affairs I shall be happy to give it you. Do not perpetuate the stupid folly of printing my name among your criminals. I am far beyond the reach of your petty colony laws; and I really wish to preserve something of a kindly and respectful memory of your country in which I have some dear friends. Should you ever visit the Republic [United States], I shall be happy to see you. As your Gazette is 'published for police information only', please tell your officers, especially Sergeant Kelly, once of Bunbury, that I send them my respects.
> Yours very truly,
> John Boyle O'Reilly[46]

The Police Superintendent of Western Australia, M. S. Smith, dutifully added the letter to the files on O'Reilly's escape. However, all that lay in the future. The 24-year-old Irishman who had been a reporter, soldier, rebel, convict, and who was now a fugitive had yet to reach America. To get there he had to partake in one of the great seafaring industries of the nineteenth century. John Boyle O'Reilly was to go hunting whales.

The Whaling Ship

As O'Reilly stood on the deck of the *Gazelle* that day in 1869 he was probably unaware that he had joined an American industry that, according to the historian Margaret S. Creighton, 'represented seafaring at its extreme'.[1] Voyages routinely lasted for up to four years and whaling ships spent much of their time sailing through the most dangerous seas in the world. The heart of this global industry lay in the American port of New Bedford, Massachusetts and, each year, hundreds of whaling ships sailed from the so-called 'Whaling City'. In August 1866 the *Gazelle* had been one of these ships and had been over two years at sea by the time it picked up O'Reilly.[2]

Throughout the nineteenth century these American ships mostly hunted four types of whale: the sperm whale, often referred to as a cachalot, was hunted mostly in the warm tropical and subtropical waters of the Pacific, Indian, and Atlantic Oceans; the right whale, hunted in the more temperate regions of the world's oceans; the bowhead whale, also called the Arctic whale, which was hunted in the cold waters of the Arctic circle; and the humpback whale, which was hunted all over the world but most heavily in the Atlantic Ocean. The bodies of the whales caught and slain by the whaling ships provided a range of important products. From the sperm whale came sperm oil. That oil was traditionally burned in lamps, especially street lamps, and had been used to illuminate cities across Europe and the United States for much of the eighteenth and early nineteenth centuries. By the middle of the nineteenth century street lamps were more often fired by gas but sperm oil remained in demand as a lighting fuel. Sperm oil was also used as machine lubricant. Other types of whale likewise furnished whale oil but this was heavier and of poorer quality than sperm oil and was used more often as a lubricant rather than for illumination.

The vagaries of fashion provided another ready market for whale products. A commercially important substance provided by sperm whales was called spermaceti and was extracted from the animal's head. The hunters would cut a large hole in a captured whale's skull. One of the sailors would then crawl through this hole and manually remove the fluid. The spermaceti was placed in barrels for the rest of the voyage. This substance was used in the manufacture of candles and soaps. Sperm whales were also harvested for ambergris, an ash-coloured secretion found in the creature's intestines and was used as a fixative in perfumes. Other types of whale were killed for their baleen, a comb-like structure in the animal's mouth that served to filter seawater for food. Baleen, also commonly known as whalebone, was light, strong, flexible and perfectly adapted to the manufacture of corsets, dress hoops, umbrellas, and other similar items.

The most heavily hunted families of whales suffered grievous population losses from the eighteenth century onwards but they were to receive some respite in the second half of the nineteenth century with the rise of kerosene as a competitor to whale oil. By 1858 the North American continent's first oil well had been drilled at Oil Springs in Canada. During the following year the US petroleum industry began with the drilling of an oil well in 1859 at Oil Creek in Pennsylvania. The petroleum industry had a ready-made market and over the following decades, as its production methods improved, the industry was able to increase massively the volume of petroleum produced. A further advantage for the petroleum industry was the fact that it could produce oil in the US, whereas whaling firms had to purchase and equip ships which were then sent on hazardous multi-year voyages.[3] As such, the owners of the oil wells were able to supply lighting oil at a far cheaper price than the whaling industry. Whalebone remained a commercially desirable product but it was whale oil that had been the mainstay of the industry. As the demand for whale oil steadily decreased, its price per barrel followed the same trajectory.

Following these developments the whaling industry entered a precipitous decline during the 1860s and by 1869 only around 280 American whalers still plied their trade.[4] These ships were crewed by approximately 8,000 men of whom O'Reilly was now one.[5] On board the *Gazelle* were thirty-one crew: fourteen Americans, fourteen Portuguese, two Dutch and one Brazilian.[6] Added to this mix were the Irish O'Reilly and the English Bowman. The living quarters aboard a whaling ship were cramped and uncomfortable. The crew were mostly quartered in the forecastle at the front of the ship and it was here that Bowman was placed by the captain. However, Gifford insisted that O'Reilly, who he told the crew was named Brown, was given accommodation with one of the ship's mates.[7] Both the new arrivals were to take part in the ship's daily routine.

The crew of the *Gazelle* were not paid a set wage but instead received what was called a 'lay', a proportional share in the net proceeds of the voyage.[8] The ship was most likely owned by one of the many whaling firms in New Bedford and they would have taken up to 70 per cent of the net proceeds. Of the remainder, the captain received the highest share of the profits, while the mates were next and then the rest of the crew. The captain kept an individual account for each crew member and before a sailor received his pay packet, deductions were made to cover the food and other provisions required by the man over the duration of the voyage. A sailor's final pay packet was dependent on the attitude of the whaling firm to which the ship belonged. The deduction of these lays was often unwarranted and every pretext was used to diminish the payment due to the sailors. In some cases the deductions actually exceeded the lay due to a sailor who, after three or four years on the ocean, would find himself in debt to the firm for which he had been working. The whole system was skewed against the common sailor and was best described by the historian Elmo Paul Hohman in his 1920s classic *The American Whaleman*: 'Both nature and man combined to create a situation which, at its best, was hard, and at its worst represented perhaps the lowest condition to which free American labor has ever fallen.'[9]

Aside from the poor remuneration, the crew of a whaling ship faced manifold dangers other than the risks common to all sailors such as storms, shallows and dangerous seas. Accidents were common and most often happened during a hunt. Whenever a whale was sighted the chase began and most of the crew transferred to the smaller, sleeker whaleboats, of which most whalers carried four. These could be damaged or sunk by an angry whale. While in pursuit of a whale a sailor might get entangled in a piece of line attached to a harpooned animal and be ripped from the boat and into the depths. Sometimes a whaleboat, which could move much faster than its mother ship, became separated and lost. If that happened, the whaleboat could easily be sunk by any inclement weather it was unfortunate enough to encounter. On very rare occasions whales were even known to have rammed and sunk a whaling ship such as in the infamous case of the *Essex*, an American whaler sunk during 1820 while sailing the South Pacific. These dangers were made brutally apparent to O'Reilly only four days after he joined the *Gazelle*. While chasing a whale, the ship's carpenter, an American named William Freeman, was knocked overboard and presumed drowned. His body was never recovered.[10]

Over the following days the ship made slow progress northwards along the western coast of Australia. Although O'Reilly would have been keen to put as much distance as possible between himself and Australia the goal of the rest of the crew was to search thoroughly each region through which it sailed. Speed of travel was of little importance to the captain of a whaling ship and long periods of fruitless enterprise were an inevitable component of a whaler's routine. These barren spells were a curse to the crew. Not only were they the main reason why a whaling expedition could last for years but it also meant long periods of numbing boredom. This fact allowed O'Reilly to fill a niche aboard the ship. He was never one to remain inactive and not only did he become a full member of the crew but he spent the evenings acting as an impresario, organising recitals of poetry and song.[11] Many of these recitations were undertaken by O'Reilly and included examples of his own compositions. The man the sailors knew as Brown swiftly established himself as a favourite among the crew.

Over the rest of that March the *Gazelle* encountered plenty of other whaling ships but no whales. The ship's lookouts kept a constant vigil for any signs of whales, which usually betrayed their presence in one of a variety of ways: by spouting (blowing a mixture of water vapour and mucous into the air); by breaching (leaping out of the water); or by lobtailing, in which the animal raises its huge flukes (horizontal tail fins) and slaps them down hard on the surface of the water. It was 29 April, almost two months after O'Reilly had joined the ship, before whales were sighted at a close enough distance to give chase.[12] On that day O'Reilly and the crew would have heard one of the lookouts shout 'There she blows!' This was the signal for the sailors to scramble into action. The hunt was on.

Most of the men now transferred themselves from the *Gazelle* to its whaleboats. These smaller craft were admirably adapted to the whaler's need for combined speed, strength, and seaworthiness. They were around 30 feet long, strongly built with a small mast and sail, which could be raised or taken down at will, and a long, heavy steering oar.[13] Each boat's crew consisted of six men. The boat-steerer occupied the extreme forward position in the boat and pulled the bow oar until close to the whale. At that point he stood and readied himself to hurl the harpoon. The bowman handled an oar and assisted the boat-steerer in setting and taking in the mast. The midship oarsman pulled the longest and heaviest oar and the tub oarsman was responsible for the harpoon line as well as for his share of rowing; the stroke oarsman rowed, bailed the boat when necessary, and assisted in handling the mast; and the boat-header, or mate, manned the steering-oar, and commanded the small crew.[14]

A whale hunt could proceed for hours and it was often the case that the hunters would not get a clear shot at their quarry and would have to return to their ship empty handed. However, if they could get within striking distance they would attempt to harpoon the whale, a scene which was described by Elmo Hohman:

> In coming to close quarters with a whale it was customary to approach either from the rear (known as 'going on the flukes') or from the front (termed 'taking it head and head'). This was because the animal's eyes were so situated on the sides of its huge body that it could see neither directly ahead nor directly behind, but only to the side. Hence the obvious advantage of avoiding its field of vision as far as possible. When within a short distance of the goal the mate warned the boat-steerer to stand up in the bow and to prepare for the dart. The latter braced himself and, with harpoon poised, awaited the most propitious moment. This was often delayed until the prow of the boat was only a few feet from the body of the whale, when the harpoon was sunk deep into the yielding blubber and flesh; and if time permitted a second harpoon, attached to the same line, followed the first.'[15]

The harpoon that would have been used aboard the *Gazelle* was called a toggling harpoon. There were numerous variations of the toggling harpoon but its basic design was an iron shaft, 3 feet long, attached to a wooden pole. The harpoon carried a two-part point, which could swivel on contact and would lodge itself under the animal's skin. That would have caused the whale intense pain but it was merely the first of many wounds inflicted by the hunters. It took an average of seven harpoons to bring a whale to a stop and even then the animal was still alive. It was at this stage that the mate in charge of the boat came to the bow (while the boat-steerer went to the stern and took control of the steering oar). He brought with him the whaling lance, an iron shank 6 feet long topped by a large oval blade, with which he stabbed the whale. The iron shank was mounted on a long wooden pole and was pushed several feet into the creature's body. This was done with the aim of piercing the lungs and was repeated until the whale's spout showed quantities of heavy, dark blood. This signified that the whale had been mortally wounded although, in what was a prolonged torture, it could still take hours before the animal finally succumbed to its multiple injuries.

Not every harpooning ended with the death of the whale and, once harpooned, the animal would usually take one of three courses of action. It might turn at once in an attempt to demolish the boat; it might swim along the surface at a tremendous speed, while towing the boat and its occupants by means of the whale line attached to the harpoon; or it might descend with great rapidity taking with it the 300 fathoms (each fathom was equal to 6 feet) of line that each whaleboat carried. In the history of whaling, the first case (in which the whale attacked the boat) was relatively rare, and was confined to what sailors called 'ugly' whales.[16] These were the great fear of whalers and when such a creature was encountered the only option open to the hunters was to attempt to evade the jaws and flukes of the whale until it tired or moved on. Unluckily for O'Reilly and his shipmates, the whale they had started chasing would prove itself to be a very ugly whale.

A few years after the event Henry Hathaway, with whom O'Reilly had become good friends and who was commanding one of two whaleboats, wrote a description of that day's hunt. Hathaway later gave a copy of this account to Roche.[17] As the boats were being lowered into the water, O'Reilly pleaded with Hathaway to be allowed join the chase. Hathaway initially told O'Reilly to stay on the ship but with no time to argue the matter he relented and allowed his new crewman to come aboard just before the whaleboats began the pursuit. The first boat to reach the whale was commanded by another of the mates, Frederick Hussey. One of Hussey's men fired a harpoon into the whale's back. The whale turned and made directly for Hussey's boat but 'settled' and disappeared beneath the waves. There were a few moments of silence before the whale reappeared but now it was closer to Hathaway's vessel. He cried at his boat-steerer to 'give it to him'. The sailor, a man called Lambert, flung his harpoon into the creature's back. The whale reacted to this second attack by raising its flukes and crashing them down on Hathaway's boat. The wooden craft was almost ripped in two by the force of the blow. Water was now pouring through the breach and the crew clambered into the sea, carrying their oars with them as flotation devices. Only O'Reilly remained aboard, slumped over the side of the boat. Hathaway had seen the Irishman's head drop as the first blow was struck. While the other sailors strove to make distance between themselves and the furious whale the animal again attacked the boat. The whale hit the vessel twice more before pausing and then striking it a fourth and final time. Then, with its assailants vanquished and the boat in pieces, the animal descended beneath the waves.

With the whale gone, the men swam back to the detritus that was formerly their boat. Hathaway was hanging onto the stern 'the only piece large enough to hold a man up'. He could no longer see O'Reilly but as he looked around he heard one of the crew shout: 'There he is, on the other side, under water.' O'Reilly was floating face down, bobbing up and down with each wave. He was unconscious. Hathaway swam to the other side of the wreckage and, while holding onto the boat's keel with his left hand, reached over and grabbed O'Reilly by the hair with his other hand. He dragged his friend towards him and placed him awkwardly on a large piece of wreckage. O'Reilly was bloodied and 'froth was running from his nostrils and mouth'. Hathaway, realising that O'Reilly was in real danger of drowning, pulled his friend up and over his shoulder so that the Irishman's stomach lay across the mate's shoulder. He later recounted, 'I kept punching him as much as possible to get the salt water out of him.'

The crew of the sunken boat were soon picked up by Hussey's boat but it took 'several hours' for the *Gazelle* to appear. The mother ship had been unable to keep pace with the whaleboats and, by the time of the battle with the whale, had fallen around 12 miles behind. O'Reilly seems to have been unconscious for all this time but he was eventually returned to the ship and taken to his bunk. He was the only casualty of the incident. Hathaway recalled visiting O'Reilly after the injured man had regained consciousness the next day. O'Reilly was in poor spirits and he asked his saviour, 'Oh, Hathaway, why didn't you let me go?' The third mate tried to cheer up

O'Reilly and told him 'that he would live to see better days'. Hathaway's words had no effect on O'Reilly who remained despondent. Despite his fierce energy and the amusement he provided for the crew it was only four months since his suicide attempt and the enormous stress and excitement of his escape from Western Australia. What scars had the separation from his family, his imprisonment and his failed relationship with Jessie Woodman left upon his psyche? Perhaps during idle moments dark thoughts threatened to overwhelm him. Is that what drove him onwards and contributed to the fierce energy he displayed aboard the *Gazelle*? Those questions cannot be answered. Perhaps O'Reilly's mind was often host to negative thoughts – whether or not that was the case it can be said with certainty that he was a man of positive actions. Within a few days he was on his feet, working among the crew and again providing entertainment during idle hours. When the *Gazelle* next encountered whales O'Reilly insisted again on joining the chase. Hathaway, as he had on the previous occasion, refused but relented after O'Reilly's protestations that he wanted retribution. This hunt was less dramatic for the crew of the *Gazelle*. Hathaway wrote: 'We were lucky enough that day to get a good big fellow, and I think he [O'Reilly] had his revenge, as we minced him up pretty well.' It was probably these two hunts that were the inspiration for O'Reilly's poem 'The Amber Whale'. The poem ends with the lines 'It's just fifteen years gone, shipmates, said old Mat, ending his tale / And I often pray that I'll never see another Amber Whale.'[18]

That was one of a few pieces that O'Reilly wrote or started to write while on the *Gazelle*. Hathaway kept a private log of events aboard the *Gazelle* and this contained many poems and short compositions written by the Irishman, usually under the name 'Old Blowhard'. O'Reilly may well have suffered intense emotional turmoil while aboard the *Gazelle* but he kept it well hidden behind a mask of relentless good humour. His writings in Hathaway's log were all light-hearted pieces, such as lampoons of the ship's rules and the terminology that had initially been so confusing to a landlubber like O'Reilly:

Dimensions of various parts of a ship – By Old Blowhard
The main top-gallant cross-tree is twice as long as the flying jib-boom.

    The jib-boom should be half as long again as the steer oar of the larboard boat. If the larboard boat has no steer oar, make the jib-boom short accordingly.

The mainyard, in all fast sailing vessels, should be about as long as a rope.

The foreyard is half as long as the mainyard, and three times as thick.

In large ships, where brown paper is used instead of canvas for top sails, it is not necessary to lace the back-stays.

The right bower anchor should be as heavy as a large stone, and she should always be kept warm.

The chimney of the cook's galley should be eight times as long as the spanker boom. In clipper ships this length may be doubled.

Mizzen top-gallant yard should be a little larger than a log of wood, and heavy in proportion.'[19]

The following weeks were relatively quiet for the crew as the *Gazelle* continued northwards towards the Sunda Strait, which divides the Indonesian islands of Java and Sumatra. The *Gazelle* entered the strait on 23 June 1869, hoping to make its way through to the port of Batavia to restock its dwindling supplies of fresh water and vegetables. This is the modern-day Indonesian city of Jakarta on the island of Java but at that time the city and surrounding area was a Dutch colony. The *Gazelle* would not make it to Batavia. The Sunda Strait is infamously hazardous, combining shallows, sandbanks and small islands, such as the volcanic island Krakatoa, in a manner that has proved fatal to shipping throughout the centuries. On that June day in 1869 Captain Gifford was unable to navigate the strait and was forced to turn back his ship and head west.[20] Its new destination was the island of Rodrigues, one of the Mauritius group of islands, near Madagascar. The *Gazelle* would stop here to restock. Unlike Batavia, however, Rodrigues was a British colony.

On hearing the news that the *Gazelle* was sailing to Rodrigues, O'Reilly was a worried man. Less than five months after he had escaped from British territory the fugitive would once again be within reach of British law. O'Reilly would have been further perturbed had he been aware that Henry Wakeford, the Comptroller General of Fremantle Prison, had sent a letter to the governors of Mauritius and Rodrigues and asked that they search the *Gazelle* should the ship arrive in their territory.[21] Wakeford had no proof that O'Reilly was aboard the *Gazelle* and he had sent out similar requests regarding other whaling ships that had been at Bunbury at the time of O'Reilly's escape, including the police's main suspect, the *Vigilant*. At this time the police in Western Australia were also looking for Bowman and maintained an open file on other escaped convicts. Around the same day that the *Gazelle* arrived at Rodrigues the local police had pulled two escaped convicts from another whaling ship anchored in the port. These fugitives, two Englishmen named Edward Connor and Brian McGuiness, had absconded from Western Australia.[22] With O'Reilly and Gifford unaware of all these developments, the Gazelle anchored near the main settlement of Port Mathurin on 10 July.

Once the ship was anchored off the coast, Captain Gifford took one of the rowing boats and a few men and went to Port Mathurin to purchase supplies. While he was so engaged, a boat containing the island's resident magistrate pulled alongside the *Gazelle*. Once this man was aboard, he questioned the ship's mates: 'Have you a man on board named John Boyle O'Reilly?'[23] Hathaway responded that he had never heard the name but asked the inspector to give a description. On hearing the description Hathaway declared that he recognised the man. He was named 'Brown' and had died a few months earlier. The magistrate seemed suspicious of Hathaway's story and demanded that the crew be mustered on deck. Although O'Reilly came on deck with the rest of the crew it seems that the description of the Fenian in the possession of the magistrate was not a very good one. O'Reilly remained unrecognised. Neither did the magistrate appear to have an accurate description of the other fugitive aboard the *Gazelle*. Although Bowman was on deck with O'Reilly, he too went unnoticed. Bowman, though, lacked the respect and friendship that O'Reilly had developed among the crew. On the contrary, he had been a source of endless trouble aboard the ship and had turned much of his aggression on one of the younger sailors. This man decided to take the opportunity that now presented itself to remove his tormentor and 'with a jerk of his thumb and a knowing look' pointed out Bowman to the magistrate.

The magistrate and his men took Bowman aside and, after re-examining their descriptions of the missing convicts, realised that they had indeed found one of the fugitives. Bowman was arrested on the spot and the magistrate then inspected the remainder of the crew before satisfying himself that everything was in order. With his mission completed, the magistrate ordered his men back to their boat but as Bowman was dragged away he turned to O'Reilly with a sneer and said loudly 'Goodbye, shipmate.' Bowman had singled out the Fenian and it seemed probable that he would use his knowledge of O'Reilly's true identity as a means of bargaining with his captors. Hathaway later remembered O'Reilly's 'half-crazy' reaction to Bowman's arrest:

> 'My God! It's all up with me! What can I do? They'll come back for me, but I'll never be taken alive.' I knew he meant what he said; for the priest [Father McCabe] had told me he'd tried to commit suicide, and if he shouldn't escape had determined to kill himself. I calmed him down and told him to go below and keep out of sight and I'd try and think up something.[24]

Any plan that Hathaway created would have to fulfil two functions: protect O'Reilly and protect the ship. The *Gazelle* had already been found to be carrying one escaped convict and the discovery of others on board, especially a Fenian, would certainly cause problems for Captain Gifford in any future dealings with the authorities in British territory.[25]

By nightfall Hathaway had a plan of action. At this time the men were all below deck except two men on the anchor watch. Hathaway ordered these men to watch the water for 'Brown' in case he decided to swim for the shore. This was a ruse. Hathaway had told O'Reilly to come on deck, bringing his hat and a small grindstone with him. While O'Reilly made his way on deck Hathaway chatted to one of the watchmen, all the time making sure the man's back was to the deck. The other watchman was out of sight at the other end of the ship. When O'Reilly was sure that he was unobserved he leaned over the side and flung both objects into the sea. Hathaway had already prepared a hiding place for O'Reilly in a locker under the cabin companionway (stairs from one deck to another), which was used occasionally by the cook to store dishes. It was just large enough to hold a person and its door was covered by one of the stair boards. Once the splash had caught the attention of the watchmen, O'Reilly stealthily climbed down this stairs and squeezed himself into the locker.[26] As O'Reilly hid, the two watchmen tried to discern the cause of the splash. Hathaway suggested that it may have been 'Brown' and when one of the watchmen saw a hat floating in the water he shouted 'Man overboard!'[27] This call brought the crew on deck and they quickly lowered one of the three remaining whaleboats into the water. They searched the area for an hour but all they recovered was a hat, which the men recognised as O'Reilly's. When Hathaway brought his whaleboat back to the *Gazelle* he saw the second mate leaning over the side of the ship and waving O'Reilly's soaking hat. The mate was certain O'Reilly had drowned, telling Hathaway: 'He's gone, poor fellow! Here's his hat. The men have just picked it up. We'll never see him again.'

The next morning the crew of the *Gazelle* mourned their lost comrade. This included captain Gifford, who had no idea that the supposedly dead O'Reilly was hiding on board his ship and he ordered that all the flags be flown at half mast. Hathaway's elaborate plan was shown to be necessary later that morning when the police returned to the ship in full force. O'Reilly, listening through the door of the locker, could hear what he described as the 'great John-Bullish majesty and awfulness' of their arrival.[28] On board was the magistrate who had examined the crew on the previous day and sitting prominently in the police boat was Bowman. As O'Reilly had feared, Bowman had struck a deal with the magistrate and had agreed to pinpoint the Fenian fugitive aboard the *Gazelle*. Bowman's scheming would fail. Once on the ship the magistrate told Gifford he had returned for the 'traitor', whereupon the captain solemnly informed the official about the unfortunate death of O'Reilly.[29] Surveying the crew, the magistrate could see the genuine sorrow among the men and this seems to have convinced him that O'Reilly had indeed drowned.[30] The magistrate's policemen made only a cursory search of the ship and, with that done, they departed. The magistrate's last act aboard the *Gazelle* was to offer his condolences to Gifford and tell the captain that O'Reilly 'was better where he is than in prison'.[31] Once again O'Reilly had fashioned an unlikely escape. Bowman, however, was sent back to Western Australia where he was sentenced to three years' hard labour, with six months of this time in solitary confinement and irons.[32] A small cabin hidden beneath a set of stairs was all that prevented O'Reilly from sharing this abysmal fate.

Later that same day the *Gazelle* departed the island of Rodrigues. As soon as they were clear of the land, Hathaway released O'Reilly from the locker. The third mate recalled that O'Reilly was trembling and his face was as 'white as chalk'.[33] To O'Reilly's anguished plea of 'What now?' Hathaway answered, 'Don't stop to ask questions, man, get out of that and come up; you're safe for this time. Land is almost out of sight.' Hathaway and O'Reilly returned to the deck where, amid the general astonishment, Gifford 'wrung O'Reilly's hand, and burst out crying, just like a baby'.[34] O'Reilly's lifelong ability to make friends had saved him again but this success was unlikely to be repeated. The ship's next landfall was to be in the south Atlantic Ocean; the Island of St Helena, famed as the site of Napoleon Bonaparte's final exile and another possession of Britain.

This posed a real danger for O'Reilly. If the ship was searched by the police on St Helena there was no guarantee that they would be as easily fooled as those at Rodrigues. Besides, every member of the crew, if they had not known before, was now fully aware of O'Reilly's identity and of the British government's desire to capture the escaped Fenian convict. Despite the fact that O'Reilly was well liked among the crew, there remained a chance that one of the sailors would take the opportunity to supplement his meagre 'lay' with any reward money that might be available. He discussed the issue with Captain Gifford who decided that it would be necessary to transfer O'Reilly to another ship, as soon as a suitable candidate could be found. Gifford also thought it advisable to disguise O'Reilly's identity by giving him the name and papers of another former crewman, John Soule, who had deserted from the *Gazelle* earlier in its current voyage.[35]

Gifford found a promising candidate for O'Reilly's new ship on 29 July 1869, during a 'gam' with an American vessel named the *Sapphire* a few hundred miles east of Durban on South Africa's eastern coast.[36] A gam was when two whalers met each other on the open sea and exchanged visitors over the course of a few hours. It was an opportunity to relax and maybe even pass letters to the other ship, depending on its destination. Gifford took O'Reilly, Hathaway and some of his crew in a whaleboat and rowed to the *Sapphire*. Once aboard, they met with the ship's captain, E. J. Seiders. This gam would provide Gifford with an opportunity to assess the character and temperament of the captain and crew of the other ship. Over the course of their relaxation it became apparent to Gifford that he had found the perfect ship for O'Reilly. Not only did Captain Seiders appear to be a trustworthy individual but it also happened that the *Sapphire* was carrying a load of cotton from Bombay to Liverpool.

It would have been natural for O'Reilly to have felt anxious about the prospect of landing in England but a return to Liverpool, although potentially perilous, had advantages. O'Reilly had his false papers and nobody in the city would recognise him. More importantly it was one of the busiest ports in the world and O'Reilly would have little difficulty in arranging a passage or getting a job aboard a ship heading to the United States. Gifford asked Seiders if he would take his crewman 'John Soule' to Liverpool, a request to which Seiders agreed. However, sometime during their conversation, Gifford abandoned the pretence of O'Reilly's false name and papers. This was a shock for O'Reilly but Gifford was a shrewd judge of character. On hearing O'Reilly's background story, Seiders reacted warmly to the Irishman. Not only would he allow O'Reilly travel aboard the ship but Seiders also offered him a stateroom in his quarters.[37]

This was to be yet another enforced goodbye for O'Reilly. He had formed a close bond with Henry Hathaway even before the *Gazelle's* third mate had saved O'Reilly's life during the whale hunt. The two men would remain in contact for the rest of their lives. O'Reilly owed an equal debt of gratitude to Captain David Gifford who had rescued the fugitive from his Australian hideout. As he bade farewell to the captain, Gifford put twenty guineas into O'Reilly's hands. With that, Gifford and Hathaway returned to their ship.[38] It was a sad loss for Hathaway, who wrote to his friend that same day:

> Dear Old Fellow:
> I am now seated at the old donkey, where we've sat side by side for the last five months, more or less, and have been reading over some of your pieces of poetry, and it makes me lonesome, although we have not been parted as yet hardly three hours, and thank God we have lived and parted as friends; and thinking, perhaps, in after years you would like to know the transactions of the remainder of this voyage, I shall endeavor to write a little, once in a while, hoping it may prove interesting to you. Most everybody on board is talking about you, and they all wish you good luck in your undertaking, and all that I have got to say is, 'Good speed, and God bless you!'[39]

O'Reilly was now a part of the *Sapphire's* crew but only Captain Seiders and his first mate, John Bursley, knew O'Reilly's identity.[40] O'Reilly's journey aboard this ship was uneventful, although he did strike up another friendship, this time with an English passenger on the ship called Bailey. Remarkably, O'Reilly told Bailey his whole story. Such honesty posed obvious risks but O'Reilly had benefited from the kindness of strangers throughout the whole escape from the penal colony. Bailey was to be another stranger who almost immediately became a firm friend of the Fenian. When the *Sapphire* docked in Liverpool on 13 October 1869 he provided O'Reilly, whom he knew to be an escaped convict and a member of the hated Fenian movement, with some money to help him pay for passage to the United States.[41]

O'Reilly never left a recollection of how he felt stepping down the gangway from the ship onto English soil. He had been transported from England just a day over two years earlier on 12 October 1867. Then he had been in chains as he was herded onto the *Hougoumont*. Now he was a fugitive from the law but with his false name and papers he was at least free to walk about and John Bursley, the first mate of the *Sapphire*, had secured a hiding place for the Fenian with an English family.[42] He was not far from Preston, the backdrop to so many happy memories, and his beloved aunt Crissy. There was, at times, a reckless streak in O'Reilly and he may well have been tempted to visit his family in Preston. However, he knew that it was too risky, both for him and for the family who were affording him space in their home. He did write a letter to his aunt, which Bursley promised to deliver as soon as O'Reilly was on board a ship to the United States.[43] This was quickly arranged when O'Reilly sought a job aboard an American ship, the *Bombay*, bound for Philadelphia, informing his new prospective captain, F. C. Jordan, of his history as a Fenian and a convict. This did not deter the captain from hiring O'Reilly and he even made his new crewman a third mate.[44]

The exact date of O'Reilly's departure from Liverpool is uncertain but he had remained in the city for only a few days. He did take time to send a letter to the Dublin newspaper *Nation* telling the editor, Alexander Martin Sullivan, that 'one man who was condemned to suffer for the "old country's cause" has escaped from prison and is on his way to liberty.'[45] This was a presumptuous act on O'Reilly's behalf, considering the fact that he had yet to reach the United States, but Sullivan would wisely wait a few weeks before publishing the letter. By the time O'Reilly's account of his escape appeared in *Nation*, the Fenian would be halfway across the Atlantic. On the morning that the *Bombay* departed Liverpool, O'Reilly was seen off by

Bailey and Bursley. It was a quiet journey except for one heart-breaking moment that remained with O'Reilly for the rest of his life. On the evening of the second day's sailing, as the sun was setting on a late autumn evening, Captain Jordan called O'Reilly on deck and told him they were near the coast of Ireland. A few months later O'Reilly described the moment at a lecture in the Music Hall, Boston:

> They were sad words; Ireland was there, under the sun; but under the dark cloud also. The rays of golden glory fell down from behind the dark cloud – fell down like God's pity on the beautiful, tear-stained face of Ireland – fell down on the dear familiar faces of my old home, on the hill, the wood, the river, lighting them all once more with the same heaven-tint that I loved to watch long ago. Oh! How vividly did that long ago rise up before me then! the happy home, the merry playmates, the faces, the voices of dear ones who are there still, and the hallowed words of dearest ones who are dead – down on all fell the great glory of the setting sun, lighting that holy spot that I might never see, a mother's grave, and lighting the heart with sorrow-shaded devotion. Home, friends, all that I loved in the world were there, almost beside me – there, 'under the sun' and I, for loving them, a hunted, outlawed fugitive, an escaped convict, was sailing away from all I treasured – perhaps, forever.'[46]

After a while Ireland receded from view. As the *Bombay* pushed its way through the Atlantic Ocean, the fugitive considered all that he had experienced and all that he had left behind. He was still an absconder from the British penal system, a criminal on whatever land or sea belonged to the British Empire. O'Reilly sensed also that he would never return to his place of birth. Ireland, England and Australia were all in the past. His future, America, was just a few weeks' sailing into the horizon.

9

The Pilot

John Boyle O'Reilly arrived at Philadelphia on 22 November 1869, his only possessions being the clothes he wore, '30 dollars and a bag of whale's teeth'.[1] That morning, he presented himself at a courthouse in the city to begin the naturalisation process and once that was done, and with nowhere else to stay, he returned to the *Bombay*.[2] O'Reilly would not be alone for long as he would find that his reputation had preceded him. Not only had O'Reilly sent a letter to the *Nation* newspaper that detailed his escape to the United States, but a few months earlier he had also written of his escape to *The Irishman*, another Dublin paper.[3] This information had made its way to the US where American Fenians had started preparations to welcome their fugitive hero to the Land of the Free. That afternoon, a Fenian delegation eagerly clambered aboard the *Bombay*. O'Reilly was working on deck at the time. He was approached by one of the Fenians who excitedly asked if John Boyle O'Reilly was on the ship. When O'Reilly answered 'I'm the man' he was met with genuine incredulity from the Fenians.[4] Given the nature of O'Reilly's story to date they may have expected a man aged by his experiences; haggard and frail as would befit someone thrown into an English prison, transported aboard a convict ship, forced to escape from the confines of a penal colony and now working aboard a whaling ship. What they found was a healthy fresh-faced man, 25 years old and enthusiastic to make a new start in the United States.

O'Reilly spent a few days in Philadelphia before he departed the city for the more dynamic environs of New York. There, O'Reilly was given a reception befitting his status as a public hero to Irish Americans. Over 2,000 people attended the Cooper Institute where O'Reilly spoke of his incarceration and subsequent sufferings at the hands of the British Empire. Telling his audience that he had joined the British army in order to further the cause of Ireland, he declared that in taking the British army oath 'it was the lips and not the heart . . . that performed the act.'[5] The crowd loved his speech and it was widely reported across the Irish-American press in the following days. During this time O'Reilly seems to have stayed with Denis F. Burke, a former commander of the 88th New York Regiment of the Union army during the American Civil War.[6] He also spent some time in the company of the Fenian founding father, John O'Mahony.[7] While with O'Mahony, O'Reilly reaffirmed his commitment to the Fenians by joining the John Savage wing of the Brotherhood.[8] He also joined Jerome J. Collins' secret revolutionary organisation, Clan na Gael, a group which Collins had founded following the failed 1867 rising in Ireland, partly out of frustration with divisions within the Fenian Brotherhood.[9] O'Reilly was a man in demand and he was likewise inducted into the ranks of the newly formed Legion of St Patrick, a militia group composed mostly of Fenians and to whom O'Reilly would act as a drill instructor. The Legion's members pledged 'to be faithful to Ireland and to obey their officers'. Each member was to learn a soldier's duties so that they would be ready for 'when the time comes when he may be wanted.'[10]

As the enthusiasm that surrounded O'Reilly's arrival began to ebb away over the following weeks, he was left with much the same problem as any other newly arrived immigrant: how and where to find a job. O'Reilly made it known to his new acquaintances in New York that he wished to return to his first trade, that of journalism. Someone advised O'Reilly that he should head to Boston and try his luck in the journalistic and literary circles of Massachusetts. So on 2 January 1870, barely over a year after his suicide attempt in the Western Australian bush, John Boyle O'Reilly boarded a train for Boston. He had with him some money and two letters of introduction afforded him by Fenians in New York. One of these letters was for Thomas Manning, the other for Dr Robert Dwyer Joyce, a County Limerick-born poet and author of 'The Wind that Shakes the Barley'.[11] Manning welcomed O'Reilly into his house and over the following weeks the new arrival was introduced to Boston's Irish community. Through these introductions O'Reilly met with such figures as Patrick Collins, a Cork-born lawyer and aspiring Democrat politician, with whom he became good friends.[12] O'Reilly moved to Collins' house for a short time before moving to a lodging house near Bunker Hill in Charlestown.

Collins introduced O'Reilly to Merrick S. Creagh, another Irish immigrant and the Boston manager of the Inman Line, at that time one of the main shipping companies sailing the North Atlantic. Creagh, after receiving recommendations from both Collins and Joyce, gave O'Reilly a position as clerk within the company.[13] It was O'Reilly's first job in the US but this welcome development would be swiftly followed by disappointment. O'Reilly had followed his talk at the Cooper Institute with a series of similar lectures on his trial, imprisonment and escape. These had been widely reported in papers such as the *New York Times* and the story of O'Reilly's escape was noticed by the management of the Inman Line, which was a British company. Shortly after O'Reilly joined Creagh's office the manager was informed by head office in England that it was impolitic for the company to have hired a Fenian fugitive as an employee. Creagh was forced to dismiss O'Reilly. Within days the Fenian had found himself a new job, utilising his old newspaper skills from Drogheda and Preston, as a printer with a small company in the centre of Boston.[14] It was through this work that, in the spring of 1870, he got a much better job offer from Patrick Donahoe, the owner of the Boston newspaper *The Pilot*.[15]

This paper had been published in Boston for over forty years but it had undergone a number of renewals during its existence. It made its first appearance on 5 September 1829 as a paper for Boston's Catholics under the title of the *Jesuit*. The paper was renamed the *United States Catholic Intelligencer* in October 1831 before returning to its original title in January 1833. It had yet another name in 1835, the *Literary and Catholic Sentinel*, before becoming *The Pilot* in 1836. All these name changes are a demonstration of the financial difficulties the paper faced in its first years. These difficulties culminated in April 1837 when the paper was forced to cease publication. Its story would have ended at that point had it not been for the efforts of businessman Patrick Donahoe. He took complete control of the paper and on 28 January 1838 *The Pilot* restarted publication.

Under Donahoe's guidance *The Pilot* would establish itself as the foremost Catholic paper in the United States.[16] Donahoe was born in Cavan in 1811 and had emigrated to the US when aged ten. He attended school in Boston where he so often fought back against other children who mocked his Catholicism that he remembered his childhood as 'the days of the discoloured eyes and the swollen lips.'[17] By fourteen he was forced to leave school as a result of his family's financial difficulties. Donahoe began an apprenticeship as a printer with the *Columbian Sentinel* and eventually made his way to the *Jesuit*. When he restarted *The Pilot* as a weekly newspaper in 1838, the paper had a circulation of only 600 subscribers out of '20,000 Catholics' in the New England area, but six years later this figure had increased to 7,000 readers, located across the United States.[18] Donahoe later credited this circulation increase to his policy of printing regular updates on Daniel O'Connell and the 'Repeal agitation in Ireland'.[19] Such news was a feature of *The Pilot*'s reportage and extensive coverage of Ireland was printed in every edition of the paper.

In the decades before O'Reilly's arrival at the paper, *The Pilot* played an important role for immigrants, linking their old society to their new one. The paper, as did other immigrant papers, sought to maintain the self-esteem of the immigrants and offered advice on the political, social and economic environment that now surrounded the new arrivals. Donahoe was well aware of the potentially vital power of newspapers and he was especially keen to fight the sense of defeat that afflicted so many Irish immigrants as well as what one *Pilot* editorial described as their tendency to 'assume the air and action of inferiors'.[20] *The Pilot* also printed notices from freshly arrived immigrants who sought information on the whereabouts of family members who had preceded them to the US. In doing all this the paper provided a sense of community and sanctuary to Irish immigrants, a service that was vitally important in those early years and especially in the face of the anti-immigrant and anti-Catholic nativism of the 1840s and 1850s. This nativism was most infamously encapsulated in the form of the 'Know Nothings', a political grouping that often resorted to violence against Catholic immigrants. The historian Francis Robert Walsh has well described *The Pilot* during this time as a sort of 'fortress', which 'reflected the insecurity of the Irish in the years before the Civil War.'[21] This insecurity, so exacerbated by the anti-immigrant sections of US society, deepened the sense of group identity among the Irish, as can be seen in the pages of *The Pilot* throughout the middle decades of the nineteenth century. In an attempt to counter racist and sectarian propaganda, which claimed the Irish were a threat to the United States, the paper lost no opportunity to highlight and frequently embellish the role of Irish immigrants in the early development of the nation. This aspect of the paper's reportage, acting as 'guardian of the good name of the Irish',[22] would continue during O'Reilly's time at *The Pilot*.

As the number of Irish immigrants to the US exploded during the 1840s, the market for such Irish-American newspapers greatly expanded. *The Pilot*'s circulation expanded to meet this demand and by the 1860s the paper was long free of its early financial fragility. Donahoe had flourished along with his paper and had used his new-found wealth to extend his business interests. These included two banks: he was co-founder of the Union Institution for Savings in 1865 and founder of the Emigrant Savings Bank in 1870.[23] He was also a steamship agent and by 1870 he was estimated to be worth around $500,000 dollars and was making a $40,000 annual profit from *The Pilot*.[24] Donahoe used this money to help others and to further his reputation. He was involved in many charitable causes and had sponsored Irish regiments during the Civil War. *The Pilot*, his flagship business, had lavish headquarters on Franklin Street in the centre of Boston. The value of this building, one of many properties he owned, was $150,000.[25] Donahoe was an outstanding businessman and he saw the value that O'Reilly could bring to his newspaper. O'Reilly had arrived in the United States as an Irish-American sensation and had continued to burnish this reputation through regular and well-attended public lectures. The ex-convict was talented, hard-working and had already been a journalist. More than that, O'Reilly had arrived in Boston specifically to pursue a career in writing and Donahoe had little trouble persuading the Fenian to join *The Pilot*.

Donahoe's offer was a joy to O'Reilly. On 5 April 1870 the new chief reporter of *The Pilot* wrote to his aunt Crissy informing her of his life in America and his already burgeoning success:

> I was thinking of you when I was in Liverpool. I dared not go to Preston. It is strange how I love Preston – I felt it then, and I feel it now. I am a very fortunate fellow to pull clear through. I am likely to become a prosperous man in America. I write for the magazines and report for the Pilot, drill the Irish Legion, make speeches at public meetings, lecture for charities, etc., etc. This course in the old countries would soon make a fortune: and, after a time, here it will have the same effect; but, at present, all this must be done to establish a reputation. I just manage to live as a gentleman. I have

paid my debts to the captains who brought me here [O'Reilly had already returned the money that Captain Gifford had given him aboard the *Gazelle*]. In a few years it will be my own fault if I do not make a name worth bearing. And how are all my friends in Preston? I am glad you liked Mr Bursley [Bursley, the first mate of the *Sapphire* had kept his promise and had travelled to Preston with a letter from O'Reilly to his aunt]. He is a noble fellow. He knew who I was from the first day I went on the ship. Send on your pictures, Aunt, dear, I'm eager to see you all again. Tell me all about the Preston people whom I knew. I will order some cartes to-day. I don't like the style of the present ones – they will do for people I don't care about . . . Does Uncle James go to sea yet? It's time he gave up; he has lots of money made now. And do you sit down quietly and rest yourself? or do you still go on with the old, old toil? Now, Aunt, you must write me long, very long letters. A lady correspondent of your ability and taste is invaluable to a literary man. Now, don't laugh – I'm in earnest. Write often. I'll send you some papers. I lecture to-night in a city called Quincy, near Boston. I have four lectures this week. I inclose a ticket for one. I wish I could see you there.[26]

This was an exciting time for O'Reilly and a few weeks after this letter he began his first major assignment for *The Pilot*. On 19 April O'Reilly travelled to New York for the latest Fenian Convention.

The roots of the convention that O'Reilly attended went back to the Fenian Convention in Philadelphia during 1865. Through that gathering the Fenians in the US had reorganised themselves in a manner that roughly resembled the government of the United States, with an elected president and senate, for example. This had begun a process whereby John O'Mahony was deposed from his role as Head Center of the American organisation, and which broke the Fenians into a 'Senate Wing' and an 'O'Mahony Wing'. It was the Senate Wing under Cork-born William Randolph Roberts who proposed a Fenian invasion of Canada. As we have seen in earlier chapters there were, in these years, tens of thousands of battle-hardened Irish veterans of the Civil War. It was initially proposed to utilise these soldiers for an incursion into Canada that could be timed to coincide with a rebellion in Ireland (of which John Boyle O'Reilly, then working as a Fenian recruiter in the 10th Hussars, would have been a part).

Thus the British would be engaged in two widely separated theatres of war. When it became apparent that the hoped-for rising in Ireland was not to take place, the goal of the invasion was changed. The Fenians now hoped that they could engineer a border incident that would entangle British forces in a war with the United States. At the time the US government had a frosty relationship with their British counterparts: a remnant of the British Empire's partiality towards the Confederacy during the Civil War and the role of British shipyards in providing raiding vessels, such as the notorious *Alabama*, for the South. While this was highly unlikely to lead to full-scale conflict, the US government was in no mood to provide any aid to the British in Canada. President Andrew Johnson was aware of the Fenian's plans but did little to hinder them.

The two competing Fenian factions, almost equally motivated by a desire to strike a blow against the British and a sense of one-upmanship, would launch separate operations. In April the O'Mahony Wing attempted to seize Campobello Island near New Brunswick but the Fenian attackers were easily dispersed by US naval forces. Shortly after this skirmish, James Stephens arrived in the US. Stephens had fled Ireland to Paris a few months after his escape from Richmond Bridewell and on his arrival in America he attempted to unite the Fenian factions. He opposed a raid into Canada but, given his failure to lead the promised uprising in Ireland during 1865, Stephens was now a discredited figure in the eyes of many Fenians and he failed to have any influence on events. The Senate Wing launched its attack on Canada under the command of General John O'Neill on 1 June 1866 (at this time John Boyle O'Reilly was in Arbour Hill prison awaiting his court martial). O'Neill was a Civil War veteran of the Union army and he led a force of over 1,000 men into Canadian territory near Fort Erie in Ontario.

His invading army had some initial success, wining two engagements including the so-called Battle of Ridgeway with about ten fatalities (with a similar number on the Canadian side).[27] O'Neill's troops kept their discipline and local civilians were respected, as were Canadian prisoners of war. One soldier, Lance Corporal William Ellis, later wrote 'the Fenians' treatment of myself and the other prisoners was kind and considerate in the extreme'.[28] Yet, O'Neill was aware that far larger Canadian forces were approaching and on 3 June felt it prudent to take his army back to American territory, where they would await reinforcements. However, the

US government was now fearful that events were spiralling out of control. Once back across the border, O'Neill's army was met by American troops who intervened to prevent the Fenians from making any further attacks. Over the following days the Fenian army was broken up by American forces while O'Neill was arrested by US Marshalls and temporarily incarcerated.[29] A second slightly smaller incursion into Canada followed on 6 June. This attack was commanded by General Samuel Spears but he proved a less capable commander than O'Neill and he ended the incursion after a few days of skirmishing. His army was also broken up by US forces when back on American soil. The Fenian invasion of Canada was over.

The whole invasion, while not the debacle that is often claimed, demonstrated the futility of the Fenian strategy. It proved that the Canadians would fight to preserve their territory and that they could mobilise tens of thousands of their population to do so. There was little hope that the Fenians could muster the required number of troops necessary to seize and then to hold Canadian territory. Most importantly, there could be no doubt now that the US government would not, despite its tempestuous relationship with the British Empire, offer any support to a Fenian invasion. Nor would the US government allow itself to be embroiled in a border war with British or Canadian forces. Nevertheless, these lessons were ignored by some Fenians for whom the idea of attacking Canada remained a worthwhile objective over the next few years. The 1870 convention that O'Reilly attended took place amid more internal wrangling within the Brotherhood. What had been the Senate Wing had now ruptured into two groups: one in support of John O'Neill, the other opposed to him.[30] Consequently the convention was attended by only 200 delegates but it resulted in a resolution to launch another raid into Canada. The Fenian force would be commanded by O'Neill and its goal was to capture two small towns on the Canadian side of border. O'Reilly was the only member of the press to be admitted to the convention and it seems likely that he was a supporter of the resolution.[31] He would be a part of the invasion, ostensibly as a reporter but also as a soldier if needed.

The invasion was set for 25 May 1870 and O'Reilly joined with the Fenian force that day. He described his experience of the whole affair in a blunt manner that did nothing to glorify what would be another defeat for the Fenians. His first paragraph set the tone:

Your reporter left Boston . . . en route for St. Albans, Vt. [Vermont], and having provided himself with diverse morning papers had his imagination inflated to extreme tightness before his second cigar was finished. Each paper had distinct and detailed accounts of thousands of men and trains of war material; and so precise were they in their statements, that even the officers commanding were named. These statements were all false. There were no thousands of men moving on St. Albans, nor on any other point, as the sequel shows. The best way to give a correct idea of the numbers of the Fenian 'armies', is simply to state what was seen by a man who was there.[32]

O'Neill, as general, mustered his forces near the town of Franklin in Vermont, a short distance south of the Canadian border. His army consisted of 400 Fenians. Hundreds more Fenians had congregated in the area but O'Neill did not have equipment for more than a few hundred men. Typically, the Fenians had been infiltrated by British agents. In this instance the most damaging spy was Thomas Billis Beach, more commonly known as Henri Le Caron.[33] Consequently, the Canadians had prior knowledge of the Fenians' plans. This was unknown to O'Neill as he marched his men, whom he called the 'advance guard of the Irish American army for the liberation of Ireland' towards Canada.[34] The Fenians crossed the border around noon, at which point they came under fire from Canadian militia units, many of them located on a high point called Eccles Hill. These militia units pushed the Fenians back across the border after a few hours of skirmishing. O'Reilly, the war correspondent, was at the front, and left this description of the combat:

As soon as the column had reached the brow of the hill overlooking the line, Capt. Cronan's and Capt. Gary's companies were sent forward by the road as skirmishers, with orders to deploy when they had reached the base of the hill where stood Alvah Richards's farmhouse. This house is about fifty rods from the line. On the Canadian side of the line, for about five hundred yards, the ground is flat, and then rises abruptly into a steep, rocky hill, on which the Volunteers were strongly posted. From Richards's farm on the west side of the road, rose another abrupt hill covered with trees.[35]

According to O'Reilly, O'Neill intended to make a flanking on the Canadian right and advance on a village about 2 miles to the west of their current position. However, the Canadians moved to prevent this and, soon after, the two forces engaged each other.

> When the first files had crossed the line, and before the company could deploy, the Canadians opened a heavy fire on them. Almost at the first discharge, Private John Rowe, of Burlington, Vt., was shot through the head, and fell dead in the center of the road. The Fenian troops, without deploying, returned the fire for a short time, and then fell back in rear of Richards's house, where General Donnelly commanded a reserve of about fifty men. The Canadians then turned their fire on the troops, which were taking up positions on the hill. The men were filing over the exposed ground between the road and the hill, when the heaviest firing of the day was opened on them. Francis Carraher fell by the roadside, shot through the groin, and, in an instant after, Lieutenant Edward Hope went down in the field, and Mr. O'Brien fell dead, with a Canadian bullet through his heart. When the troops gained the hill, they got the order to advance to the front and open fire. They advanced but before they had reached the position which General O'Neill wished them to occupy, they fell back again under the close, steady fire of the Canadians. The Fenians also kept up a steady fire, but all the energies of their officers could not get them to advance. Major Murphy, Col. Sullivan, and Capt. Fitzpatrick did all that brave men could do to inspire the men with confidence. It was evident then that the troops were too few to achieve anything. The men felt that they had no support to fall back upon, and that even if they drove the Canadians back, they were too weak to hold a position against any considerable force. Gen. O'Neill, who had been in their front under the hottest fire, cheering and rallying the men, then formed them up under cover and addressed them. After some ineffective attempts by the officers to rally the men and lead them to the position on the hill which O'Neill wanted, the men fell back in rear of the hill. This was virtually the end of the fighting.[36]

Once back on American soil O'Neill found that he had a new foe behind his front line. The current US President, Ulysses S. Grant, had become fearful that if his government was seen to do nothing while an attack was launched from US territory the relationship between the United States and Canada could be seriously damaged. He therefore had issued an order allowing for the arrest of any Fenian violating Canadian territory or involved in 'sundry illegal military enterprises'.[37] O'Neill, having contravened that order, was arrested by US Marshalls. Remarkably, before he was taken into custody O'Neill placed O'Reilly in command of the Fenian army.[38] Although O'Reilly may have supported the idea of an invasion, there is no evidence to suggest that he had been involved in its planning. Once in command he had little impact upon events. Henri Le Caron, seemingly part of the Fenian invasion force, remembered O'Reilly holding a 'council of war' with senior officers.[39] Some of the men, he wrote, made 'a strong attempt' to get O'Reilly 'to lead an attack at some other point, but in the end nothing was done'.[40]

Although fresh Fenian troops were still arriving at the invasion point, it is hard to see how O'Reilly could have succeeded where his general had failed. Even if O'Reilly had been able to motivate the troops it was not long before he too was arrested. His latest incarceration would be brief. Despite the order that Grant had issued against the Fenians, the US government was not excessively disturbed by their activities and was content to prevent the attack from developing into a large-scale confrontation. Although O'Neill and a few others were prosecuted for violating the presidential order, they were pardoned a few months later by Grant.[41] O'Reilly, like most of those arrested, was released from custody without charge after a few hours.[42] During the fighting four Fenians had been killed (another would die of his wounds). The Canadians suffered no casualties. Some desultory skirmishing began on the next day but this soon came to a halt.[43] O'Reilly's account continued:

> On the 27th, and following day, men continued to arrive in Malone from various places. They met with a sorry reception from the mass of weary men who crowded the depot; but, as a rule, they expressed their disbelief in the statements of failure, and would go to the front and see for themselves; and go they did, and came back sadder and wiser men.[44]

O'Reilly may well have been describing himself in that last sentence. It had become clear to him that not only were the Fenians incapable of putting together an army but the poisonous factionalism of the organisation had sickened it beyond cure. A few days later *The Pilot* launched a ferocious editorial attack on Fenianism within the United States. It is not certain that this editorial was written by O'Reilly but, even if not, the piece was undoubtedly based on his reports of the invasion:

> Fenianism now stands before the world with all its jagged corners clear and bare as the peak of Tenerife, and forming as decided a landmark to the people of the Irish race as does the lofty spire to the mariner. Fenianism has lost its mystery, and with that has lost its power but Mokanna like, before it would allow the veil to be torn from its hideousness, it would complete its career by the exercise of the most baneful influence. Fenianism, so far as relates to the invasion of Canada, ceases to exist, but it has done all the evil it could do. It has torn thousands of men away from their homes and their employment in a wild and futile enterprise. It has caused the deaths of several brave men, and the imprisonment, perhaps death, of many others, and it has given occasion to the enemies of the Irish people to renew the slurs which such enterprises have given birth to before now. Its evil effects are multiform, but its most dangerous result consists in the instability, the recklessness which it tends to impart to the young and the least reasoning part of our people. The men who framed and executed this last abortion of war-making have proved themselves to be criminally incompetent.[45]

O'Reilly left the Fenians around this time. Not only was he disgusted by the divisions within the American Fenians and the incompetence that resulted in such poorly conceived escapades as the invasion of Canada but he was particularly perturbed by the negative publicity that resulted from such events and which was heaped upon the whole Irish population in America. Throughout his life in the United States O'Reilly remained very sensitive to criticisms of the Irish and seemed to take personal insult in the condemnations that followed a debacle such as the Fenian invasion.

The decision to leave the Fenians must have been a profoundly important moment for O'Reilly. After all, he had devoted so much to the Brotherhood and suffered as a consequence; not only had he been imprisoned and exiled, but his own brother, William, had died a Fenian convict in an Irish prison. Yet O'Reilly took the decision quickly and seemingly without regret. Despite departing the organisation, he did not sever his personal relations with many leading Fenians and he remained in agreement with the Fenians' goal of an independent Ireland, although he now believed them to be incapable of delivering that goal. Also, he was not opposed to violent insurrection that had a reasonable chance of success. At the end of July he explained this in a letter to 'The officers and men of the Fenian Brotherhood in Boston':

> On reviewing my course since I landed in America in November, 1869 I find no political act of which I am ashamed now, or which could earn for me the enmity or reproach of honest national men . . . After experience in the ranks of both [Fenians and Clan na Gael], and learning how great was the change in the aspect of organized working from that which existed before my arrest and imprisonment, I determined to leave the Fenian Brotherhood. I was convinced and I am now that I was doing no good for Ireland. Therefore, I left it, at a regular meeting of my circle (The O'Donovan Rossa). I was then a member in good standing. The Center of that Circle and the members present on the night of my resignation fully agreed that I was justified in leaving if I chose. Whatever other objections I had were of a minor character, and related to the working of the organization . . . Had I remained a member of your organization, when I did not believe in it (as I might, advantageously to myself, have done) I think I would deserve more ill-feeling from you and all honest men than I have earned by severing the connection . . . I am no enemy of Fenianism . . . I wish the Fenian Brotherhood all the success it ever aimed at.[46]

O'Reilly departed the Legion of St Patrick and Clan na Gael at this time. He had done this, according to John Devoy, at the behest of the Bishop, later Archbishop of Boston, John J. Williams.[47] Devoy may have been correct in this. O'Reilly and Williams would become friends and, later, business partners. Also, the Catholic Church had a long antipathy towards secret organisations such as the Clan. For O'Reilly this may well have been an added reason to leave both the Clan and the Fenians. O'Reilly had always been a devoted Catholic and perhaps he felt it was time to follow the counsel of the Church.

However, it is in this part of O'Reilly's life that the historian John Duffy Ibson has discerned a duality in the Irishman's personality that he believes explains O'Reilly's new course. Once O'Reilly had established himself in Boston, Ibson writes that O'Reilly's main impulse was to gain acceptance in that society.[48] The upper levels of society were still overwhelmingly Protestant, the so-called Boston Brahmins whose descendants were among the first settlers in Massachusetts. Therefore, he argues, O'Reilly took on the persona of the reputable Irishman. Yet, O'Reilly's actions suggest a more deep-seated reason than the wish to obtain a veneer of respectability. He could have privately departed the Fenians and maintained the conciliatory approach evident in the above letter but O'Reilly's decision to publicly and fiercely criticise his former comrades suggests that he had a fervent, albeit newly discovered, belief that the secret machinations of the Fenians were the wrong path to Irish freedom. Besides, in openly criticising the Fenians, O'Reilly showed courage. Only two years earlier a former editor of The Pilot, Thomas D'Arcy McGee from County Louth, had been assassinated in Canada by a Fenian sympathiser. McGee, a veteran of the Young Ireland rebellion in 1848, had been targeted due to his criticism of the Fenians, especially their 1866 invasion of Canada.[49]

O'Reilly's unsentimental accounts of the Fenian invasion of 1870 were enormously influential. He was a public figure, beloved by many Irish people in the US and Ireland and known as a man who had worked and suffered for Fenianism. His reports set the pattern by which the invasion would be covered in other papers both in the US and Ireland. No heroism or moral victory could be gleaned from what O'Reilly had written and within weeks Irish newspapers such The Freeman's Journal and Nation would write of 'The Fenian Fiasco'.[50] O'Reilly's articles on the Fenian invasion also convinced Donahoe that he had found a great talent and, in the early summer of 1870, he promoted O'Reilly to the editorial department of the paper. O'Reilly's first editorial assignments came later that summer when he involved himself in further controversy following an Orange Order march in New York on 12 July 1870. This march had degenerated into a riot when the 3,000 marchers had been confronted by protestors. O'Reilly described the event and castigated all those who were involved in the fighting:

Events have at intervals occurred in the history of this country which have justly called up a blush of shame on the faces of patriotic

Irishmen; but we doubt if they ever have received so great a reason for deep humiliation as during the past week. On the 12th of July the 'American Protestant Association' – in other words, the Orange Lodges of New York, had advertised their intention of celebrating the anniversary of the Battle of the Boyne . . . On the line of march they lost no opportunity of goading to intensity the bitter feelings of their Catholic fellow-countrymen whom they passed. This resulted in a general banding of the laborers of the vicinity, who set upon the Orangemen with sticks and stones, which were answered by them with pistol bullets. A terrible mêlée was the consequence, in which four lives were lost, and numbers endangered. Is not this cause for deep humiliation? Earnest men have labored for years to remove that bitter old taunt of our enemies – 'You cannot unite'. Patient workers have tried to teach the world, and even ourselves, that this reproach was not the truth. This is the reward of their labor. Our own people, in a strange land, have insultingly turned on their benefactors and flung their labor in their faces. Oh, what a national degradation is this! We talk of patriotism and independence! We prate and boast of our 'national will'! What evidence is this? What are we to-day in the eyes of Americans? Aliens from a petty island in the Atlantic, boasting of our patriotism and fraternity, and showing at the same moment the deadly hatred that rankles against our brethren and fellow-countrymen. Why must we carry, wherever we go, those accursed and contemptible island feuds? Shall we never be shamed into the knowledge of the brazen impudence of allowing our national hatreds to disturb the peace and the safety of the respectable citizens of this country? . . . Both parties are to be blamed and condemned; for both have joined in making the name of Irishmen a scoff and a byword this day in America.[51]

This editorial can be linked to another piece on the same theme that O'Reilly wrote a year later. This came after another Orange Order demonstration descended into violence and during which the US army fired on protestors. O'Reilly was certainly appalled by those events but he was more disturbed by the universally negative press commentary on Irish affairs which followed the riot:

We do not speak to either party in the late riots – we have neither Orange subscribers nor rowdy readers: but we speak to the great class – the Irish in America – who are made to bear the blame and the shame of the disgraceful proceedings that have marked the 12th of July in New York for two years past. But let us return to the main consideration. How is a recurrence of this disaster to be avoided? . . . The question is, Do we or do we not defend the New York rioters? As Irish-American Catholic citizens, we answer, we condemn the rioters, and ignore them both as Irishmen and Catholics. By making ourselves responsible for their acts, which we do by a vain attempt to justify them, we give the 200 Orangemen who walked in New York the satisfaction of knowing that they have destroyed all friendly feeling between Irish Catholics and native Americans; in a word, we play into their hands, and give them more than they could ever have hoped for[52]

The editorial then continued to argue that the Orange Order had the right to parade in so far as that Fenians regularly paraded through New York and other cities. Therefore, it was futile and hypocritical to attack the Orange marchers:

Really, we are almost forced to the conclusion that the whole ground of objection consists in the fact that the Orangemen play, 'Croppies Lie Down'. We admit that this is, and should be considered, an insulting tune by the Irish people; and we should deeply regret to see them lose their detestation of it. But, let us ask, is it sufficient cause to warrant a violation of the law and a sacrifice of life? We have written this article with a most oppressive feeling of its necessity . . . Certain it is that the Orange procession is not a pleasant sight to any Irish Catholic, however unprejudiced; but it is just as certain that the Irish Catholics of this country, as a body, condemn all breach of the law in attacking an Orange procession, just as honestly as they would condemn a riot of any other criminal nature. There are two ways of getting rid of this apple of discord. The first is, by an agreement between the general Irish population and the Orangemen foregoing all right to parade, and expressing their determination never to hold processions for Irish political objects alone. This we may rest assured, will not be easily agreed to. The second one is the best, and the one that must come in the end, when America, tired out and indignant with her squabbling population, puts her foot down with a will and tells them all – Germans, French, Irish, Orange – 'You have had enough now. There is only ONE flag to be raised in future in this country and that flag is the Stars and Stripes.

Perhaps there is evidence in this editorial of Ibson's claim that O'Reilly had already assumed a respectable public face through which he was to further his success within Bostonian society.[53] To back his assertion, Ibson cites O'Reilly's response to a letter from a reader who was angered by the above editorial. O'Reilly replied, 'When we wrote that editorial we were fully aware that it would not be acceptable to certain people in the community. But we knew that therein we expressed the opinions of the calm, rational, and respectable Irish Catholics of America.'[54] However, while O'Reilly may well have been partly motivated by the 'ethnic anxiety over making the "right appearance"',[55] his disillusionment with the Fenians and with the divisions within Irish nationalism was still a source of personal anger. That cannot be overlooked when explaining the role that O'Reilly made for himself as a commentator on Irish issues.

Another possible explanation for O'Reilly's editorials is that he had formed a niche for himself within Irish-American journalism and that he enjoyed the abundant fame, tinged with notoriety, which now surrounded him. Within an astonishingly short time he had gone from being an anonymous convict, a tiny cog in the British penal system, to a figure of great influence and visibility within the dynamic world of journalism and the wider Irish-American community. Edward Page Mitchell, the writer and future editor of the *New York Sun*, knew O'Reilly during the Irishman's early days in Boston. Mitchell, who adored O'Reilly, nevertheless remembered his friend as a restless individual who 'talked much of himself, of what he had done, what he was doing and intended to do'.[56] There is more than a hint of this energy and exhilaration in a long letter which O'Reilly wrote to O'Donovan Rossa around this time:

I've made one thing a specialty – to fight this confounded praise of everything Irish and hatred of everything un-Irish, and try to induce other men to do the same. We must criticize our own people, Rossa, if we want to raise them. They will not bear criticism from outsiders, which is thrown to them as a bone might be to a dog not offered them as from a man to his fellow-man with a good intent . . . Man alive, there's a sort of heroism in pitching into a friend. When I do it I feel so like the Galway judge, who hung his own son [according to Galway tradition a judge named Lynch was once supposed to have hanged his son for the crime of murder], that I'm sorely tempted to be always doing a little that way.[57]

Those articles and editorials on the Orange marches were widely quoted at the time both within and outside of the Irish-American press and they remain among the most famous pieces of O'Reilly's journalistic work. This is not to say that the articles in themselves were ground-breaking, since Irish-American newspapers carried a wide variety of opinions and argument. However, such was O'Reilly's fame and the high circulation of *The Pilot* (anything from 55,000 to 103,000 copies a week) that the articles aroused great debate.[58] They also played a vital role in keeping O'Reilly at the forefront of Irish-American consciousness. If he had remained famous for nothing other than being a daring and triumphant escaped convict, then O'Reilly's fame would have quickly faded away with the next newsworthy event. His work with *The Pilot* showed him to be a much more complex figure and a forceful commentator on Irish and American affairs. His reputation was such that in 1871 Horace Greeley, soon-to-be presidential candidate and one of the most influential newspaper editors in the United States, offered O'Reilly a job as a reporter on his *New York Tribune*.[59] The New York paper had a long history of support for varied reform movements and had counted Karl Marx and Margaret Fuller among its contributors.

This opportunity to work with such a prominent paper may well have tempted O'Reilly but Patrick Donahoe moved quickly to stymie Greeley's plan. O'Reilly's fame and his often controversial journalism had added to the reputation and the circulation figures of *The Pilot*. The newspaper owner was not willing to lose his star acquisition and he trumped Greeley by giving O'Reilly a substantial increase in his salary.[60] More than that, Donahoe also advanced the young journalist to the position of editor. The internal politics of *The Pilot* during this time are unclear but O'Reilly seems to have been made editor during the summer of 1871 and it may have been Greeley's attempt to entice the ambitious young reporter that forced Donahoe to make this decision. Whatever the reasons behind it, O'Reilly's progression to the editor's chair was a remarkable achievement.

During this time, as O'Reilly worked to build his journalistic career, there were many changes in his personal life. In early 1871 O'Reilly heard news that his father, William, had died and been buried in Glasnevin Cemetery, Dublin. William David O'Reilly had died in near poverty although, in his last years, he was financially supported by Alexander Sullivan of the *Nation* newspaper and some Dublin Fenians.[61] The Fenians provided for his burial but the epitaph they composed for William David was more of a paean to his son's life rather than a testimonial to the father:

> *William David O'Reilly, Aged sixty-three years*
> Died February 17, 1871 – Deceased was father of John Boyle O'Reilly, A good Irish soldier. Convicted by English court martial, and self-amnestied by escaping from Western Australia to America. May the brave son live long, and may the remains of the noble father rest in peace![62]

John Boyle O'Reilly had known that his father was in poor health but he had no hope of visiting him since he was still a fugitive in the eyes of British law. It remained a source of sadness to O'Reilly that he never had a last chance to visit his father. William O'Reilly's death, only a few years after that of Eliza Boyle, had cut another of the Irishman's ties to Ireland but as O'Reilly's Irish family faded away he had begun to create his own American family.

In May 1870 O'Reilly had the first of many poems published in *The Pilot*. It was called 'Pondering' but it was a not a new composition. It was one of the 'Night Thoughts' poems that O'Reilly had written in the Western Australian bush.[63] Why O'Reilly chose this poem is impossible to say. Did his thoughts still dwell on Jessie Woodman? Perhaps they did but later that same summer he was to begin a new relationship with a twenty-year-old local journalist named Mary Murphy. Mary, whom O'Reilly described as 'the very nicest girl in New England', wrote for a Catholic magazine called the *Young Crusader* under the pseudonym 'Agnes Smiley'.[64] It seems doubtful whether O'Reilly ever told Mary of Jessie Woodman or his attempted suicide, although she cannot have failed to notice the scar that would have snaked its way across his left arm. If she did know of Woodman, it did nothing to dampen her relationship with O'Reilly. James Jeffrey Roche, who was later a friend of the couple, wrote that 'a mutual love soon grew up between them'.[65] The two were married on 15 August 1872 at St Mary's Church in Charlestown. After a short honeymoon travelling through New Hampshire and Maine they settled at 34 Winthrop Street in Charlestown. Those first few months of married life were a happy time for the couple but their circumstances came close to a disastrous reversal only a few months later with the Great Boston Fire. The fire could have put *The Pilot* out of business and left O'Reilly without an income. Yet it would ultimately prove to be the financial undoing of Patrick Donahoe and would give O'Reilly with the opportunity to provide for his family and to further his already remarkable progress into Boston society.

Large fires were a plague that regularly visited American cities throughout the nineteenth century. Much of Chicago had been devastated by a conflagration in 1871 and civic authorities in Boston were fearful that a similar calamity might strike their city. Still, little was done to prepare Boston for such a scenario. Water supplies to the city centre were inadequate and many fire hydrants were not fully pressurised. Building codes in the city were almost totally ignored, leaving many narrow streets whose busy pathways were towered over by wooden-roofed buildings too tall for their upper storeys to be reached by rescue ladders. The fire began on the night of 9 November 1872 just after 7 p.m. in a warehouse on the corner of Kingston Street and Summer Street. The timing was particularly unfortunate since the building was empty and the fire had almost consumed the interior of the warehouse before it was noticed by a passer-by.[66]

The flames had quickly taken hold of the warehouse and in their hunger for new fuel had spread to the wooden roofs of nearby buildings. Further spread was now inevitable, but on that night a number of factors coalesced to turn a damaging but still controllable fire into a conflagration that would annihilate much of the city. Perhaps the most important of the factors was an outbreak of horse flu that had hit Boston. The disease had first been noticed in Canada during early October 1872 and spread with astonishing speed throughout that country and the US. Infection rates were almost 100 per cent and it meant that, on the night of the fire, the Boston fire department had almost no horses to pull their equipment. The department was forced to organise civilians into teams to get their fire wagons to the scene of the fire. The delay that resulted from this was crucial and allowed the fire to spread unchecked through Kingston Street and Summer Street.

Once in position the firefighters were further hampered by the poorly pressurised fire hydrants, panicked home and business owners, looters and huge crowds of spectators. All of these combined to leave the city defenceless as the fire raged in an expanding ring of destruction. By 11 p.m. it had reached Franklin Street and the head office of *The Pilot* as well as the Emigrant Savings Bank.[67] Franklin Street had long been considered by the city's firefighters to be among Boston's prime fire hazards and so it proved. Most of the street, including the Pilot Building, was destroyed. The fire continued to spread through the city. Under pressure from city officials and citizens Mayor William Gaston authorised the use of gunpowder to demolish buildings in the path of the fire. In theory they hoped to make a fire break and deprive the flames of their fuel. In practice, buildings were packed with gunpowder by people with no experience of explosives. The resulting explosions showered adjacent buildings with burning embers creating miniature versions of the main fire. The explosions had to be stopped by the city's chief firefighter, John Damrell.

It took twenty hours for the fire to be quenched only a short distance from Boston landmarks such as the Old South Meeting House, Faneuil Hall, and the Old State House. Thirty people had been killed, hundreds made homeless and thousands more jobless. After the fire the writer and later acquaintance of O'Reilly, Oliver Wendell Holmes, left his home on Beacon Street to assess the damage. In a letter to a friend he described the scene:

> everything flat to the water, so that we saw the ships in the harbour
> . . . here and there a tall chimney – two or three brick piers for safes,
> one with a safe standing on it as calm as if nothing had happened –
> piles of smoking masonry, the burnt stump of a flagstaff in Franklin
> Street – groups of people looking to see where their stores were, or
> hunting for their safes, or round a fire-engine . . . cordons military
> and of the police keeping off the crowds of people who have flocked
> in from all over the country, etc., etc.[68]

Patrick Donahoe and his staff were one of the groups on Franklin street picking through the remains of their former headquarters. By a sad coincidence Donahoe had been addressing the Boston Press Club on the night of the fire. The subject of the lecture had been the successful history of his newspaper. Of that paper, all that remained was a sorry collection of charred roof beams and little else. Around the site of what was once the magnificent Pilot Building the whole street was nothing other than 'huge piles of cracked and powdered brick and stone'.[69]

The Pilot, though, would continue publishing. Donahoe had contracted the printing of the paper to another company, Rand and Avery, on Cornhill Street, a street which had been left unscathed by the fire. Rand and Avery's office building served as a temporary headquarters for the paper over the following days and from here the staff missed only one edition and got the paper onto news stands by 23 November. Under the headline 'Boston's heart torn out' *The Pilot* estimated that the devastation of 120 acres of the city had cost Boston a loss of $100,000,000.[70] *The Pilot*'s losses amounted to $500,000 and, while the paper had been insured, the scale of the destruction and the consequent claims threatened to bankrupt insurance companies. The editorial of that edition promised that *The Pilot* would carry on: 'We have long known that nothing cannot be accomplished by energy and hard work [sic]. If every insurance office in the country declares bankruptcy, we shall look only to the rising sun, trust in God, and go on working.'

These were heroic sentiments but by that stage events had intervened as if to scorn *The Pilot*'s optimism. With sickening bad luck the offices of Rand and Avery caught fire on the night of 20 November. *The Pilot*'s printing presses, supplies of newspaper and that week's edition of the paper, which had already been typeset, were all destroyed. The damage cost the paper another £350,000 and must have been a personal devastation for Donahoe.[71] He still managed to get the paper into production, although O'Reilly and the staff had not time to give an account of the second fire until the 30 November edition. *The Pilot* now moved to another premises on Washington Street without missing an issue.[72] Donahoe's plight and the determined manner in which he and his staff responded to the disaster made them a symbol of hope to many in the city, as can be seen from an 1873 book about the Great Fire written by the journalist and future founder of Temple University, Russell Conwell:

There is much controversy as to which class of Christians will be tenants of the 'burnt districts' in the next world; but all publishers, at least, have a tender feeling for any of their brethren of the press who may happen to get into this. Mr Donahoe has been so brave, resolute, cheerful, and confident in meeting the calamity which destroyed his magnificent building on Franklin Street, that the hearts of all of us go out to him in cordial sympathy. The burning, afterwards, of a whole edition of 'The Pilot' in Rand and Avery's fire, made most of us have a semi-Catholic interest in the paper. Any third dispensation of Providence in the same direction will make some Protestants sympathize with the creed as well as the man.[73]

Providence, unhappily, dispensed a third blow to Donahoe and his paper less than a year later. Another fire hit Boston on 30 May 1873.[74] It was far smaller than the Great Boston Fire of the previous November but *The Pilot's* temporary office on Washington Street was destroyed. O'Reilly admitted in an editorial that the fire was another disaster for the paper but he did inject some gallows humour into his piece: 'When a fire comes to Boston now-a-days it goes looking round all the corners for its old friend, the Pilot. It is evident that the fire has a rare appreciation of a good newspaper and a companion to pass a brilliant hour.' Donahoe now moved production of *The Pilot* to a building on Boylston Street, which he had purchased earlier in the year and which was then being renovated. The November 1872 fires had resulted in the production of *The Pilot* being conducted in at least four different locations across Boston. The new building on Boylston Street would see all the paper's staff reunited and would also serve as *The Pilot's* new headquarters.

While *The Pilot* endured the vicissitudes of fate, O'Reilly's personal life continued to flourish. On 18 May 1873 Mary gave birth to the couple's first child, a girl they christened Mary although she would be known to family and friends as Mollie.[75] A second child, another girl, followed on 25 July 1874. The new arrival was christened Eliza in honour of O'Reilly's mother.[76] His poetry was also proving to be a success and in 1873 he published his first book of poetry, *Songs from the Southern Seas*. This collection, dedicated to his rescuer from Western Australia, Captain Gifford, was comprised partly of his very early poems such as 'The Old School Clock' and partly of poems written during his time aboard the *Hougoumont* and the *Gazelle*.[77] There were also a few poems written in or about the penal colony of Western Australia, a land, he said in the introduction to the collection, that was, 'blessed by God and blighted by man'. On 7 September 1874 he brought his 'Dear Aunt Crissy' up to date on his accomplishments thus far:

It was like listening to you and looking at you, to read your kind letter. It has made me so happy and yet so sad that I do not know which feeling is uppermost. I know you were pleased to see my poor book; but what would my own dear patient mother have felt when she saw me winning praise from men? Thank God! I have her picture – the girls and Edward [O'Reilly's younger brother] were kind enough to send it to me – and I have it grandly framed, and hung in our parlor. My little Mollie loves to kiss it, and I can only allow her to kiss the frame for fear of injuring the picture. Mary loves to look at it as much as I do, and she loves you, dear Aunt, from your one or two letters. Please write her a letter as soon as you can. She is getting strong again, from the birth of our second baby – our Eliza Boyle O'Reilly. Is it not strangely touching to see this new generation with the old names – springing up in a new land, and cherishing as traditions all that we knew as facts? Somehow, I feel as old as you and Uncle James. It seems so long since I was a boy that I really do not, cannot, accept young men or their ways of thinking. It gives me the sincerest pleasure to know that Uncle James is doing so well. He has a good book-keeper when he has you; but I am sure he knows that God has blessed him with that greatest of all blessings – a good wife. Willy's good fortune is as dear to me as if he were my own brother. I always knew he would be a clever chemist, and I am sure he is. Please God, sometime, when the Government lets me, I shall walk into his shop and ask for a bottle of medicine. He would never know the bearded man [from 1874 to 1880 O'Reilly sported 'long hair and a full beard'[78]], with streaks of gray, from the thoughtless boy he knew long ago. Nobody in England would know me but you: you could see the Boyle in me.

It will please you, I know, to know just how I am doing. I inclose a lot of extracts from the leading papers of America, which will show you that I do not lack literary reputation. My position in Boston – which is the chief city in this country for literature and general culture – is quite good. I am chief editor of the Pilot –which is the most influential Catholic paper in America, probably in the world. My salary is $3,000 a year (£2 a day); $4,000 next year. Besides, I write when I please for the leading magazines and literary papers – which also adds to my income. Of course, $3,000 a year does not represent its equivalent in English money in England. Everything is sold at a higher rate here. However, Mary, who is a wonderful manager, has saved a few thousand dollars (I give her all the money), and we are prepared for a rainy day. My health is excellent. I have just returned from a vacation, which I spent in the glorious Southern States of Maryland and Virginia. I visited Baltimore and Washington, and had an invitation to stay with the President of the Jesuit University, at Georgetown. I do not know what you think of America, Aunt, but it may surprise you to hear that the cities here are far greater and grander than those in the Old World, always excepting London for size, of course. Washington is the most magnificent city I ever saw. But what do you care for America! Give my love to all.[79]

Crissy Watkinson would soon have had further reasons to be proud of her nephew. Within two years of this letter O'Reilly would be a part-owner of *The Pilot*.

Patrick Donahoe had been put under intolerable financial strain as a result of the fires that had consumed his businesses. His insurance had been adequate to cover the losses incurred as a result of the fire of 9 November 1872. However, the claims resulting from this fire had subsequently bankrupted many insurers and Donahoe did not recoup his losses for the fires of 20 November 1872 and the following May.[80] When *The Pilot* moved to its new head office on Boylston Street, Donahoe was forced to take out mortgages on a number of his properties, including his own home.[81] His business suffered further strain as result of the financial panic of 1873 and the depression which subsequently hit the US economy. As an immediate consequence of that panic there had been a series of bank failures 'owing to exorbitant real estate loans on inflated values'.[82] Following these bank failures, the provision of credit to businesses vanished. From 1874 to 1876 business failures rose from 6,000 to 9,000 per annum.[83] The Massachusetts economy was not spared the turmoil and Donahoe's commercial empire steadily lost its ability to maintain itself. Especially damaging to Donahoe was a loss of $170,000 that resulted from his endorsement of loans to Gustavus Finotti, a Boston-based businessman.[84] Finotti, whom the *New York Times* described as 'a dreamer and a theorist', had lost all the money in 'experimenting and speculation' and had been unable to repay the loan, leaving the burden to fall on Donahoe.[85]

By 1876 Donahoe was $569,000 in debt.[86] He still believed that, given time, he could make good these debts and had made efforts to sell off his substantial real estate holdings, including his home, but with land prices and property prices having collapsed, *The Pilot*'s owner was unable to cover his liabilities. On 2 March 1876 his creditors filed an involuntary petition for bankruptcy against him. Donahoe's estate was taken over by these creditors who assigned control of his business interests to Charles Kendall, Charles Shepard and the politician Patrick Collins.[87] Over March and April 1876 the collapse of Donahoe's commercial empire was covered in detail across all the Boston press and the *New York Times*. Their reports made for grim reading. Disaster for Donohue was also to become a disaster for some former depositors in the Emigrant Savings Bank. Donahoe had resigned as president of the bank after the Great Fire of 1872 (to be replaced by Irish lawyer Charles F. Donnelly) and had agreed a series of deals with a section of the bank's depositors whereby he acted as their private banker.[88]

These depositors seem to have been entirely comprised of small investors who did not trust anyone other than Donahoe to manage their money. During 1874 and 1875 they invested a combined total of almost $73,000 with him.[89] The exact purpose of these deposits is not clear although it was widely acknowledged in the press that Donahoe had not been involved in any criminality; the *New York Times* described him as 'An Honest Man' bankrupted by 'Careless business habits and the Boston fires'.[90] However, in 1875, Donahoe was also a desperate man and it is unlikely that his depositors fully understood the risks they had undertaken by investing in his private bank. Donahoe lost the entire sum in a futile effort to prevent his bankruptcy by paying off 'the tremendous interest account which had accumulated on his loans, mortgages and securities of various kinds'.[91] His one performing asset was *The Pilot* and in this O'Reilly saw an opportunity that would benefit both himself and Donahoe. O'Reilly planned to take control of the paper and if he was successful, he told a friend, 'the old man [Donahoe] will come saved'.[92] O'Reilly could not afford to buy *The Pilot* but he put a proposal to the Archbishop of Boston, John J. Williams, that the Diocese of Boston take part ownership of the paper.

The archbishop was a Boston native and he was eager to see such a renowned Catholic paper remain in publication. On that basis the two men were able to forge an agreement whereby Williams would pay $21,000 for the paper and its offices, O'Reilly $7,000.[93] The deal was closed on 15 April 1876 and it contained a number of stipulations to which both Williams and O'Reilly had agreed. One of these was that they would take on an existing loan of $6,500, plus interest, which Donahoe had taken against *The Pilot*. They would also take none of the profits, above expenses and salaries, until the $73,000 was repaid to Donahoe's unfortunate investors. Their extraordinary generosity was acknowledged by Donahoe a few days later when he issued a public statement expressing his gratitude to Archbishop Williams and especially to O'Reilly for 'his untiring efforts in my behalf since misfortune fell upon me'.[94] Williams and O'Reilly then printed the terms of the agreement in *The Pilot*; an act which not only advised the investors in Donahoe's private bank that they would recoup their losses, but which also helped to lessen the damage caused to Donahoe's reputation.[95]

The terms of the deal were lauded across Boston, leading one commentator to write a few years later: 'Is it any wonder that, throughout the diocese of Boston, the Archbishop is regarded with double reverence, and that next to him, in the hearts and the prayers of the poor, stands John Boyle O'Reilly, the poet?'[96] Archbishop Williams also announced that in tribute to Donahoe's 'honorable work in behalf of his church' he hoped to eventually hand back to Donahoe 'a large and profitable interest in the Pilot'.[97] Until such a time, editorial policy would remain completely in the hands of O'Reilly who would receive an annual salary of $5,200 (the average salary of 'non-farm employees' in the US during 1876 was $403).[98] Over the previous six years *The Pilot* had come to be dominated by O'Reilly's voice. Now the 31-year-old was not only the editor of the paper but also its co-owner and we need to take some time to look at what kind of newspaper *The Pilot* would become under O'Reilly's control.

Civil Rights and Wrongs

O'Reilly had a clear vision of how the press should function and from the beginning of his time with *The Pilot* he used the newspaper to do battle on behalf of America's underprivileged. In 1879 he gave a speech to the Boston Press Club in which he described this vision to his audience of fellow editors and reporters. In O'Reilly's eyes, the journalist held an august and vital position in society. Journalism, he believed, should be something more than mere muckraking and manufactured outrage. The press should seek to move beyond sensationalism and to explain the world to its readers in an honest manner:

> All who teach are ours. The priests of all future dispensations shall be members of the press. Ours is the newest and greatest of the professions, involving wider work and heavier responsibilities than any other. For all time to come, the freedom and purity of the press are the test of national virtue and independence. No writer for the press, however humble, is free from the burden of keeping his purpose high and his integrity white. The dignity of communities is largely intrusted to our keeping; and while we sway in the struggle or relax in the rest-hour, we must let no buzzards roost on the public shield in our charge.[1]

In his attempts to make these ideals a reality O'Reilly had devoted much of his reforming zeal to supporting workers' rights and black civil rights. Throughout the 1870s O'Reilly's writings on these issues had helped to expand the Irishman's fame across the United States. In making the issue of civil rights a keystone of *The Pilot*'s coverage of American affairs, O'Reilly was working against a wider tradition within the Irish community of the United States. The historian Dennis Clark has written that 'Of all the ethnic antagonisms that have arisen in the turbulence of American social development, few have such a distinctively rancorous history as that between Black man and Irishman.'[2] Much of this antagonism resulted from competition for employment as Irish and black labourers clashed in cities across the US, especially in dockyards on the east and gulf coasts. In the words of the novelist Peter Quinn, it was 'a contest over which group would find itself relegated to permanent status as impoverished and oppressed outsiders'.[3]

As a consequence of this rivalry, Irish Americans had, before the Civil War, repeatedly resisted efforts to abolish slavery or improve the lives of free blacks. Their hostility towards abolitionism was part of a wider Catholic ambivalence towards slavery. The Catholic Church in the US had not taken an official stance on slavery, although Pope Gregory XVI had officially denounced the African and international slave trades in 1839. The position of the Catholic hierarchy in the US was exemplified by the Cork-born Bishop of Charlestown, John England. Over the winter of 1840–41 he wrote a series of letters on the subject of slavery to the US Secretary of State, John Forsyth.[4] These letters, as can be seen below, were designed to demonstrate Catholic loyalty to the laws of the United States, including those that allowed slavery. England's letters were not challenged by other members of the hierarchy and in the decades before the American Civil War the letters came to be understood as explaining the Church's attitude to slavery and abolitionism. Slavery, according to Bishop England, was a human creation and was subject to corruption and abuse whereby the slaves were mistreated or deprived of their dignity. However it was not intrinsically evil and not in contravention of 'natural law':

> I may perhaps here close that part of my observations which were intended to show that by Scripture and by tradition we discover that the existence of domestic slavery is perfectly compatible with the practice of true religion. In the Scriptural evidence, we have seen the laws regarding it, made for his chosen people by God himself. We have found that amongst the various crimes denounced by the Saviour, he never directly or indirectly either mentions or alludes to

this, yet he not only was fully aware of its existence, but it was alluded to and spoken of by slave-holders, upon whom he conferred great favors and to whose high virtues he bore ample testimony. His apostles distinctly show their respective duties to the slave-holder and to the slave, who are both members of the church of Jesus Christ, and strongly as they recommended kindness and mercy to one, they inculcate obedience and humility upon the other.[5]

While the Irish in America were hostile to abolitionism, the position of the Irish across the Atlantic was markedly different during the 1840s and the years of O'Reilly's childhood.

Daniel O'Connell had long been an opponent of slavery and in 1842 he signed a petition, along with the famous temperance reformer Father Theobald Mathew and 70,000 other Irish people, entitled an 'Address of the people of Ireland to their countrymen and countrywomen in America'.[6] The petition called upon the Irish in America to join with abolitionists in opposition to slavery:

> The object of this address is to call your attention to the subject of Slavery in America – that foul blot upon the noble institution and the fair fame of your adopted country. But for this one stain, America would indeed be a land worthy of your adoption; but she will never be the glorious country that her free Constitution designed her to be, so long as her soil is polluted by the foot-prints of a single slave. Slavery is the most tremendous invasion of the natural, inalienable rights of man, and of some of the noblest gifts of God, 'life, liberty, and the pursuit of happiness'. What a spectacle does America present to the people of the earth!'[7]

O'Connell was a hero to Irish Catholics on both sides of the Atlantic and the appeal was a shock to Irish Americans, many of whom assumed the petition was a hoax. Indeed, the Tyrone-born Bishop of New York, John Hughes, declared that O'Connell's signature was a forgery.[8] When the document was shown to be authentic the shock was replaced by anger. This anger was rooted in the belief among Irish Americans that O'Connell and the Irish in the Old World did not appreciate the situation facing the Irish in America.

The petition had left Irish Americans in an awkward position. In the 1840s Catholics were still insecurely placed within American society. That decade witnessed a burgeoning nativist movement that resulted in anti-Catholic violence across the United States. As justification for their violence, and as part of their campaign to stop Irish and Catholic immigration, nativists routinely decried Catholics as disloyal. In response immigrant groups such as the Irish reacted by trying to prove their loyalty to the United States and especially the constitution. Since slavery was a feature of the law in many American states, the Catholic hierarchy judged that its existence was a natural law of the land and, as such, that the Church had nothing to gain from seeking its destruction. It was in that context that Irish Americans were so resistant to the efforts of Irish abolitionists like O'Connell. Indeed, Bishop England's first letter to Forsyth had ended with the declaration that 'Pope Gregory XVI is not the associate of abolitionists and that Catholics . . . should not be rendered objects of suspicion to their fellow citizens.'[9] Yet O'Connell remained steadfast in his hostility to slavery and in the following year he issued a call to the Irish in America: 'Turn not a deaf ear to the cry of the slave but let him feel, in the future and forevermore, that in every Irishman he has a friend.'[10]

O'Connell's persistence on the issue encouraged the Irish in the United States to respond. In 1844 Bishop England's letters to Forsyth were collated into a book, edited by George William Read. He provided an introduction which explained the book's purpose:

> It is more than probable, that Mr. O'Connell little dreamt of the mischief he was doing, to a still holier cause than that of injured Ireland, when, in the ardour of his vituperation against America, he ventured to misconstrue the Pope's denunciation of the African slave trade (denounced no less by our own and almost every civilized government) into a denial of the compatibility of domestic slavery, as existing in this country, with the practice unto salvation of the Catholic Religion . . . To our fellow-citizens of Irish origin, therefore, and the candid and intelligent of every persuasion, these letters on slavery, by the great apostle of this western world [Bishop England], incomplete as they fell from his hurried pen, and sealed by death midway his argument [England had died in 1842], will yet prove of inestimable value, as exhibiting the true doctrine of Christianity, on

the fundamental principle of involuntary servitude, and her ameliorating influences on a state ordained of God, yet liable, like most other social institutions, to manifold and great abuses.[11]

Such attitudes regularly appeared throughout the Catholic press and, unsurprisingly, the insidious euphemism of 'involuntary servitude' found its way onto the pages of Patrick Donahoe's *The Pilot*. Donahoe was no supporter of slavery but he was not so perturbed by the peculiar institution that he was willing to challenge its existence. In 1855 his paper considered the issue of slavery and the manifold indignities that accompanied it, such as: 'Inhuman treatment – separation of families – deprivation of right to perform ordinary Christian duties – violence done to the marriage relation – refusal to recognize in the negro a man'.[12] Yet, like Bishop England, the paper argued that slavery was not, in itself, wrong and that these abuses could and should be removed from its application. The editorial continued, 'When you have stripped slavery of those abuses which are accidental and do not necessarily belong to it, you have simply involuntary servitude.' In fact, the paper claimed, when slavery was properly administered it provided food, clothing and shelter to the slave. It was, the editorial concluded, 'like making him a member of the family'.

Such statements could seem almost like a parody of the reality of slavery except for the fact that Donahoe was entirely in earnest. His paper's musings on slavery were an inevitable outcome of the Catholic ambivalence towards the practice and the hierarchy's rationalisations of its existence. Through such articles newspapers like *The Pilot* hid the immorality of slavery. This attitude became less tenable during the closing years of the 1850s as the associated issues of slavery and states' rights became the most vital questions facing the United States. As that dispute became increasingly bitter, the hostility towards freeing slaves became more openly racist. After the abolitionist John Brown led the infamous raid on the military stores at Harper's Ferry in 1859 *The Pilot* put in verse its prediction of the dire results that would follow the end of slavery: 'When the negroes shall be free / To cut the throats of all they see / Then this dear land will come to be / The den of foul rascality.'[13]

Despite such sentiments, when the conflict between the states erupted into outright civil war, *The Pilot* and the wider Irish community of the North openly and vociferously supported the Union.[14] There were many reasons that the Irish volunteered to fight in the Union army; some wished to offer support to the country that had taken them in, others believed that the skills learned on the battlefields could some day be used in gaining Irish independence; others simply needed employment. Whatever their reasons, they did not join to fight slavery, a position summed up in the crude line of a song popular among the Irish: 'we're not for the nigger but we are for the war'.[15] It was during the Civil War that the relationship between Irish and blacks reached a nadir with the violence of the New York Draft Riots of July 1863. Ostensibly, the crowds who rioted in New York were protesting against the provisions of a new law drafting soldiers into the Union army. These provisions were designed in such a manner that the bulk of the draft would unfairly fall upon the poor immigrant communities, including the Irish. That was what brought thousands of Irish onto the streets, but the protest quickly became violent with New York's black community bearing the brunt of attacks from Irish mobs. In the chaos twelve black men were murdered.[16]

When the war ended two years later the black population had broken free of slavery and their position as citizens of the US was solidified during the following year with the Civil Rights Act of 1866, the first civil rights measure of the US Congress. This conferred equality before the law on blacks, with respect to the protection of the fundamental rights of person and property. The Catholic press was, for the most part, hostile to the Civil Rights Act of 1866, with *The Pilot* claiming that the Act was a Republican Party plot to maintain its political dominance.[17] The paper had long considered that party to be anti-Catholic and anti-Irish and it now believed that Republicans planned to use black voters as a means to overcome the solidly Democratic Irish vote. *The Pilot* also raised the fear that freed and newly enfranchised black slaves would pour north and east and undercut the Irish in competition for jobs. It warned that: 'We have nothing to say against efforts to elevate the Negro; but we do most earnestly protest that those efforts must not be put forth at the expense of our race.'[18] *The Pilot* was not alone in such views and the Catholic Church remained hesitant in its attitude to blacks. When the Second Plenary Council of American bishops met at Baltimore during October 1866 it had little to say on the current or future status of blacks in the US although it did advise that priests should make efforts to preach to black communities.[19] While there were many individual priests such as Father (later Cardinal) Herbert Vaughan who took this advice and worked hard to welcome African Americans into the Church, Catholics and blacks remained wary of each other.

In spite of this troubled history, O'Reilly came to the issue of civil rights at a time when there were some hints that the mutual resentment of Irish and blacks may have passed its high point. Just six months after the end of the Civil War, the California State Convention of Colored Citizens met at Sacramento where, amid other issues, it debated Irish independence. Most contributors to the debate argued in support of Irish independence and in October the Convention passed a resolution declaring 'That, notwith-standing the opposition we receive from Irish immigrants in America, whose prejudices are existed against us by the misnamed Democratic Party, every effort to rid Ireland of English bondage and establish Irish independence meets our cordial approbation.'[20] Daniel O'Connell remained a hero to black Americans and they also had other links to the Irish in Ireland. Frederick Douglass, the great civil rights campaigner and former slave, had travelled to Ireland in late 1845. He spent six months in the country where he had befriended Daniel O'Connell and enjoyed some of the 'happiest moments' of his life.[21] Douglass' Irish journey was an important period in the development of his political thought. After his eventual return to the United States Douglass had become an open supporter of Irish independence and influenced many other black leaders to think likewise. Another prominent black politician, George Downing, was similarly eager to encourage cooperation with the Irish: 'I would cultivate toward all who have been our enemies – toward the Irishmen who have been so brutal in outraging us – a forgiving spirit, if they will henceforth be, in reality, our and our country's friends.'[22]

There were even some public manifestations of this new spirit throughout the 1870s with Irish and black politicians working together on occasion. In 1875 the city of St Paul, Minnesota, hosted a large public celebration of the centennial of the birth of Daniel O'Connell. The event was organised and attended by both the Irish and black communities of the city during which they listened to a speech from Robert Banks, a black barber, who had once met with O'Connell.[23] The event was judged by all in attendance to have been a great success. O'Reilly would capitalise on any cooperation between Irish and black communities, such as the Minnesota celebration, to forge relationships with black politicians and public figures. Even so, the two groups still viewed each other with suspicion and the

Detroit Plaindealer complained that the Irish were too quick to forget that they had been victims of prejudice, writing that 'almost their first Americanism polished with the brogue is "down with the Nagur"'.[24]

There was more than a little truth in this statement and O'Reilly was to spend much of his time as editor combatting such attitudes, whatever their source. There does not seem to have been any specific incident which converted O'Reilly to the cause of civil rights. However, there can be little doubt that his experiences in Ireland, of prison life, his subsequent transportation and his convict existence in Western Australia were key factors in the development of his thought on democracy and civil rights. Also, although we have little knowledge of his childhood, O'Reilly cherished the memory of his mother and perhaps the kind manner in which she administered to the orphans in her care was a formative influence. Whatever his influences it is certain that by the time he arrived in the US O'Reilly's concern for the welfare of disenfranchised groups was already an inherent part of his character, a core value which was the overriding influence on how he saw the world around him.

Throughout the early 1870s O'Reilly was relatively moderate in his support of black civil rights but once it became apparent to him that such moderation was being used, by many politicians and newspapers, as an excuse for delaying or preventing civil rights he became more forceful in his criticisms. From 1874 onwards O'Reilly began to write more frequently on anti-black prejudice. In February of that year he explained to his readers the importance of what was generally referred to as the 'negro question':

> The destiny of the colored American is one of the big problems to be worked out in the life of this Republic. The day is fast coming when this man's claim cannot be answered by a jest or a sneer. The colored American of to-day may not be equal to his position as an enfranchised man. He has still about him something of the easy submission and confessed inferiority of a race held long in ignorance and bondage. But this man's children and grandchildren are coming, and they are receiving the same education in the same schools as the white man's children. In all things material before God and man, they will feel that they are the white man's equal. They are growing above the prejudice, even before the prejudice dies: and herein is the opening of the problem.[25]

O'Reilly's writings on this subject were not always welcomed by the subscribers to his paper. One of these readers, from Georgia, wrote to O'Reilly to condemn the editor for his support of race integration. The letter writer was especially dismayed by O'Reilly's criticisms of the Franklin Typographical Society, an organisation which had recently refused admittance to a black man. These men, the letter writer asserted, 'have too much respect for their race to associate with Negroes'.[26] O'Reilly was unrepentant and replied to the letter via an editorial:

> We are sorry that such sentiments should come from one who boasts of belonging to the 'faithful Irish'. There is nothing Irish about his principles; and we are glad to receive the 'stop my Pilot' of such a man. We glory in the very things he hates ... The Pilot holds that the colored man stands on a perfect equality with the white man.[27]

This statement was to be a guiding principle of *The Pilot* under O'Reilly's editorship and it was a principle that would similarly inspire him to defend Native Americans and other beleaguered groups in the United States.

O'Reilly's first opportunity to write in their defence came in 1873 following the death of General Edward Canby at the hands of the Modoc tribe in California. Canby was a casualty of the so-called Modoc War fought across California and southern Oregon from 1872 to 1873 and his death elicited an extraordinary outpouring of grief in American newspapers. Amid all this emotion there was little room for rational argument with newspapers and politicians clamouring for vengeance against the Modoc Indians. There were exceptions to this combative consensus. The *New York Times* advised against a hasty response to the death of Canby and chastised those who were demanding 'the inauguration of an exterminating war'.[28] *The Pilot* was another exception, with O'Reilly denouncing the attack on Canby while placing his death in the context of the sustained misgovernment of the Indians by the US government and its agents: 'We have too much and too old a sympathy with people badly governed, to join in this shameful cry for Madoc blood. We grant that they have committed murder, and they are unstable, treacherous, and dangerous. Who should not be so, with the robberies and outrages of generations boiling in their blood?'[29]

O'Reilly would again defend Indian tribes following the defeat of the

7th Cavalry at the Little Bighorn in June 1876. At the end of that month Lieutenant Colonel George Armstrong Custer had led the 7th Cavalry to destruction at the hands of the Lakota and Cheyenne. The news of the battle, fought near the Little Bighorn River in the Montana Territory, stunned an American public that had been enjoying the celebrations of the United States' centennial. Practically all the press was united against the 'Red Devils' who had won the battle. Custer's reputation had grown in tandem with the rising public anger and many newspapers glorified the dead commander. O'Reilly was far less enamoured by Custer, whom he called 'the pet of the army',[30] and he penned an accurate depiction of that soldier's often reckless nature and his excessive love of fighting. 'War to him was more than half-sport', wrote the editor.

O'Reilly was an antidote to the maudlin and often false accounts of the battle that filled the newspapers. At a time when allusions to Greek and Roman history were a stock-in-trade of journalists, it was sadly inevitable that newspapers would draw comparisons between 'Custer and his brave three hundred' and the last stand of the 300 Spartans at Thermopylae.[31] As an analogy it was particularly useless and it was an analogy that O'Reilly dismissed. He was one of the comparatively few commentators that sought to place to Battle of the Little Bighorn in its proper setting:

> The story of the Sioux Indians is one of record of cruel injustice on behalf of the United States. Treaties have been made with them and broken ere the ink was dry; grants have been voted by Congress to pay their claims, and the money stolen by rascals . . . The death of the most dashing officer in the army . . . will prevent for a time, the righteous consideration of this question. The border-cry of vengeance is heard already, and it is probable that an attempt will be made to extirpate the entire Sioux. But the day will come when these things cry to Heaven against the United States. The treatment of the Indians has been a red record of rascality and crime; and it is worse than ever to-day. The Sioux warriors did not murder Custer and his soldiers. They met him in a fair fight, out-generalled him, and cut him to pieces. He tried to do the same to them.[32]

This was a sober and accurate assessment at a time when many newspapers were demanding revenge and when the story of the battle was already being transformed into legend. O'Reilly derided claims that the 7th Cavalry had been ambushed or that their commander had somehow been tricked, two reasons for the defeat that were steadily becoming a part of the official version of the battle. 'Custer's bravery outran his caution'[33] was O'Reilly's judgement of the 7th's commander but appointing blame for the US army's defeat was not the editor's main concern. He was far more interested in defending the Lakota and Cheyenne's reputation and in trying to prevent the punitive reprisals that were certain to occur over the rest of the summer. O'Reilly finished the editorial with the hope that some good might come from the battle: 'There is no justice in this cry for vengeance. There is far more need of a cry for fair play. If the death of Custer brings about an honest consideration of the Indian's rights, the blood of the brave soldiers has not been supplied in vain.'

Native American issues were never to be given as prominent a position in The Pilot as that of black civil rights but O'Reilly always maintained a close eye on government actions towards them. He would, throughout 1886 and 1887, use his newspaper to campaign, albeit unsuccessfully, against the Dawes Act, which divided up reservation lands, against the wishes of most tribes, into privately owned allotments.[34] By that time O'Reilly had emerged as a consistent public adversary of racism and he was often asked by civil rights groups to speak or write on race relations. He was, for example, an open opponent of anti-Semitism and on one occasion the American Hebrew magazine asked O'Reilly to provide his analysis of anti-Jewish sentiment in the United States. O'Reilly replied to the magazine that he was baffled by the continuance of prejudice against Jews although he was at pains to dismiss Christianity as a factor in its persistence:

I do not believe that the cause of this prejudice is the religious instruction in Christian schools, because the most prejudiced are least religious or Christian. Part of the prejudice is inherited from less intelligent times; part comes from the exclusiveness of the Jews as a race, and the largest part from the marvelous success of the Jewish race in business. In this country, I think, the anti-Jewish prejudice is not at all religious. From personal experience, I should say it was wholly racial and commercial.[35]

He told the editor of the *American Hebrew* that he had many Jewish friends and business acquaintances: 'I know three men who are my ideals of mercantile honor, integrity, and business character: one is a Christian and two are Jews.' He concluded by saying that: 'I do not know how to dispel the anti-Jewish prejudice except by expressing my own respect, honor, and affection for the greatest race – taking its vicissitudes and its achievements, its numbers and its glories – that ever existed.'[36]

Amid all O'Reilly's writings and activity in support of minorities of one form or another, it was the issue of black civil rights to which he would most often return, although it would take him a few years to clarify his thoughts on this subject. During the 1870s, while O'Reilly had consistently supported civil rights, he had displayed some sympathy towards the claims of southern whites that they were suffering unfair treatment from the government. In *The Pilot* he printed letters from whites stating that the black population of the South was far better treated than was commonly reported in northern newspapers. As late as 1879 he had agreed with the decision of the United States Circuit Court in Virginia to overrule the legality of a marriage between a white man and a black woman. This was despite the fact that O'Reilly supported inter-racial marriages in *The Pilot* writing that 'The race that shuts out humanity is like a lake compared to the ocean.'[37] O'Reilly backed the court decision because he was a proponent of states' rights against the central power of the federal government (see below), even when he believed laws such as Virginia's prohibition of inter-racial marriage to be unjust.

By the 1880s O'Reilly had become far more sceptical of claims by southern whites regarding the racial situation in the South. He had taken note of the speeches of Frederick Douglass and other black leaders such as Blanche Kelso Bruce which had laid bare the failure of the government to protect civil rights in the South.[38] O'Reilly now realised that laws such as Virginia's proscription of inter-racial marriage were not merely quaint southern customs, which could be excised from the statute books by reasoned debate, but were actually part of a system designed to subjugate the South's black population. This realisation would lead him to make his own investigations of the situation. In 1885 the editor travelled through the southern United States and was sickened by the enduring discrimination against blacks. The ubiquitous segregation he witnessed during his journey made him wonder whether 'something was the matter either with God or humanity in the South.'[39]

In December of that year O'Reilly told a predominantly black audience at the first meeting of the Massachusetts Colored League that it was their duty to oppose discrimination all over the United States and especially the racial segregation laws in the former Confederacy. They would not lack his support: 'If ever the negro question comes to the front while I live,' he declared, 'I shall be counted in with the black man.'[40] Not only did he fight anti-black prejudice in the columns of his paper but he also sought to instil a sense of self-respect among the black population and he would often print advertisements and notices for black social and cultural events. To read *The Pilot* of these years is to read O'Reilly's regular exposures of prejudice. On one occasion he displayed his abhorrence at two examples: the refusal of New York policemen to admit black men to the force, and the refusal of girls in an Indianapolis high school to share their graduation ceremony with a fellow black student:

> To insult and degrade a free man and tie his hands with social and statute wires, that cut and burn as well as restrain, is worse than to seize him bodily and yoke him to a dray as a slave . . . The girls who have disgraced themselves and their city ought to be marked with a scarlet letter. Every fair-minded man and woman and child in America ought to seize these shameful facts as a reason to make up their minds on the negro question. They ought to say that every policeman in New York or elsewhere, who dared to say he was better than his colored fellow-citizen, was unfit to wear the uniform of an American city; and that every school-girl who was so un-Christian and so unladylike as to ostracize a fellow-student because her skin was dark, was utterly unworthy of a diploma from the public schools.[41]

One of his most famous public speeches on race relations came following the 'Carrollton Massacre' in Mississippi of March 1886, during which a white mob attacked a courthouse and murdered at least eleven black men.[42] The news of the event led to protests across the United States and Boston's black community invited O'Reilly to address a public 'indignation meeting' on the events of the massacre. This speech, which is very similar to a version he had previously given to the Massachusetts Colored League, is worth quoting at length since it details much of O'Reilly's attitude to race relations, his ambivalence towards political parties and his belief in the power of the written word. It had become clear over the previous decade that neither of the two major parties could be trusted to work on behalf of black voters:

> I know nothing and care nothing about your politics or party preferences; but I know that if I were a colored man I should use political parties, as I would a club or a hatchet, to smash the prejudice that dared to exclude my children from a public school, or myself from a public hall, theater, or hotel. The interest you have to protect and defend is not that of a party, but of your own manhood. Use party as they use you – for your own best interests. But the thing that most deeply afflicts the colored American is not going to be cured by politics. You have received from politics already about all it can give you. You may change the law by politics; but it is not the law that is going to insult and outrage and excommunicate every colored American for generations to come. You can't cure the conceit of the white people that they are better than you by politics, nor their ignorance, nor their prejudice, nor their bigotry, nor any of the insolences which they cherish against their colored fellow-citizens. Politics is the snare and delusion of white men as well as black. Politics tickles the skin of the social order; but the disease lies deep in the internal organs. Social equity is based on justice; politics change on the opinion of the time. The black man's skin will be a mark of social inferiority so long as white men are conceited, ignorant, unjust, and prejudiced. You cannot legislate these qualities out of the white – you must steal them out by teaching, illustration, and example. No man ever came into the world with so grand an opportunity as the American negro. He is like new metal dug out of the mine. He stands on the threshold of history, with everything to learn and less to unlearn than any civilized man in the world. In his heart still ring the free sounds of the desert. In his mind he carries the traditions of Africa. The songs with which he charms American ears are refrains from the tropical deserts, from the inland seas and rivers of the dark continent . . . He has all the qualities that fit him to be a good Christian citizen of any country; he does not worry his soul to-day with the fear of next week or next year. He has feelings

and convictions, and he loves to show them. He sees no reason why he should hide them. The negro is the only graceful, musical, color-loving American. He is the only American who has written new songs and composed new music. He is the most spiritual of Americans, for he worships with his soul and not with his narrow mind... The negro is a new man, a free man, a spiritual man, a hearty man; and he can be a great man if he will avoid modeling himself on the whites.[43]

O'Reilly gave variations of this speech throughout 1885 and 1886. He ended one talk with a stirring declaration that thrilled his audience: 'every heart that beats for humanity beats for the oppressed.'[44]

There are elements of this speech that show O'Reilly was not entirely free from the tendency to mark certain characteristics as inherent to particular races but that is a minor issue. Many white civil rights activists framed their arguments in terms that were paternalistic or patronising towards blacks. What was different about O'Reilly was that he always encouraged black Americans to remain true to their history and culture. By so doing, he maintained, they could retain a sense of personal pride as well as a communal pride that would aid their quest to achieve true equality within society. In a later speech O'Reilly declared that his 'colored fellow-citizens' could achieve this goal by becoming 'their own protectors' and establishing 'a brotherhood of race': 'Make it so strong that its members will be proud of it – proud of living as colored Americans, and desirous of devoting their energy to the advancement of their people.'[45] He also stated his hope that 'the bonds of ignorance and prejudice' would be broken forever within 'the next twenty-five years'. As shall be seen later (chapter 14), O'Reilly became a hero to many black Americans during the 1880s. However, he would become bitterly frustrated by the widespread discrimination that permeated American culture and the resulting slow progress towards complete civil rights for black citizens of the United States.

Despite all O'Reilly's writings in support of civil rights and in opposition of prejudice he would play a different role in the long-running campaign to obtain voting rights for women. It was a role that would upset many of his friends and fellow reformers since O'Reilly was a vehement and consistent opponent of women's suffrage. Boston and the state of Massachusetts had a long history of providing leaders to various American reform movements and, in this spirit, the state had held the first National Women's Rights Convention during 1850. Massachusetts was home to some of the most influential campaigners for women's suffrage such as Abby Kelley and Susan B. Anthony and, in the years after the Civil War, the issue was never far from the public consciousness. This reform movement, however, provoked a strong reaction in Massachusetts and the state would delay the enfranchisement of women until 1920. In his resistance to this reform O'Reilly was very much in line with the views of the Catholic hierarchy. The traditional Catholic stance on this issue was that each sex had its distinct spheres of activity. The woman's duties revolved around her role as the centre of the family and as the mother of children. It was a system, in the words of one historian, 'designed by God, revealed by a Pauline interpretation of scripture and/or the natural law, re-enforced by biological differences, and supported by a historical tradition which proclaimed the political supremacy of man.'[46] This 'natural law' could be rent asunder by any attempts to alter the traditional roles of men and women.

Opposition to women's suffrage was not merely a Catholic phenomenon and it was a common occurrence to see preachers of various faiths working in concert to prevent the enfranchisement of women. They marshalled a variety of justifications to aid their cause, other than that of 'natural law'. A commonly stated view was that women were intellectually inferior to men and so it was futile to provide them with a vote. As the future Bishop of Fall River, German-born William Stang, pointed out on more than one occasion, 'smartness is not becoming women.'[47] Others stated that they did not consider women as intellectual inferiors to men but argued instead that women were hamstrung by their supposedly capricious and irrational natures. Women, in this argument, would prove an unstable element in the political compound and could not be trusted with the ability to use the vote wisely. O'Reilly did not subscribe to the assertion that women were intellectually inferior to men but he was a firm believer that a woman's place as, to use the popular phrase of the time, 'queen of the household' would be destroyed by any grant of suffrage. This belief manifested itself in *The Pilot* on many occasions over the 1870s and into the 1880s. A lady, he once opined:

is simply the highest type of woman. She will be gentle and modest, mistress of temper and curiosity. She will be pure of heart, for the sweet memory of her mother, and for the sake of her own motherhood, and, therefore she will love religion for God's sake and the sake of poor humanity. She will know and honor her own place in the social order, as the divinely appointed moulder, teacher, and refiner of men and out of this beautiful and noble place she will not seek to move.[48]

The perfect lady, in other words, would provide an example to other women by knowing her place and keeping to it. Unlike the Irish, blacks, Jews, Native Americans, working classes and others who railed against the fact that they were not afforded full membership of society, women were supposed to remain content with their pre-assigned role.

Unsurprisingly, Archbishop Williams, *The Pilot*'s co-owner, was in full agreement with O'Reilly. Williams rarely gave press interviews but in 1885 he discussed women's suffrage with the *Boston Advertiser*. The archbishop did not address the arguments of those who sought to enfranchise women but, instead, declared that there was no popular mood among women in favour of voting rights. He suggested that the whole idea was being pushed forward by a noisy minority:

Not only is there no such movement among the women, but there has been no attempt by the Catholic Church in Boston towards organizing such a movement. There have been no efforts at persuasion in this direction either in private conversation or publicly from the pulpit to the whole congregation. I am sure there is no general movement among Catholic women towards voting. It has never been advised by the Church. In fact, I do not believe in the Church meddling with politics in any shape, and the Church leaves the question alone. But beyond this, theoretically I do not think that women ought to take part in politics; they can be much better employed.[49]

Williams was correct in saying that there were many women who opposed women's suffrage. This was especially true among Irish Catholics. However, their antagonism towards suffrage, as the historian Hasia Diner notes, was not merely a result of the Catholic Church's attitude to this reform. She lists many issues, such as involvement in trade unionism and attendance at public schools, in which Irish women ignored Church directives.[50] Irish women's opposition to suffrage was more a consequence of the economic and cultural divisions that separated immigrant women from the middle and upper class Protestants who dominated the pro-suffrage movement. Most female Irish immigrants were too busy trying to make a life in the United States. Those Irish women who were active trade unionists, for example, were far more upset by the vast economic disparities in the US rather than what they perceived as a misguided focus on inequality between the sexes. The gulf that separated many Irish women and the women's suffrage movement was further widened by a strong strain of anti-Catholic and anti-Irish prejudice that ran through the movement, and which gave the clear indication that some women were more suited to equality than others. It is unlikely that Williams or O'Reilly were interested in these complex reasons behind Irish women's hostility to suffrage. O'Reilly, in particular and as can be seen below, had very specific justifications for his aversion to women's participation in the political process. However, the archbishop and the newspaper editor would use the lack of enthusiasm displayed by Irish Catholic women towards this reform as a means with which to attack the concept of women's suffrage.

In 1886 O'Reilly made one of his rare forays into direct political action as part of an anti-suffrage lobby group. This group, headed by the transcendentalist Octavius Brooks Frothingham, was roused to action by pro-suffrage attempts to put a suffrage motion before the Massachusetts state legislature. Frothingham organised a group of journalists, politicians and religious figures to compose a pamphlet which outlined their position under the succinct title *Woman Suffrage – Unnatural and Inexpedient*.[51] O'Reilly contributed the following:

> For the sake of men and women, we ought to ask the legislature to refuse the woman suffrage motion. Women deceive themselves in thinking that they can cure the evils of society by the ballot. The evils are spiritual and social: the ballot is only intellectual and political. All men's political issues are based on compromise. Political movements, parties, aims, are not, and cannot be, ideal or ultimate. The only ultimate ideal in society, as it is to-day, is the infallible 'Right' and 'Wrong' of good women. Their souls are at the judgment, when men can only use their minds. To compel women to vote would be to

reduce the whole human race to the secondary or intellectual level of the male half. The uncompromising spiritual sight and sense of the female half is the reservoir of morality and equity. To compel women to vote is to excite the brutal in men, and to engender disregard for law. Women cannot enforce an ideal equity, when they have enacted it. The physical weakness of woman is her strength when it appeals to the spirit of man; but let it attempt to control or obstruct his physical or intellectual movement, he will push it aside or trample on it.

Ideal statutes openly disregarded is barbarism and anarchy – the rule of the stronger appetite. It would be no more deplorable to see an angel harnessed to a machine than to see a woman voting politically, giving up her divine intuition for a vulgar material compromise. It is not fair to let women make laws they cannot enforce. They could set the world by the ears, and leave the men to fight it out. Political excitements will injure their health, and interfere with their family duties. Natural law makes them weaker than men: they ought not to assume an equal strength, for the outcome of failure is inevitable.

The logic of O'Reilly's contribution, if carried to its end, is chilling. It is clear from his writings on many topics that O'Reilly believed civilisation was ultimately underpinned by force; that society was a fragile blend of competing interests, each of which were backed by men willing and able to fight for what they believed. 'Moral force', he stated, 'has always a threat in reserve' (as can be seen in later chapters he would warn the black population of the US as well as the Irish in Ireland that they might have to fight in order to defend their rights).[52] It was those competing interests that were the driving force of history and if the disparate groups that formed the social order failed to compromise then violence was the inevitable result. According to O'Reilly, the delicate balance of society would be skewed by women's suffrage. His reasoning was that women are physically the weaker sex so it was worse than futile to give women the vote. They would never be able to protect their interests through force and would be trampled upon by men. The ensuing disregard for law would set a brutal and dangerous precedent that would spread anarchy throughout the land. 'A vote, like a law', he once declared, 'is no good unless there is an arm behind it; it cannot be enforced. This is a shameful truth, perhaps, but it is true.'[53]

The pamphlet was actually a calmer statement of his position than had previously appeared in some of his editorials. On one occasion he had written:

> Women's suffrage is an unjust, unreasonable unspiritual abnormality. It is hard, undigested, tasteless, devitalized position. It is a half-fledged unmusical Promethean abomination. It is a quack bolus to reduce masculinity even by the obliteration of femininity. It would quadruple the tongue-whangers at a convention, without increasing the minds capable of originating and operating legislation. It would declare war on the devil and all wickedness, and leave the citizens in shirts to do the fighting. It would injure women physically. Who shall say that at all times they are equal to the excitements of caucus rows, campaign slanders, briberies, inflammable speeches, torchlight parades, and balloting on stormy days?[54]

O'Reilly did temper his rant with the statement that 'Women ought to be fully guarded by law in all rights of property, labor, profession, etc.; but, roughly stated, the voting population ought to represent the fighting population.'[55] Given O'Reilly's belief that civilisation was underpinned by violence, he may well have rationalised his anti-suffrage stance in the belief that he was protecting women, both from the dangers of upsetting the balance of society and from what he viewed as the dishonest and morally corrupting nature of politics. O'Reilly had always kept *The Pilot* closely allied to the Democratic Party and was a firm supporter of representative democracy as the best form of government. Nevertheless, he retained a wariness of politicians of all political hues and of a political process that contributed to the social ills that he saw all around him. He often wrote of what he considered to be women's moral superiority over men, a superiority that would be sullied by political action. They were safer and more useful in the home, where they could mould the next generation of men.

This was a man who had argued against the education of women in 1876, complaining that 'Instead of learning how to sew, our girls must be sent to high school to learn astronomy. They imbibe a smattering of Greek, and a corresponding hatred of ironing and mending. They practice on a piano but never on a pie.'[56] The early to mid-1870s saw some of O'Reilly's most vicious attacks on women's suffrage but it may be that this overt sexism was lessened by the birth of his daughters. They all received an expensive education, including piano lessons, at the Elmhurst Academy of the Sacred Heart in Providence, Rhode Island.[57] He evidently supported their learning and his eldest daughter, Mary, would become a crusading journalist in her own right.[58] O'Reilly encouraged women journalists to enter male bastions such as the Press Club. He employed women writers such as Katherine Conway (also a keen opponent of women's suffrage) as an assistant editor and the poet Louise Imogen Guiney as a staff journalist during the 1880s.[59] In doing so, O'Reilly was working against the consensus within Boston newspapers at the time. One of the region's most successful newspapers, the *Boston Daily Globe*, had 'a definite bias' against women journalists despite the fact that its editor, Charles H. Taylor, was ostensibly a dedicated supporter of women's suffrage.[60] It was 'a bias widely shared in newspapers then and long after', according to that paper's historian Louis Martin Lyons.[61] O'Reilly also advanced the literary careers of Conway and Guiney (she would dedicate her first book of poetry to O'Reilly), saying on one occasion that 'at least in literature and art, bright minds cease to be classed as men and women, and are seen only in the rich neutral light of authorship.'[62]

However, O'Reilly did not waver in his opposition to women's suffrage. Although he would not have seen it this way, O'Reilly was a man who toiled on behalf of so many of the disenfranchised groups of the United States but who was willing to deprive women of the chance to live a full life. It was an attitude that confused and appalled many of his contemporary reformers. Reverend Thomas Wentworth Higginson, a friend of O'Reilly and a collaborator in many campaigns, later said of the newspaper editor: 'In some ways Boyle O'Reilly was not enough of a reformer for me. I never could quite forgive him for not being – like my friend and his associate, Col. [Charles H.] Taylor – a strong advocate of woman suffrage.'[63] In his defence of the Irish, blacks, Jews and others O'Reilly was continually vigilant for those commentators and politicians who sought to limit the freedom of achievement of particular groups or who resorted to ignorant racial stereotypes: 'violent' Irish, 'childlike' blacks, 'greedy' Jews, and so on. This vigilance was absent when it came to suffrage for women and O'Reilly repeatedly resorted to listing virtues and characteristics that he believed were inherent to women and which made them perfectly suited to their historical mission as 'queen of the household'. For O'Reilly they often seemed to be wholly defined by these supposed characteristics:

> We want no contest with women; they are higher, truer, nobler, smaller, meaner, more faithful, more frail, gentler, more envious, less philosophic, more merciful – oh, far more merciful and kind and lovable and good than men are. Those of them that are Catholics, are better Catholics than their husbands and sons; those who are Protestants are better Christians than theirs. Women have all the necessary qualities to make good men; but they must give their time and attention to it while the men are boys.[64]

O'Reilly's attitude would persist in the pages of *The Pilot* long into the future. James Jeffrey Roche, who joined the paper in 1883 and who later followed O'Reilly as editor of the paper, revered his friend and former boss. Roche followed his idol's line on many issues, including that of women's suffrage.[65] The above passage from O'Reilly he considered to be 'one of the best ever' responses to the supporters of women's suffrage. O'Reilly, Roche and others like them would remain unmoved by the arguments of women who sought to climb down from their pedestal and who refused to let such lists be the limits of their lives.

Workers' rights and the immense divide between rich and poor were the other great issues that appeared in the pages of *The Pilot* during O'Reilly's tenure. From the end of the American Civil War in 1865 to the beginning of the twentieth century the United States underwent a period of rapid industrial expansion. It was America's 'Gilded Age', a period when big business pushed itself to the forefront of American life and it was an era when industrialists and railway magnates such as George Hearst, John D. Rockefeller and Andrew Carnegie forged great corporations and huge profits. It was also a time when labour and employers engaged in a protracted struggle over the rights of workers. O'Reilly was not blind to these developments and he was gravely worried by their implications. He had experienced the dangerous working conditions aboard whaling ships and had seen the poor financial rewards given to the sailors who served on them. This pattern, he believed, was being replicated throughout US industry and in 1872 he wrote: 'Never before in this country has the unnatural gulf between labor and capital been so wide as at present'.[66]

Throughout its earlier existence *The Pilot* had had an ambivalent, often antagonistic, attitude towards unions but under O'Reilly's editorship the paper would become a strong proponent of workers' rights. However, O'Reilly would often equivocate on the role that unions and strikers should play in the promotion of those rights. During 1871 he contributed a piece to *The Pilot* in support of Pennsylvania miners who were then on strike: 'It must be remembered that the miners have interests to protect as well as the owners, and the only effective way for the worker to protect his interests is by association.'[67] Two years later he reversed this position and warned that any worker who joined a union 'throws away the great gift of individuality which God has given to him.'[68] He was dubious about the efficacy of strikes, writing in the same editorial that 'The idea of working men protecting their interests by strikes is a blind and suicidal one.' In any protracted struggle between workers and employers, he believed, it was the employers who were destined to triumph. They could live on their accumulated wealth while the workers would soon be left destitute. That same year made such tidy assumptions less easy to maintain. The depression that hit the US in 1873 caused O'Reilly to modify his thoughts on this matter and he came to believe that his hostility to unions was untenable.

As the economic conditions in the US grew steadily worse O'Reilly became convinced that workers across the country, of all ethnic backgrounds, were being exploited by railroad companies, factory owners, mining companies and industrialists. According to O'Reilly it was employers, acting in concert to preserve their mutual interests, who were driving down the worker. They had used the ongoing economic crisis as pretext to cut wages to 'starvation levels.'[69] Therefore workers had every right to group together in furtherance of their own interests and to protect themselves from the owners and industrialists who employed them. One of his original reasons for opposing unions was that many of those organisations were secret societies and, since leaving the Fenians, O'Reilly had followed the Catholic Church's line on such organisations. Yet, as workers across the US saw their attempts to unionise quelled by intimidation from bosses and company owners, O'Reilly realised that many unions were being forced to operate secretly.

His changing attitude to strikes could be seen in April 1876 when hundreds of Irish workers in Newton, near Boston, began a strike against their pay and conditions. Each week the workers at the Newtown waterworks construction site saw two-thirds of their pay packet deducted by the contractor. This deduction was supposedly to pay for food and board but the workers were provided with 'the cheapest and coarsest fare, and lodgings in the rudest shanties'.[70] O'Reilly took up their cause, writing, 'No wonder the poor men should strike when ground by such rascally extortion. Herded like cattle and worked like slaves, the men have been driven to rebellion to save their manhood.' However, the legal advantage in such disputes lay with the bosses rather than the workers; the contractor, one Mr Moore, publicly stated that 'Not another Irishman will be employed on the Newton water-works while we control their construction.' Within a few days of the strike beginning he had arranged for the transportation from New York of 250 Italians as strike-breakers.

O'Reilly was angered by the use of strike-breakers although, in such cases, he laid the blame with the contractors rather than the workers who took the jobs of strikers.[71] In the above instance, the Italians who had replaced the Irish workers were to suffer just as badly as their Irish forerunners and so followed them on strike. In June 1876 *The Pilot* gleefully reported that Moore, the contractor, had lost his contract and that a new employer had taken control of the project; the striking labourers, 'most of them Irish' were back to work.[72] In O'Reilly's eyes this episode was a lesson on how a strike could be effective in righting a wrong. It also demonstrated how he could use his paper to publicise the cause of maltreated workers. Yet the victory of the workers at Newton was a rare occurrence in the United States at the time. By the mid-1870s strike-breaking was just one of the tactics that industrial companies employed against discontented employees. O'Reilly was dismayed by rail and mining companies who used hired militias against their workers. This had become common practice in labour disputes across the US. Pennsylvania, for example, had passed legislation in 1865 and 1866 that allowed companies to form private police forces. These 'Coal and Iron Police' were supposed to operate as guards for the mines but by the 1870s they were being engaged by the Philadelphia and Reading Railroad Company (this company also owned coal mines across Pennsylvania) as a paramilitary force against miners.

The anthracite coalfields of north-eastern Pennsylvania had been wracked by violence since the 1860s as workers protested against their low pay and extremely dangerous working conditions; in September 1869 a fire in the Avondale mine had killed over 100 hundred workers.[73] One manifestation of this unrest was a group called the Molly Maguires. They were comprised almost entirely of Irish Catholic miners but it was not a trade union. The Molly Maguires were a secret society that had sprung from the tradition of Irish agrarian secret societies such as the Whiteboys and Ribbonmen.[74] Those groups had routinely used violence against their enemies and, displaying a similar mode of operation, the Molly Maguires had been responsible for a number of assassinations of mining company officials over the previous years. In 1873 the Philadelphia and Reading Railroad Company hired the Pinkerton Detective Agency to combat the Molly Maguires. The Pinkerton Agency, founded by Scottish-born Allan Pinkerton, not only provided a detective service but it also supplied private militias to its clients. In Pennsylvania the Pinkertons would use undercover agents, especially James McParlan from Armagh, to infiltrate the Molly Maguires. Pinkerton agents on the ground were also, with Allan Pinkerton's blessing, supplying names of suspected Molly Maguires to vigilantes in the pay of the mining companies. Through this combination of infiltration and intimidation they were able, over the subsequent years, to bring a number of Molly Maguires to trial, facing charges of murder.

In 1877 O'Reilly offered an editorial defence of the Molly Maguires. The editor did not justify their actions but, perhaps remembering his own court martial in 1866, deplored the use of paid informers against the defendants. Following the hanging of ten leaders of the group in June of that year he argued that the real criminals were the mine owners: 'The Corporations of Pennsylvania first drove the miners into Molly Maguirism and murder, and then virtuously hounded them to the scaffold. The same Corporations have caused the present strikes, and have dragged down on themselves the fire of their burning wealth and the blood of many victims'.[75] Despite the fact that the trial of the Molly Maguires had been a shoddy affair and had probably led to numerous miscarriages of justice, O'Reilly was one of the few commentators to offer any defence of the condemned men. Press commentary, which mostly emanated from the point of view of 'corporate capital or American middle-class society',[76] was overwhelmingly hostile to the strikers and had applauded the executions of the Molly Maguires. The Molly Maguires, according to the historian Kevin Kenny, were 'also shunned and condemned by the clergy and hierarchy of the Catholic church to which most of them belonged.'[77]

O'Reilly maintained his attack on the mine and railroad owners over the rest of 1877, accusing large corporations of having 'large pockets but no souls'.[78] Only a month after the execution of the Molly Maguires, rail workers in West Virginia began a strike action against the decision of their employers, the Baltimore and Ohio Railroad Company, to cut their wages for a second time that year. Within days the strike had spread throughout the US, with more railroad workers and miners joining the action. It was the first national strike in American history and would last for a further six weeks before it was eventually supressed with great violence by a combination of government troops and private militias hired by mine and railroad companies. These militias, especially the Pinkertons, whom O'Reilly would later categorise as 'murderous thugs', were a regular target of *The Pilot*.[79] A year after the railway strike O'Reilly again defended the strikers from claims in other newspapers that they were a mere mob. 'Capital cannot totally disregard the rights of humanity and then hold itself blameless when humanity breaks the law,' he responded.[80]

By 1880 O'Reilly had reversed his earlier opposition to strikes. He now concluded that not only were strikes 'a necessity' but that 'When wisely managed their effect is almost invariably good.'[81] From this premise, O'Reilly became a supporter of the Knights of Labor, at that time the most prominent labour organisation in the US. O'Reilly's opinions on unions were replicated by the paper's labour correspondent, who wrote under the by-line of 'Phineas'. This correspondent claimed that 'As a result of the Knights of Labor's aggressive policies, labor can no longer be ignored'.[82] It is not certain who Phineas was but the reporter was brought into *The Pilot* by O'Reilly. Through the 1880s Phineas was usually more radical than O'Reilly in his or her support of unions and strike actions. On one occasion Phineas advised readers that the interests of labourers 'and the interests of the capitalistic class are antagonistic'.[83] This kind of language and analysis, which O'Reilly usually avoided, was a regular feature of the Phineas articles.

Having accepted the right of workers to strike, the editor increasingly turned his ire against the factory, mine and railroad owners. Men such as the railroad developer and speculator Jay Gould and Franklin B. Gowen, president of the Philadelphia and Reading Railroad Company, had been targets of O'Reilly since the late 1870s. He wrote that these men and others like them 'believe that nature has selected them to do the governing, while the only right of the common people is to be governed.'[84] O'Reilly concluded, although reluctantly, that the government had to intervene to combat the growing power of such industrialists and their dominance of the economic landscape. During 1879 he issued a rallying cry to his readers and dismissed commentators and politicians who claimed that any attempts to curtail the activities of large corporations would damage the economy: 'It would not interfere with the return of "good times" if the American people took advantage of their power and strangled a few monopolies'.[85] It was a theme he returned to repeatedly over the next decade, becoming more antagonistic towards the so-called 'robber barons' with each passing year:

> Well, paternalism is better than intolerable and irresponsible tyranny and there seems to be no other alternative. Paternalism supported by State power is better than Monopoly upheld by the private mercenaries whom Pinkerton lets out to the service of the money kings. Anything is better than the rapacity of the insolent highway robbers who control the total supply of a prime necessary of life, anything even anarchy.[86]

These were strong words from a man who genuinely believed in 'the least government for the people' (see below) but, as he judged it, the existence of fantastically wealthy individuals who held monopolistic power over vital industries and who maintained their supremacy through the use of hired militias such as the Pinkertons was a grave threat to democracy. These corporations, O'Reilly claimed, were practically private fiefdoms within the United States. They were damaging to the worker, customer and the political process and had to be broken up, even if that meant heavy state involvement in certain industries, such as the postal, telegraph and railroad services, as well as legislation to protect workers' rights.[87]

Aside from O'Reilly's belief in human rights and concern for the underprivileged his analysis of the conflict between labourers and industrialists was also influenced by socialism. Indeed, the historian Arthur Mann has written that O'Reilly's views on these matters were 'socialist in spirit and source'.[88] It is necessary, however, to examine what socialism meant to O'Reilly. As Francis G. McManamin has pointed out, O'Reilly was often kindly disposed even to those social reformers with whom, ultimately, he disagreed.[89] It is clear from his writings in *The Pilot* that, for

O'Reilly, any person who seriously examined society and its problems was worthy of respect and due consideration. When Karl Marx died in March 1883, O'Reilly praised the German for his efforts at reform. According to O'Reilly, Marx had shown that capitalism 'fattens on the misery of the poor'.[90] This conciliatory approach had its limits and O'Reilly remained implacably opposed to those who advocated violence as a means of remaking the world. One notable target was Johann Most, a German political activist and journalist, who had entered the US in 1882. Most had long supported violent action against political and economic targets and would continue to do so throughout his life. He was an extraordinarily controversial figure and O'Reilly joined in the general condemnation: 'The word "socialism" which ought to stand for the noblest philosophy, is a hissing and an abomination in the ears of men, because of such moral and intellectual monsters as Herr Most.'[91]

O'Reilly had much sympathy with the claims of socialist thinkers that selfish, materialistic and acquisitive behaviour among people were the products of a culture that encouraged such behaviour rather than an inherent feature of humanity. Socialism concerned itself, not only with the conditions in which people found themselves, but also with what they had the capacity to become. This led some theorists to create utopian visions of society as they believed it should be and it was a mode of thinking that attracted O'Reilly:

> So long as misery and poverty exist, so long will man speculate and devise for their removal. It is wiser to listen to the proposals even of dreamers than to try and put them down by brute force. There may be a grain of wheat hidden in the chaff of even the wildest theorists. There is only one thing that can stop them: the satisfaction and contentment of the people.[92]

Even so, O'Reilly had many reservations about socialism, especially concerning those thinkers who attacked religion. For example in 1883 he criticised Marx for ignoring the 'spiritual life in man and communities'.[93] Later that year he returned to the subject and explained:

> Socialism is the great problem of the present and the future: how to raise humanity to a higher and more equitable civilization. To this

world movement there is only one safe guide – the Catholic Church, the spiritual test, for the revolution must be spiritual as well as intellectual. Socialism is the hope of the People. How deep the crime of those who have made the world synonymous with Atheism and disorder. The shallow reasoners of Europe who have dissociated Socialism and Religion have committed an almost unpardonable sin. With the deepest equities underlying the social order, the Catholic Church must always be in the deepest sympathy.[94]

Socialism, as O'Reilly understood it, meant a more equal society and a higher level of protection for workers amid the laissez-faire ethos of the time. He recognised that this would necessitate some level of government involvement in labour disputes but, in general, O'Reilly was opposed to state intervention on any large scale unless it was absolutely unavoidable. Nor did he support any reformer who called for the abolition of private property or the forcible appropriation of land (see below).

Despite his positive mentions of socialism and his policy of reviewing works such as Edward Bellamy's *Looking Back*, a novel set in a socialist utopia, O'Reilly was wary of radical solutions to the problems he described. He was most caustic when attacking a target, especially some corrupt politician or greedy corporate figure, but was far less assured when it came to providing answers to the societal problems that he described. O'Reilly had, since his early years as editor, been an advocate of cooperative movements whereby workers would group together and take control of business and divide the profits among themselves. He advised, 'Instead of a strike let the dissatisfied workmen start a shop or a store of their own, and meet the masters on their own ground by becoming masters themselves.'[95] This was also a policy embraced by Terence Powderly, the Irish-American head of the Knights of Labor. Cooperation appealed to O'Reilly and many of the Knights 'precisely because it aimed to ameliorate specific labor problems such as low wages, insecure employment, and declining craft control.'[96] In one speech Powderly advised that 'a system of cooperation will eventually make every man his own master – every man his own employer; a system which will give the labourer, a fair proportion of the products of his toil.'[97] Although in 1880 the Knights would set up a fund to establish cooperatives they proved to be an ineffective proponent of the idea. The fund was hampered by divisions within the Knights and the opposition of its members to a compulsory tax that was designed to keep the cooperative fund alive. While there would be some successes over the next decade, many of the cooperatives which were established struggled to survive amid the poor economic climate of the time. Despite those problems, O'Reilly remained a consistent supporter of the cooperative movement in his paper.

One of the editor's clearest ideas was his advocacy of arbitration as a means of dealing with labour disputes. O'Reilly's proposal, which he had adopted in the 1870s, was that the government could provide an independent mechanism whereby workers and industrialists would meet and undergo a process of arbitration. This should be done, he argued, through 'a constitutional law'.[98] He believed that this would have the benefit of protecting the workers by affording them an opportunity to air their grievances before the law. Thereby it could save them from a prolonged struggle, such as a strike through which they would lose their only means of income. O'Reilly was willing to let the government legislate for a system of compulsory arbitration if corporations refused to involve themselves in the process. As an addendum to his arbitration idea O'Reilly urged the government to legislate to protect workers' wages: 'Mathematicians can tell us the point where strength ends and weakness begins in a beam; so should the legislators find out and fix the market point at which profits should cease and wages begin.'[99]

A less practical solution that O'Reilly offered to workers, especially Irish workers, was his support of the 'colonization' of the American countryside.[100] He encouraged Irish city dwellers to leave their urban surroundings and head west to begin a new life as farmers, believing that they would have a better quality of life and thus free themselves from the clutches of industrialists. O'Reilly was not a farmer, nor was he from a farming background, and like many of the supporters of western colonisation he idealised the lifestyle. This had been a strand within American Catholic thought throughout the nineteenth century, at least as far back as the Irish Emigrant Association in 1817. At the height of nativist prejudice during the 1850s Catholic clergy in Buffalo had examined plans for a colony in Nebraska. That scheme came to nothing but the possibility of Catholic settlements in the American midwest and west persisted as a topic of discussion in the subsequent decades.[101]

During O'Reilly's time as editor of *The Pilot,* John Ireland, the Kilkenny-born Archbishop of St Paul, Minnesota, founded the Irish Catholic Colonization Association of the United States.[102] That body, founded in 1879, was followed a year later by the publication of Bishop John Lancaster Spalding's *The Religious Mission of the Irish People,* which urged the Irish in the overcrowded cities to settle their own farms in the countryside. Only there, Spalding wrote, could they protect 'the sanctity of the family, preserve the purity of childhood, and promote the growth of religious character.'[103] Despite such exhortations the Irish in the cities almost totally ignored the activities of the Colonization Association. Although Archbishop Ireland established a few small settlements in Minnesota, the numbers of urban Irish involved in settlement schemes were pitifully small.[104] Farmers were likewise suffering as a result of the prolonged economic turbulence that followed the financial crisis of 1873 and it was evident to Irish immigrants that plans to settle colonies in the west were no panacea for the difficulties facing workers in the cities.

O'Reilly continued to expose corruption and the mistreatment of workers into the 1880s but he was becoming frustrated by the lack of progress in solving these issues or in closing the gap between rich and poor. He had always stressed his belief that the US, despite its flaws, was a far more equitable and dynamic nation than any which existed in Europe. By 1883, however, the editor was so disillusioned that he described a New World that was little different from the Old:

> The King, the noble, the aristocrat have yielded to the railway magnates, the great incorporated owners of mines and mills and factories, the speculating capitalists. The law of the monarch's will is substituted by the law of the bribed legislature. The people are the prey, ever the dazed workers in the valley, the voiceless ones. There is no change except in the masters.[105]

This sense of disillusionment seeped into O'Reilly's other writings and can be seen in his 1881 book of poetry *The Statues in the Block and Other Poems.* It is a volume that contains some of his angriest verse such as 'Prometheus – Christ' and 'From the Earth, A Cry'. That lengthy poem, which comes with an introduction detailing the violence that had afflicted various parts of the globe from 1870 to 1880, begins by asking 'Can the Earth have a voice?'[106] The poem then imagines the planet calling out to the oppressed masses that teem across its surface:

> Insects and vermin, ye, the starving and dangerous myriads,
> Listen to the murmur that grows and growls! Come from your mines
>   and mills,
> Pale-faced girls and women with ragged and hard-eyed children,
> Pour from your dens of toil and filth, out to the air of heaven –
> Breathe it deep, and hearken! A Cry from the cloud or beyond it,
> A cry to the toilers to rise, to be high as the highest that rules them,
> To own the earth in their lifetime and hand it down to their children!
> Emperors, stand to the bar! Chancellors, halt at the barracks!
> Landlords and Lawlords and Tradelords, the spectres you conjured
>   have risen –
> Communists, Socialists, Nihilists, Rent-rebels, Strikers, behold!
> They are the fruit of the seed you have sown – God has prospered
>   your planting. They come
> From the earth like the army of death. You have sowed the teeth of
>   the dragon!
> Hark to the bay of the leader! You shall hear the roar of the pack
> As sure as the stream goes seaward. The crust on the crater beneath you
> Shall crack and crumble and sink, with your laws and rules
> That breed the million to toil for the luxury of the ten –
> That grind the rent from the tiller's blood for drones to spend –
> That hold the teeming planet as a garden plot for a thousand –
> That draw the crowds to the cities from the healthful fields and
>   woods –
> That copulate with greed and beget disease and crime –
> That join these two and their offspring, till the world is filled with
>   fear,
> And falsehood wins from truth, and the vile and the cunning
>   succeed,
> And manhood and love are dwarfed, and virtue and friendship sick,
> And the law of Christ is a cloak for the corpse that stands for Justice!
> – As sure as the spirit of God is Truth, this Truth shall reign,
> And the trees and lowly brutes shall cease to be higher than men.
> God purifies slowly by peace, but urgently by fire.

O'Reilly's poetry lashed out at the same targets as his editorials but often in a more zealous manner. He also expanded on some of his more far-reaching proposals to improve society in *Moondyne*, a novel he dedicated 'to all those who are in prison for whatever cause.' It was serialised in *The Pilot* from November 1878 before being published as a book in 1879 (it was also published in Australia the next year).[107] Amid its often implausible plot, peopled with angelic heroes and pantomime villains, the novel contains serious criticism of the English prison system and the policy of transportation to the British colonies. As we have seen, it has clear elements of O'Reilly's own life story. While at least two of the characters in *Moondyne* are partly based on O'Reilly and his life, it is Mr Wyville who most closely resembles the Irishman. In the story, Wyville endures prison and transportation to Australia before escaping into the bush where he befriends local Aborigines. They bring the convict into their community and reveal to him the secret of a stupendously wealthy gold mine. With this knowledge Wyville remakes himself as a successful businessman and an influential campaigner for penal reform.

One scene from the book is particularly instructive. It involves Wyville discussing the ills of society with a group of London parliamentarians and public figures. One of these, Lord Somers, questions Wyville as to how poverty could be alleviated by any other means than the 'spread of charity and religion among the wealthy?'[108] Wyville answers:

> Ah, pardon me; I consider these things from another standpoint. Charity among the rich simply means the propriety of the poor being miserable – that poverty is unfortunate, but not wrong. But God never meant to send the majority of mankind into existence to exercise the charity and religion of the minority. He sent them all into the world to be happy and virtuous, if not equal; and men have generated their evils by their own blind and selfish rules.

Somers and his companions are dismayed by Wyville's statement and one of them interrupts: 'Surely, Mr. Wyville, you do not believe in the American absurdity that men are born equal?'[109] Wyville explains his position by saying: 'I do not think the Americans mean that in your sense. I do believe that every generation of men should have a fair start, and let the best lives win.'

The conversation continues with Wyville stating that if he had the power to reshape society he would start 'By burning all the law-books', followed 'By burning the title-deeds'.[110] Lord Somers then asks, 'Could society exist without the law?' to which Wyville replies, 'Not just yet; but it could have a better existence with better laws. At present the laws of civilization, especially in England, are based on and framed by property – a depraved and unjust foundation. Human law should be founded on God's law and human right, and not on the narrow interests of land and gold.'[111] The effect of this, Wyville explains, would be 'To raise all men above insecurity, which is the hot-bed of lawlessness.' He then proposes a redistribution of land whereby no would be allowed to 'hold unproductive land while a single man is hungry . . . till every acre of land in England is teeming with food.' Wyville, though, does not advocate 'that the estates of wealthy men be wrested from them' by force. 'No inherited nor purchased land should be taken for the benefit of the people without giving a fair recompense to the aristocrat,' he assures his listeners. For urban dwellers he proposes 'a system of technical education, which would enable the town and city populations to manufacture to advantage the produce of the fields and mines.'

Even with those changes, Wyville continues, humanity would be only at the beginning of its journey: 'At present, the level of society is insecurity, poverty, misery; from which spring fear, ignorance, disease, and crime. Under a better system, the lowest point would be at least sufficiency, enough for all the human beings in the country; and this, in time, would eradicate much of the evil, perhaps most of it.'[112] Wyville's vision was hardly a call to arms. He judged that it would take thousands of years for these changes to come into effect:

> no man who sees the truth, however distant, can conscientiously go on as if it were not there. Thousands of years are vast periods; but the love of human liberty and happiness shall reach out and cling to the eternal. Let every man who believes, faithfully do his share, sow the seed that he has received, and in God's time the glorious harvest will come of a pure and truthful people, whose aristocrats shall be elevated by intelligence and virtue, and the love of humanity, and not by accident of birth and superiority in vice and pride.[113]

Wyville's speech has many similarities with aspects of O'Reilly's thought on labour and social issues as he described them in *The Pilot*, especially in regard to the suggestion that all land should be put to productive use by smallholders. Also, in his involvement with the Irish Land league and its American subsidiary O'Reilly would argue for a similar approach to land redistribution (see chapter 13). However, the social criticism in *Moondyne* is directed at the prison systems of England and Australia. The United States plays no part in the novel and O'Reilly's apparent wariness in proposing solutions to the social ills afflicting America led Arthur Mann to the conclusion that O'Reilly was 'uncompromisingly radical as regards England, but moderate with respect to the United States.'[114]

Perhaps O'Reilly would not have disagreed with that description. His personality was that of a natural mediator whose instinct, at least with regard to workers' rights and economic issues, was towards piecemeal progress. Throughout O'Reilly's editorship of *The Pilot* he regularly lauded himself and the paper's readers as being 'calm', 'rational' and 'respectable'. Whereas Karl Marx had castigated those who had sought only to interpret the world rather than to change it, O'Reilly confined his role to that of critic, stubbornly exposing the tribulations afflicting society. 'The first duty of the social reformer,' he once wrote 'is to teach – not to do.'[115] This trait within O'Reilly's character was noted by a contemporary and friend of the Irishman, an editor of the *Atlantic Monthly*, George Parson Lathrop. He suggested that O'Reilly sometimes used writing (Wyville's speech in *Moondyne*, for example) as a means of testing ideas and of highlighting inequalities rather than as definite proposals for social change:

> He was a revolutionist always: but he was much more than that. He was reconstructive, also. I have never known anyone who showed such deep and searching and wide interest in the welfare, comfort and progress of the whole human race. He had an almost infinite compassion for the sufferings of mankind, and an unlimited hope for the alleviation of those sufferings. Sometimes, however, he uttered terrible theories looking towards the destruction of human society as it now exists. These theories were only a sort of rendrock, intended merely to blow up the granite wall of inert prejudice, and make an opening for broader paths of progress and enlightenment; but they caused him to be misunderstood.[116]

Eric Foner, who has analysed politics and ideology in the US during O'Reilly's time, has also commented on the Irishman's cautious attitude to social change.[117] In regard to labour issues Foner has compared O'Reilly unfavourably with Patrick Ford, the only Irish newspaper editor then working in America who could match O'Reilly's potent mix of fame, influence and talent. Ford, born in Galway during 1837, was a veteran of the American Civil War and formerly had been a printer's devil in William Lloyd Garrison's abolitionist newspaper *The Liberator*. After the Civil War Ford returned to journalism and in 1870 was the founding editor of the New York-based *Irish World and Industrial Liberator* (usually referred to as simply the *Irish World*). Like O'Reilly, Ford was a consistent opponent of racism as well as a proponent of workers' rights. The editor of the *Irish World*, however, was more radical than O'Reilly in his analysis of the problems facing workers in the United States and Ford's paper would often criticise the Catholic Church's stance on labour issues as well as that of the Democratic Party. Whereas O'Reilly had criticised the Fenians out of his frustration at their factionalism and because of some personal unease with secret societies, Ford criticised the Fenians for having no agenda of social change other than insurrection. 'Fenianism saw only a green flag', he once complained and it was this attitude that was repeated in the *Irish World*.[118] Indeed, as Foner points out, when it came to writing about the struggles between workers and industrialists the *Irish World* made *The Pilot* seem tame by comparison.[119]

O'Reilly's Catholicism played a role in how he perceived labour issues. He looked to the Catholic Church for moral guidance but there were divisions within the hierarchy on how best to protect workers' rights. Some bishops effectively wanted to do nothing. The Tipperary-born Archbishop of Philadelphia, Patrick J. Ryan, offered his solution to 'the social question' at the Third Plenary Council of Baltimore in 1884: 'Christian kindness to the poor and the working men and women and the inculcation of patience in poverty, after the example of Our Lord, are the best securities against the communism and anarchy that seem to threaten society.'[120] Ryan's ascription of nobility to poverty and his support of the status quo were commonly stated positions within the clergy. In this view, social inequalities were divinely ordained and charity rather than reform were the best means with which to support the poor. Such opinions negated any attempts at analysing poverty and inequality. It can be seen from O'Reilly's writings in *Moondyne* and in *The Pilot* that he opposed this strand of Church thinking. O'Reilly believed that charity without any accompanying attempts to alleviate the causes of poverty was useless, serving merely to salve the conscience of the donor while leaving the recipient dependent on help and incapable of advancement.

O'Reilly's sentiments were more in tune with those of Cardinal James Gibbons who travelled to the Vatican in 1887 to successfully defend the Knights of Labor from a possible papal censure:

> That there exist among us, as in all other countries of the world, grave and threatening social evils, public injustices which call for strong resistance and legal remedy, is a fact which no one dares to deny ... the heartless avarice which, through greed of gain, pitilessly grinds not only the men, but even the women and children in various employments, make it clear to all who love humanity and justice that it is not only the right of the laboring classes to protect themselves, but the duty of the whole people to aid them in finding a remedy against the dangers with which both civilization and social order are menaced by avarice, oppression and corruption.[121]

O'Reilly was an admirer of Gibbons and the Cardinal's sentiments were regularly echoed by *The Pilot*.[122] It has sometimes been claimed that O'Reilly's cautiousness was entirely a result of his Catholicism but, while religion is part of the explanation, he did not blindly follow wherever the hierarchy led. Nor was the Catholic Church in nineteenth-century America a monolithic organisation whose clergy and congregation all marched in step.[123] On issues such as unions and strike actions O'Reilly was willing to ally himself with the more reform-minded elements in the Church. In a similar vein the editor criticised commentators who invoked the secular religion of 'the survival of the fittest' to explain the inequities afflicting society as natural, inevitable and in no need of further analysis. Proponents of this idea, such as the English sociologist Herbert Spencer, took theories that Charles Darwin had applied only to the natural world and used them to develop the principle that human societies had always been, and should always be, based on 'the survival of the fittest'. Such beliefs, which would later be termed Social Darwinism, were utterly contradictory to what O'Reilly advocated in *The Pilot*.[124] The surest way of making communists, he once warned, was for industrialists and bankers to act in concert 'to grind the working men down to the starvation point and then assume a patronizing air of superiority.'[125]

O'Reilly's Irish background is another explanation that has been invoked for his positions on social reform. As will be seen in chapter 13, O'Reilly often stressed the need for unity within the Irish-American population. This fact was used by Thomas N. Brown, in an influential 1950s article on Irish-American nationalism, to argue that O'Reilly's 'limitations as a liberal reformer derived from his role as immigrant leader.'[126] He contended that O'Reilly believed that 'the advance of Irish-America depended upon the solidarity of its members and the impregnability of its fortress.'[127] Brown was correct in this part of his analysis, although O'Reilly's dreams of Irish-American unity never prevented him from criticising those, such as the Fenians, with whom he disagreed. However, Brown then stated: 'If pursuit of reform divided the immigrant community, the effort was abandoned and the divisions were denied.'[128] That statement, while it has validity with regard to O'Reilly's stance on land reform in Ireland (see chapter 13), does not hold true as a general assessment of O'Reilly the reformer. We have seen how he maintained his reforming impulse throughout the 1870s and 1880s, even when the Catholic Church was divided over strikes and other social matters. Civil rights for blacks, for instance, was not exactly a goal that found much support among the Irish in America and O'Reilly became more strident on the subject as the 1880s progressed.

There are other reasons why he was relatively restrained when advocating solutions to social problems. O'Reilly strongly believed in individual rights as being the foundation stone of democracy and far preferable to the potentially overweening power of government. He once said that 'When men talk about rights they must be willing to go to the foundation. The bottom right is the right of a man, not of a state.'[129] His experiences of Ireland, in which there was lots of government but little democracy, played a part in the development of his thought on this issue. Also, being a former convict, O'Reilly knew what it felt like to lose one's rights as a citizen. This commitment to individual rights was expanded upon by O'Reilly in The Pilot when he described his political philosophy as 'Jeffersonian Democracy.'[130] The editor went on to explain what this meant to him:

Democracy means to use the least government for the people, instead of more or most.

It means that every atom of paternal power not needed for the safety of the Union and the intercourse of the population should be taken from the Federal Government and kept and guarded by the States and the people.

It means the spreading and preserving of doubt, distrust, and dislike of all sumptuary and impertinent laws.

It means that law shall only be drawn at disorder, and that all affairs that can be managed without disorder should be managed without law.

It means that all laws not called for by public disorder are an offense, a nuisance, and a danger.

It means watchfulness against Federal legislation for such State questions as education, temperance, irrigation, and all other questions that may arise and are sure to arise in the future.

It means the teaching of absolute trust in the people of the States to understand and provide for their own interests.

It means home rule in every community right through our system, from the township up to the State Legislature; and above that, utter loyalty to the Union.

It means antagonism to all men, classes and parties that throw distrust and discredit on the working or common people, and who insinuate or declare that there is a higher, nobler, or safer patriotism among the wealthy and more book-learned classes than the common people possess or appreciate.

It means that Democratic principles must be followed by individual citizens as well as by the aggregated party, that they must oppose the petty boss in their own caucuses, and the arrogant majority in their own town, when these attempt to coerce the rights of the masses or change the self-governing principle of the free town.

That was how O'Reilly saw himself but he was not always rigid in his thought and was often willing to change his mind when the facts changed. There are consistent values in his thinking on social issues while at *The Pilot*: his passionate advocacy of black civil rights; his opposition to women's suffrage; his belief that the rights of workers were not adequately protected; his wariness of radical solutions to societal problems; and an attendant distrust of political and economic ideologies that claimed their own correctness at the exclusion of all others. Although an opponent of what would now be called 'Big Government' O'Reilly spent his time at *The Pilot* combatting the laissez-faire philosophies that allowed industrialists to both lord it over their workers and to threaten American democracy through their incredible economic power. Many of his solutions to these problems, such as arbitration and legislation to protect wages, involved government intervention. *The Pilot* under O'Reilly's editorship had become an extension of his personality and a vehicle for his beliefs and social concerns. Of course, the issues of civil rights, discrimination, women's suffrage and workers' rights did not comprise all of the paper's reportage. It remained primarily an Irish Catholic paper and, as we shall see throughout later chapters, O'Reilly never forgot Ireland and the Irish.

The Queen's Prisoners and the King's Men

In 1875 and 1876 the Fenians and Western Australia would again play a major part in O'Reilly's life. The Australian colony was still the location for Fenian convicts and the newspaper editor would contribute to an audacious scheme to free these prisoners. The roots of this rescue attempt went back to 1866 when the wives of some of the convicts had begun a campaign for the relief of the prisoners' families. Over the following years this had morphed into a campaign for the release of the prisoners, culminating in the launch of an amnesty committee and then, in 1869, the Amnesty Association with Isaac Butt as president. This organisation stirred huge support across Ireland although the Catholic hierarchy refused to endorse the campaign. Despite the lack of Church support the Association achieved much success and in May 1869 the British government released thirty-four of the prisoners in Western Australia. Remarkably, this decision was made after O'Reilly had escaped aboard the *Gazelle*. However, had he still been a convict, O'Reilly would not have benefited from this amnesty; the military Fenians were explicitly excluded and were to serve the remainder of their sentences. This point was reinforced in 1870 when William Ewart Gladstone's government provided a general amnesty to the civilian Fenians arrested in the mid-1860s. He too overlooked the military Fenians, eleven of whom remained in Western Australia. However, Gladstone's amnesty for the civilian Fenians had conditions, the most important of which was the stipulation that required the amnestied prisoners to spend the remainder of their sentences outside of Ireland or Britain.[1]

The United States was the primary destination for these exiled Fenians and the first group arrived in America aboard the passenger liner *Cuba* in January 1871. This group included Jeremiah O'Donovan Rossa, John McClure, Charles Underwood O'Connell, Harry Mulleda and O'Reilly's former comrade John Devoy. The 'Cuba Five', as they were called in the press, were the object of a tug of war between the various Fenian factions. Much to the disappointment of the five men, they were witness to the same divisions which had so upset O'Reilly in 1870. Shortly after their arrival in New York they composed a letter to 'The Gentlemen of the Several Deputations for Receiving the Irish Exiles', in which they expressed their frustration with disunity among the Fenians.[2] This did nothing to heal those divisions and O'Reilly wrote to Devoy to warn the new arrival that he would be better off to leave the Fenians. A few months later he advised Devoy to 'keep out of these Irish or American political "rings". Work for yourself. It pays in the end.'[3] Devoy was not deterred by O'Reilly's disillusionment with Irish revolutionary groups and he made efforts to reunite the opposing factions within America. This proved a fruitless endeavour and so Devoy left the Brotherhood and joined the rival revolutionary group Clan na Gael.

Devoy, of course, needed some form of employment and, like O'Reilly, he became a journalist. For the next decade he would work with the *New York Herald*, eventually rising to the position of foreign editor. Aside from his journalistic work Devoy remained an active revolutionary and, in 1871, he became preoccupied with freeing the remaining military Fenians in Western Australia. As he later put it, 'Most of the evidence upon which the soldiers were convicted related to meetings with me, and I therefore felt that I, more than any man then living, ought to do my utmost for these Fenian soldiers.'[4] Devoy continually pressed the idea with colleagues in Clan na Gael but it was not until the Clan's 1874 convention in Baltimore that he obtained formal support. During that convention a resolution was passed in support of rescuing the Fenians and of forming a plan to do so.[5] Control of this mission was given to Devoy.[6]

It was a wise decision by the Clan leadership. As T. W. Moody has written, Devoy had developed into the 'most clear-headed, realistic, implacable, and incorruptible'[7] of all the leaders of Clan na Gael or the Fenians. Devoy began planning the rescue with his characteristic thoughtfulness and sought guidance from a number of former convicts, men who had been aboard the *Hougoumont* and had since been amnestied, such as Thomas Fennell and John Kenneally.[8] But it was John Boyle O'Reilly, a man who had been self-amnestied, who would prove to be Devoy's most important adviser. Devoy's decision to involve O'Reilly in discussing the rescue mission would later be a source of anger to some members of the Boston branch of Clan na Gael. They were still wary of O'Reilly following his departure from the Clan in 1870 and when Devoy met with the Boston branch during late January 1875 he quickly ascertained that 'the less I said about calling on O'Reilly the better'.[9] Sensibly, Devoy ignored their distrust of O'Reilly and, on 1 February, he met with his former Fenian comrade at the offices of *The Pilot*.

Devoy brought O'Reilly up to date on the discussions within Clan na Gael and outlined the plan that had been agreed whereby the group would purchase a ship, fill it with a team of armed men, travel with it to Western Australia, attack Fremantle Prison, save the convicts – and sail away to glory. Devoy was justifiably dubious of this plan and O'Reilly concurred. A month earlier O'Reilly had written to Devoy, 'The only way to do your work clean, sure and well is by a New Bedford whaler. The more I think of it, the easier it does appear to me.'[10] O'Reilly also pressed upon Devoy the vital need for secrecy. 'Not half a dozen men should know' the means by which the rescue was to proceed. This was another piece of common ground between the two men: memories of their arrests in February 1866 and the British infiltration of the Fenians before and during the invasions of Canada testified to the damage that informers could pose.

A few days after that first meeting, Devoy again met O'Reilly, this time in the company of another former convict aboard the *Hougoumont* – Denis Cashman. Following the amnesty given to the civilian Fenians in 1869, Cashman had made his way to the US and O'Reilly had welcomed his friend, an able writer, onto the staff of *The Pilot*. The three men spent hours discussing the intricacies of a plan involving a whaling ship. It was during these meetings that the final outline of the rescue emerged. But O'Reilly had something more than advice to offer Devoy: he had a contact in the whaling community. After they had agreed a strategy, O'Reilly gave Devoy a letter of introduction to the chief of the night police force in New Bedford.[11] This police chief happened to be Henry Hathaway, the former third mate of the *Gazelle* and the man who had saved O'Reilly's life during the whale hunt.[12] Hathaway had retired from seafaring a few years previously and had become a respected figure in New Bedford. He certainly impressed Devoy, who travelled to meet with Hathaway in early February: 'When I gave him O'R[eilly']'s note I saw a good effect produced at once . . . Splendid physique; handsome, honest face; quite English-looking. Wears only side-whiskers; very reserved in manner; speaks low and slowly, but every word fits. Never without a cigar in his mouth.'[13]

Devoy stayed in New Bedford for the next few weeks and had frequent discussions with Hathaway, in which he brought the police chief fully into his confidence. Hathaway provided his expertise to the scheme and by the middle of February Devoy was ready to set the plan into action. This revised plan was to purchase or hire a whaling ship that would hunt for whales on its way to Western Australia. Doing this would have a number of benefits: it would hide the fact that the ship was involved in anything other than whaling; it would make it far easier to find an experienced captain and crew; and it offered the possibility that, if enough whales were caught, the expedition could cover all its costs. The ship was only one part of Devoy and Clan na Gael's grand strategy. While the whaler made its way to Australia, the Clan would send agents to Fremantle with the intention that they would make contact with the prisoners and arrange a rendezvous point. That month Devoy wrote to a colleague in Clan na Gael, James Reynolds: 'We want $15,000 to start with, but can recover nearly all, and in fact all, if the ship whales enough. She could then either be kept and sent whaling again to raise a fund or sold off.'[14] Hathaway also assisted Devoy in finding a captain to lead the proposed voyage. The man they found was George Anthony, a greatly experienced captain whom Hathaway assured Devoy could be relied upon to complete the mission.[15]

Devoy's next task was to find a ship for Anthony to captain. While Devoy searched New Bedford, O'Reilly searched the docks in Boston. Devoy was the more successful of the two men and located a 202-ton whaling barque called *Catalpa*, which he purchased for $5,250 of Clan na Gael's money (Devoy had also received a loan from a New Bedford businessman named John T. Richardson).[16] News of the acquisition worried O'Reilly since he had wanted to examine any potential purchase before the money was paid. Yet he was extremely busy with *The Pilot* and had not been able to devote much time to finding a suitable ship. 'A hundred unexpected things have prevented me from going to see you', he apologised to Devoy.[17] O'Reilly had, however, obtained the services of another friend of his, an officer in the US navy named Tobin. He told Tobin that the *Catalpa* was to be used as a merchant ship and asked that the officer inspect the vessel's seaworthiness. On 15 March O'Reilly and Tobin travelled to New Bedford and met with Devoy aboard Clan na Gael's newest acquisition. Tobin spent hours examining the ship with a nervous Devoy in tow. Fortunately, Tobin was impressed with what he saw and pronounced that the ship was fit to sail anywhere. He reckoned the *Catalpa* to have a potential value of $10,000, almost twice what it had cost Devoy. The vessel's only flaw, he advised, was that it was a little slow.[18]

Captain Anthony took control of the ship from that point and organised the necessary equipment as well as a crew. At that stage, the captain was the only member of the crew to know the real purpose of the voyage. The rest of his men would not be informed until the rescue was in progress. When Anthony was satisfied that the ship was ready, the *Catalpa* left New Bedford on 29 April 1875. Since the *Catalpa* was to operate as a normal whaling ship it would spend much of its time hunting and was not due to arrive at Western Australia until April 1876. As planned, two Clan na Gael agents, John J. Breslin and Thomas Desmond, arrived at Fremantle a few months in advance of the *Catalpa*.[19] They travelled under the aliases of Collins and Johnson and posed as businessman assessing potential opportunities in Western Australia.[20] Breslin had some previous experience of prison breaks, having played the key part in the breakout of James Stephens from Richmond Bridewell in November 1865. His role at Fremantle was more subtle. Along with Desmond he made contact with the prisoners to prepare them for the escape.

At this time, of the eleven military Fenians who had been refused an amnesty by Gladstone, eight remained in the locality of Fremantle. Two others, John Shine and James McCoy, were on ticket-of-leave and far from the town. One of the convicts had died; Patrick Keating, who had welcomed O'Reilly aboard the *Hougoumont*, had succumbed to illness during January 1874.[21] Of the eight Fremantle prisoners, six would take part in the escape: Martin Hogan, Robert Cranston, Thomas Hassett, James Wilson, Michael Harrington and Thomas Darragh (the last two had been court martialled alongside O'Reilly during June and July 1866). Two of the Fenians, Thomas Delaney and James Keilley, were not to be included. Delaney had been sentenced, in June 1875, to twelve months' hard labour and was under constant guard. There was no way he could be told of what was happening without compromising the whole strategy. Keilley's situation was somewhat different. The other prisoners had suspicions that he had offered the police information on Fenian comrades during the arrests of 1866. Whether he had or not is unknown, but it was decided by Breslin and the others to leave Keilley out of the escape. He would die in 1918, having lived the rest of his life in Western Australia where he was known to locals as 'the man the Fenians left behind'.[22]

This rescue plan was one of the few Fenian or Clan na Gael operations that was not infiltrated by British spies. Even so, intelligence had reached the British government that there might be an attempt to liberate the Fenians at Fremantle. On 13 April 1876 the Secretary of State for the Colonies, the Earl of Carnarvon, contacted the governor of Western Australia about these reports. The governor, William H. Robinson, guaranteed Carnarvon that there was no cause for alarm: 'I think I may assure your Lordship that any scheme of the nature referred to which may possibly be set on foot, will end in total failure.'[23] Events would soon expose Robinson's assurances as worthless. The *Catalpa* had docked at Bunbury on 28 March, from where Captain Anthony had contacted Breslin via a prearranged telegram code. Anthony had then travelled to Fremantle and met with Breslin and Desmond. Together they selected the spot where the escapees would meet the ship, a place called Rockingham Beach, about 20 miles south of Fremantle on the road to Bunbury. The escape began only a few days after Robinson's telegram when, on Monday 17 April, the six convicts slipped away from their work camps. By the next morning all six had met with Breslin and were aboard a rowing boat en route to the *Catalpa*.[24]

Their boat narrowly avoided a police vessel before making its rendezvous with the *Catalpa* on Tuesday afternoon. Unluckily, that morning as Breslin and the others sailed form Rockingham Beach they had been spotted by a woodcutter named John Bell. He rushed to Fremantle and raised the alarm.[25] That same night the governor of Western Australia ordered an armed steamship, the *Georgette*, to pursue the *Catalpa*. The *Georgette* was a far faster vessel than the whaling ship and by 8 a.m. on Wednesday 19 April it had moved alongside its target. A report in *The Pilot* described what happened next:

> The Georgette came up with the Catalpa and fired a shot across her bows, but she would not stop. Coming within hailing distance, a

parley commenced. Superintendent Stone [commander of the
Georgette] demanded in the name of the Government of Western
Australia that 'there are six escaped convicts on board your vessel,
and if you don't give them up you must take the consequences'.

Captain Anthony: "I have no prisoners on board".

Superintendent Stone: "You have. I now see three of them on
deck".

Captain Anthony: "I have no prisoners; all are my seamen
belonging to my ship."

Superintendent Stone: "I will give you fifteen minutes to consider
my request."

After that interval Superintendent Stone again demanded the
convicts, and the captain ruled he had none on board.

Superintendent Stone (pointing to a gun and men ready to fire)
said that "if you do not I will fire into and sink you".

Captain Anthony: "I am on the high seas and that flag (pointing
to the stars and stripes) protects me."[26]

John Breslin also recalled that the captain added the warning that 'if you
fire on this ship you fire on the American flag'.[27] This confrontation took
place in international waters and, when Captain Anthony refused to accede
to Stone's demand, it became apparent that the superintendent was not
willing to risk an international incident. This left him with no option but
to order the *Georgette* back to Fremantle. The prisoners were free.

The *Catalpa* returned to New Bedford on the afternoon of 24 August
1876 after a stop at New York a few days earlier. The ship had arrived at
New York amid great jubilation and those scenes were repeated at New
Bedford. Thousands of people crowded the wharves and when the ship
docked 'men and women swarmed aboard and carried away everything
which was not too large for souvenirs'.[28] On the following day there was a
public reception to honour the *Catalpa*'s crew. O'Reilly was the keynote
speaker. The event was opened by Dr Stephen W. Hayes who spoke of his
'gratitude that the political prisoners were now in the land of the free,
where the flag which protected them on the Catalpa would continue to
protect them as long as it waved.'[29] This was the theme that O'Reilly would
carry through his speech. Zephania Pease, who wrote a book on the
Catalpa in the 1890s, described O'Reilly's address on this occasion 'as one

of his most eloquent efforts'. Pease regretted that the entire speech had not been preserved, writing that 'The summaries which were printed in the newspapers [even *The Pilot* only printed an abridged account] do him very inadequate justice.'

From what is left of O'Reilly's speech, we can see that it was a panegyric, not only to the rescuers and the rescued but also to the United States, their new home. He spoke at length about New Bedford and its sailors and the debt of gratitude that he owed to men such as David Gifford and Henry Hathaway of the *Gazelle*: 'Seven years of liberty, wife, children, and a happy home in a free country were his debt of gratitude, and when the close of his sentence came, in 1886, his debt to New Bedford might be grown too heavy to bear.'[30] Referring to Captain Anthony, O'Reilly said:

> The self-sacrifice and unfailing devotion of him who had taken his life in his hand and beached his whaleboat on the penal colony, defying its fearful laws, defying the gallows and the chain-gang, in order to keep faith with the men who had placed their trust in him – this is almost beyond belief in our selfish and commonplace time.

O'Reilly then disputed the claims of the British government that the rescue was an act of lawlessness:

> If these men were criminals, the rescue would be criminal. But they were political offenders against England, not against law, or order, or religion. They had lain in prison for ten years, with millions of their countrymen asking their release, imploring England, against their will to beg, to set these men at liberty. Had England done so it would have partially disarmed Ireland. A generous act by England would be reciprocated instantly by millions of the warmest hearts in the world. But she was blind, as of old; blind and arrogant and cruel. She would not release the men; she scorned to give Ireland an answer.

This cruelty had marked O'Reilly's own life and he described some of his experiences as a convict. Then he spoke of the links between Ireland and the United States and, finally, he pointed at the American flag which hung over the speaker's podium and declared before his audience:

It was in obedience to this supreme law that Captain Anthony rescued the prisoners, and pointed his finger at the Stars and Stripes, when the English commander threatened to fire on his ship. The Irishman, who could forget what the Stars and Stripes have done for his countrymen, deserves that in time of need that flag shall forget him.

O'Reilly's speech was answered by a rapturous applause. He had come to New Bedford not only to praise Anthony but to remind his listeners that the captain had risked and sacrificed so much in the pursuit of an Irish cause. O'Reilly had brilliantly achieved that goal. Amid the excitement, members of the crowd rushed forward pledging donations to the captain. That night 'a considerable sum of money was contributed' and it was the beginning of a successful fund-raising campaign.[31]

After the speech O'Reilly continued to laud Anthony in the pages of *The Pilot*. He reminded the paper's readers that 'Captain Anthony has destroyed his career as a whaleman. He has placed himself beyond the pale of every British harbour in the world'.[32] The aftermath of the *Catalpa* episode was a triumph for Clan na Gael and it was a time of hectic activity for O'Reilly. He was already famous as a result of his own exploits and when the *Catalpa* expedition became public knowledge, O'Reilly's office at *The Pilot* was besieged by American and international journalists seeking a scoop from a man they all reckoned to be the main organiser of the escape. London's *The Times*, for example, reported in June that O'Reilly was the key figure among a small group who had 'managed the affair' while, in August, Perth's *Western Australian Times* assured its readers that O'Reilly and Denis Cashman were the masterminds of the escape.[33] O'Reilly tried to deflect this attention by using *The Pilot* to credit others as having been more important but, since the Clan was technically a secret organisation, he was limited in what he could say about Devoy.[34] Also, although Devoy was the true leader of the project, he was not well known outside Irish circles and ultimately the *Catalpa* escape added an extra gloss to O'Reilly's reputation in the United States and further afield.

O'Reilly was extraordinarily busy over the next few years, not only through his editorial work but also as a result of his literary career. His personal life was no calmer as he and his wife tried to raise their small children. The family had expanded again on 19 May 1877 when Mary had given birth to the couple's third child, a girl whom they named Agnes Smiley after Mary's nom de plume.[35] In 1879 the writer and architect Arthur Gilman included O'Reilly in his book *Poets' Homes*. The book was a soft-focus collection of articles on various writers and their domestic lives. O'Reilly's inclusion shows the heights to which his reputation as a poet had now climbed. Walt Whitman, Oliver Wendell Holmes, Ralph Waldo Emerson and other luminaries of the east coast literary scene were also in the book. In his introduction to the O'Reilly chapter Gilman provided a pen portrait of the newspaper editor:

> Change of fortune has not altered him much in manner, and seems to have made little difference in his disposition. He still sits silent in company, immovable except as to his restless dark eyes, until somebody asks him a question; but then the heavy brows are lifted, the head is raised, and the answer comes usually in the Milesian form of another question, sometimes paradoxical, sometimes a little dogmatic, but always striking. Unless one wants to rouse him to vehemence, it is best to avoid saying anything snobbish, and, above all, not to insinuate that his beloved workingmen are not perfect; and it is also well not to say anything against Ireland.[36]

Gilman gave a detailed description of the O'Reilly household near Winthrop Park. 'Most of his poetical work', Gilman wrote, 'is done in his study, a long room occupying half of the first floor':

> The arrangement of the room shows a hundred signs of womanly taste, and its planning is really more his wife's work than his own, although it suits him perfectly. The moldings and panelings of the walls are of a warm crimson, repeated in the heavy curtains and the cover of the long desk at one end of the room, and in the comfortable lounge that invites him to rest when he has worked too long. A book-case, containing the volumes that he needs for reference, stands at the left of his chair, and another fills the space between the chimneys. Upon the top of the latter are statuettes, vases and small pictures innumerable, and others line the walls; each one having a history for its owner, not ancestral, but of his own talent and energy.[37]

At the right side of O'Reilly's desk there was a picture of Dowth Castle, made for him by his friend, Robert Joyce. Alongside that picture there stood a little engraving of a scene of military life. O'Reilly's study was no ivory tower but 'the favorite resort of all the family'.[38] Mary, called 'Mamsie' by the children as well as her husband, likewise used the study as a writing room and the children regularly made the room a playground. Gilman enjoyed his time with the O'Reilly family and he affectionately described the hustle and bustle of the household:

> Here come his three black-haired little girls to ask papa's advice on various profound topics, and are chased out by mamma, only to return again and coax for an answer, and to receive it, no matter what becomes of the rhymes meanwhile. Here, too, in the evening, come the Papyrus men [O'Reilly's fellow members of the Papyrus Club, see below] to chat, to discuss their coming poems and books, and, if the truth must be told, to smoke while they talk until long after midnight.[39]

'Up-stairs', continued Gilman, 'are his wife's parlor, the nursery whither his babies beguile him as often as they can, and the bed-rooms.' Clearly the O'Reilly family was happy. They were also financially comfortable, a fact which was underlined that same year when they purchased a summer residence in Hull, a short ferry ride across the bay from Boston.

The periods of domestic bliss which Gilman had observed in the O'Reilly household were, unfortunately, regularly punctuated by illness. Mary had been suffering bouts of ill health since the birth of her second child in 1874. By the end of the decade these episodes were becoming steadily more severe and she was often confined to bed. It is uncertain what she suffered from. All that can be discerned from the mentions she receives in O'Reilly's letters and elsewhere is that she seems to have endured periods of sleeplessness and underactivity, remaining bedridden for days at a time.[40] Her doctor regularly prescribed rest, trips to health spas and various sedatives but, at that time, such prescriptions were routinely advised to combat a wide range of diseases. A. G. Evans has suggested postnatal depression as a possible cause of Mary O'Reilly's symptoms.[41] In an age where many mental illnesses were still unnamed, there is a chance that she did suffer depression, which remained untreated and developed into a chronic condition. Ultimately, we can only speculate and it is unlikely that the true cause of her suffering can be revealed at this stage. Mary's ill health did not prevent the couple having a fourth child, another daughter, on 18 June 1880. They named the girl Blanid, after the heroine in Robert Joyce's epic poem of the same name.[42] Sadly, Blanid was to be chronically ill throughout her childhood. Like her mother, it is uncertain what she suffered from, but the little girl was often bedridden and fever-stricken.[43]

Professionally, though, O'Reilly was thriving. He had published another volume of poetry in 1878, *Songs, Legends and Ballads*, which incorporated all of his earlier work from *Songs of the Southern Seas* along with new poems. This volume he dedicated to his wife: 'To My Dear Wife, whose rare and loving judgement has been a standard I have tried to reach, I Dedicate This Book.' *Songs, Legends and Ballads* would be highly successful and reached eight editions by 1891. O'Reilly followed that work with another volume of poetry in April 1881, *The Statues in the Block*, dedicated 'To the Memory of Eliza Boyle, my Mother'. He also made his first venture into fiction during this period. As we have seen, *Moondyne* was being serialised in *The Pilot* from 1878, before being published as a book in 1879.

Much of this work O'Reilly had completed in the literary and social clubs of which he was a member. Alexis de Tocqueville, on his travels through the US earlier in the century, had noted the American predilection for forming clubs of all sorts: 'As soon as several of the inhabitants of the United States have taken up an opinion or a feeling which they wish to promote in the world, they look out for mutual assistance; and as soon as they have found each other out, they combine.'[44] This was an aspect of American culture that dovetailed perfectly with O'Reilly's character. From his days in Preston when he had joined the local militia, O'Reilly had always been involved in formal groups of one sort or another. He adored the companionship of associations as well as the opportunities they offered to pursue goals common to all the members. Throughout his time in the US O'Reilly was involved in dozens of clubs, ranging from benevolent organisations such as the Charitable Irish Society to those that sought to help destitute children, to groups opposing women's suffrage, sporting associations such as boxing and hurling clubs (see chapter 14) or social groups such as the Union Boat Club and the exclusive Somerset Club. Yet, it was the literary clubs that were most dear to his heart.

O'Reilly had joined the Boston Press Club soon after beginning work at *The Pilot* and by 1872 was practically running the organisation. When the world-famous journalist, Henry Stanley (of 'Dr Livingstone, I presume' fame), visited Boston in December of that year, O'Reilly led the official press reception. It was a gala evening, during which a marvellous time was had by all the assembled hacks. Such was their enthusiasm that the members of the Press Club voted to hold similar events every month and so formed a new group which they named the Papyrus Club.[45] This club was a home from home for O'Reilly over the following years and it was where much of his poetry was first heard. These clubs were not only a social outlet for men like O'Reilly but a valuable opportunity to associate with influential figures across a range of professions. The friendships and associations formed in these clubs could prove of vital aid to the members. George M. Towle, a journalist with the *Boston Post* and a friend of O'Reilly, described the fraternal nature of the Papyrus Club: 'I suppose most of us feel a kindlier interest in a man when we know he is a Papyrus man. I think we are more ready to help him when he is in trouble, to regret his calamities, to rejoice in his good fortune.'[46]

The Papyrus Club, being an offshoot of the Press Club, was primarily a club for journalists and in 1880 Boston's 'leading authors, artists, and other men of distinction' combined to form a new artistic organisation they called the St Botolph Club, modelled on New York's famous Century Club.[47] James Jeffrey Roche wrote that 'Its success was assured from the beginning, for it possessed the happy combination, so seldom found, of brains and money'.[48] Alongside O'Reilly, who was a founding member, there was the writer and editor of the *Atlantic Monthly*, William Dean Howells, and the publishers Henry Houghton and George Mifflin. Artists were represented by Frank Hill Smith and John Singer Sargent among others. There were politicians such as the future Republican Party senator, Henry Cabot Lodge, although at that stage he was recognised more for his writing and editing. It was through such friendships that O'Reilly had firmly established himself among the social and literary 'elites' of Boston. The St Botolph Club was also the backdrop to O'Reilly's friendship with Walt Whitman. The American poet developed a strong regard for O'Reilly whom he described as 'clean, clear, afire with ideals of justice'.[49] Both men would sometimes be critical of each other's work over the following years and, although Whitman never fully reconciled himself to the Irishman's Catholicism (see the final chapter), they remained friends.

O'Reilly also used his positions in the Boston literary world and as an editor to support the work of other Irish poets. Poems by Thomas William Rolleston, Douglas Hyde, Katherine Tynan, Fanny Parnell and William Butler Yeats appeared in *The Pilot* at various times during O'Reilly's editorship of the paper. In 1887 O'Reilly would go so far as to release an edited collection called *The Poetry and Song of Ireland*, a huge gathering together of works by Irish poets that ran to over 1,200 pages.[50] Through his efforts in support of Irish writers O'Reilly became an occasional correspondent with Lady Jane Wilde and her son Oscar. Lady Wilde, who published her writing under the pen-name of 'Speranza', was the first of the Wilde family to appear in *The Pilot* when, in February 1876, O'Reilly printed her poem 'To a Despondent Nationalist'.[51] O'Reilly and Oscar Wilde corresponded later that same year when *The Pilot* carried Wilde's poem 'Rome Unvisited'. Wilde was moved to write from his Dublin home: 'I esteem it a great honour that the first American paper I appeared in should be your admirable Pilot . . . I hope always to be able to keep up my connection with the Pilot. Lady Wilde sends you her compliments and best wishes.'[52]

Wilde and O'Reilly met for the first, and probably only, time in 1882 when Wilde made his celebrated tour of the United States.[53] The two men spent a few days together in late January after Wilde's journey brought him to Boston. They attended a performance of *Oedipus Tyrannus* at the city's Globe Theatre and O'Reilly helped to arrange Wilde's introductions to Walt Whitman, Oliver Wendell Holmes and Wendell Phillips. O'Reilly and Wilde departed each other's company on good terms and maintained an irregular contact thereafter. Later that year Wilde wrote to O'Reilly to discuss the possibility that a volume of Speranza's verse could be printed in the United States. Wilde made the case for his mother's poetry: 'I think my mother's work should make a great success here: it is so unlike the work of her degenerate artistic son. I know you think I am thrilled by nothing but a dado. You are quite wrong, but I shan't argue.'[54] Wilde suggested that one of Boston's main printers, Roberts Brothers, could be enlisted as the publisher but, although O'Reilly was interested in the idea, nothing came of the proposal. However, it may be that O'Reilly's contacts within the Roberts Brothers firm had already been of use to Oscar. That company had worked with O'Reilly on a few occasions and in 1881 they had brought out the authorised American editions of Wilde's *Poems*. They would also win the American rights to Wilde's 1888 collection of children's stories, *The Happy Prince*.

While O'Reilly always offered a helpful hand to other authors, he remained observant for potential opportunities to further his own writing career. In 1883 his participation in the St Botolph Club was to lead one such literary opportunity. As a member of the Papyrus and St Botolph Clubs, O'Reilly had become friendly with three other authors: Robert Grant, Frederic Jesup Stimson (a fellow campaigner with O'Reilly against women's suffrage), and John Tyler Wheelright. These men were familiar figures in the Boston literary scene. Towards the end of 1883, perhaps as a result of the creative brainstorming that such clubs were supposed to facilitate, the idea of a collaborative novel to which they would all contribute was agreed on by the four writers. It is possible that the project may have been the idea of Charles Taylor, editor of the *Boston Daily Globe*, and in whose paper the finished book was serialised.[55] The publication of the novel, which became known as *The King's Men*, would prove a financial windfall for Taylor's paper, although, after publication, it was Grant who retained the copyright for the work.[56] This may suggest that he was the driving force behind the book or that he contributed the most work.

Stimson, however, later said that it was O'Reilly who instigated the book and this may well be accurate.[57] Many of the themes of *The King's Men*, such as penal reform and the corruption of democracy by powerful or radical interests, were themes that O'Reilly habitually addressed in his paper and his literary works. Not only was the 39-year-old the most famous of the group, he was also an established writer whose life story left the other three collaborators in awe. Certainly, the novel's Dartmoor Prison scenes are based on O'Reilly's own life but it is hard to judge how much of the finished book flowed from his pen. Throughout early 1884 the four men worked together on the story. Each author spent a week working on their assigned section and they met every Saturday night at the St Botolph club. During these meetings they would assess their progress to date and agree which chapters to work on over the following week. It seems to have been a remarkably harmonious arrangement and the novel was completed within a six-week period.[58]

The King's Men was set in the future, sometime around the 1960s, at a time in which the British monarchy has been replaced by a British republic. The first president of this imagined republic had been a kind-hearted

Irishman by the name of O'Donovan Rourke. As Charles Fanning has surmised, this was almost certainly an inside joke as the name is very similar that of O'Reilly's friend, Jeremiah O'Donovan Rossa (at that time Rossa was the focus of much public anger in Britain due to his role in the dynamite campaigns of the 1880s; see chapter 13).[59] In the novel, O'Rourke's government is succeeded by that of the populist demagogue, Lemuel Bagshaw, an 'atheist and an anarchist' who is chosen as president by an alliance of radicals and former aristocrats.[60] A cabal of aristocrats see, in Bagshaw, an opportunity to restore the monarchy. They smuggle the deposed King George V, who had fled Britain and had been living as a commoner in Boston, back into the country. This strategy, led by a former lord, Sir Geoffrey Rippon, is betrayed by a woman, Mrs Oswald Carey. She is in love with Rippon but is scorned by him and in her bitter fury she informs the government of the conspiracy. The republican government pre-empt the coup and, amid much violence, save British democracy. The former king, conspicuously lacking moral fortitude, flees the country and abandons his supporters to their fate. Rippon is sent to Dartmoor Prison where, despite the degrading and brutal environment, he learns how to be a better man. He eventually escapes and travels to Boston where he renounces the monarchy. Meanwhile back in Britain, the corrupt Bagshaw is replaced by one of his senior ministers, the noble Richard Lincoln, who safeguards the future of Britain's republic.

The historian Susanna Ashton has made a strong case for the historical importance of *The King's Men*, as an example of a multi-authored novel. It is a less melodramatic and more tightly plotted work than *Moondyne*. However, while that book had received generally favourable reviews, *The King's Men* received a lukewarm, at times hostile, response from critics following its 1884 publication. The collaborative nature of the novel was the aspect on which most critics commented, with one reviewer calling it 'a four-headed baby at a show'.[61] In the *New York Times* a reviewer accused the four authors of writing 'rather for their own amusement than the delectation of the public' and concluded that 'it verifies the old adage of too many cooks spoiling the broth'.[62] If the authors felt any annoyance at these criticisms it may well have been alleviated by the financial rewards that accompanied the publication. According to Roche, the four men received $5,000 for the work, which they presumably divided equally amongst themselves.[63] The serialisation of *The King's Men* in the *Boston Daily Globe* proved a particularly successful endeavour for the newspaper. Charles Taylor claimed that it brought the paper an extra 30,000 subscribers.[64] While this figure is probably exaggerated, there is no doubt that *The King's Men* was extremely popular with the reading public; O'Reilly and his fellow authors would soon make another $5,000 when the chapters that appeared in the *Globe* were republished in book form by a New York company.[65] Much of this success came as a result of O'Reilly's involvement in the project. He was the best-known writer among the group and we need to survey O'Reilly's literary career to see why this was so.

Poet

In 1988 the rock band U2 released *Rattle and Hum*. The album contains a song, written by The Edge, called 'Van Diemen's Land'. It is a poignant tale of a man 'who fought for justice and not for gain' but who was ripped from his family by the British army and transported to what was then a convict colony and is now Tasmania. The sleeve notes of the album show that the song was inspired by O'Reilly's life and contain the line: 'Dedicated to John Boyle O'Reilly, a Fenian poet deported from Ireland to Australia because of his poetry. (It wasn't very good . . .!)'.[1] That line, humorous if blunt, would probably be the standard interpretation of O'Reilly's poetry today. Yet, during the 1870s and 1880s, O'Reilly was one of the most famous poets in the United States. In this chapter we will take a little time to assess O'Reilly's poetry and literary endeavours, not so much from a critical viewpoint but to see how they reflected on the man himself.

From the early days of O'Reilly's life in Boston, he was heavily involved in the city's literary scene and between 1873 and 1886 he would publish four volumes of poetry: *Songs from the Southern Seas* (1873); *Songs, Legends and Ballads* (1878); *The Statues in the Block and Other Poems* (1881); and *In Bohemia* (1886). His novel *Moondyne* was serialised in *The Pilot* from 1878 and published as a book in 1879, while in 1884 he collaborated on the novel *The King's Men*. O'Reilly's literary fame would prove ephemeral. By the twentieth century nearly all O'Reilly's poetry, unlike his writings in *The Pilot*, was virtually forgotten. Almost none of his poetry appeared in anthologies, although a handful of his poems made it into Kathleen Hoagland's mammoth 1947 collection *One Thousand Years of Irish Poetry*.[2] Of the few poems that were anthologised, the most popular was 'A White Rose' from *In Bohemia*: 'The red rose whispers of passion / And the white rose breathes of love / Oh, the red rose is a falcon / And the white rose is a dove.'[3]

O'Reilly's literary career had been progressing well since his publication of *Songs from the Southern Seas*. Although he was never a darling of literary critics, O'Reilly was popularly and commercially successful. Many of the poems that appeared in his published volumes also appeared in newspapers and poetry magazines. He was very well paid for many of these, receiving $150 from Joseph Pulitzer for the publication of his poem 'America' in *World* magazine.[4] This is one factor in O'Reilly's career that is often overlooked. He published practically every word he wrote and, being a successful businessman, he had a keen awareness of his own value as a literary commodity. After all, he had an ill wife as well as four children to provide for. The Irishman's attitude to his own work was summed up by correspondence with a journal named *Literary Life* in 1886.

That summer he received a letter advertising the arrival of this new journal, which was to be edited by Rose Cleveland, sister of the then President of the United States, Grover Cleveland. The publisher of this magazine informed O'Reilly that as one of the country's 'ablest writers' they wished him 'to contribute a short article of from 1,000 to 2,000 words for Miss Cleveland's Magazine, *Literary Life*, on any subject of interest to our readers.'[5] For this commission they offered him a rate of one cent a word.[6] This was far below the going rate for authors and O'Reilly composed a sharp response, which he printed in his newspaper. 'I cannot see why you should appeal to the charity of literary people for the benefit of your magazine. If your letter is not an appeal for charity it is a humiliation and a disgrace to the literary profession.'[7] O'Reilly ended his letter by quipping, '*Literary Life* is "a young magazine" and if this be its method of living it is to be hoped that it may be spared the burden of old age.'[8] He was also an active member International Copyright Association and of the American Copyright League, both of which sought to protect the rights of authors, and which included Harriet Beecher Stowe, Oliver Wendell Holmes, Mark Twain and Walt Whitman among its members.[9]

Another factor in his literary life was the sheer amount of work that lay before O'Reilly at any one time. His editorship of *The Pilot* meant that

O'Reilly was perpetually busy and he once wrote to a friend explaining that 'I never get an hour ahead of the printers and that's awful'.[10] Consequently he often failed to revise his literary work. This all conspired to give a rushed, unfinished edge to much of his poetry and it was noted by the critics. In an otherwise glowing review of *Songs from the Southern Seas* the *Literary World* complained that 'His verse is sometimes careless; and often lacks finish'."[11] Similar comments, whether from admirers or detractors, greeted every volume written by O'Reilly. Speaking of his own 1878 work, *Songs Legends and Ballads*, the poet admitted, 'I write at white heat and I never revise.'[12] His third and fourth volumes, *Statues in the Block* and *In Bohemia*, although they received much praise, were criticised for their 'formlessness', 'lawlessness' and for containing 'rough drafts of poems'.[13] While these comments on the later volumes were also directed at the 'Whitmanesque turn' of some of O'Reilly's verse, the perception among reviewers that he rushed his poetry into print remained a cause for criticism.[14]

Often his poetry has no subtext and there is a clear lesson for the reader to learn. James Jeffrey Roche wrote approvingly of this aspect of O'Reilly's verse: 'He never wrote a line which the most innocent might not read with safety. He never used a vile word; there was none such in his vocabulary.'[15] It was a point that was picked up by Martin Carroll, who wrote that much of O'Reilly's poetry showed the poet to 'be the skillful dealer in the comforting phrase, the moulder in words of what he considered to be home truths and eternal wisdoms.'[16] This can make O'Reilly's poetry bland, sometimes self-righteous, but it leaves the reader in no doubt as to his beliefs and goals. However, there is another aspect to these poems; perhaps O'Reilly's poetry was designed to be read aloud, almost as sermons. Poetry and song were a large component of O'Reilly's childhood and schooling. One of his boyhood contemporaries described the young O'Reilly's extraordinary knowledge of poetry and his mastery of recitation: 'he had dozens of them off by heart . . . he could roll them out until you'd think every tree and flower along the Boyne were repeating the words after him.'[17] Carroll suggests that any analysis of O'Reilly's poetry must be cognisant of the fact that most of O'Reilly's 'verse must be listened to rather than read quietly. In the declamation of it the most expert spell-binder was O'Reilly himself'.[18]

Public performances were an integral part of O'Reilly's literary career and he regularly recited his poetry for admiring audiences: aboard the

Hougoumont and the *Gazelle*; in the Papyrus and St Botolph Clubs; and in lecture halls across the US. He was a relentless presence on the lecture circuit and he reached huge audiences as a result. Once O'Reilly travelled to give a talk at Minneapolis where he expressed his disappointment that 'the audience was good, not large, around 1,100 people'.[19] Robert Grant, a collaborator on *The King's Men*, described his experience of an O'Reilly recitation:

> he was certain to carry any audience off its feet by the intensity he put into the delivery of his poems. I shall never forget his delivery of his 'In Bohemia' at . . . the Papyrus Club, when, though not unaware that the creed was fustian, I subscribed unreservedly under the spell of the moment to the ardor of his rapturous eloquence . . . With what passionate faith did he proceed, and when he reached the glowing, relentless close, it was impossible not to feel that one was listening to a seer . . . What a tumult of applause when he sat down. I was stirred to the depths, though dimly aware that I was under a spell.[20]

This feeling of being enraptured was a common response among O'Reilly's audiences. Another critic described the thrilled applause that followed one O'Reilly performance: 'It was perfectly plain that he had accomplished his poet's mission in touching the hearers' hearts rather than their reason.'[21] O'Reilly, the critic wrote, was born 'with the art of getting at the real sentiment of human beings.' Perhaps that partly explains O'Reilly's success as a poet and the speedy demise of his literary reputation after his death; maybe the poetry and the poet could not be separated and what can appear dull and formless on the page took on a vital power when proclaimed by its creator.

His poetry frequently used religion as a theme and many of his verses, especially in *Songs, Legends and Ballads*, were written with religious instruction in mind. O'Reilly acts as a lay priest in such poems as 'Macarius the Monk' and 'The Trial of the Gods',[22] where faith in God is advocated by the poet. The poem 'Peace and Pain' advises, 'The star that led the Magi still can teach us / The way to go if we but look to Him.' The same poem encourages readers to remember and atone for their sins. In 'A Seed' O'Reilly writes of the heavenly benefits of earthly kind deeds. Like Gerard Manley Hopkins, O'Reilly sees the hands of God in nature and religious allusions are scattered throughout his work. O'Reilly was devoutly Catholic throughout his adult life but his religious poems were occasionally political. The subjugation of Ireland, of the poor, or of minorities was wrong in O'Reilly's view, not only because it offended human dignity, but also because it offended God.

This religious poetry was rarely spiritual and more often didactic, advising that mankind should strive to live a Christly life. It was in this vein that O'Reilly defended religion in his poetry. These sentiments were mirrored in *The Pilot* by such means as his paper's occasional criticisms of Charles Darwin.[23] O'Reilly seems to have been wary of the concept of evolution by natural selection as expounded by the scientist, but his reservation was not the same as that of the modern-day creationist who believes in the literal truth of the Christian Bible and therefore refutes the concept of evolution. Rather, he was unnerved by any theory that threatened to remove a creator-god from the realm of human experience. For O'Reilly, an existence without God was an existence devoid of meaning or beauty. This is not to say that O'Reilly was an opponent of scientific and technological progress. Indeed, he regularly used *The Pilot* to advocate that scientific and technical subjects should be given a much more prominent role in Catholic schools.[24] Yet there is an occasional ambivalence towards scientific enquiry in his poetry. This can be seen in 'Star-Gazing', in which the poet suggests that the knowledge gleaned by science may lead to answers but not always fulfilment: 'Let be what is: why should we strive and wrestle / With awkward skill against a subtle doubt.'[25]

The difference between O'Reilly the poet and O'Reilly the editor was often slight but he was sometimes more bitterly critical of society in his poems, especially in the later volumes, *The Statues in the Block* and *In Bohemia*. In these works there was a focus in his writing on social inequality. There were no shades of grey but a Manichean distinction between light and darkness, between right and wrong. It was these energetic verses that endeared him to many of his contemporaries. Writing in 1886 for *The Irish Monthly*, a magazine published by the Jesuits, the poet and critic Daniel Connolly declared that 'In all his literary work the quality of forceful expression is paramount. But with the expression there always is vigorous thought; the writer never speaks unless he has something to say.'[26] There is a thematic link in these political poems to Percy Bysshe Shelley's (he was a favourite of O'Reilly's) 'England in 1819' and that poem's attack on the 'Rulers who neither see, nor feel, nor know / But leech-like to their fainting country cling.' In O'Reilly's 'The City Streets' the narrator journeys through a city and contrasts the lives of the rich and poor. Geographically, the two groups are only feet apart but socially they inhabit parallel universes:

> The men of the city who travel and write, whose fame and credit are known abroad,
> The people who move in the ranks, polite, the cultured women whom all applaud.
> It is true, there are only ten thousand here, but the other half million are a vulgar clod;
> And a soul well-bred is eternally dear – it counts so much more on the books of God.
> The others have use in their place, no doubt; but why speak of a class one never meets?
> They are gloomy things to be talked about, these common lives of the city streets.[27]

The rich may have isolated themselves in their salubrious neighbourhoods but the narrator had a warning: 'Beware with your Classes! Men are men, and a cry in the night is a fearful teacher / When it reaches the hearts of the masses, then they need but a sword for a judge and preacher.' In the same poem O'Reilly deplores the tendency of the powerful to claim that all crime results from the supposed 'criminal taint' of the poor and thus ignore the fact that theft and other offences are often a result of desperation and necessity. In the game of life 'the poor man's son carries double weight.' This theme was threaded through his poetry, fiction and newspaper editorials; those on the bottom rungs of society were being punished, not because of any inherent flaws in their character but through the bad luck of being born into poverty or into a country that had been colonised. In 'The Three Queens' the poet fears that the world had become 'a monstrous corporation' and had been corrupted beyond repair. The 'selfish, strong and shrewd' have designed the laws of this new world: 'Her teachers taught the justice of oppression / That taxed the poor on all but air and sun / Her preachers preached the gospel of possession / That hoards had rights while human souls had none.'[28]

O'Reilly also feared the repercussions of ethnic and racial divisions in US society and he argued that the social exclusion of ethnic minorities was tantamount to chaining them to a yoke.[29] In 1888 he was asked by a committee of Boston civil rights campaigners to provide a poem for the dedication of the Crispus Attucks monument in the city. Attucks, a black man, had been shot dead by the British army during the 'Boston Massacre' of March 1770. During later decades abolitionists and civil rights advocates had used the memory of Attucks as an example of black patriotism and to stress the role of black people in American history. O'Reilly's 'Crispus Attucks' uses this theme of black patriotism to proclaim: 'Indian, Negro, Saxon and Celt, Teuton and Latin and Gaul / Mere surface shadow and sunshine; while the sounding unifies all / One love, one hope, one duty theirs! no matter the time or ken / There never was a separate heartbeat in all the races of men!'[30] This poem denounced those who would foster artificial distinctions of race in order to maintain their superiority and who would deny civil rights to others:

> Patrician, aristocrat, tory – whatever his age or name,
> To the people's rights and liberties, a traitor ever the same.
> The natural crowd is a mob to him, their prayer a vulgar rhyme;
> The freeman's speech is sedition, and the patriot's deed a crime.
> Wherever the race, the law, the land – whatever the time, or throne,
> The tory is always a traitor to every class but his own.
> Thank God for a land where pride is clipped, where arrogance stalks
>   apart;
> Where law and song, loathing of wrong are words of the common
>   heart;
> Where the masses honor straightforward strength, and know, when
>   veins are bled,
> That the bluest blood is putrid blood – that the people's blood is red!

This sentiment was replayed in other poems such as 'Wendell Phillips' where O'Reilly declares that: 'There are no classes or races, but one human brotherhood'.[31] However, in the same manner that O'Reilly's support of civil rights found a home in his poetry, so did his hostility towards women's suffrage.

That men could change the fortunes of the world through their strength was, to him, obvious and natural. Women could not join in this pantheon since, while men could exist in a brotherhood of man, a woman could never form, according to O'Reilly, a similar friendship with another woman. In an unnamed poem from *The Statues in the Block* he claims: 'A woman – does she tell her sins? Ah, no! / She never knew a woman she could trust.'[32] Sections of *Watchwords from John Boyle O'Reilly* (a collection of his poems, aphorisms and journalism that was edited by Katherine Conway and published after his death) portray women as fickle, while the patronising 'Her Refrain' sees the poet afflicted by an insecure lover who repeatedly asks if he loves her.[33] In O'Reilly's poetry, women were more suited to acting as pillars of support to men in their forging of new worlds and as a rein on men's more atavistic tendencies. Romantic love rarely features in the poetry and when it does it is often compromised by female duplicity.[34]

Women were sometimes idealised by O'Reilly in his love poems but, as so often with those held up as perfection, flaws are found and the women are both loved and scorned: 'her heart was a cinder instead of a coal', bemoans the poet in 'A Disappointment'.[35] Sex, outside of the merest hints, is absent from his poetry. Indeed, it is also absent from his fiction apart from one instance where O'Reilly displays a grim and guilt-ridden attitude to sexuality. In *Moondyne* he had described the reaction of the novel's heroine, Alice Walmsley, to her first 'moment of communion' with her husband (one of the novel's villains, it must be said): 'she knew that for ever she had parted from the pure and beautiful, and was buried in an ocean of corruption and disappointment, rolled over by waves of unimaginable suffering and wrong.'[36] Yet the poet is at times intoxicated by love and in 'Jacqueminots' he pleads: 'And tell her, tell her, roses, that my lips and eyes are dying / For the melting of her love-look and the rapture of her kiss.'[37]

O'Reilly's poetry was often praised for its 'manliness' and 'virility'. This was a comment not only on the terse nature of much of O'Reilly's verse but also his masculine subject matter. This 'manly virtue' was one of the most common strands across his work. O'Reilly wrote in 'The Patriot's Grave' of the Irish revolutionary Robert Emmet: 'He teaches the secret of manhood – the watchword of those who aspire / That men must follow freedom though it lead through blood and fire.'[38] On another occasion he claimed that 'The greatest service a man can do for a good cause is to die for it.'[39] It was a point that was repeated in his poem 'John Mitchel' following the Irish nationalist's death in 1875 (in his elegy for Mitchel, O'Reilly overlooked the fact that the former Young Irelander had been a fervent proponent of slavery in the United States). Mother Ireland had called and he 'gave her his life as men should do.'[40] If necessary, men should fight to the last against injustice. His 'A Song for the Soldiers' tells of a battle between the US cavalry and the Cheyenne. The Indian warriors, although outnumbered, refuse to surrender and are all killed. 'God, they are brave,' cries one of the soldiers in awe at the Cheyenne's fortitude.[41] O'Reilly, though, was not blind to the darker side of such masculinity. In 'Dolores' the poets wonders: 'Is he well blest who has no eyes to scan / The woeful things that shadow all our life / The latent brute behind the eyes of man / The place and power gained and stained by strife.'[42] In 'Prometheus-Christ' man is held to account for his venality and brutality: 'Man's soul is dual – he is half a fiend'.[43] In the same poem the poet cries: 'Let us confess: by Nations first – our lines / Are writ in blood and rapine and revenge / Conquest and pride have been motive and law.'

O'Reilly did not revel in war for its own sake and his poems on militaristic themes are not merely tales of audacity and patriotic fervor. Rather, they are a means of showing his reader or listener that wars are sometimes worth fighting, especially those wars in defiance of oppression or those that result in a new birth of freedom. Walt Whitman once claimed that 'the proof of a poet is that his country absorbs him as affectionately as he has absorbed it'.[44] O'Reilly would certainly absorb his adopted country in works like 'America', which he read before the Army of the Potomac in 1882. The poem looked forward to a day when Europe would have developed to resemble the United States. Then, all Europe's monarchies would be toppled and Europe would be unified: 'Without a barrier and without a throne / Of one grand federation like our own.'[45] Poems such as 'America', among others, reveal a poet who is immersed in the United States as an idea, in the belief that American independence could be a new dawn in human history. In return for such verses, the country absorbed O'Reilly and he was often invited to compose poems for national occasions. Joseph Pulitzer's *New York World* commissioned a piece from O'Reilly to celebrate the Statue of Liberty's dedication in 1886. His 'Liberty Lighting the World' has the statue call out: 'I am she who the ages prayed for / Heroes suffered undismayed for / Whom the martyrs were betrayed for.'[46] In 1889 he was commissioned to compose a poem for the dedication of the Pilgrim Fathers Monument. The epic poem, 'The Pilgrim Fathers', is a hymn to the United States containing lines such as: 'Here, on this rock, and on this sterile soil / Began the kingdom not of kings, but men / Began the making of the world again.'[47]

The Old World of O'Reilly's birthplace also featured in his poetry, although much of his poetry on this subject is maudlin, sometimes dolorous. In 'My Native Land' he described Ireland as 'My first dear love, all dearer for thy grief! / My land, that has no peer in all the sea / For verdure, vale, or river, flower or leaf'.[48] Amid his poems on Ireland, however, there are political verses. A few years after he had departed the Fenians O'Reilly wrote 'The Priests of Ireland'. The poem is practically propaganda for the Catholic clergy who had denounced the Fenians before their congregations during the 1860s: 'Ah, you told them – it was cruel – but you said they were not true / To the holy faith of Patrick, if they were not ruled by you'.[49] In this poem there is a tacit acknowledgement from O'Reilly that he now believed he had been on the wrong side of the argument when he had joined the Fenians:

O, God bless you, Priests of Ireland! You were waiting with a will,
You were waiting with a purpose when you bade your flocks be still;
And you preached from your altars not alone the Word Sublime,
But your silence preached to Irishmen – 'Be patient: bide your time!'
And they heard you, and obeyed you, as well as outraged men could
    do –
Only some, who loved poor Ireland, but who erred in doubting you,
Doubting you, who could not tell them why you spake the strange
    behest –
You, who saw the day was coming when the moral strength was best.

It has often been claimed that O'Reilly became opposed to violent insurrection against Britain during his time in the United States. That is generally accurate but, while he was opposed to poorly planned and supplied risings like that of 1867, O'Reilly never abandoned the idea that a rebellion might be necessary if Britain refused to concede self-government to Ireland (see chapter 13). In 'The Statues in the Block' the poet sees the personification of Ireland with 'Thy hand raised to ward the cruel blow' of its English master.[50] The poet, heartbroken by the vision, looks forward to a day 'In which thy colors shall be borne through fire / And all thy griefs washed out in manly blood / And I shall see thee crowned and bound with love / Thy strong sons round thee guarding thee'. At the end of 'The Patriot's Grave' O'Reilly writes of Robert Emmet 'That sacrifice is the bitter draught which freemen still must quaff / That every patriotic life is the patriot's epitaph'.[51] The cruelty of the British Empire is stressed in 'Ireland 1882', in which O'Reilly imagines the personification of the Empire striding across the country:

> Thou canst stand by the way ascending, as thy tyrant goes to the base:
> The seeds of death are in her and the signs in her cruel face.
> On her darkened path lie the corpses of men, with whose blood her feet are red;
> And the curses of ruined nations are a cloud above her head.[52]

He continues the theme in 'Erin', in which the poet proposes a toast: 'May no weak race be wronged, and no strong robber feared / To oppressors grow hateful, to slaves more endeared / Till the world comes to know that the test of a cause / Is the hatred of tyrants and Erin's applause!'[53]

O'Reilly's poetry was a complement to the concerns that were a leitmotif in his fiction and editorials. That was the motivation behind his verse. There was 'very little attempt at fine literary finish', as *The Irish Monthly* wrote in 1887 during an approving review of O'Reilly's poetry.[54] Critics noted that some of O'Reilly's poetry, such as 'From the Earth, A Cry', owed a debt to Walt Whitman but his greatest literary influences were in the past. Roche described how O'Reilly 'would read for hours every evening to his little ones' and that he 'taught them to understand, Shakespeare, Milton, Dante, Shelley, Byron, Keats, and all the masters of English verse.'[55] It was the Romantics among these poets who were O'Reilly's favourites. He was part of a movement within American Catholic literature that sought to protect, as they saw it, the Romantic tradition from modern influences, especially realism and naturalism as exemplified by the French writer Émile Zola. Charles Fanning has shown that opposition to Zola and realism 'was an article of faith in Catholic cultural circles' during these years.[56] O'Reilly explained his thoughts on this subject in an 1889 article for the *New York Herald*:

Romantic literature belongs to the domain of art on the same level as sculpture, painting, and the drama. In none of these other expressions is the abnormal, the corrupt, the wantonly repulsive allowable. The line of treatment on these subjects is definitely drawn and generally acknowledged. The unnecessarily foul is unpardonable. Why should not the same limit be observed in romantic literature? All art deals with nature and truth, but not with all nature and all truth. A festering sore is part of nature; it directly affects the thought and action of the sufferer, and it is as unsightly, as deplorable, and as potent as the festering vice on the soul. Why should the latter be allowed and the bodily sore forbidden? The average middle-class American reader, male or female, is a Philistine – unquestionably the most impervious and cloaked conventionality known to all nations, not even excepting the 'lower middle-class' English. He wants his fiction to be as proper, as full of small exactitudes in demeanor, as 'good an example' on the outside, as he is himself. Humbug as he is, he is far preferable to the 'natural' type of the morbid morality mongers, who teach the lesson of an hour by a life-long corruption. The Philistine has a right to his taste, and he is right in voting down the Zola school as the best for his children. Being a Philistine myself, I vote with him.[57]

O'Reilly believed moral enrichment – the good example – to be a vital component of art. This attitude had been an important influence on his poetry through the preceding two decades. Outside of the debate on realism, literary arguments and developments had only a tangential influence on O'Reilly's poetry. He was not attracted to poetic experimentation. Karen Conway wrote in 1892 that O'Reilly was 'intensely earnest, and the merely droll or fantastic or ingenious never appealed to him' and she demonstrated that that he found little favour with elaborate poetic forms.[58] Daniel Connolly similarly wrote of O'Reilly: 'His work is all his own. There is no echo, not even a suggestion of any other poet in any part of it.'[59] That would be taking the argument too far but it is true to say that O'Reilly was not interested in emulating other poets. His main goal was to communicate ideas and this may also be a part explanation for the plainness of his poems; evidence of a desire to be a man of the people.

The many people who praised his poetry concentrated on O'Reilly's social conscience as well as the drama and inspiration of his work. In an 1894 collection of American poetry the critic Arthur Beaman Simonds wrote that 'The name of John Boyle O'Reilly is recognized in American literature as synonymous with the word heart.'[60] The same critic stated: 'O'Reilly has many gifts in the matter of poetry – keen analysis, an eye for landscape, and sharp, vivid expression; but, more than anything else, stands out his sure, sententious judgement of character.' Francis McManamin well described this trait when he wrote that O'Reilly's poetry was full of 'terse, graphic and manly expressions which were concerned more with conveying his own pent-up emotions and humanitarian ideas than they were with the mechanics of versification.'[61] It was a side of O'Reilly's poetry that wooed his contemporaries. In 1881 the *New York Times* gave its opinion on *The Statues in the Block*. It was a mixed review with the critic complaining at one point about 'Muley Malek, The King' that 'Mr. O'Reilly is not up to this complicated rhythm.'[62] The critic forgot all these reservations in the conclusion:

> In fact, we have in Mr. O'Reilly the case of a man who has something to say. He has had experiences; he loves and hates; and if perhaps he does not love to much purpose, his hates are inspiring and contagious. It is the easiest work in the world to pick flaws in his verses, but the sovereign fact remains that he thrills you as you read.

O'Reilly's poetry was one medium for his humanitarianism. His verse was designed to illustrate virtue, expose the hypocrisy of the powerful and to stress his belief that the divisions in humanity engendered by imperialism, race, creed and money were as stupid as they were wicked. That others should be entitled to dignity is a profound yet uncomplicated message. O'Reilly took it upon himself to deliver it and made his name as a poet in so doing.

All Things Irish

While O'Reilly had become renowned as a newspaper editor and writer he had maintained a heavy involvement in Irish affairs both in Ireland and within the United States. His adopted home of Boston was the centre of a dynamic Irish community. Those Irish who had settled in the US over the early decades of the nineteenth century were drawn, primarily, to the big cities of New York, Philadelphia, Chicago and Boston. However, Boston, in those decades, was an unwelcoming destination for the Irish. The historian Thomas O'Connor, in the introduction to his study of the Boston Irish, described the reality of immigrant life in the city for those first immigrants:

> It was an American city with an intensely homogenous Anglo-Saxon character, an inbred hostility toward people who were Irish, a fierce and violent revulsion against all things Roman Catholic, and an economic system that precluded most forms of unskilled labor. Boston was a city that rejected the Irish from the very start and saw no way in which people of that ethnic background could ever be fully assimilated into the prevailing American culture.[1]

In the eighteenth century the city's Irish-born Catholic population would have been tiny.[2] However, as Irish immigrants arrived in steadily increasing numbers over the first half of the nineteenth century tens of thousands of them chose Boston as their new home. By 1850 over a quarter of the city's population had been born in Ireland.[3]

The increasing numbers of Catholic immigrants from Ireland and other countries resulted in a vicious backlash from the predominantly Protestant population of the United States. Although some of the worst anti-Catholic violence was seen in Philadelphia, Boston was not immune to this plague of discrimination. Patrick Ford, long before he rose to prominence with the *Irish World*, lived in Boston for a time during 1850s. While there, he discovered that the local population held 'the fact that I was Irish and a Catholic against me.'[4] It was a humiliating time for the Irish and it left Ford with the fervent belief that 'it was necessary for everyone of Irish blood to do all in his power to change that state of things.'[5] Such a change would take time and over the rest of that decade the religious and racial discrimination experienced by immigrants contributed to a ghettoisation of the Irish into the slums of the North End of the city as well as South Boston.[6]

This prejudice had by no means disappeared by the 1870s but O'Reilly had arrived in the United States at an opportune moment for the Irish. Since the 1850s the Nativist movement had withered and the Irish involvement in the Union army during the Civil War had done much for both the self-confidence and the public image of the Irish. The Irish were also making inroads into the civic life of the large cities and in Massachusetts the Irish had begun to establish themselves as a visible and vital part of Boston. O'Reilly was proud of this fact and eager to support the social advance of the Irish in America. He frequently preached the value of education as the best means of social improvement for the Irish. In 1875 he warned his readers: 'We learn that while the Irish have nearly twice as many children as the Americans – the latter have nearly twice as many at school as the former. This is where the Irish are making a grievous mistake. They keep their children at home or send them too early to work.'[7] On this topic O'Reilly clashed with the writer Orestes Brownson, one of the most famous Catholic converts in the United States. Brownson openly doubted the necessity of education for immigrants. O'Reilly disputed Brownson's arguments although he did have a preference for Church-run schools, which he claimed were superior to public schools; a belief that was fully in accord with the official position of the American Catholic Church.[8]

When it came to the topic of Catholic students in Boston's schools, Francis McManamin described *The Pilot* under O'Reilly as 'a kind of vigilance committee'.[9] The paper was forever watchful of instances of discrimination, of which it found some genuine examples.[10] In 1885 he noted that although over half the schoolchildren in Boston were Catholic only 'two hundred of the 1,341 teachers are Catholic'.[11] His commitment to this issue led him down some strange paths. On one occasion in 1871 O'Reilly reported on the work of a Harvard professor who had researched why some Boston women had become prostitutes. The professor concluded that the public school system had been a decisive factor. O'Reilly wrote admiringly of the Professor's work: 'To his utter surprise a large number of the unfortunate girls traced their fall to the influences which surrounded them in the public schools. They described the obscene books and pictures passed through the school.'[12] Yet over the next two decades O'Reilly would prove to be a thoughtful observer of the school system. He was especially insistent that the range of subjects needed to be widened and that less stress should be placed on subjects such as Latin.[13]

O'Reilly took every opportunity to highlight Irish achievements. As we have seen in earlier chapters he was very generous in promoting the literary work of other Irish authors. In a similar manner *The Pilot* regularly reported on the material success of the Irish, such as when, in 1877, it published a list of 200 wealthy Irish citizens of Boston. Each of these people held property worth over £15,000.[14] Population statistics were another key piece of evidence that he utilised to prove the advance of the Irish. He also had another goal in using population statistics. As Francis Walsh has demonstrated, O'Reilly used statistics to bolster his argument that Catholics would soon replace Protestants as the main religious group in the United States.[15] O'Reilly looked forward to this day with apparent glee. In 1874 he assured his readers that 'it was best for humanity that the grim and narrow minded Puritan should go to the wall from the strong progress of stalwart, liberal but faithful Irish.'[16] This topic, in which *The Pilot* displayed hints both of insecurity and triumphalism, was a feature of the paper's reportage throughout the 1870s.

In 1877 O'Reilly offered his prediction for the fate of the American republic over the forthcoming century and the corresponding decline of the country's Protestant population. In *The Pilot*, he charted the 'Pilgrim's Progress':

1620   He lands with other Pilgrims on Plymouth Rock.
1808   He asks where is this to end? The Pope has sent a Catholic
         bishop to Boston.
1856   He joins the Know-Nothings for protection.

1870	He is startled at being told by statisticians that his race is dying out.
1890	He goes to the State House and finds eighty-six per cent of the members 'foreigners'.
1893	Tries to marry his daughter to a 'foreigner' of three generations in Boston but can't find one to take her.
1940	Asks the President of the United States, Mr Chang Wung, for a position as postmaster and gets it.
1960	Draws up his will to preserve the ruins of South Church.
1970	Attends lecture on great Americans of the past century. Schlieffen the astronomer, McNeill of the electrical engine, Donnelly and the principle of perpetual motion.
1976	A monument is erected to the last Puritan.[17]

While such an article has triumphalist overtones it should be seen more as a satirical piece. Also, during the 1880s O'Reilly became less concerned with the idea of one population group replacing another. Instead, while always disputing claims that the United States was an Anglo-Saxon country, he declared that the United States was witnessing something new and wonderful, the amalgamation of the world's races: 'A race that differs in many ways from the old races is growing up in America . . . the best of all races.'[18]

The Irish, as O'Reilly happily noted in *The Pilot*, were benefiting, albeit unevenly, from increased affluence and educational status and it was inevitable that they would translate their new confidence into the realm of politics. By the 1880s, in the words of Thomas O'Connor, the previous 'docility of the Irish in political matters was fast becoming a thing of the past.'[19] O'Reilly was fully attuned to this development and he continued what had long been *The Pilot's* policy of involvement in American politics. In 1877 O'Reilly explained his attitude towards American politics:

> There is not one Irish person in 10,000 who will ever return to live in Ireland . . . Is it right to tell these people . . . that they must live solely for that country's politics, and that until she is free they must not become good citizens of this country? Is it not plainly the duty of the 9,999 to become good American citizens?[20]

Under Patrick Donahoe's ownership *The Pilot* had been a supporter of the Democratic Party and O'Reilly retained this policy. As O'Reilly explained in an 1884 speech he regarded the Democratic Party as historically more kindly disposed to the Irish in the United States.[21] The Republicans, he declared, were not only antagonistic to the Irish but were also inextricably wedded to big business and the political elites. This analysis was unlikely to have upset any of *The Pilot*'s readers since the Irish and the Democratic Party had become interdependent over the preceding decades. The Irish had originally joined the party to gain a measure of protection from hostile groups such as the Know-Nothings of the 1850s. In return for votes the Democrats gave the Irish access to opportunities for social and political advancement that they would otherwise have been denied. Membership of the Democratic Party also, as Kerby Miller has shown, gave the Irish 'a sense of belonging to a powerful *American* institution.'[22]

In the 1876 presidential election O'Reilly had supported the Democratic candidate, Samuel J. Tilden.[23] That election had been highly controversial and had seen Tilden win the popular vote but lose in the Electoral College to his Republican rival, Rutherford B. Hayes. In 1880 O'Reilly supported the Democratic candidate, civil war general Winfield S. Hancock, only to be again disappointed by the narrow victory which the electorate handed to the Republican candidate, James Garfield. The following presidential election, however, would offer the first real test of O'Reilly's Democratic Party credentials. During that party's primaries, O'Reilly had opposed the ultimate winner of the nomination, Grover Cleveland. He then found that the Republicans were running a candidate, James G. Blaine, whom some quarters termed an 'Irish candidate'. Blaine's attempted grab for the Irish vote was based on the fact that his mother was a Catholic and that he supposedly possessed sympathy for Ireland. O'Reilly urged his readers to ignore such cosmetics, although he took solace from the fact that the Irish had emerged to a level at which both parties were competing for their vote: 'A few years ago it would have been desirable for a Republican candidate to be antagonistic to the Irish ... But this will never again occur.'[24] *The Pilot* backed Cleveland and methodically disputed Blaine's Irish credentials as well as his candidacy in the run-up to the election. O'Reilly even went on the campaign trail and made what was publicly described as his 'First Campaign Speech' to urge voters not to vote for Blaine.[25]

Despite O'Reilly's efforts Blaine did receive support from major Irish figures such as Patrick Ford and John Devoy but this was more to do with Blaine's promise to protect American labour and industry through tariffs on imports rather than his Catholic background.[26] In the event, Blaine would scupper his chances with Irish voters. Only a few days before the election, Blaine attended a rally where Reverend Samuel J. Burchard, a Presbyterian minister and a member of the Republican Party, made a disparaging remark about Catholics to the effect that they represented 'Rum, Romanism and Rebellion'.[27] Blaine somehow failed to renounce Burchard's comment, which, by the following day, the Democrats had turned into a countrywide news story. Cleveland won the election.

Away from national level politics O'Reilly was more open to the idea of breaking from the Democratic Party establishment, such as in 1878 when he supported Benjamin F. Butler as an independent Democratic candidate for the governorship of Massachusetts. Butler canvassed on the promise to break up monopolies but was defeated by his Republican opponent.[28] Butler did have a partial victory in that, mainly because of *The Pilot's* support, he trounced the official Democratic candidate. That result made Boston's Democratic leadership fully aware of the growing power of the Irish within the party. Four years later, Butler ran as the official Democratic candidate and, again supported by *The Pilot*, won the governorship. O'Reilly was also a part of other political victories. In 1884 he backed Hugh O'Brien's campaign in the Boston mayoral election. O'Brien, a Democrat, triumphed and became the city's first Irish mayor. This was a clear example of growing Irish power but the United States was not the only country in which the Irish wished to see political progress. For O'Reilly and his readers, the old country of Ireland and its domination by Britain signified unfinished business. During O'Reilly's editorship of *The Pilot*, much of his personal energy and his newspaper's columns were devoted to political developments in Ireland.

Although O'Reilly had left the Fenians and Clan na Gael in 1870, he had maintained a personal interest in Ireland and had supported the establishment of Isaac Butt's Home Government Association in Dublin. He had then backed the Association's 1873 successor, the Home Rule League.[29] Nevertheless, O'Reilly had not completely abandoned his erstwhile comrades and remained friends with men such as John Devoy and Jeremiah O'Donovan Rossa. As we have seen, it was his friendship with Devoy that resulted in O'Reilly playing an important role in the *Catalpa* rescue of 1876. Indeed that triumph seems to have spurred O'Reilly to involve himself more directly in the politics of Ireland. The rescue of the Fenian convicts had been a source of joy to Irish communities around the world and Irish nationalists of various hues. O'Reilly now sought to capitalise on this sense of achievement by making an appeal for unity among the many groups that were motivated by Irish issues:

> The Home Rulers are as honest as the Fenians, and as intelligent. One should say to the other, 'We travel the same road; but when you stop, we go further. If we succeed you can join us; if we fail, we shall return to you for support.' This is true nationality; and when this spirit grows among the Irish people, there cannot be a doubt of the results.[30]

O'Reilly's desire for Irish-American unity would be a constant factor in his writings on Irish issues over the following decade. He was, however, never convinced by Isaac Butt's leadership of the Home Rule League, believing the politician to be honourable but too supine in the face of British governmental intransigence.

O'Reilly was far more impressed by a small cadre of Irish members of the British parliament who had, since 1874, occasionally disrupted the work of the House of Commons by filibustering. Initially the 'obstructionists', as they were called, were led by Joseph Biggar, a Belfast-born Member of Parliament for Cavan. Biggar combined his role as MP with being a senior member of the Irish Republican Brotherhood and he had little patience with what he saw as the failures of Butt's conciliatory policy. Biggar's obstruction campaign was soon joined by other Members of Parliament, such as Charles Stewart Parnell, a newly elected and highly ambitious politician.

The two MPs combined with great efficiency in 1877 and led a prolonged campaign of obstructionism that brought the House of Commons to a legislative standstill. Watching their efforts from Boston, O'Reilly was moved to write:

> If Ireland does not fight in the field, she must fight all the harder in the British Parliament. She has never received anything from

England for the humble asking. These young and strong men, disgusted with the decent humility of Isaac Butt when his face was slapped and his country sneered at, have adopted a more virile course. They know the lesson of Irish history. The best prophet of the future is the past.[31]

O'Reilly discerned a new spirit of opportunity in the emergence of Parnell and the 'young and strong men' among the Home Rulers, but it was a Fenian who was to bring O'Reilly into the fold of Irish politics. This Fenian was Michael Davitt who travelled to the United States in the summer of 1878.

The two men had much in common, although Davitt's life to date had been far grimmer than O'Reilly's. Davitt had been born on 25 March 1846 in the Mayo village of Straide, the second of five children. His family survived through the Famine but, in doing so, Davitt's father had accumulated debts that he was unable to pay off. The family were evicted from their home in either September or October 1850. It was a defining moment in Davitt's life. Although only four and a half years old when it happened, he later described the scene: 'the remnant of our household furniture flung about the road; the roof of the house falling in and the thatch taking fire; my mother and father with four young children, the youngest only two months old, adding their cries to the other pangs'.[32] The family emigrated to the north of England and settled in the Lancashire town of Haslingden, about 15 miles east of Preston, O'Reilly's home from 1859 to 1863. Michael Davitt would remain in the town until 1868, but his life in Lancashire had been very different from O'Reilly's enjoyable four-year residency in Preston. As a nine-year-old, Davitt had begun working in local cotton mills before finding longer-term employment at Stellfoxe's Victoria Mill near Haslingden where, on 8 May 1857, his right arm was mangled in a spinning-machine accident. Later that day, the arm was amputated below the shoulder.

In 1858 Davitt restarted his education by taking night classes and by 1861 he was a wage earner once more, working in a Haslingden printing office. Like O'Reilly, he worked for a time as a printer's devil. It was a period when the Irish Republican Brotherhood and the *Irish People* were first emerging into the public consciousness and Michael Davitt was not immune to these developments. In late 1865, around the time that

O'Reilly had been working as a Fenian recruiter in the British army, Michael Davitt joined the Brotherhood. He was an active member and, in February 1867, took part in the abortive Fenian raid for arms stored in Chester Castle; a raid that was supposed to have been a precursor to the main rising, which took place in Ireland a month later. By 1868 Davitt had quit his job in Haslingden and had become a full-time 'organising secretary' for the IRB, a role that required him to act as an intermediary between the supreme council of the Brotherhood and individual 'circles'. It was an important job, which he combined with a second, much more dangerous, role: that of smuggling weapons. Through his smuggling activities Davitt became a target for police surveillance and he was arrested in May 1870. Davitt was tried, convicted and sentenced to fifteen years' penal servitude. As we have seen, he spent around ten months in Millbank before being transferred to Dartmoor in May 1871.

As a result of the ongoing Irish amnesty campaigns Davitt was released, on a ticket-of-leave, from Dartmoor Prison during December 1877.[33] He left prison to find that he had become a public figure and when he arrived in Dublin in January 1878 he was given a public reception headed by Charles Stewart Parnell. Davitt then headed to Mayo where, for the first time since he had been forced from Ireland as a child, he was able to assess conditions in the west of Ireland. While there, he met with James Daly, editor of the *Connaught Telegraph* and a brilliant advocate of agrarian reform. Davitt also met with Matt Harris, a Fenian who had recently started a group called the Tenants Defence Association in Ballinasloe, County Galway. This trip was vital in the development of Davitt's thought. Beforehand, his political philosophy had been based almost solely on the Fenian goal of separation from Britain but he began to think deeply on the condition of tenant farmers in Ireland. Davitt returned to England in the spring of 1878 and, while he pondered the issue of land reform in Ireland, he continued to make a name for himself through describing his experiences of prison life. In a similar manner to O'Reilly, Davitt became a powerful opponent of the British penal system and an activist for its total reform.

In July 1878 Davitt travelled to the United States. His intention was to visit his family who now resided in America but outside of that goal he had no definite political agenda. This changed when Davitt met John Devoy a few days after his arrival in New York. The two men established an immediate affinity and Devoy took Davitt to a meeting of the Clan na Gael executive on 5 August 1878.[34] Here, the Clan persuaded Davitt to remain in the United States for the next four months and to undergo an extensive speaking tour, during which he would talk of both his own experiences as a Fenian and the state of Ireland. It was through Devoy and another Clan na Gael leader, Dr William Carroll, that Davitt was introduced to John Boyle O'Reilly on 18 September.[35] Their first meeting was not very productive, since Davitt was disappointed by O'Reilly's disavowal of Fenianism and what he regarded as the editor's moderate tendencies. Davitt stayed only a few days in Massachusetts and, while he toured the United States, he had little contact with O'Reilly over the following months.

Davitt's lecture tour would have profound consequences for the future politics of Ireland, since it was during this tour that he began to explain publicly his new thinking on Irish issues. By far the most important of Davitt's early speeches was one he delivered in Brooklyn, New York, on 13 October. In this speech Davitt began with the standard Fenian criticisms of the Home Rule Party in Westminster, especially of Isaac Butt. Most of the party were useless, he declared, except for a few members such as Charles Stewart Parnell. The popularity of Parnell in Ireland, he said, was proof that the MP expressed the sentiments of the people. Davitt told his audience that 'self-government is the chief want of Ireland'.[36] To aid the work of Parnell and to push forward the cause of Ireland throughout the world Davitt advocated: that Irish representatives in Westminster should 'oppose the government, tooth and nail, in every effort to coerce Ireland'; that 'there should be agitation for settlement of the land-question on the basis of security against eviction (except on the non-payment of a just rent)'; and 'that Irish industries should be developed'.

Davitt's speech was the first time he had publicly promoted the involvement of Fenians in constitutional politics. He also offered a future whereby constitutional action could be taken in tandem with public agitation on the issues of land and landlordism. Remarkably, Devoy followed Davitt to the rostrum and reiterated these points. In fact, he went much further than Davitt. By 1878, Devoy had realised that groups like the Clan and the IRB had to become more practically involved in Irish affairs and so end the 'isolation from the public life of the country' that had hampered such groups since the end of the 1860s.[37] It was in Brooklyn that he first made public these sentiments. He called on the Irish people to vote against candidates who did not work towards Irish self-government or who did not espouse policies that were for the benefit of the public. The whole political system in Ireland needed changing and he advised that Irish nationalists should seek to infiltrate local public bodies across the country and thus make those bodies serve the Irish people. He concluded by saying that:

> I believe in Irish independence but I don't believe it would be worthwhile to free Ireland if that foreign landlord system were to be left standing . . . I know it is a solution that cannot be reached in a day, and therefore I think we should, in the meantime, accept all measures looking to the prevention of arbitrary eviction and the creation of a peasant proprietary as a step in the right direction.[38]

Devoy's speech was particularly important as, since the success of the *Catalpa* rescue in 1876, Clan na Gael had utterly eclipsed the Fenians as the natural home for Irish revolutionaries in the US. This was recognised even by the IRB in Ireland, who had agreed to cooperate with the Clan in revolutionary activities. The audience, among whom was Patrick Ford of the *Irish World*, reacted enthusiastically to these speeches. Davitt met Ford for the first time that night and the editor of the *Irish World* would become one of the most influential supporters of the land agitation in Ireland as proposed by Davitt and Devoy.

In the aftermath of the Brooklyn speeches, events moved with great speed. Just over a week later the Home Rule Confederation of Great Britain held a meeting in Dublin and, against Butt's wishes, re-elected Parnell as its president. Devoy seems to have believed that this marked a split between Butt and Parnell. Although no such split had occurred, it was clear that Parnell was in the ascendancy and had become the leader of Irish constitutional nationalism. Devoy judged that it was time to make an offer to Parnell. On 24 October, on his own initiative and while Davitt was lecturing elsewhere, Devoy sent a telegram to Parnell, via Charles Kickham, the chairman of the IRB's supreme council. The telegram, which was signed by Devoy and the other leaders of Clan na Gael, contained five points:

Nationalists here will support you on the following conditions:

(1) abandonment of all federal demand and substitution of general declaration in favour of self-government;

(2) vigorous agitation of land question on basis of peasant proprietary, while accepting concessions tending to abolish arbitrary eviction;

(3) exclusion of all sectarian issues from platform;

(4) Irish members to vote together on all imperial and home questions, adopt aggressive policy and energetically resist all coercive legislation;

(5) advocacy of all struggling nationalities in British Empire and elsewhere.[39]

On the following day Devoy had the telegram published in the *New York Herald* under the heading 'An Irish New Departure'. Two days later the same paper carried a series of articles, all written anonymously by Devoy, which offered their support to the New Departure.[40]

The publication of this telegram resulted in much debate in Ireland and among the Irish in the United States. In Boston, O'Reilly wholly endorsed Devoy's publication of the New Departure. It matched his desire for unity of purpose among Irish nationalists, although initially he misunderstood the nature of Devoy's proposal. O'Reilly assumed that the telegram had come from both Devoy and Davitt and that it recommended an immediate course of action. On 2 November he editorialised in *The Pilot* that the 'Parnellites' in Westminster 'are to demand home rule and cooperate in blocking the House of Commons until the demand is granted or they are expelled'.[41] Although he quickly realised that this was not, in fact, the case, O'Reilly retained his enthusiasm for the proposal over the following weeks and at the end of November he contacted Devoy to arrange another meeting with Davitt.

Davitt, in the company of Devoy, returned to Boston on 2 December where he met with O'Reilly at Robert Dwyer Joyce's house. Here, the group discussed Devoy's publication of the New Departure. Davitt may have been originally disappointed with O'Reilly's moderation but this was the first occasion on which the two men had had time for a detailed conversation about Irish issues. By the end of the meeting Davitt was fully aware that O'Reilly's determination to gain self-government for Ireland remained undimmed. Over the next week Davitt spent much time in

O'Reilly's company and, like so many others, he fell under the spell of the editor's contagiously friendly manner. By the week's end he was full of admiration for O'Reilly: 'Remarkably successful man. Immense influence as editor of Pilot. Nominated for state treasurership – declined. President of press and literary societies. Poet of no mean order. Forcible writer. Thinks deeply on national affairs. Vigorous speaker. Fine head, alive with genius. Compact figure.'[42]

On 7 December O'Reilly, Davitt and Devoy reconvened at Joyce's house. The subject of the meeting was once more the New Departure. The result of this meeting, according to Davitt, was that 'land should be made the basis of the national fight, and that all nationalist energies should be enlisted in a contest with the English landlord and political garrison for the ownership of the land and the control of the public bodies in the country.'[43] This new concentration on land was made explicit in a seven-point programme, which was agreed by the four men but which was mostly a more detailed version of Davitt's Brooklyn speech two months earlier:

(1) National self-government as the chief want of Ireland.

(2) Irish representatives in Westminster to be thoroughly nationalist in conviction, and opposed to all coercive measures.

(3) A demand for the immediate improvement of the Irish land system by such a thorough change as would prevent the peasantry from being further victimized by landlordism. This change to lead up to a system of small proprietorship similar to what at present obtains in France, Belgium and Prussia. Such land to be purchased or held directly from the state. The state to buy out the landlords and to fix the cultivators in the soil.

(4) Legislation for the encouragement of Irish industries; the development of Ireland's national resources; substitution as much as possible of cultivation for grazing; reclamation of waste lands; protection of Irish fisheries; and improvement of peasant dwellings.

(5) Assimilation of the country to the borough franchise, and reform of the grand-jury laws, and also those affecting (penalizing) the right of convention in Ireland.

(6) Vigorous efforts to improve and nationalize popular education; and
(7) The right of the Irish people to carry arms.[44]

Davitt later wrote that 'No one entered more heartily into the idea of the new policy than O'Reilly'.[45] He recalled how the editor of *The Pilot* made his contribution to the meeting in an impassioned speech:

> Throw down the gage of battle to landlordism, as the source of Irish poverty, eviction and emigration, and a mighty power will be enlisted in the fight against English rule. America's moral support would be won for a practical Irish proposal that would link a solution of the social problem with the national question, while the financial help of the Irish in the States would be forthcoming in a land-for-the-people struggle in Ireland. I am confident that this is going to be the greatest of Irish revolutionary movements.[46]

On the following night O'Reilly chaired the final lecture of Davitt's tour at the Mechanic's Hall in Boston. In this speech Davitt made the case for the seven-point Boston programme and explained to his audience why Irish nationality could only be advanced through showing the tenant farmers of Ireland that the goal of nationalists should be 'the social well-being of our people'.[47] He also told his audience, in terms similar to those argued by O'Reilly in 1873 (see above), that it was futile for nationalists to keep themselves outside the political process. Now was the time for Fenians, Home Rulers and all those who believed in Irish nationality to unite in pursuit of a common goal.

> No party has the right to call itself national which neglects resorting to all and every justifiable means to end the frightful misery under which our land-crushed people groan . . . In the name of the common good of our country . . . let the two great Irish parties agree to differ on party principles while emulating each other in service to our impoverished people.[48]

It was the culmination of Davitt's first tour of the United States. He returned to New York from where he left for Ireland on 11 December

1878. Following Davitt's departure both *The Pilot* and the *Irish World* sustained a fervent support for the new programme of land reform being attempted in Ireland. Even at this stage, however, O'Reilly was looking beyond the land issue. In *The Pilot* he assured his readers that the land reform programme was a vital goal on the road to independence but not an end in itself.[49]

Devoy had left New York on the same day as Davitt aboard the steamship *Canada*. He arrived in Paris shortly before Christmas and waited until joined by Davitt on 11 January 1879. On the 19 January Davitt, a member of the IRB's supreme council since his release from Dartmoor, brought Devoy to a meeting with the other ten members of the council, including the Brotherhood's leader, Charles Kickham. For a week Davitt and Devoy put the case for the New Departure to Kickham and the rest of the council. It was a torturous series of negotiations, much complicated by the fact that Kickham had been left almost blind and deaf by a childhood accident. One of the council members, John O'Connor, conveyed words to Kickham by spelling them out with the fingers of Kickham's left hand. Despite the efforts of Devoy and Davitt, the IRB rejected the idea of an alliance with constitutional nationalists in Westminster. Only Davitt, among the council, favoured this proposal. The council also rejected the notion that the Brotherhood should involve itself in agrarian agitation, fearing that such participation would divert the Irish public from the goal of independence. The Galway land reformer Matt Harris was the only member of the council who supported Davitt's proposal for IRB involvement in land agitation.

Davitt, undeterred by the IRB's disinterest, arranged a meeting between Devoy and Parnell. This meeting eventually took place in the city of Boulogne in the north of France over 7 and 8 March 1879. Davitt was not present but Devoy left the meeting with a belief that Parnell, while hesitant towards the New Departure, was not outrightly opposed to the proposal. Devoy then secretly travelled to Ireland. In doing so, he took a great personal risk since he was breaking the terms of his 1871 amnesty and, if discovered, he would be re-arrested and imprisoned. In April Devoy met with Parnell again, this time in Dublin and in the company of Davitt. The trio met in Dublin again during June for another discussion of the New Departure. No notes were taken of this meeting although Devoy later claimed that a verbal agreement on the New Departure was reached between the three men.[50] That may or may not have been the case but it is very unlikely that Parnell committed himself to anything as specific as an alliance with Clan na Gael or the Fenians.[51] It is more likely that Parnell gave Devoy vague assurances that an independent Ireland would be his ultimate goal. It is uncertain what knowledge O'Reilly had of these developments although it seems likely that Devoy, once he returned to the United States in August 1879, would have told O'Reilly of the meetings with Parnell. If so, he may also have given O'Reilly the idea that the New Departure had been formally agreed.

Davitt had also been busy in the west of Ireland since his return from the United States. During February 1879 he travelled to Mayo and found that conditions for tenant farmers had deteriorated over the previous twelve months. Since 1877 bad weather and poor harvests had combined to create an agricultural and economic crisis that left the country fearful that the nightmare of the Great Famine was about to be repeated. The grave problems facing tenant farmers were encapsulated in the Bourke Estate in Mayo, whose tenants were in debt and under a looming threat of eviction. These tenants contacted James Daly in the hope that he would report on their plight in the *Connaught Telegraph*. Daly, though, was wary of possible libel action from the Bourke family and advised the tenants to hold a public meeting to present their grievances. This meeting, primarily organised by Daly, took place at Irishtown on 20 April 1879. Davitt was not in attendance, presumably out of fear that he could be arrested for violating his ticket-of-leave from Dartmoor. He missed a momentous event, attended by a crowd of around 7,000 people.[52] The meeting was a triumph for the tenants and resulted in all eviction notices being withdrawn and their rent reduced by 25 per cent.[53] In the weeks after Irishtown other landlords in the locality also granted rent reductions.

A similarly successful meeting took place at Westport on 8 June, this time with both Davitt and Parnell as speakers. Parnell had not yet entirely committed himself to land reform but he could not ignore what was happening in the west of Ireland. His presence at Westport was important because, as F. S. L. Lyons has written, he 'had lent the already considerable prestige of his name to what was still a struggling agitation'.[54] Parnell's speech, in which he warned the crowd that 'You must not allow yourself to be dispossessed as you were dispossessed in '47', was given much coverage in the national press.[55] Not all of this was favourable and many newspapers criticised the Westport meeting. The *Dublin Evening Mail* described the event as 'communism in Connaught'.[56] At this stage in the burgeoning land movement's development, any publicity was good publicity. More mass meetings were held in Mayo and Galway in the weeks after Westport. On 16 August 1879 this public sentiment was brought together in the form of the National Land League of Mayo, a body which proved the model for a national organisation.

By now, Davitt had become utterly focused on land reform as the vital necessity of the Irish tenant and he made a concerted effort to gain Parnell's commitment to the land movement. Through Davitt's efforts Parnell was engaged in a series of negotiations by which the Land League of Mayo was transformed into a countrywide organisation, the Irish National Land League, on 21 October 1879. The new organisation needed money and, as Davitt had realised since he had first travelled to the United States a year earlier, O'Reilly would have an important role to play in this regard. The day after the League was founded, he wrote a letter to O'Reilly in which he implored *The Pilot's* editor to use his influence with 'wealthy Irish-Americans' and thus gain their support for the new movement: 'What we want is money for without it the present spirit of our people cannot be kept up.'[57]

In Boston O'Reilly took to his assigned role with relish and lavished praise on the Land League, which he compared to 'anti-slavery agitation' in the United States. 'The Irish', he wrote, 'only demand that the laws be passed compelling the absentee owners of large estates in Ireland to sell the land to the farmers who till the soil and who pay its produce in rents that are spent out of the country'.[58] Davitt, who was in regular contact with O'Reilly during these months, informed him in November that Parnell, as part of the fund-raising effort, would soon make a tour of the United States. This news delighted the editor as it offered an opportunity to advance both Irish and Irish-American agendas. O'Reilly saw in the Irish Land League the potential to unify Irish America and to garner support for an Irish cause among the wider American population. This can be seen in a letter he wrote to Devoy while organising the committee: 'I called a meeting yesterday, I send you a circular. Asked about 80 of our best men – all parties and classes – your fellows [Clan na Gael], Fenians, Clerics, Protestants, to make a representative committee'.[59] This committee met later in the month and it chose O'Reilly to lead the delegation that would greet Parnell.

Parnell arrived at New York on 2 January 1880 where, on the following day, he was met by O'Reilly, Patrick Collins and Joyce among others. O'Reilly was suitably impressed by the Irish leader, whom he described to *The Pilot*'s readers as a man with an august destiny:

> Great needs evolve men equal to their emergency. Unquestionably this man is marked for his age. He fit his place admirably. Already he is in full harmony with the times. Already he has struck a note of tremendous omen – Irish politics must be settled by reason and adjustment, not by arbitrary will on one side, or passionate refusal on the other. This method has the deepest significance for both England and Ireland.[60]

From New York Parnell embarked on a fruitful tour of the east coast over the following month. Parnell's American sojourn was heavily and sympathetically covered in the American press, even outside Irish-American circles. In Boston O'Reilly convinced his friend Wendell Phillips to speak alongside Parnell. Phillips offered his public support to the Irish politician: 'I do say that I honor citizens that won't lie down tamely under wrong and oppression . . . I do honor the efforts to make the government so uncomfortable that it at lasts consents to make the people comfortable.'[61] This tour, which combined lectures and fund-raising, culminated in his speech to the United States House of Representatives in early February (he was the first foreigner to do so since 1851).

Michael Davitt, writing in 1904, claimed that three men were of vital importance to the American land movement in these early days. The most important of these had been John Devoy who 'brought most of the leading members of Clan na Gael round to his views' but it was the 'corresponding labour by Patrick Ford of the Irish World and John Boyle O'Reilly of the Boston Pilot in their respective papers and widely influential entourage which paved the way' for Parnell's successful tour.[62] The enthusiastic coverage that Parnell obtained in those newspapers also helped create a climate in which an American version of the Land League could flourish. Before Parnell departed for Ireland he assembled a group of prominent Irish Americans and put to them a plan for an American Land League, a move which O'Reilly supported. This organisation, the Irish National Land League of America, came into existence in March 1880. The following month O'Reilly was elected treasurer of the Boston branch of the American Land League, with Collins as President.[63] The League in America would become a much broader church than either the Fenians or Clan na Gael. Parnell's visit to the United States had added a layer of respectability to the Irish Land League and the American version attracted the support of many wealthy Irish Americans who had shunned the revolutionary bodies. It also attracted wide support within the Catholic Church as well as across Irish-American newspapers. With such support in place, branches of the Land League were formed across the country and by the summer of 1880 the organisation was a national phenomenon, with enough branches for a national convention.

This convention met over two days from 18 May 1880 in Trenor Hall, New York, and, not surprisingly given their high profile, it was dominated by the delegates of the Boston branch. In the course of the two days O'Reilly and Patrick Collins presided over the various meetings and were instrumental in choosing the new national leadership: James J. McCafferty as president; William Purcell as vice-president; Michael Davitt (who had just returned to the US from Ireland) as secretary; and the Reverend Lawrence Walsh as treasurer. McCafferty, a relatively unknown figure, had not been the convention's first choice as president.[64] They had initially voted for O'Reilly as the League's national president but he had declined the offer, perhaps because he wished to remain an independent figure within the movement who could cajole or mediate between different factions. Nonetheless, O'Reilly played an important role at the convention when, influenced by Devoy, he successfully made the case that control of the disbursement of funds should be the remit of the national treasury rather than allowing individual branches access to those funds on an ad hoc basis.[65] He also advised the delegates of his opinion on how the American Land League should operate:

> He who should strike the true tone for the Land League of America must be one who looked over the whole field of Irish political, social, and industrial interests, and who should speak a word to linger in the mind and smelt into harmony every healthy element of the race. This convention was essentially one of unification. To-day, with millions in America, Irish nationality was only a sentiment. To-morrow it should be a system. The duty of the Convention was to reduce into

operative form the best aspirations and principles of the people. When this is done, a danger is averted. It is wiser to follow organized principles than to follow men, however excellent they be. When the masses follow men, they may be dangerous to the enemy; when they follow principles, they become terrible. Impotent action breeds contempt and pity. Too much of Ireland's national action has been futile and impotent. It is time to reduce the fight to reason and science, and take advantage of every opportunity. Ireland must plead her case and make her charges against her powerful enemy – not in the dark, where she may be strangled and gagged, as heretofore – but in the market-place, before the world.[66]

That statement also described the role O'Reilly took upon himself: that of a publicist. It was in this role as an advocate for the organisation that he was most influential. Nevertheless, in his private correspondence, O'Reilly admitted that there were problems within the League. The organisation was riven by leadership struggles from its inception and it also contained an element that wished to exclude Clan na Gael. O'Reilly, in his desire for Irish unity, was keen to work in the spirit of the New Departure and keep the revolutionaries as part of the process. In a letter to Devoy during March 1880 O'Reilly assured his friend that the Land League was little more than a fund-raising and publicity machine:

It is at most a paper mountain: it will have a certain effect on English opinion, just to show that Parnell has left tracks in America. But there is no more to it. Do not let your fellows [Clan na Gael] regard it so seriously to make a rupture, or give reason to objectors to say that they meant to rule or ruin. That would do more harm than good, even if the L. League were partly objectionable.[67]

Despite any reservations he may have held, O'Reilly remained one of the League's loudest promoters over the next twelve months. In this effort he had the full backing of *The Pilot*'s co-owner, Archbishop Williams. In early 1881, after the second national convention of the Land League, Williams gave his blessing to the movement: 'justified by religion and morality, we extend our earnest and heartfelt sympathy and cooperation to all those who are laboring in such a just and righteous cause'.[68]

POLICE BOAT.   SHIP'S BOAT WITH THE ESCAPED FENIANS.   BRITISH SHIP GEORGETTE.

BARK CATALPA, OF NEW BEDFORD.

Contemporary sketch of the Catalpa *rescue, with the* Georgette *in pursuit (US Library of Congress, LC-USZ62-12755).*

Walt Whitman c. *1887 (US Library of Congress, LC-DIG-ppmsca-07550).*

Oscar Wilde in 1882, during his visit to the United States (US Library of Congress, LC-USZ62-69512).

Charles Stewart Parnell during his trip to the United States in 1880 (US Library of Congress, LC-USZ62-86689).

Michael Davitt and scenes from his life, drawn in 1881 (US Library of Congress, LC-DIG-pga-01262).

John Boyle O'Reilly in Father Teeling's summer house, c. 1888 (Donahoe's Magazine, September 1893).

John L. Sullivan, famous boxer, c. 1883 (US Library of Congress, LC-USZC4-3040).

Thomas Wentworth Higginson, Civil War veteran and civil rights campaigner, c. 1870 (US Library of Congress: LC-DIG-ppmsca-11424).

Wendell Phillips, the great abolitionist, in the 1860s (US Library of Congress: LC-DIG-cwpbh-01978)

At 17

At 26

At 32

At 36

John Boyle O'Reilly.

The year of his death.

Images of John Boyle O'Reilly throughout his life (Donahoe's Magazine, *September 1893*).

By 1881 Ireland was in the midst of the 'Land War'. From the summer of 1880 the Land League had spread into Munster and Leinster and had copied the Mayo tactics of mass meetings in attempt to reduce rents. Landlords had responded to agrarian agitation by evicting an increasing number of their tenants. In some instances large crowds disrupted these evictions and land agents who enforced evictions were socially ostracised by local communities, most famously in the case of Captain Charles Boycott. There was also, despite condemnations by the Land League, a rise in violent agrarian crime. The Liberal government of William Gladstone, at the urgings of the Chief Secretary of Ireland, William Forster, responded to the violence with the Coercion Acts of February and March 1881. This legislation allowed the police to arrest 'reasonably suspected' persons and, as a result, hundreds of local leaders of the Land League were arrested. The police, as is often the result when given such wide-ranging powers, arrested the very people who were working to restrain others from violence. Michael Davitt, who had repeatedly condemned agrarian violence as wrong and damaging to the tenants' cause, was stopped by a police officer while walking across O'Connell Bridge in Dublin on 3 February 1881. Two days later, Davitt was in Portland Prison in Dorset and would remain there until May 1882.[69]

Parnell strongly protested the introduction of these acts and, along with thirty-five other Irish members, was temporarily ejected from the House of Commons in February 1881. He resisted the urgings of many of his colleagues to secede from the House and return to Dublin to form a parliament from the expelled Irish MPs. In making this decision, Parnell believed that the policy of coercion could not continue without the British government having to make some gesture towards the Irish MPs and the Land League. Parnell's instincts were proved correct when the British government brought a land bill before parliament during April 1881, which was passed into law in late August. Gladstone's Land Act, although it was not immediately apparent, was a major reform: it effectively granted fair rent, fixity of tenure and freedom of sale for tenants. An Irish Land Commission was established to make loans to tenants for the purchase of their land and to maintain fair rents. The Land League was uncertain as to the merits of the act and a convention of the organisation held in Dublin agreed to 'test' its provisions. This would be done by sending selected tenants before the rent tribunals created under the act. While this was happening the Land League kept up its agitation across Ireland. Parnell, eager to keep the Land League from losing momentum, publicly denounced the Land Act as unsatisfactory.

Gladstone's government seemed uncertain as to how to react to Parnell's actions but, from Dublin, William Forster advised the Prime Minister that it was necessary to arrest the Irish leader. On 2 October 1881 he wrote to Gladstone: 'If we strike a blow at all it must be a sufficiently hard blow to paralyse the actions of the League, and for this purpose I think we must make a simultaneous arrest of the central leaders'.[70] Parnell was arrested on 13 October 1881 and confined without trial in Dublin's Kilmainham Jail. He retaliated by issuing the 'No-Rent Manifesto' on 18 October. The Manifesto called for a rent strike, in which tenant farmers were to withhold all rents. The statement was released to the public on 18 October and it caused a sensation in Ireland. Gladstone's government retaliated by suppressing the Land League as an illegal organisation. Parnell had been nervous about the idea of a rent strike and the document exposed divisions within the movement. In Ireland, practically all the bishops and clergy of the Catholic Church condemned the Manifesto, as did newspapers such as *The Freeman's Journal* and the *Nation*.[71] Prominent among the hierarchy in his condemnation was Archbishop Thomas Croke, who had previously been a strong supporter of the League.

The Manifesto also widened pre-existing divisions within the American Land League. Patrick Ford and the *Irish World* represented a 'radical' section within the wider movement. Ford, through a combination of his powerful personality, prodigious fund-raising and a long-standing commitment to the idea of 'the land for the people' had become the Irish Land League's most influential supporter in America.[72] He had founded the 'Spread the Light Fund' to pay for free distribution of the *Irish World* in Ireland and, every week, thousands of copies of the paper were distributed throughout the country.[73] Ford was also somewhat hesitant towards Parnell and would later become a critic of the politician. Then there was the 'conservative' group centred upon O'Reilly and Patrick Collins who allied themselves completely with Parnell and who were determined to prevent Ford's social radicalism from becoming the dominant aspect of the League. The third element within the League was the revolutionaries of Clan na Gael and the Fenians. For this element, land reform in Ireland was a means to unify nationalism in Ireland and thus undermine British rule.

Whereas O'Reilly was friends with Devoy, most of the conservatives in the American Land League were antagonistic towards a secret society such as Clan na Gael. Despite their mutual distaste, the conservatives had more in common with the Clan than they did with Ford and other radicals. Unlike Ford, both those groups, including O'Reilly, saw the Land League as merely a step towards the ultimate goal of Irish self-government, whether that be through Home Rule or outright independence.

In late 1881 two Irish MPs, Thomas Power O'Connor and Timothy Healy, as well as the prominent Land League activist Father Eugene Sheehy, arrived in the United States with the aim of uniting the differing sections of the American Land League. To aid this endeavour O'Reilly, along with Patrick Ford, Patrick Collins and T. P. O'Connor, issued a public call for a national convention to be held in Chicago on 30 November 1881. Although O'Reilly would not be able to attend this convention due to illness he stated his political position in *The Pilot*. It was the first of two important articles by O'Reilly in which he indicated that his focus had now moved from land issues to Home Rule. In this first article he called for Home Rule, while also trying to appeal to Clan na Gael in the United States and the IRB in Ireland:

> It must be remembered by the Chicago Convention, and all other Irish-American conventions, that there is to be no dictation to Ireland as to what line she is to pursue. The five and a half millions there are the people to judge. It would be better and manlier for the millions here who have left Ireland forever to cut away from her altogether than to attempt to coerce or decide for her. If Ireland chooses to agitate for a federal union with England, depending on her great natural advantages, and on her native militia or volunteers to insist on them, we Irish-Americans should promise her continued sympathy and support. This is her choice at present in her own words. We believe it is a wise one; she will be better able to demand and secure more, if necessary, after ten or twenty years of Home Rule. Nevertheless, it is far from our wish to see the physical force men, the separatists, disband their organizations, and come on to the constitutional platform. There could be no surer way of preventing Ireland from getting any improvement what-ever. All countries keep a force party, an organized army, as a threat behind the spoken word.

The country that is struggling for existence surely needs this in a special manner. The Irish Nation irrefutably says that it was the armed volunteers behind Grattan who secured the Parliament of 1782. Therefore we trust that as Irish unity proceeds there will be one allowance made on all sides of the necessity of a party of physical force to which all Irishmen can fall back should England refuse Ireland's coming demand for Home Rule. Until the Home Rule idea is tried to the uttermost, and refused by England, the physical force party can never depend on the whole Irish people. In case of that refusal there is only one course for earnest Irishmen to take.[74]

In the same article he wrote that if Ireland was given 'a home government' the country would become 'a quiet part of the empire, as Hungary entered into the life of Austria, and grew at a bound to be the most important part of the empire.' This was the way forward for Ireland, he argued. England, he warned, 'fears entire separation, and will coerce and lie and murder to oppose it.' Therefore he urged the Irish to respond by making a 'firm and intelligent demand for a federal union between the countries' which would 'be supported by the public opinion of the world.'

The Chicago convention was dominated by the conservatives and it passed a resolution in support of the No-Rent Manifesto. However, the Manifesto was endorsed, as Thomas Brown put it, only 'as a political expedient; without reference to its social and philosophical implications.'[75] This decision ruptured the League, and the Catholic hierarchy in the US condemned the resolution. Especially critical was Bernard J. McQuaid, the Catholic Bishop of Rochester. McQuaid, originally from County Tyrone, was a conservative member of the hierarchy who had always been suspicious of the Land League. Even so, he was particularly fierce in his opposition to the No-Rent Manifesto and he rebuked the priests who had been delegates at the convention.[76] Bishop Gilmour of Cleveland proclaimed that the Manifesto was a communist doctrine and violation of the Fifth Commandment.[77] These developments left O'Reilly facing a personal dilemma and it may be that his decision to miss the convention due to 'illness' was a tactical move. He was perturbed by the actions of the Catholic hierarchy in Ireland and the United States who were almost completely antagonistic to the No-Rent Manifesto. Yet, independent of the hierarchy's position, O'Reilly thought that the No-Rent Manifesto should be nothing other than a temporary arrangement, a bargaining chip which would lead to the release of Parnell and the other imprisoned leaders as well as the introduction of legislation to deal with tenants' arrears. In *Moondyne*, written throughout 1878 and 1879, O'Reilly had already shown his belief that, during any period of land reform, the landowners should be compensated. The No-Rent Manifesto, he believed, ran counter to that idea.

A month later O'Reilly returned to the topic of Home Rule in an article for the American Catholic Quarterly Review, entitled 'Ireland's Opportunity'. It was a remarkable piece that marked O'Reilly's break with the Land League. The article began with his assertion that the work of the League had been completed:

> The arrest of Parnell and the other leaders – and even the lawless shattering of the Land League in Ireland by armed and ruffianly force, have been futile work for the English Government . . . because there are now, in this country alone, more organized Irish societies, and twice as many Irishmen as there are in Ireland . . . The Land League has succeeded. It has compelled the passage of a law that will lower rents, more or less. It has raised the Irish question into cosmopolitan attention. It has crystalized the national sentiment of the Irish people and their descendants in America, Australia, Canada and other countries. But above all its good results, it has nationalized the Irish farmers, traders, priests and well-to-do classes, and they stand now ready and waiting for the next act in the national drama. It is time for the curtain to rise again. When the Land League, aided fearfully by the famine, began its agitation, its timeliness and force were acknowledged by all Irish parties. The Home Rulers virtually subsided, giving the newcomers their place. The Revolutionists looked on with unfriendly eyes, at first fearing that the land movement, which only aimed at a detail, would distract attention from the National idea. But as they watched, they saw that the new agitation was raising the farmers and tradesmen into activity, and after a time the Land League was left alone in the field to work out its purpose as best it could.[78]

O'Reilly derided suggestions that 'the Land League means to abolish rent altogether'. In fact, he stated, the League had never worked towards such a goal. He called the idea 'a social theory which no country has yet accepted'.[79] Nobody, he continued, could expect Ireland who was 'struggling for very life', to 'voluntarily burden herself also with a socialistic mill-stone that would probably sink the United States'. The purpose of the Land League had been served and it was time to agitate for Home Rule:

> Ireland in 1882 ought to agitate for and demand her own government. No matter by what name the movement is called, whether Home Rule, Repeal or Federation. The result will be practically the same . . . The official life will no longer be an alien and inimical network spread over the island. The insolent presence of soldiery and armed constabulary will disappear. The dignity of a people upholding a nationality they are proud of will take the place of the servile helplessness of an almost pauper population. We do not fear for Ireland's future in a federal union with England . . . And if, after a fair trial of the Federal union, it were found that Ireland suffered by the bond, that she was outnumbered in council, harassed and injured by imperial enactments, that in fact it was an unequal and unbearable contract, then still there remains the ultimate appeal of an oppressed people – separation – even by the sharp edge of violence.[80]

Such violence, he stressed, was not the correct option for Ireland at this point in time. In the midst of his article O'Reilly chastised those who 'declare that they will have nothing less than utter separation from England, with a republican and socialistic government for Ireland'.[81] Although he did not name the groups, he also warned Clan na Gael and the Irish Republican Brotherhood that separation from the British Empire was militarily unfeasible. It would require an Irish army 'of at least one hundred thousand men, equipped with engineers and artillery' as well as a fleet of ships and he posed the question: 'What earnest revolutionist is prepared to wait until all this can be done before Ireland obtains a Parliament of her own?' He urged them, as he had urged the Land League, to work for Home Rule:

> The next step for Ireland is obviously not revolution. She has been for the past four years a model to the world of intelligent, peaceful

agitation . . . The people of Ireland are to-day without a national policy. The splendid Land League organization goes on grinding, but it is not grinding toward nationality. Its great-hearted work for the present winter is to protect the evicted families of farmers who refuse to pay rent because England has outraged even her own laws. But Ireland cannot go on forever fighting with all her forces against a minor evil. The sooner Ireland in America speaks on this point the better . . . Even the revolutionary party in America [Clan na Gael] condemn as absurd the 'No Rent' proposition. This party, too, sees that Irish Home Rule in no way conflicts with their own more consummate settlement. Another, and a very grave reason for an expression of policy, is that the best intelligence, both in Ireland and America, will withdraw from a movement that either cloaks its ultimate purpose, or has none. Already the Land League has suffered deep loss by the vagueness of its drift. One American bishop has publicly uttered his disapproval of an organization which he could not understand; and the Catholic clergy generally have, it is believed, a secret and a growing feeling in regard to the Land League, that they are dealing with an occult and uncertain organism. To allow so great an organization to collapse through blind management and lack of purpose would be calamitous.[82]

O'Reilly concluded with an address to the Irish people, writing that it was 'not enough' to fight the landlords and support evicted tenants. He urged the Irish, through their representatives in parliament, to make a demand for Home Rule. This demand would gain sympathy 'from the Catholic hierarchy and priests, both in Ireland and America, and from intelligent and conservative men, who have hitherto avoided all Irish national movements.' Now was the time to make this demand or 'an opportunity such as Ireland has not seen for a century will be lost.'[83]

O'Reilly's public abandonment of the Land League and his backing of Home Rule brought him bitter criticism from within some sections of Irish America. The Boston branch of the League accused him of being a traitor to the movement, although they later withdrew this accusation.[84] Patrick Ford also criticised O'Reilly in the *Irish World* claiming that the editor of *The Pilot* was 'killing the Land league.'[85] O'Reilly ignored these comments and continued to participate in the League. He attended the national assembly of the organisation in Washington during April 1882. Despite the furore that greeted *The Pilot*'s editor after his 'Ireland's Opportunity' article, he was made a member of the convention's resolutions committee, a fact which suggests that he retained much personal support within the organisation.[86] However, the controversy that surrounded O'Reilly would soon be overshadowed by news from Ireland of the Phoenix Park murders. On 6 May 1882, a previously unknown secret society called 'The Invincibles' assassinated the Chief Secretary for Ireland, Frederick Cavendish, and the Undersecretary, Thomas Henry Burke. The two politicians were stabbed to death while walking through the Phoenix Park.

This event presaged a political crisis in Ireland. Parnell had been released from prison only a few days earlier under the terms of the Kilmainham Treaty. This agreement between Parnell and Gladstone had been a victory for the Irish leader. He had given little of value to Gladstone other than a promise to condemn agrarian violence. In return, Gladstone had given assurances that the policy of coercion would end and that arrears of rent would be dismissed. This would be a vital step in allowing tenant farmers to take advantage of the previous year's Land Act. Cavendish had been brought to Ireland specifically to implement these new policies. All that progress was threatened by the stunning news from the Phoenix Park. Parnell made an immediate public denunciation of the murders and he had this statement telegraphed to John Boyle O'Reilly so as to achieve 'the widest publication in America'.[87] Across the Atlantic O'Reilly was appalled. On 7 May the editor and Collins chaired a meeting of the Boston Irish in Faneuil Hall where they agreed a resolution to send Parnell $5,000 dollars, which could be offered as a reward for information on the murderers.[88]

When O'Reilly had first heard the news of the Phoenix Park murders, he had denied that the assassination had been committed by any Irish group but this belief was quickly shown to be unsustainable. In *The Pilot* he used the event to warn of the dangers of secret societies. The actions of such groups were the opposite of the 'patient, moral agitation'[89] that O'Reilly urged as the way forward for Ireland:

> There is an awful lesson both for Ireland and England in the discovery of these murderers. It is no victory for England to lay bare the abominations of her own misrule. She may use the appalling fact to justify still further coercion. Blind, cruel, and fatuous, will she

never learn that such measures cannot have other effect than to increase secret retaliation? The lesson for Ireland is one that has been taught before. Secret organization to commit violent crime is an accursed disease. It has blighted Ireland, under the names of Ribbonism, Orangeism, and Whiteboyism. It has blasted every country that ever resorted to it. It is the poison of patriotic action. Passion and ignorance are its parents, and its children are murder and cruel crime. The voice of the Church is always against it, and the wise leaders of the people have everywhere abhorred it. The country that allows it to become rife, which sympathizes with its dark deeds, is not fit for freedom. Ireland has not so sympathized. It is heroic to prepare for war with a tyrant power. Patriots will always win the admiration of mankind for daring to meet the bloodshed of battle for their country's liberty. But the patriot who is willing to go to that sacrifice will be the first to condemn the aimless and secret shedding of blood in time of peace.[90]

There is a seeming contradiction in O'Reilly's thought on this issue and his writings on physical force have caused confusion to those who have studied his life.[91] Months earlier, he had written that revolutionary bodies were a necessary part of any national struggle and that groups such as Clan na Gael were a legitimate expression of Irish nationality. Such sentiments appeared in *The Pilot* on a few occasions over O'Reilly's editorship of the paper.[92]

Those editorials in which he argued that there was a place within Irish nationalism for revolutionary bodies have usually been portrayed as O'Reilly's passion overruling his cautious nature. That conclusion is misguided and O'Reilly did have a coherent policy on the use of physical force. He never advocated violence as a means of furthering land reform in Ireland or in regard to gaining Home Rule. O'Reilly was publicly critical of secret societies and violence against civilians. Instead, his advocacy of physical force was in the sense that he believed that a willingness to fight was the ultimate safeguard of a people's rights. He argued that in the future an Irish army might have to take the field in pursuit of Irish independence but this was only after all other methods had failed. He once said, 'I want to say, for my own self-respect, and for the self-respect of my countrymen, that behind all their constitutional effort is the purpose to fight, if they don't get what they now ask for.'[93] His thoughts on physical force in Ireland cannot be divorced from the approach that O'Reilly took to other issues that concerned him. We have seen in his attitude to women's suffrage that he believed civil society and individual rights to be ultimately underpinned by force of arms; that the voting population should correspond to the fighting population. He similarly advised blacks in the American south to defend themselves against attacks from white vigilantes (see chapter 14). His statements on the existence of Irish revolutionary groups such as Clan na Gael are thus consistent with his wider world view.

Irish nationalists in Ireland and the United States rallied around Parnell in the aftermath of the Phoenix Park murders. His position was further strengthened in August 1882 with the introduction of the Arrears Act. This relieved tenants of crushing debt and allowed them to take advantage of the Land Act to have their rents fixed. Parnell, in the words of T. W. Moody, 'in effect called off the land war after securing an immediate settlement of the arrears question . . . and accepting as a long-term settlement of the land question the development of dual ownership under the land act and of occupying ownership through an improved system of land purchase'.[94] The Land League had achieved many of its aims and set in place a pattern through which additional land reforms would be achieved in later years. Parnell now felt confident to move away from land agitation and turn towards Home Rule. In October 1882 the Irish National League was formed in Dublin, replacing the Land League and the old Home Rule League. Although the National League utilised much of the regional structure and branches left behind by the Land League, the National League was a very different body. This new league would be directly controlled by Parnell and would be very closely tied to the Irish MPs in parliament rather than a mass movement. Davitt, who had been released from Portland Prison following the Kilmainham Treaty, called it 'the overthrow of a movement and the enthronement of a man'.[95]

Despite his reservations Davitt supported Parnell and was made a member of the League's organising committee. However, Davitt had passed the high point of his influence in Irish politics and by the end of the year he had become completely enmeshed in land reform to the exclusion of Home Rule. In doing so Davitt would rupture his friendship with Devoy and would also, albeit to a much lesser degree, distance himself from O'Reilly. Davitt, like O'Reilly during 1870, had become disillusioned with the Fenians and had left the Brotherhood by 1882. That alone, as evidenced by the continuing friendship between Devoy and O'Reilly, would not have been reason for Davitt to become estranged from Devoy. The real reason was that Davitt's approach to land reform was fundamentally different from that of Devoy and O'Reilly. By 1882 Davitt had become influenced by Henry George, a prominent American political economist. George, in his 1879 work *Progress and Poverty*, had blamed private property for existence of inequality in the economy and society: 'From this fundamental injustice flow all the injustices which distort and endanger modern development, which condemn the producer of wealth to poverty and pamper the nonproducer in luxury.'[96] The landlords, according to George, were the worst of these non-producers as they contributed nothing to the economy and achieved wealth through monopolising land and levying taxes on the earnings of capital and labour. George's theories were mostly ignored by the American Land League but he had a highly influential devotee in Patrick Ford. In October 1881 Ford had hired George as the *Irish World*'s 'special correspondent' in Ireland.

From George's writings Davitt formulated an approach to Irish land reform that was, to many of his colleagues, dangerously innovative. Davitt now proposed land nationalisation, which he described as 'the land of Ireland to be national property with the state as the only landlord'.[97] He was accused by nationalists in Ireland and the United States of being a mere pawn of Henry George and the *Irish World*. Parnell dismissed the land nationalisation idea as incompatible with Land League policy. In America, Clan na Gael and the conservatives in the American Land League rejected land nationalisation proposals. O'Reilly was at the fore of this American opposition to land nationalisation. Although he remained personally friendly with Davitt, O'Reilly joined the consensus that claimed the Land League's founder had become seduced by impractical and radical ideas. In *The Pilot* O'Reilly warned that George wished only to use Ireland as a test case for his theories and urged the Irish to ignore land nationalisation: 'Henry George and his school care nothing about Irish nationality. They only want to see their communistic ideas put into practical operation.'[98]

Davitt's land nationalisation ideas fell on stony ground in the United States. As had occurred in Ireland, Home Rule replaced land reform as the goal of Irish nationalists. In April 1883 the American Land League convened in Philadelphia and merged itself with the newly formed Irish

National League of America. O'Reilly could have, if he had wished, forged a central role for himself in the new National League but from that year onwards he 'functioned chiefly as a self-appointed critic of the Irish scene'.[99] O'Reilly was often a perceptive political analyst and he had played a leading role in the American Land League but he took little pleasure in political manoeuvring. He preferred to raise issues and cover events as an editor and campaigner rather than as a political practitioner. O'Reilly had proved this in 1878 when he had refused the nomination of State Auditor for Massachusetts, which had been offered to him by the Democratic Party. In declining the offer O'Reilly wrote that if elected: 'I would have to choose between filling the Auditor's or the Editor's chair. I prefer the latter.'[100] In a sense, O'Reilly's involvement in the events surrounding the New Departure was accidental, as was the strong political role he held in the American Land League. They came about solely through his friendship with John Devoy and then Michael Davitt.

When it came to the National League O'Reilly returned to his favoured roles of publicist and fund-raiser. The new League, he wrote, would build upon the work that the land reform movement had started. In July 1883, in Boston, O'Reilly explained his viewpoint to a meeting of the National League:

> We have come here to prevent the repetition of such a scene of shame as that which happened in New York on the 12th of July, 1871; to prevent such an iniquity as that of importing paupers from the Irish subject country; to destroy the wicked and ruinous drain on the finances of the people of this country, which are sent every year to fill the pockets of the rack-renting landlords of Ireland; and to take such measures as are best calculated to win to our cause our fellow-citizens and the entire American race. We can do this by appealing to the justice and to the intelligence of our fellow-citizens. It will be our first duty to prevent American citizens from misunderstanding the purposes of the Irish National movement, and from believing the misrepresentations of the English papers and their agents in this country. It is our duty to make it known to America that the National League is based on a reverence for law and order, and we hope to win for our cause the conscientious conviction of every good man in America, no matter of what race.[101]

Such sentiments have often been described as an example of O'Reilly's conservatism and as evidence of his desire to appear respectable before an American audience. However, his speech was an accurate analysis of the situation in the United States. The Fenians had been obsessed, throughout the 1860s and 1870s with the idea of utilising the military manpower of Irish Americans in support of Irish nationality. O'Reilly had once dreamt that dream but he had seen the limitations of such a strategy. The Fenians' insistence on military action had damaged the reputation of Irish nationalists in the United States. O'Reilly was also speaking at a time in the 1880s when O'Donovan Rossa was using his base in the United States to sponsor bombing campaigns in England (see below). These bombings were proving to be similarly damaging to Irish nationalism in America and threatened to undo the broad-based support that had been achieved by the Land League in that country. O'Reilly could see the potentially awesome influence of the Irish in America on any future settlement that Ireland might obtain from a British government, and that insight was apparent in all his writings on the National League and Home Rule. That was one reason why O'Reilly continually counselled reverence for law and order among the members of the Land League and then the National League.

Where O'Reilly advocated 'moral influence', or what today might be termed soft power, others within Irish America, especially O'Donovan Rossa, sought to use the sharp edge of violence to defeat the British Empire. As far back as 1875 Rossa had been a proponent of sending teams of 'skirmishers' to England to launch small-scale attacks. He first espoused this notion in a letter to the *Irish World* in which he established what he called a 'Skirmishing Fund'.[102] The idea of a skirmishing fund was given credibility during the following year by the success of the *Catalpa* rescue. That operation, albeit one in which Rossa and his fund played no part, had suggested that properly resourced operations involving a relatively small number of people could achieve outstanding results. After the rescue Clan na Gael took over Rossa's fund and renamed it the National Fund. The Clan, under the control of men like John Devoy, showed little appetite for sending men to wage war in England and instead poured much of its money into supporting land agitation in Ireland and schemes such as John Phillip Holland's submarines, which they hoped to eventually use against the British navy.[103]

Rossa had opposed the New Departure and been a loud critic of the Land League. He suffered further disappointment with Clan na Gael's refusal to use the National Fund as means of launching attacks in England. So, in 1880, he began a new fund which he advertised in the *United Irishman*, a newspaper he founded that same year. This fund, as he had originally intended for the Skirmishing Fund, was designed to pay for a bombing campaign against English targets. He had no organisation, other than his own efforts, with which to maintain this fund but by 1881 Rossa had received enough donations and volunteers to begin sending strike teams from the United States to Britain. Rossa's campaign would be a major deviation from the type of warfare that had been an inherent part of Fenian and Clan na Gael military thinking. The Fenians, in particular, had anticipated open warfare between an Irish army and its British enemy. The limitations of this strategy had been demonstrated on many occasions, most recently in the 1867 rebellion. To adequately arm and train such an army until it was in a position to triumph against the British Empire was simply beyond the resources of any Irish revolutionary group. However, when Rossa spoke of skirmishing he was not proposing guerilla warfare such as would be successfully conducted by the Irish Republican Army during 1919 to 1921.

The skirmishing which Rossa envisioned was the use of dynamite against targets in Britain. Dynamite was a new weapon, having only been invented in 1867 by the Swedish chemist, Alfred Noble. It was originally a commercial explosive but its ability to be transported relatively safely, allied to the fact that its explosive power far exceeded that of gunpowder, made it an increasingly common choice among revolutionaries and anarchists across the world. Rossa personally trained many of the bombers whom he was about to send to Britain. His teams would use this new weapon as part of a strategy to terrorise the British public through bombings of public amenities and symbols of the British government. This campaign was planned in the full knowledge that it would result in civilian casualties and that it would cause a backlash against Irish communities in Britain.[104] Rossa's strategy, as Owen McGee wrote in his history of the IRB was 'denounced by almost all figures within the Irish revolutionary movement as irrational, wasteful of revolutionary funds and highly immoral.'[105] One of Rossa's few supporters was Patrick Ford who, in the *Irish World*, regularly defended the use of dynamite as a legitimate response to the overwhelming power and brutality of imperialist powers.[106]

O'Donovan Rossa's dynamite campaign began in 1881 with an attack on Salford Barracks in Lancashire. The dangers that such bombings posed to civilians had been demonstrated at Clerkenwell during 1867 and the attack on Salford had similarly dire results. Four civilians were injured and one these, a seven-year-old boy, died a few days later. Further bombings, none of which caused major damage, were carried out in British cities over the rest of 1881 and 1882. Glasgow was the site of an attack on a gasworks in January 1883, which caused huge property damage. O'Donovan Rossa's men were emboldened by that feat and, during March, attacked the headquarters of *The Times* newspaper and government offices in London. While the attack on *The Times* resulted in very little damage, the explosion at the government offices almost destroyed a building that housed various sections of the British civil service. Remarkably, no one was seriously hurt.

While O'Donovan Rossa had been running his campaign, Clan na Gael had been preparing for its own attacks in England. By 1883 John Devoy was no longer a power broker in Clan na Gael. During 1881, with his prestige in the movement damaged by his support for the New Departure, Devoy had resigned from the Clan's Revolutionary Directory and started his own newspaper, the *Irish Nation*.[107] The Clan then became dominated by 'the Triangle' of Alexander Sullivan, Michael Boland and Denis Feely. These three controlled Clan na Gael during the 1880s and they decided to organise a bombing campaign in England. The British government had some intelligence on these developments but not enough to prevent the Clan from launching two, almost simultaneous, bombings in the London Underground on 30 October 1883. There were many injuries but no deaths in these attacks. A similar bombing in Victoria Station on 26 February 1884 likewise caused extensive damage, multiple injuries, but no deaths. These incidents caused panic in London and public anxiety was deepened by a series of attempted bombings over the subsequent months. On 30 May 1884 the Clan carried out one of their most effective attacks when they badly damaged the office of the Irish Special Branch in Scotland Yard.

The attack on Scotland Yard, a symbol of the British authorities, was an undoubted coup for the Clan. It was a very public embarrassment for the police who, thus far, had failed to end the bombings and who had now failed to protect their own headquarters. In December Clan na Gael ramped up their operation when they made an unsuccessful attempt to destroy London Bridge. This was followed, in January 1885, by bombs at the Tower of London and Westminster. No civilians were killed in these attacks but their audacity shocked the British public and the political establishment. Yet those explosions were the zenith of the campaigns and the police, through a combination of surveillance and informers, soon managed to disrupt or arrest most of the bombing teams. There was much relief among the Irish on both sides of the Atlantic that the violence had ended. In Ireland and Britain, the IRB had disapproved of dynamite attacks and, although individual members may have assisted Clan na Gael and O'Donovan Rossa's campaigns, the organisation, as a whole, had not participated in the bombings. In America, Devoy berated Clan na Gael for engaging in 'terrorism to force concessions from the British government rather than starting a fight for independence to drive the British out of Ireland.'[108]

The dynamite campaign was a source of great personal anguish to O'Reilly.[109] He had condemned the bombings and the reasoning behind them. News reports from England that told of a rising tide of anti-Irish animosity horrified him. During the height of the violence in early 1885 the New York Times reported that the moment was near when a mob 'will fall upon the Irishmen in London'.[110] The paper urged the bombers to stop before the whole Irish population of the city was imperilled. On 2 February 1885 English outrage manifested itself in the United States when a young Englishwoman, Yseult Dudley, fired five shots at O'Donovan Rossa as he walked down a New York street. At least a couple of the bullets hit Rossa before his assailant turned and attempted to leave the scene. She was apprehended by onlookers before she could escape.[111] Rossa was not seriously hurt in the attack but the reaction in England to news of the attempted assassination was one of untrammelled joy. The New York Times reported that newspapers carrying the story were 'selling like wildfire on the streets in every city and town throughout Great Britain' and that 'nearly every person seems jubilant'.[112] In response to these developments O'Reilly penned a passionate, yet coherent, plea for an end to the historic enmity between Ireland and England:

> The madmen were at the helm a week ago, and the nations seemed to be rapidly drifting into a war of races more appalling than the world has ever seen, for the limits of such a conflict, should it ever

come, will extend round the planet, wherever there are Irishmen and English interests. The madmen are at the helm yet. When thirty million English people wildly cheer a half insane and wholly disreputable murderess, and thirty million people of Irish blood half sympathize with the desperate lunatics who would burn down London – it is time for both sides to pause. It is time for both England and Ireland to answer this question: Is it too late to be friends? In the present hour of her calamity and grief, we say to England that she can steal the exultation out of Irishmen's hearts by granting the justice that they now ask, but will soon demand, from her... One magnanimous statesman in England, one leader with the courage and wisdom of genius, would solidify the British Empire to-day with a master stroke of politics. He would abolish the Union, and leave Ireland as she stood eighty-five years ago, a happy, free, confederated part of the Empire. Such a policy would silence the dynamiters and radicals, satisfy and gratify the Irish people throughout the world, strengthen the British Empire, and make America thoroughly sympathetic. There are twenty million people in the United States who as kindred feel the rise and fall of the Irish barometer; and the policy of America must largely respond to their influence in the future. It is only a question of a few years till Ireland obtains all that she now asks, and more, without England's consent. Nothing can stop the wave of Irish nationality that is now moving. At the first rattle of the conflict in India or Europe, Ireland's action may mean the ruin or salvation of the British Empire. England may think that an offer of friendship from her would now come too late. She knows her own earning in Ireland, and may well doubt that her bloody hand would be taken in amity by the people she has so deeply wronged. But let her offer. She is dealing with a generous and proud and warm-hearted race. We know the Irish people; we gauge their hatred and measure their hope; and we profoundly believe that the hour is not yet too late for England to disarm and conquer them by the greatness of her spirit, as she has never been able to subdue them by the force of her armies.[113]

It was a theme that O'Reilly returned to throughout 1885. The basic argument always remained the same: the British government should release Ireland from the stranglehold of the Union and so begin the process by which centuries of mutual antagonism could be ended. He called on Gladstone to 'Send an olive branch to Ireland . . . It is not too late to win Irish loyalty for a union which leaves her as free as England – the only union that can satisfy Ireland and make the British Empire more powerful than ever.'[114] In April O'Reilly described to his readers how the injustices of British rule in Ireland meant that 'every Irishman' carried in his heart a hatred of England: 'He had in him, whatever land may be his home, a force that drives him to passionate mediation and action, a poison that frets his own soul, and is handed down to his children's children.'[115] This antagonism, according to O'Reilly, left Ireland without hope, portended doom to the British Empire and threatened to foul the lifeblood of American society. In October 1885 he explained why justice for Ireland was also an American issue:

> The elements of our population are mainly in the East descended from England and Ireland, and they inherit a prejudice, an unfriendliness – an unnatural, artificial, ignorant antipathy on both sides. That unnatural condition of distrust and dislike should cease in America, and we should amalgamate into one race, one great unified, self-loving American people; but that condition will never come until peace is made between the sources of the two races. Their descendants in this country will always be facing each other in antagonism, discontent, and distrust, until England sits down and shakes hands freely with Ireland.[116]

Although O'Reilly, throughout 1885, used his paper to urge an end to hostilities between Ireland and England, that same year the British government signalled that they were not yet ready to end hostilities with John Boyle O'Reilly. In December 1884 the Irish community in the Canadian city of Ottawa had invited O'Reilly to deliver the St Patrick's Day oration on 17 March 1885.[117] According to Roche, the Canadian government consented to this invitation and promised they would take no action against O'Reilly who was an American citizen, even though the one-time Fenian had been part of an invasion of their territory in 1870.[118] O'Reilly was keen to accept the invitation but wary of entering a British Dominion lest he be arrested as an escaped convict. O'Reilly contacted a friend of his, Thomas Sexton, the Member of Parliament representing Sligo. Sexton advised him to make a request to the British Home Secretary, Sir William Vernon Harcourt, for a guarantee of safe conduct. This O'Reilly did, and he also asked the American Secretary of State, Frederick T. Frelinghuysen, to intercede with his British counterpart. Frelinghuysen duly contacted the British government but both requests were rejected.[119]

Sexton then raised the matter in the House of Commons. In a superb speech he argued that it had been O'Reilly's duty to escape from his confinement in Western Australia: 'If by any conceivable turn of fortune the Home Secretary came to suffer penal servitude himself, would he not make an attempt to escape? He might have shown as much ingenuity as Mr Boyle O'Reilly; but it was doubtful whether he would have shown as much courage.'[120] Sexton was followed by Thomas Power O'Connor who told the House that O'Reilly was 'one of the best known, most respected, and eminent citizens of the United States'. The government's refusal to accede to O'Reilly's request, said O'Connor, and its failure to debate the issue properly was symptomatic of the 'tone of insolence, of arrogance, of mean and snobbish contemptuousness, which in a great measure accounted for the acrimony which unfortunately characterised Irish discussions in that House.' Sexton and O'Connor, however, failed to change the government's stance. The Home Secretary maintained his refusal to allow O'Reilly into Canada. In the eyes of the British government, according to Harcourt, O'Reilly was still a criminal who had 'committed the offence known as prison breach.'[121] O'Reilly's cause was not aided by the dynamite campaigns, which had led to a hardening of attitude among the British authorities. During 1883 a group of Irish prisoners had been convicted of bombing and had all received life sentences. In such a climate even O'Reilly's request to enter Canada was judged to be unacceptable by the British government, not least because it would have led to a political backlash from the Conservatives on the opposition benches.

While all this had been happening, O'Reilly had confirmed his commitment to Home Rule by backing the creation of the American Irish Parliamentary Club, an organisation which sought to provide funding to Irish parliamentarians in Westminster.[122] In December 1885 O'Reilly was given hope by the results of the British general election, in which eighty-six Parnellite MPs were elected and thus held the balance of power between the Liberals and the Tories. After the election Gladstone's son, Herbert, signalled that his father was moving towards supporting Irish Home Rule and by January 1886 it seemed certain that the Liberals in alliance with Parnell would bring Home Rule legislation before Parliament. Watching these developments from America, O'Reilly contributed a piece entitled 'At Last' to the *North American Review*. In this journal he provided a history of Irish struggles since the twelfth century, a story which was now, he believed, nearing its long-delayed denouement. The man who was pushing Ireland and England to this endpoint was Parnell who, O'Reilly wrote, 'has drawn together the forty millions of people who respond to the Irish barometer, in all lands, and made them into one marvelous, moral, organized nationality, supporting Ireland with public opinion, agitation, and money.'[123]

England, he continued, had two choices with regard to Ireland: 'another Cromwell must sweep Ireland with fire and sword, or that England must grant her constitutional demand for Home Government.' He was certain that England would, eventually, take the second course: 'England is learning the great lesson. Ireland is saved by the twenty million Irish-blooded Americans; by the five million Irish and their descendants in England, Scotland, and Wales; by the vast numbers of Irish sympathizers in Australia, New Zealand, Canada, and other countries.' O'Reilly concluded his article with a prediction:

> In returning eighty-six Nationalist members to Parliament, the Irish have not ended, but just begun their national struggle . . . Parnell, with fifteen or twenty votes, was not a power; he was only a voice, an emphasis, an appeal. He was an agitational influence. With eighty-six votes he is a controversial force. 'He has compelled John Bull to listen', as Wendell Phillips said of him. In 1889, I predict, the legislative stage of the Irish question will have arrived; and the Union with England, which shall then have cursed Ireland for nine-tenths of a century, will be repealed.[124]

By now O'Reilly's involvement in Irish politics was beginning to wane. As we shall see in the next chapter, the second half of the 1880s was a trying time in O'Reilly's personal life. His wife and youngest daughter were both ill and his own health had begun to fail. A more pessimistic tone now characterised his writings on civil rights and labour reforms. The idealism and hope with which he had supported the New Departure and the Land

League had become diluted over the subsequent years. The British policy of coercion in Ireland and the dynamite attacks in England were two causes of his dissatisfaction, but it was the divisions among the Irish in the United States which he found most dispiriting. The Irish-American unity that had marked the birth of the Land League in America was long gone. In a personal capacity he tried to restore Irish unity through dialogue with disputing factions and he even remained friendly with those who had planned the bombing campaigns in England and whom he criticised in *The Pilot*: Jeremiah O'Donovan Rossa and Alexander Sullivan. In May 1886 he wrote to Devoy, 'I am sick to death of the deadly bitterness of these fights, and I think that as a journalist the interests of the Irish people are best served in ignoring them.'[125] O'Reilly's letter laid bare his frustrations:

> I despise [Patrick] Egan's judgement; but I am sure he means well. I dislike [Alexander] Sullivan's intense planning and manipulating; but it his natural way, and his whole career, so far as I have seen it, has been highly beneficial to Ireland. I have a sincere affection and respect for John Byrne; but I abominate his method of making a personal fight at every corner. I have a tender friendship for Rossa; but I think he ought to be killed for a darned fool... They have each written pages of hatred against the others, to me; but charge and counter-charge cannot be true – so I have concluded that neither is quite correct – and that both had better be forgotten.[126]

O'Reilly was also disappointed by Gladstone's Home Rule Bill, which was brought before the British Parliament in April 1886, writing that it 'promises life but enacts death'.[127] The bill was indeed a half-hearted measure that promised a single legislative body in Ireland composed of two 'Orders': one based on the Irish peers already sitting in the House of Lords and the other based on the existing Irish MPs sitting in the House of Commons. The bill would never become law, ultimately being voted down in the House of Commons, a victim of Conservative and Unionist opposition. After 1886 O'Reilly continued *The Pilot*'s policy of giving broad coverage to Irish developments but he had less of a personal involvement in Irish politics. He remained a firm supporter of Parnell and an advocate of Home Rule for Ireland but American and personal issues were to be the main focus of his life.

'The Word Must Be Sown'

Throughout the 1880s O'Reilly seems to have been engaged in a terrible battle to stay one step ahead of time. He was overworked and constantly striving to reach one deadline after another. Yet he was unable, perhaps unwilling, to break free of this cycle. During 1882 O'Reilly had described to a friend, the writer Charles Warren Stoddard, his wish 'to be listless and dreamy, and idle, and regardless of conventionalism'. In the same letter he had predicted: 'It can never be. I am chained to the wheel. I shall never lie down in the sunny grass till I lie in the churchyard.'[1] The hub of this wheel and the centre of O'Reilly's working life was his office at *The Pilot*'s headquarters. Arthur Gilman described the room:

> His journalistic work is done in the queerest little den ever seen – a tiny room in the fourth story of the Pilot building; made tinier by being lined with book-cases, and by a litter of old newspapers and magazines. His desk is a wild confusion of first proofs, 'revises', copy, slips cut from exchanges, old letters, poems, and leading articles for the Pilot, and piles of dust.[2]

Such was the state of the office that the editor routinely scribbled facts and memos on any available surface, including the desk and the window frames. One day, O'Reilly happened to be away on business when an enterprising assistant decided to give the office a thorough cleaning. (This assistant was probably Dan O'Kane, the orphaned son of a former employee in *The Pilot* whom O'Reilly had made his personal secretary in 1877.) In doing so, he washed away O'Reilly's scribbles and left the editor bereft of contacts and other 'valuable memoranda'.[3] From that time onwards, the assistant 'would sooner think of dropping out of the window than he would dare to touch anything in the room higher than the floor'.[4] The paper's staff had learned that amid O'Reilly's chaotic office there was an order that was explicable only to their boss. This room was an apt symbol of O'Reilly's increasingly frantic life and during exceptionally busy periods the editor would even sleep there.

As the 1880s progressed O'Reilly's health was to become less robust. He regularly suffered colds and, while this may have been a result of stress and work, he may also have had a more serious condition. What that condition was and whether it was physical or psychological is a matter of conjecture but, especially in the second half of the decade, O'Reilly was struck by repeated and debilitating bouts of insomnia. Roche also makes mention of O'Reilly suffering at least one bout of vertigo.[5] He tried to combat this through regular activities such as canoeing but it was boxing that was his favourite means of maintaining fitness. In 1880 O'Reilly had been a founder member of the Cribb Club (Tom Cribb had been a prominent English prizefighter earlier in the century), an exclusive boxing club which catered to only twenty-five active members, 'men distinguished in art, literature, and statesmanship'.[6] Over the next decade the newspaper editor trained at the club's gym whenever he had the opportunity and in the ring he developed a reputation as a fearsome opponent. Justin McCarthy, the Irish Home Rule MP and writer, gave a description of O'Reilly's prowess as a boxer that would have befitted a mythological hero:

> Although he is not more than common tall, he has the breadth and the thews [muscles] of a Viking of the days when Olaf Tryggveson dwelt by the Liffey in Dublin town and wooed and won the fair daughter of an Irish royal house. He excels in all manly arts and accomplishments in a way that we are almost afraid to chronicle ... Who among amateurs can ride better, row better, walk better? Above all, who can box better?[7]

A more prosaic description came from the pen of Edward A. Moseley, a good friend of O'Reilly and a fellow member of the Cribb Club. O'Reilly, he wrote, 'always entered into every sport with the heartiest enthusiasm. He did not have the slightest sympathy for a man in full vigour who could not take as well as give a blow.'[8] The Irishman had a punch 'almost forcible enough to knock an ox down'.[9] Moseley knew what he was talking about. He had once stepped into the ring against a professional and, to quote an observer of the fight, 'got the worst end of it, but he simply did not know when he was whipped.'[10] The fight had to be stopped to prevent the still eager Moseley from getting seriously hurt. On another occasion O'Reilly had sparred with Boston-born John L. Sullivan, at that time the Heavyweight Champion of the World. O'Reilly and Moseley regularly boxed together and they carried their enthusiasm for the sport into their confrontations. Moseley's biographer, James Morgan, gave an account of one of their bouts as described by a club member: 'I well remember holding the watch for an event between O'Reilly and Moseley, and there were no love pats about it either. Both men were stripped to the buff. The blows came hard and fast, and were given with all the strength the opponents could muster.'[11]

Boxing and canoeing were not O'Reilly's only sporting passions. He was an accomplished swordsman, a skill he developed while with the 10th Hussars. On his arrival in the US in 1869, the jobless Fenian had briefly considered earning money 'by giving lessons in broad-sword, single-stick, and foils'. The former soldier would often, as Moseley remembered, challenge his friend to a duel: 'Ned, on guard! Now run me through. Thrust me anywhere you can. Kill me if you can.'[12] Moseley always lost these bouts: 'And then with a smile upon his face he would ward off my lunges until, suiting his purpose, he would send my sword flying across the room.' O'Reilly was also a devotee of Irish sports and in 1879 had been a founding member of the Irish Athletic Club of Boston (IACB), which thereafter held annual athletics meets in the city.[13] He had a particular affinity for hurling and in 1880 had presented the IACB with the 'John Boyle O'Reilly Hurling Cup', described in the press as 'a magnificent silver cup, superbly ornamented, unique in design, and of great value'.[14] By the 1890s, partly as a result of O'Reilly's support, the city would play host to five hurling and two Gaelic football clubs.[15]

O'Reilly was never able to devote as much time as he would have wished to his personal fitness. The publication of *The King's Men* in 1884 had added to his workload and he spent much of the next two years giving public lectures and poetry recitals, while also working in support of the various American and Irish causes in which he had involved himself. This had an adverse impact on his editorial work. O'Reilly admitted in print that, as a result of his demanding schedule, he had 'neglected his work on the Pilot and increased it by allowing it to accumulate in his absence'.[16] It was not a good time for the editor to have taken his concentration off the paper. By 1886 O'Reilly's old boss Patrick Donahoe, now aged seventy-six and freed from debt, had resurrected his business career. It was a remarkable turnabout in his fortunes. Ten years earlier the former proprietor of *The Pilot* had been almost broken by the misfortunes that had plagued him but in 1878 he had started the monthly publication, *Donahoe's Magazine*.[17] That publication was now at the centre of a new empire, which included a travel agency and a foreign exchange service. Donahoe, however, was still missing his former flagship, *The Pilot*. Sometime in early 1886 Donahoe contacted O'Reilly's co-owner of the paper, Archbishop John J. Williams. When Williams had purchased the paper in 1876 he had publicly stated that he hoped to return some day to Donahoe 'a large and profitable interest in the Pilot'.[18]

Donahoe now intended to convince the archbishop to make good on this promise and, through an intermediary, he approached Williams about purchasing the paper.[19] The news shocked O'Reilly who was understandably fearful of his position on the paper, especially as Boston gossip at the time conveyed as fact the rumour that Donahoe would soon take ownership of *The Pilot*. Williams was the major shareholder and could, if he wished, respond positively to Donahoe's approach. It now appeared to O'Reilly that Donahoe could cause him to lose the enterprise in which he had invested so much time and effort and which was his main source of income. O'Reilly's nervousness was palpable in a letter he wrote to Williams:

> I am constantly reminded by strangers and acquaintances that Mr. Donahoe is to have the Pilot and that I am to stay on for a time and I am tired of it. I wish to know where I stand. The Pilot is worth $100,000 if let alone ... because you saved it by purchase and I have saved it by hard work. If anyone wants to profit by this ... it is not fair. You may be able to suffer it – but it is a loss to me of ten of my best years.[20]

O'Reilly was so worried that Williams would sell the paper that he even proposed a scheme whereby the editor would have sole control of it for

1887 and 1888. His proposal stated that 'all its earnings would be mine for that time'.[21] O'Reilly calculated that this would earn him around $20,000. Once the two years had passed Archbishop Williams could then sell the paper 'without injury to me'. This, the editor believed, would serve as compensation for his loss of a stake in the paper. O'Reilly, after all, had been the driving force behind the 1876 takeover of The Pilot, which had saved Donahoe from disgrace. O'Reilly and Williams had repaid $73,000 of the paper's profits to Donahoe's creditors; money that would otherwise have been theirs. It is true that O'Reilly had done very well from the takeover. He had a very substantial salary and a place of influence within Boston society. His fame as editor of The Pilot had also allowed him to further his literary career. However, these were justifiable rewards for his courage and ambition in saving the paper.

Throughout the summer O'Reilly was genuinely concerned about a possible takeover but there is no evidence that Williams was ready to sell the paper to Donahoe. The two men's co-ownership of The Pilot remained in place and the rumours that surrounded the paper faded away by the autumn. However, the episode had upset O'Reilly and had exacerbated the strain of his working and home lives. The editor was further annoyed that, having worked for so long on Irish issues, he was a focus of public scorn for some within the Irish-American community. Among Clan na Gael and Fenian circles in Boston there remained a lingering distrust of O'Reilly even though he had played an important role in the Catalpa rescue. As we have seen, his 1882 decision to emphasise Irish Home Rule rather than land reform had earned him the enmity of the Boston branch of the Land League. O'Reilly sometimes received criticisms from within these groups and in May 1886 he was irritated by rumours that he charged large fees for his lectures and work in support of Irish causes.[22] The editor printed a lengthy riposte in The Pilot. It is curious that O'Reilly wrote of himself in the third person, as if he could not directly admit that he was overworked and exhausted. However, the article lays bare the strain that he was now under and gives an indication of his increasing troubled home life:

> he started off by subscribing his full share in ready money for the Irish Parliamentary Fund and all other Irish funds. Then he willingly gives evening after evening making speeches at Boston and

neighbouring meetings without charge, of course. Then he is asked to speak in other cities . . . In some of these places, the committees have paid his expenses, sometimes generously, sometimes insufficiently, sometimes not at all; but in no case have they ever been asked to pay anything . . . To O'Reilly, whose literary work must all be done at night, this constant interruption has entailed a very serious pecuniary loss. Since October last [1885] he has had to utterly abandon his literary work. His irregular coming and going destroyed his home life, and dangerously affected his wife's health, unhappily already impaired. In the season of greatest pressure he had to leave his home in consequence, and go and live in a hotel, thus doubling his expenses . . . and injured his health by overwork. Committees commonly say, 'O, it will do the Pilot good if you come.' This is bosh; the Pilot would be better served by constant attention. In October last, O'Reilly engaged with his publisher to have a new book [In Bohemia] ready. The book only needed a week's revision. He has not had seven days since to do it, and it stands undone, at the author's loss . . . O'Reilly has literally raised tens of thousands of dollars for the Irish fund this winter; and has sacrificed more since October in literary reputation and money, giving up his work, than he could earn by lecturing in seven years. He had nothing to gain by making speeches; it is all labour and loss. He does not want the reputation of a lecturer, speechmaker or orator. Any popularity it may give he could earn a thousand times better by and easier by literature and journalism. Indignation at the above question compels this answer. O'Reilly does his work for Ireland ungrudgingly and unboastfully, but the people who find fault are those who give one or two evenings during the winter to go to a lecture, for which they pay fifty cents, and are entertained for their money during hours that have no value to them. There are many men doing the same work as O'Reilly in this way; and for their sake and his own the next time a committee ask him to come and 'donate his services' he will see that they understand the matter.[23]

A few weeks after this letter O'Reilly managed to break free of his punishing schedule for a few days by the Merrimack River, north of Boston. The newspaper editor made the journey by canoe (which he had named the *Blanid* after his youngest daughter) to the summer house of his friend, Father Arthur Teeling. O'Reilly kept a short diary, 'Boyle's Log' of his escape to the countryside in which he praised the solitude: 'No books – no newspapers – no bores. Thank God, and Fr. Teeling!'[24] He was to spend the next five days fishing, shooting and canoeing but the trip also marked a very personal anniversary:

> June 21 – Red Letter Day. Alone in Domus Tranquilla – twenty years ago to-day I was sentenced to twenty years' imprisonment by the English Government. Had I not escaped in 1860, they would to-day open my cell door and say, 'You are free!' This is a good place to celebrate the day – alone – thinking over the changes – the men – the events of the twenty years![25]

There is a discrepancy in O'Reilly's dates. As we have seen in chapter 3 he was sentenced on 9 July 1866, although it was not until he was drummed out of the army the following September that he was made aware of his fate. It could be that O'Reilly was genuinely confused as to the dates or it could be that his sentence was due to end on 21 June 1886.[26]

This anniversary seems to have marked a period of introspection for the 42-year-old. O'Reilly's decision in September 1865 to become an active member of the Fenians had set his life on a course that he could never have had imagined. His current status as a respected newspaper editor, a prominent writer, a loving family man and a focus for the affection, almost hero-worship, of his large band of friends and admirers on both sides of the Atlantic, had all flowed from that moment. Where this contemplation took him we can only guess but, amid all the success, courage and justifiable pride, there were many regrets and worries that may have crowded his mind: never having had a final opportunity to see his now dead parents; Jessie Woodman and his attempted suicide; former Fenian comrades like Henry McCarthy and Thomas Chambers who had been destroyed by their incarcerations; his ill wife and daughter. Through the second half of the 1880s there is a sense that O'Reilly was growing disillusioned with at least some features of society in the United States and perhaps also with aspects of his own life. This can be seen in his last volume of poetry, *In Bohemia*, which was published later in 1886. The poet's disappointment is especially apparent in the title poem of the volume, 'In Bohemia'.

The poem, like many of his editorials, lashed out at inherited wealth: 'I'd rather fail in Bohemia than win in any other land / There are no titles inherited there / No hoard or hope for the brainless heir'.[27] He also targeted those native-born families of the American aristocracy who looked dismissively on those whom they regarded as social inferiors. In his imagined Bohemia there would be 'No gilded dullard native born / To stare at his fellow with leaden scorn'. In *The Pilot* O'Reilly regularly lampooned the pretensions of the rich, especially figures such as Jane Stanford, the wife of the industrialist Leland Stanford, a woman who was world famous for her outlandishly expensive taste in precious stones. In 1885 O'Reilly had told his readers: 'Mrs Leland Stanford of California in buying a $100,000 necklace of Tiffany's . . . took pains to assure the jeweler that she only wanted it for breakfast.'[28] O'Reilly's disgust at such ostentation was instinctive. He once described attending a dinner and his dismay on meeting the hostess, one Mrs Kelly: 'She was enamelled and painted and blazing with diamonds . . . She simpered and sidled like a silly duchess . . . I had an unpleasant feeling of disgust and amusement.'[29]

'In Bohemia' questioned the dismissive attitude of the rich towards the poor and how that attitude could be exhibited in charitable organisations. O'Reilly was wary of the power that charities could gain over the poor, especially those charities which sought to decide who did or did not deserve support. He was particularly dismissive of the supposedly 'scientific' means by which the Charity Organisation Society, a Protestant benevolent group, dispensed relief to the poor.[30] It was this organisation that was the target of one of his most brilliant and cutting lines: 'The organized charity, scrimped and iced / In the name of a cautious statistical Christ':

> But the thirsty of soul soon learn to know
> The moistureless froth of the social show;
> The vulgar sham of the social feast
> Where the heaviest purse is the highest priest;
> The organized charity scrimped and iced
> In the name of a cautious statistical Christ;
> The smile restrained, the respectable cant,
> When a friend in need is a friend in want;
> Where the only aim is to keep afloat,
> And a brother may drown with a cry in his throat.

Oh, I long for the glow of a kindly heart and the grasp of a
    friendly hand,
And I'd rather live in Bohemia than in any other land.[31]

'In Bohemia' was, on one level, a critique of the United States for not yet
having created a culture in which equality of opportunity was afforded to
all. But, like other poems in the volume, it also served as a cry for escape
from the pretence of the social order.

Another poem from the collection is 'The Cry of the Dreamer'. This is,
today, the poem for which O'Reilly is most well known. (It is, for example,
the title of a musical retrospective of O'Reilly's life by the Irish musician
Seán Tyrrell.) Its first verse exhibits the same desire to break free of the
daily grind: 'I am tired of the planning and toiling / In the crowded hives
of men / Heart-weary of building and spoiling / And spoiling and building
again.' The second verse is darker in tone and displays a wider
disenchantment with society:

> I am sick of the showy seeming
> Of a life that is half a lie;
> Of the faces lined with scheming
> In the throng that hurries by.
> From the sleepless thoughts' endeavour,
> I would go where the children play;
> For a dreamer lives forever,
> And a thinker dies in a day.[32]

O'Reilly's determination to address social problems in his poetry is the key
theme of In Bohemia. In that sense it is similar to his earlier works. Yet, as a
whole, the collection is of a more personal nature than his previous volume,
The Statues in the Block. In 'The Cry of the Dreamer' and 'In Bohemia'
O'Reilly is not looking down on events, as in poems such as 'From the Earth,
a Cry', but is ensconced in the midst of the society that he is criticising. The
poet is on the street and amongst the crowds. He does not like what he sees.
The world-weary view of human nature that permeates many of In Bohemia's
poems may be a reflection of O'Reilly's personal frustrations.

A number of factors had combined to dampen the enthusiasm with
which O'Reilly usually approached problems: his ill wife; the stress of

editing an influential paper; Patrick Donahoe's attempt to take over *The Pilot*; the squabbling of Irish nationalists; the slow progress towards black civil rights in the United States; and the failure of the British political system to provide Home Rule for Ireland. The periods of ill health that were becoming a regular part O'Reilly's life may also have contributed to the jaded views of *In Bohemia*. On 24 July 1886, only a few weeks after he returned from his stay at Father Teeling's summer house, O'Reilly wrote to John Devoy describing a prolonged period of poor health: 'Today after three hours work, I am unable to proceed – my first day after two weeks rest too.'[33] O'Reilly sought some solace in his religion. He had always been devoutly Catholic but it seems that, from this time, faith became a more important part of his life. According to George Noble Plunkett, who first met O'Reilly around 1880: 'he frequented the sacraments with increased assiduity'[34] during the later years of the decade.

O'Reilly was discomfited by some aspects of American culture but he still believed that the society could be improved. By the late 1880s his chosen mode of social improvement was sport. Even while O'Reilly had been composing *In Bohemia*, he had been working on what would be his next publication; the *Ethics of Boxing and Manly Sport*. The book, published in 1888, was the culmination of O'Reilly's passion for boxing, rowing and Irish sports. O'Reilly wrote the *Ethics of Boxing and Manly Sport* at a time in which Irish and Irish-American boxers were at the pinnacle of their success in heavyweight boxing. This was also a time in which gloved boxing was replacing bare-knuckle boxing. The Irishman was a proponent of gloves both for safety reasons and because he advocated the 'science' of boxing in opposition to the vicious brawls that were so often the outcome of bare-knuckle fights. In an 1882 interview that he gave to the *Boston Daily Globe*, O'Reilly declared that he had an antipathy towards professional prizefighting and that 'nothing can relieve a prize-fight, the outcome of which is the physical defeat of one of the men, from its present revolting features of cruelty and passionate brutality'.[35] Instead he argued that the sport should be based upon an amateur ethos and that contests should be judged 'depending on skill alone'. Nevertheless, over the intervening years O'Reilly had not ignored the success of John L. Sullivan and Irish boxers such as Paddy Ryan from Tipperary. By 1888 he had become a passionate advocate of Sullivan's skills as a boxer, although he still contended that safety was not a high enough priority within professional boxing.[36]

The *Ethics of Boxing and Manly Sport* was divided into four main parts: a history of boxing from ancient until modern times; a guide to training techniques, diet and exercise; a history of athletics and hurling in Ireland; and an account of some canoeing expeditions of which O'Reilly had been a part. It was typical of O'Reilly that he had personal as well as social improvement in mind when he wrote the book. It was published only four years after the founding of the amateur Gaelic Athletic Association (GAA) in Ireland and at a time when the concept of 'muscular Christianity' had become popular in Britain. These developments undoubtedly influenced O'Reilly's thoughts on sport and he was a supporter of the codification and regulation of sports that was then happening across Europe and the United States. O'Reilly maintained that sport should be enjoyed by all the population and that 'we must save athletics from the professional athletes, and from the evil association of betting and gambling'.[37] This could only be achieved through making sport 'a necessary and admirable part of general education':

> So long as large numbers of our young people, of both sexes, are narrow-chested, thin-limbed, their muscles growing soft as their fat grows hard, timid in the face of danger, and ignorant of the great and varied exercises that are as needful to the strong body as letters to the informed mind, such books as this need no excuse for their publication.[38]

There is little doubt that O'Reilly's personal experience of overwork was another key influence in writing the book. In its introduction he stressed the necessity of exercise in maintaining a healthy mind and in combating the strains of the modern world. He was particularly concerned by the heavy demands which society made of workers and schoolchildren:

> 'We have not holidays enough', says an eminent American physician. 'Five days a year is our allowance, a scanty one indeed, that seems ridiculous to our quieter neighbours across the water, who, needing rest less than we, get four times as much. But there is no time for relaxation; we must only do our best to brace up and stand the drive.' What parent, who has observed the endless studies of his children, at school during the day, and at home in the evening, with little time and

opportunity for vigorous play, and has not inwardly feared that it was too much for the boy or girl? His fears are real warnings: they are true. The studies are too much, unless offset by a proportionate amount of play and vigorous exercise. They prevent the children from developing; and they also prevent them from learning.[39]

Despite these noble aspirations, O'Reilly received some criticisms for this book from within the Irish community. Boxing, according to Denis Ryan in his study of the Boston Irish, 'was never fully accepted by Yankees or by Irishmen sensitive to outside opinion'.[40] *Donahoe's Magazine* accused O'Reilly of dredging up stereotypes of the violent Irish through his writings on boxing.[41] This could be evidence of an enduring ill feeling between O'Reilly and his old boss but it was more probably a manifestation of 'lace-curtain' Irish hostility towards a sport they considered to be a working-class pastime.[42]

These were relatively isolated criticisms and the *Ethics of Boxing and Manly Sport* was well received by the press.[43] The publicity of the book necessitated another series of public lectures and writing commissions for its author. During the course of 1888 O'Reilly was as busy as he ever was, although he was able to take a short canoeing holiday through the Dismal Swamp region of Virginia and North Carolina with Edward Moseley during the summer.[44] It was only a short respite from worry. Mary's health had markedly deteriorated over the previous few years and from 1889 onwards she would spend most of her time at the O'Reilly's summer house in Hull.[45] Blanid fluctuated between periods of normality and times of frightening illness. A month after the trip to Dismal Swamp O'Reilly wrote to Moseley: 'My little Blanid has been very ill, dying almost, for two weeks. I could not write. I was up day and night. She is better now, thank God.'[46] O'Reilly shared a particularly close bond with Blanid and her poor health was heartbreaking for him. She was the subject of one of his most tender poems, unpublished in his lifetime, 'To My Little Blanid':

> I told her a story, a fairy-story,
> My little daughter with eyes of blue.
> And with clear, wide gaze as the splendors brightened,
> She always asked me – 'Oh, is it true?'

Always that word when the wonder reached her,
The pictured beauty so grand and new –
When the good were paid and the evil punished,
Still, with soft insistence – 'Oh, is it true?'

Ah, late, drear knowledge from sin and sorrow,
How will you answer and answer true,
Her wistful doubt of the happy ending? –
Wise Child! I wondered how much she knew.[47]

We know little of O'Reilly's home life other than the occasional glimpses provided by his letters but the anxiety provoked by the poor health of his wife and youngest child was evident to those who knew him. Thomas Wentworth Higginson, who had often clashed with O'Reilly over the issue of women's suffrage, was greatly moved by his friend's commitment to his family: 'But I can tell you that when the man who is doing two men's work all day still spends night after night in attending the invalid wife to whom he owes so much . . . I am ready to sign an amnesty with him on the woman suffrage question.'[48]

Perhaps when O'Reilly contemplated the problems that filled his newspaper editorials he was now, like Blanid, plagued by the 'wistful doubt of the happy ending'. Throughout the last two years of the 1880s O'Reilly remained committed to the cause of Irish Home Rule and to improving the conditions of workers in the United States. However, it was the gradual but seemingly inexorable diminution in the civil and legal status of blacks that drew much of his attention, and which caused him great anguish. The decades after the Civil War had, despite the Civil Rights Acts of 1866, 1871 and 1875, seen a resurgence of prejudice against blacks. This was apparent all over the country but especially so in the eleven states of the former Confederacy. The end of the 'Reconstruction' period in the United States had been a disaster for the black communities in those states. Reconstruction, which had its origins in Abraham Lincoln's Emancipation Proclamation, had been designed not only to reintegrate the Confederate states into the Union and to reform an economy that had been based on slavery but also, to a lesser extent, to provide civil rights for the millions of former black slaves.

However, while it may have led to the black population of the South gaining the vote, Reconstruction did little to improve the economic conditions of blacks or to give them access to land. They remained impoverished and in thrall to whites. But it was the ever-present threat of violence from whites that was the most horrific characteristic of life in black communities across the south. Even though the federal government had crushed the Ku Klux Klan in the years after the Civil War, blacks remained subject to systematic intimidation from white vigilantes. Their dire situation was worsened by political developments in the 1870s. The Democratic Party was, at that time in the South, effectively the party of white supremacy. In the early years of the decade it had begun to regain control of southern legislatures, a process the party had almost completed by 1876. This happened at a time when there was waning Republican Party support for Reconstruction and by 1877, when the government pulled the last federal troops out of the southern states, the Reconstruction era was over. Across the whole of the United States the impetus towards black civil rights that had been apparent after the end of the Civil War had disappeared. The mood of the country was exposed during 1883 when the United States Supreme Court ruled that the Civil Rights act of 1875, which had forbidden discrimination in hotels, trains, and other public spaces, was unconstitutional.

This court ruling had effectively legalised discrimination based on race. Blacks, especially in the south, were no longer slaves but they were most definitely second-class citizens. (Such discrimination would not be declared illegal until the Civil Rights Act of 1964.) O'Reilly had opposed the repeal of the 1875 Civil Rights Act: 'the highest crime may be written in the highest law of the land', he wrote in an 1884 lament for his friend, the abolitionist Wendell Phillips.[49] He hated the pernicious hypocrisy of a society that was supposedly based on the premise that all its citizens were equal. O'Reilly had seen the results of this new mood and the discrimination that it sustained during his journey through the former Confederacy in 1885. He had undertaken a second trip to the south in 1888 and received further proof that the chasm between whites and blacks was still growing. Those journeys had confirmed to the editor of The Pilot the need to regularly highlight prejudice against southern blacks and the racial segregation that resulted from what would later be called 'Jim Crow Laws'.

Such discrimination had its defenders, especially the eloquent and highly influential southern orator Henry W. Grady. The southerner had toured the United States in the late 1880s making speeches on what he called the 'New South'.[50] In these speeches he claimed that the northern media had overplayed the poor relations between whites and blacks in southern states. Grady's speeches were about more than race-relations: he also stressed the need for the South to industrialise and make itself a vital part of the United States. Those features of Grady's thinking were laudable but his analysis of the 'race problem' was wilfully misleading and supportive of a society that was grotesquely prejudiced against blacks. In December 1889 Grady spoke at Faneuil Hall in Boston on 'The Race Problem in the South'. He told his audience, including former US President Grover Cleveland, that southern blacks 'were happy in their cabin homes, tilling their own land'.[51] He rubbished the claims of northern commentators, such as O'Reilly, that blacks were marginalised or subject to regular violence. Black 'agitators', he declared, were responsible for spreading this falsehood among gullible or anti-southern journalists. Grady evidently told his audience what they wanted to hear and his speech was interrupted for applause at least twenty-nine times. Over the following days newspapers in Boston and across the north extolled Grady's speech and the promise it offered of a rapprochement between the north and the former confederacy.[52] The positive reaction that the speech garnered gives an indication that, for all the efforts of reformers like O'Reilly, most white citizens of the United States were happy to ignore the ongoing bigotry that afflicted black communities across the country.

O'Reilly was one of the few journalists who disputed this consensus. In *The Pilot* he chastised Grady and the attitude that the southerner represented, writing, 'Never did oratory cover up the weaker points of a repulsive cause so well'.[53] O'Reilly did more than editorialise and, in his paper, he printed a series of articles that disputed the claims advanced by Grady and highlighted the realities of southern life. Throughout the 1880s black communities had to contend with increasing violence from white mobs. One particularly brutal occurrence was the massacre of eight black men by over one hundred whites in Barnwell County, South Carolina, during December 1889. O'Reilly responded to the event with one of his angriest editorials:

> The black race in the South must face the inevitable, soon or late, and the inevitable is – DEFEND YOURSELF. If they shrink from this, they will

be trampled on with yearly increasing cruelty until they have sunk back from the great height of American freedom to which the war-wave carried them. And in the end, even submission will not save them. On this continent there is going to be no more slavery. That is settled forever. Not even voluntary slavery will be tolerated. Therefore, unless the Southern blacks learn to defend their homes, women, and lives, by law first and by manly force in extremity, they will be exterminated like the Tasmanian and Australian blacks. No other race has ever obtained fair play from the Anglo-Saxon without fighting for it, or being ready to fight. The Southern blacks should make no mistake about the issue of the struggle they are in. They are fighting for the existence of their race; and they cannot fight the Anglo-Saxon by lying down under his feet.[54]

This article brought O'Reilly much criticism across the United States, some of which he printed in *The Pilot*. In reply to a claim from the St Louis newspaper *Church Progress* that 'It is neither Catholic nor American to rouse the negroes of the South to open and futile rebellion', he wrote, 'True, and the Pilot has not done so. We have appealed only to the great Catholic and American principle of resisting wrong and outrage, of protecting life and home and the honor of families by all lawful means, even the extremest, when nothing else remains to be tried.'[55] O'Reilly further defended his editorial by repeating that blacks in the south were 'fighting for the existence of their race' and that if they failed they would be 'exterminated'.

Despite the backlash from other newspapers O'Reilly was not deflected from his support of civil rights and he continued to write on the topic throughout 1890. In June of that year he composed what would prove to be his last great editorial on inequality and prejudice, in which he linked racism to the manifold hypocrisies engendered by imperialism. O'Reilly editorialised on the success of Clement Garnett Morgan, a black student who had recently graduated with a bachelor's degree from Harvard University. Whereas in previous years the editor would have written about the joy of the occasion, he now had no illusions about Morgan's future:

Clement Garnett Morgan, the colored graduate of Harvard, who delivered the class oration last week, held his own manfully. His

oration was as good as the average and very like all the others, just as
Clement Garnett Morgan is like all other Harvard graduates, except
in the color of his skin. Men who have traveled and observed and
reflected know that all men are like each other; that the same
keyboard touches all their notes; that a black, red, yellow or white
skin has no deeper significance; and that there is no greater
difference between 'races' than between individuals of the same race.
But for all that, the position of Clement Garnett Morgan is an
unhappy one; for the average American person calling himself an
'Anglo-Saxon' is the most mulish of all men in claiming superiority
for his own little part of the human family. To him the black man is
an inferior, as the brown man is to his British relative in India. If he
can throttle a man and rob his house, that proves that he was created
to 'govern' him. This colored boy was elected class orator in Harvard
partly through class dissensions and partly through the noble
instincts of youth still 'uncorrected' by society and experience.
When his oration was ended, and Morgan stepped out of Harvard
and into the world, he ceased to be a 'gentleman' and an equal, and
at one descent fell to the level of 'the nigger' who could never be
invited to one's house; or proposed at one's club, who would be
refused a room at nearly all leading hotels, even in the North, and
who would not be tolerated even in church in the half-empty pew of
polite worshipers. Clement Garnett Morgan has trials and heart-
burnings before him, and we wish him strength and wisdom to bear
them ... The Anglo-Saxon will accept him only when he has proved
his strength in the mass. The A. S. will not accept colored
individuals, simply because he need not. Negro strength is in negro
unity; and it must so continue till the crust of white pride, prejudice,
and ignorance is broken, torn off, and trampled into dust forever.
Then, and not till then, Clement Garnett Morgan can be a
cosmopolitan. Until then he must be a faithful, forbearing, helpful,
and self-respecting negro.[56]

These editorials were written at a time when O'Reilly was in increasingly
poor health. This was evident in correspondence between O'Reilly and M.
J. Harson during September 1889. Harson, who was on the organising
committee for the first Catholic Lay Congress due to be held in Baltimore

later that year, had written to O'Reilly asking if the newspaper editor would deliver a speech at the event. O'Reilly responded from a hotel in the White Mountains region of New Hampshire:

> Your letter finds me here in the mountains trying to get over the effects of a year's incessant overwork, and, however kindly you express it, you ask me to begin overworking again – before I am rested – and with too short notice to prepare a paper for the Catholic Congress. I cannot leave here, wisely, for at least ten days more. I will then return to a mountainous accumulation of work . . . I am just recovering from a repeated attack of insomnia, which has so alarmed my wife that I have promised her to abstain from all engagements, outside my editorial work, for a whole year.[57]

The true gauge of O'Reilly's poor health at this time was the fact that he had curtailed his involvement in many of his social clubs. Over the latter half of 1889 and throughout 1890 O'Reilly made only one appearance at his beloved Papyrus Club. According to Roche, his friend had grown 'perceptibly older' over the last year of the decade.[58] In January 1890 O'Reilly wrote to Edward Moseley about a possible repeat of their canoeing expedition of two years earlier: 'In May, please God, we will go down to that Eastern Shore and take a howl in the primeval. I am tired to death.'[59] That month was particularly dispiriting for the editor. He had been very ill over the winter when the O'Reilly household had suffered through an outbreak of influenza. During the winter of 1889–1890 the United States was hit by a flu pandemic, often referred to as the 'Russian flu'. The whole family, including their two servants, were bedridden by the flu. 'I never was so sick in my life,' O'Reilly had written to Moseley during December 1889, 'nor have I seen so much dangerous illness in my house before . . . pray that it may not seize you or yours.'[60]

O'Reilly was shaken by the experience but in March 1890 he could not resist the lure of a lecture tour across the midwest and west of the US. Unfortunately, this tour was badly organised by its promoter, a man named Carroll, and the lectures were poorly attended, although some of his audiences numbered over a thousand people. Carroll seems to have failed to advertise the lectures adequately and by the time O'Reilly reached California the tour had descended into farce. Only eleven people turned up to hear the speaker at Sacramento. There was further trouble when Carroll failed to pay O'Reilly the agreed fee (the editor eventually received $2,000 for his work). O'Reilly's mood had been worsened by a telegram he received in San Francisco stating that his wife was ill and he decided to return to Boston.[61] When he arrived home in April O'Reilly was suffering from a bad cold and seemed to friends to have been left utterly exhausted by the month's traveling.

A month later, still unwell after his journey westwards, he was forced to cancel his planned expedition into the wilderness with Edward Moseley. Their destination was to have been Maryland, which O'Reilly had hoped would 'be a good place for an absolute rest and a tent on the beach – shooting and fishing, and lying in the sand all day, like savages.'[62] O'Reilly remained weak throughout the summer of 1890 although he took some time to attend the athletics meet of the National Irish Athletic Association on 6 August. O'Reilly was supposed to be a judge at this event but it was a very warm day and, by the afternoon, he was feeling faint. He was taken home by some friends and spent the rest of that day recovering. The editor was busy again the next morning providing an editorial for *The Pilot*. That day he was also heavily engaged, as part of a committee of Boston citizens, in organising a parade of Union army veterans to mark twenty-five years since the end of the Civil War.

That work kept him occupied until midday Saturday 9 August, although his increasingly haggard appearance made it clear to O'Reilly's staff that their boss was in the midst of another severe bout of insomnia. He was also worried about Mary. Only a few days earlier O'Reilly had told a journalist from the *Boston Daily Globe* that 'My wife's sickness . . . has made me rather undesirous of leaving Hull.'[63] Around 2.30 p.m. on Saturday he left the office to meet with his family.[64] That evening O'Reilly arrived, by boat, at Hull where he was met by Blanid. He seemed to be in a good mood and they shared an enjoyable stroll back to their house. All the family was together: the eldest daughter, Mary, was home for the summer from Harvard's Collegiate College for Women, while Eliza and Agnes were both home from Elmhurst. O'Reilly spent the rest of the day with his wife and children and then took a late-night stroll with his brother-in-law, John R. Murphy (a former business manager of *The Pilot* from 1876 to 1885). Before the two men went their separate ways, O'Reilly arranged with Murphy that they would attend Mass together early the next morning. The editor then headed home, arriving shortly before midnight. O'Reilly had begun to prepare himself for bed when his wife told him she was unwell and asked if he would go and purchase some medicine at the nearby office of Dr W. H. Litchfield.[65]

O'Reilly walked to the doctor's house and returned with Litchfield. The doctor examined Mary and prescribed some medicine for 'a nervous trouble'.[66] Once that mission had been completed O'Reilly, unable to sleep, sat down in the study to do some reading. Mary called him once again at 2 a.m. She had spilled the medicine that her husband had recently obtained and asked if he would acquire a refill. John dutifully walked to the doctor's office where he obtained a replacement prescription and returned home. Mary, temporarily satisfied, went to sleep but awoke around 3 a.m. to see that John had not yet come to bed. This, of itself, was not unusual since O'Reilly would often spend those long hours of sleeplessness reading in the sitting room. Mary left her bed and went in search of her husband. She found him in the sitting room, seated in a chair with his left hand on the table: 'He was leaning forward, his right elbow on his knee and his hand to his mouth, holding a cigar.'

According to Roche she 'noticed an unusually pallid look on his face'.[67] Mary tried to rouse her husband from his sleep but was unable to so, although she believed that he muttered, 'Yes, my love! Yes, my love!'[68] Realising that something was seriously wrong she sent her daughter Eliza to Dr Litchfield who came to the house 'in all haste'.[69] He found O'Reilly on the floor of the sitting room with 'one of his daughters supporting his head'.[70] According to Roche, Litchfield was joined by another local doctor who had been summoned at the same time. Once there, they moved O'Reilly onto a couch in the sitting room.[71] By this stage all the children were awake and they waited in dread as the doctors tried for nearly an hour to revive their father. *The Pilot* described the end: 'It was too late to save the precious life. He revived a little, showed signs of consciousness, recognised by pressure of his hand, his little daughters at his bedside, murmured a few half-articulate words, and gave up his brave, Christian soul, to God.'[72] At 4.50 a.m., Sunday 10 August 1890, Dr Litchfield pronounced John Boyle O'Reilly dead.

Epilogue

Had O'Reilly committed suicide? It is a question that has been asked by many of those who have studied his life. He had, after all, attempted suicide in Western Australia. But that attempt had been preceded by a rush of life-changing events. In the previous thirty months he had been convicted of treason, drummed out of the army, endured spells in Millbank and Dartmoor and been transported to Australia. He had been separated from his family and had recently heard that his mother had died. Then, amid that personal maelstrom, he had been heartbroken by the end of his affair with Jessie Woodman. All he could see before him was the seventeen long years that were still left on his sentence. That combination of events could have overwhelmed any person, never mind a young man, isolated from friends and family. His attempt to end his life in Australia may have been a reaction to his situation. Also, in the weeks before it happened there were warning signs. He wrote the two 'Night Thoughts' poems, both of which showed a man on the edge of despair. From a distance we can see the events that caused his attempted suicide and the pattern that preceded it. In 1890 there is no evidence of any similarly life-changing events or any comparable pattern. There is nothing in his writings prior to his death that suggests suicidal thoughts. There is no doubt that *In Bohemia* displays an O'Reilly who is more disillusioned with the world. However, while the poems of that volume display distaste with some aspects of life in the United States they do not suggest a man battling with hopelessness.

There is one poem in the volume that could, on first glance, suggest that a dark shadow followed O'Reilly. 'A Passage' describes the journey of man from birth to death. It is a short poem that displays a cynicism usually absent from O'Reilly's work. In the poem a man's actions are driven by instinct rather than reason and a man's path in life is entirely predictable: he is born; he ignores the lessons of the past and makes mistakes; he fights; he drinks; he loves; becomes distrustful of women; he grows old. Finally, nothing is left other than suspicion and an empty sensuality: 'He grows formal with men, and with women polite / And distrustful of both when they're out of his sight / Then he eats for his palate, and drinks for his head / And loves for his pleasure – and 'tis time he was dead!'[1] It is tempting to read an autobiographical intent in these poems. But was 'A Passage', with its descriptions of an isolated and distrustful sensualist, a reference to O'Reilly's own life? It is far more likely that O'Reilly was describing the kind of superficial personality who lives life behind a veil of conventionality and was disparaged elsewhere in his writing. In that sense 'A Passage' fits perfectly with other poems from the volume such as 'In Bohemia' and 'The Cry of the Dreamer', both of which scorn the superficiality and insincerity of the wealthy. In other words, it is not an autobiographical poem.

Following O'Reilly's death there was no public mention of suicide from the family. Nor did any such claims appear in the press. That, in itself, tells us little since it is probable that, if O'Reilly had committed suicide, the family would have sought to prevent this information from creating a public scandal. No autopsy was conducted and the descriptions of his death in the press suggest that O'Reilly had suffered a heart attack. However, Roche suggested that O'Reilly had taken some of his wife's 'chloral', the medicine which she had been prescribed by Dr Litchfield that same night.[2] Chloral hydrate was regularly employed as a sedative at the time and O'Reilly may have attempted to self-medicate and accidently overdosed. This outcome was a known risk to using chloral hydrate. The drug was implicated in a number of high-profile deaths in the late nineteenth century. For example John Tyndall, the Irish scientist, died of an accidental chloral hydrate overdose in 1893.[3] Also, an overdose of chloral hydrate can sometimes lead to cardiac arrest. There is no indication that O'Reilly deliberately overdosed. We do not know for certain what happened that night but the evidence does not point to suicide. It has been proposed that O'Reilly's bouts of insomnia were a result of depression.[4] From that premise, it could then be suggested that he took his own life but it is dangerous to make such claims when given so little evidence. While insomnia can be an indicator of depression, there is no other evidence that O'Reilly suffered from depression. His insomnia could have been related to any number of issues, primarily stress. O'Reilly certainly was overworked and it seems much more likely that his insomnia was related to work-induced stress.[5] Why he worked so relentlessly hard is a question that is examined below.

On the morning of Monday 11 August John's body was taken from the O'Reillys' home in Hull to their home in the city. On the following day, he was moved to the nearby St Mary's Church. O'Reilly would have enjoyed the fact that, even in death, he was bringing Irish nationalists together. One of the pall-bearers was Denis Cashman, his fellow convict aboard the *Hougoumont*, Land League supporter and respectable Boston journalist. Alongside Cashman was the unrepentant bomber, the man who scorned anything but action, Jeremiah O'Donovan Rossa. O'Reilly's funeral Mass took place the next day amid a huge crowd; the church was full and the mourners crammed themselves into 'the sidewalks before it and the adjacent streets'.[6] His four daughters stood at the front of the congregation but their mother was not with them. Mary had been inconsolable since the night of John's death and on the day of the funeral she was 'prostrated with grief and unable to leave her bed'.[7] Father Robert Fulton conducted the funeral Mass and delivered a sermon in which he dwelt upon the sense of 'loss' that all those present so keenly felt: 'loss to his countries, loss to his creed, loss to all of us his lovers ... He owned two countries; his country by birth, his country by adoption.'[8] Fulton praised O'Reilly's 'readiness to forgive, reluctance to pain, charity of interpretation' and concluded by saying, 'He was approximating Christ, for such is our Exemplar.'[9] When the Mass was complete, the crowd accompanied the funeral cortège to the Boston suburb of Roxbury. Many of those who had played a supporting role in the epic that was O'Reilly's life helped to carry the coffin. Among them were James Jeffrey Roche, Henry Hathaway and Patrick Donahoe. In Roxbury, O'Reilly was laid to rest in a temporary vault. His final burial place in Boston's Holyhood Cemetery was not yet ready, since both his family and the city wanted to provide a suitably grand memorial to their lost leader.

The news of O'Reilly's death stunned the people of Boston and it is in their reactions to his death that we can see the immensity of the person. In the days after the funeral there were many memorial services held in honour of O'Reilly while condolences poured into *The Pilot*'s offices from Ireland and all over the United States. On 2 September Boston's City Council hosted a public commemoration for O'Reilly in Tremont Temple, a Baptist Church in the heart of the city. The temple was full to its capacity of nearly 3,000 people. A wide selection of the city's leaders spoke at the commemoration but all of them spoke of O'Reilly's humanitarianism. O'Reilly had not been alone among Irish Americans in his advocacy of civil rights and his criticisms of racial discrimination. Others such as Patrick Ford and Archbishop John Ireland were forthright opponents of these evils. Nonetheless, such figures were rare and, on this issue, O'Reilly had no peer. O'Reilly's achievement was that he had utterly changed the focus of *The Pilot* from an Irish paper that had been hostile to the abolition of slavery and sometimes racist in its commentary on civil rights into a paper that was renowned for its support of African Americans. At the Tremont Hall memorial service Edwin G. Walker gave a powerful speech in honour of O'Reilly. Walker, in 1866, had been one of the first two black men elected to the Massachusetts State Legislature. He had been a prominent black leader since that time and had known O'Reilly since the Irishman had first made his home in the city.

Walker's oration was a moving testimonial to the importance of O'Reilly. American society, he declared, may have banished slavery but it had not freed itself from the assumptions and beliefs that had made slavery possible. Walker told his audience that each day African Americans faced the bitterness of whites in the former slave states and the racism of those people, north and south, who were 'always ready and anxious to sustain and support the holding in slavery of the American black man.'[10] Yet there was an even more pervasive attitude that plagued the black American, that of the 'timid': those Americans who did not believe in slavery but who 'lacked the courage needed for its destruction, and the removal of the rubbish that its going out would leave.' O'Reilly, Walker judged, was most definitely not one of the timid: 'He was quick to grapple with the many-headed monster that had been formed out of the debris that had been left to show that slavery once had a standing in this land.' Walker spoke of how the death of the great abolitionist Wendell Phillips had demoralised 'my race in this country' but in that dark hour the loss of Phillips had been alleviated by the rise of O'Reilly as a defender of civil rights: 'as long as Mr. O'Reilly lived and spoke, we felt that we had at least, outside of our own people, one true vigilant, brave and self-sacrificing friend, who, like Mr. Phillips, claimed for us just what he claimed for himself.' He continued:

> With his pen, John Boyle O'Reilly sent through the columns of a
> newspaper that he edited in this city words in our behalf that were

Christian, and anathemas that were just. Not only that, but he went on to the platform, and, in bold and defiant language, he denounced the murderers of our people, and advised us to strike the tyrants back. It was a time when the cloud was most heavy, and more threatening than at any other period since reconstruction. At that time our Wendell Phillips was stricken by the hand of death, and then some doubted that they would be ever be able to see a clear sky. But in the midst of all the gloom we could hear Mr. O'Reilly declaring his determination to stand by the colored American in all contests where his rights were at stake.

Walker's declaration that O'Reilly had taken on the mantle of the great abolitionist Wendell Phillips was a stirring affirmation of O'Reilly's importance as a civil rights activist. Phillips had died in 1884 and over the subsequent six years O'Reilly had been the person to whom Boston's black community had turned in times of tension. Indeed, O'Reilly's reputation as a civil rights campaigner would survive long after his death. In 1945 *The Crisis*, the magazine of the National Association for the Advancement of Colored People (NAACP), published a long feature on the editor of *The Pilot*:

> One of the best friends and strongest champions the American Negro ever had was himself the victim of political and economic persecution, imprisonment and exile; 'legalized degradation' to use one of his own phrases. That man was John Boyle O'Reilly, nineteenth century Irish patriot, poet, and journalist, who escaping from prison in Australia to the refuge of America, contributed mightily to the cause of the common man of whatever race, creed or color wherever oppressed and denied the fundamental rights of humanity.[11]

The Crisis described O'Reilly as 'a man who knew his time and its issues' and also 'a poet-prophet who saw a long way into the future'. O'Reilly, the paper stated, 'saw so clearly for his own time; spoke so fearlessly and with such impassioned sense of the rights of man that he speaks to us today of our own time and its problems.' *The Crisis* had no doubt that O'Reilly deserved 'his place among our own contemporary fighters against the political and economic injustices forced upon racial minorities.'

Other speakers at Tremont Hall spoke of O'Reilly's role as a bridge between the Irish and American, between Catholic and Protestant. O'Reilly's close friend, the Unitarian minister Thomas Wentworth Higginson, spoke of a man who was both American and Irish:

> I am not one of those who can criticise a man who was so good an American for being not merely incidentally and occasionally, but steadily and underneath it all, an Irishman too . . . I cannot complain of Boyle O'Reilly, that through life, in his spirit, he kept the green flag waving beside the Stars and Stripes.[12]

It is this part of O'Reilly's career that has been most misunderstood. In recent decades something strange has happened in the assessments of O'Reilly's life. He has come to be seen as the archetype of a man torn apart by the competing tensions of being both Irish and American. Not only that but he has been held up as an example of someone who ultimately vanquished his own Irishness in a humiliating and futile attempt at assimilation and acceptance by American society.

This viewpoint was established by John Duffy Ibson, whose 1990 book on Irish assimilation in the United States devoted a short section to O'Reilly. According to Ibson: 'O'Reilly's Irishness vanished in a process of repression, of internalisation.'[13] He declares that 'It was only in his poetry that O'Reilly could contradict his own Pilot editorials and issue what in America, but not Ireland, was tantamount to sacrilege – a denunciation of economic striving, of social mobility.' It would have been news to Irish tenant farmers and the Land League to hear that economic striving and a desire for social mobility were somehow alien to the Irish. Also, O'Reilly's poetry, while it lashed out at the shallow materialism of the wealthy, never denounced social mobility. His poetry denounced the laissez-faire ethos that allowed the monopolisation of wealth and political power by a privileged few. In no sense did his poetry contradict his editorials in The Pilot. In fact, as we have seen, the poetry complemented his journalism and his fiction. In each strand of O'Reilly's writing we can see the same subjects, the same ideals, the same targets for criticism. Each of these strands was integral to the fabric of O'Reilly's life and any understanding of the whole person.

Everywhere Ibson looks in O'Reilly's American life Ibson sees 'pain', 'melancholy' and 'self-hatred'. Unfortunately his portrayal of O'Reilly does not address his subject's fiction or journalism. He judges that O'Reilly's supposedly dualistic nature was exacerbated by the fact that he 'usually kept his competing selves apart'. The 'competing selves' that Ibson sees in O'Reilly are the sentimental anti-material Irish Catholic and the rational Anglo-Saxon Protestant industrialist. This mixture of stereotypes, of matter and anti-matter destroyed O'Reilly. Ibson assumes that O'Reilly killed himself and laments that 'it was the sadly logical conclusion to his career'. He also asserts that 'A crucial element of this unstable union of opposites was the guilt O'Reilly must have felt over his "betrayal" of his ethnicity.' Such assertions are an unstable foundation on which to build an argument. There is no evidence that O'Reilly had 'competing selves', at least not those described by Ibson. It follows, then, that there is no evidence that O'Reilly 'kept his competing selves apart'. Even in a practical sense such a division would have been impossible. During his life in the United States, O'Reilly was simultaneously one of the country's most famous journalists and most famous poets. His poetry and his novels sold in huge volume and his journalism for *The Pilot* was often carried in other newspapers. O'Reilly's writings were there for all to see and they were voraciously consumed by admirers and critics alike.

In a wider sense, Ibson demonstrates in his study that assimilation into American society caused massive psychological tension for many Irish immigrants but his attempt to fit O'Reilly into that pattern does not succeed. To describe O'Reilly as a 'token Irishman' utterly misunderstands O'Reilly's place in America and the claim that his 'Irishness vanished' is untenable after any close study of his life. Certainly, there was tension in O'Reilly's life between his role as an Irish Catholic leader and his efforts to assimilate the Irish community into the political and social mainstream of the United States. O'Reilly was an atypical person and, as Francis Walsh put it, 'his work was far more complicated than merely threading his way through two conflicting forces.'[14] Nevertheless, the notion of O'Reilly as a melancholy, self-loathing, emotionally inarticulate Irish American has become the dominant image of the man. Kerby Miller, in a work of great scholarship, has shown that loneliness and alienation were a debilitating factor in the lives of many emigrants. However, Miller deals with O'Reilly only in passing and he too succumbs to the temptation of describing O'Reilly as a man alienated from America, a man filled with 'destructive, subconscious estrangement'.[15] It is no surprise then that both Ibson and

Miller have both seen O'Reilly's work ethic as resulting from the strains of assimilation.[16] Surveying O'Reilly's twenty years in the United States Ibson concluded: 'O'Reilly had been destroying himself with an Irish-American vengeance throughout his residence in Boston'.[17]

That explanation is unsatisfactory. O'Reilly's work ethic had long preceded his arrival in the United States. He had striven always to be the best; as an eleven-year-old he replaced his ill older brother as an apprentice with the *Drogheda Argus* newspaper and so saved the family; he had soon doubled his wages through his endeavours with the paper; in the Preston militia he became an officer; in the 10th Hussars he was reckoned the 'best soldier in the regiment'; as a Fenian agent he had succeeded where John Devoy had failed and recruited nearly all the Irish soldiers in his regiment; aboard the *Hougoumont* he was one of the leaders of the Fenian convicts; as a convict in Australia he had risen above his fellow prisoners to become a warder's assistant; he was one of only a few prisoners to escape the penal colony of Western Australia; and in the United States he had become the editor of the foremost Irish Catholic newspaper, a celebrated writer, and one of the most influential Irish Americans of his generation. Even then, he was not satisfied: he wanted to improve society, banish prejudice, and foster equality of opportunity. In every part of his life he pushed himself to achieve more. As Justin McCarthy wrote: 'who can ride better, row better, walk better? Above all, who can box better?'[18] Edward Moseley recalled a friend who was a blur of activity: swimming, hiking, canoeing and boxing. George Noble Plunkett most clearly remembered O'Reilly 'flying up the steep office stairs, with his hands deep in his pockets', eager to get to his desk from where 'he turned the key on the outside world.'[19]

Where did this drive come from? It might have been rooted in his childhood experiences. O'Reilly had seen how his parents' employment had protected the family during the Famine. Although others were consumed by hunger and poverty, O'Reilly's parents, while not wealthy, were able to keep the family alive. When only eleven years old O'Reilly had taken on his brother's burden and become an apprentice in the *Drogheda Argus* and a wage-earner for the first time. Work, responsibility, ambition and the ability to progress his career were hallmarks of O'Reilly's life ever after. Perhaps that internal drive was reinforced by his experiences in Western Australia. Through his own hand he almost lost his life. He had faced a twenty-year sentence, which seemed to him like a living death. But he had escaped and grasped freedom to start his life again. Did that confrontation with his own mortality drive him onwards? Ultimately, the question of what fuelled O'Reilly's fierce energy is impossible to answer in a definitive manner. Perhaps a useful concept with which to approach this aspect of his life is the ancient Greek idea of *pothos*. This concept had many meanings but it was sometimes attributed to historical figures who displayed a longing, an unquenchable drive, to achieve and succeed. The roots of O'Reilly's *pothos* are unknown but its manifestations are clear throughout his life from childhood to death.

Was O'Reilly's life marked by personal angst? We have no direct evidence that it was but if he suffered a hidden torment where are we to search for its root cause? The most likely place to start is not the United States but Western Australia and especially those few months he spent with Jessie Woodman. Perhaps his lost love haunted his thoughts for the rest of his days but then again perhaps not. We can never know what scars were left upon O'Reilly's psyche by his imprisonment and his enforced exile from Ireland. Of course *Moondyne* was devoted to prison reform and *The King's Men* contains an extended section set in Dartmoor Prison. But O'Reilly's writings, outside these fictionalised accounts, did not dwell on his personal experiences of prison. Nor does he seem to have talked about prison in great detail while in the United States. Yet there are hints that at least some part of him remained bitter over his imprisonment and transportation. In 1888 Walt Whitman recalled an occasion on which O'Reilly described his experiences as a convict: 'I shall never forget the first time he spoke to me about his prison life. He was alive with the most vivid indignation – he was a great storm out somewhere, a great sea pushing upon the shore.'[20]

O'Reilly did try and seems to have succeeded in forgiving his jailers. Roche recounted O'Reilly's attitude towards a particularly severe warder whom he had encountered in Australia. This was the warder who had refused to give O'Reilly the letter containing news of his mother's death. O'Reilly told Roche that he had did not bear the man any malice and that he had forgotten his name.[21] George Noble Plunkett, who first met O'Reilly around 1880, noted the same lack of bitterness in his friend.[22] In 1872 or 1873 O'Reilly was visited in his office by a former comrade in the 10th Hussars. It was not a happy reunion since his visitor was Patrick Foley, one of the two informers who had proved most damaging to O'Reilly during his 1866 court martial. Following O'Reilly's conviction Foley had been shunned by his fellow soldiers and, after deserting the army, fled to America. Here, according to Roche, he found that 'the story of his treachery had preceded him'.[23] Penniless and without support, Foley was left 'starving in the streets of Boston' when he called upon O'Reilly. As Roche put it, most people 'would have enjoyed the spectacle of the traitor's misery' but O'Reilly gave Foley enough money to 'supply his immediate wants, and pay his way to some more propitious spot'.[24]

O'Reilly, despite claims to the contrary and his occasional swipes at the Anglo-Saxon, was never motivated by a hatred of England or the English people.[25] O'Reilly always spoke and wrote fondly about his time in Preston, where he spent some of the happiest days of his life. He had an admiration for many aspects of English culture, especially its literature. Large portions of both *Moondyne* and *The King's Men* are set in England and most of those novels' heroes are English. It would be more correct to say that O'Reilly harboured a hatred of the British Empire. How could it be otherwise? The foundations on which O'Reilly built his intellectual and moral life were the ideas of individual rights and democratic freedom. From that premise he drew the conclusion that all people, all races, are essentially the same. Empire, with its ideologies of racial superiority and its use of force to demean and subjugate others, was the antithesis of O'Reilly's philosophy. He saw those forces at work in Ireland and they hurt him deeply; it was an open sore that festered throughout his life. Also, it cannot be forgotten that it was the British Empire that had imprisoned both himself and his brother. It was the British Empire that had transported him to Australia, and which, nineteen years later, refused to allow him entry into British territory. At the time of his death, O'Reilly was still officially classed as a criminal by that same Empire. In that sense, O'Reilly and the British Empire had a mutual resentment towards each other. O'Reilly gave full vent to his anger in June 1887 during Queen Victoria's fiftieth year as British monarch. He led a public demonstration against the city council's decision to allow Faneuil Hall play host a celebration of the golden jubilee.[26] Even then, his hatred had a limit and he never allowed it to become an all-consuming passion that blinded him to decency and political realities. He condemned attempts to terrorise the British public through bombing and he was willing to accept Home Rule for Ireland, either as an end in itself or as a stepping stone to independence.

That aspect of O'Reilly's personality, his ability to forgive, was recognised by his contemporaries. In the Tremont Temple memorial many of the speakers testified to how 'love' had been a dominant trait of O'Reilly's character. The Democratic politician, Charles Levi Woodbury, told the congregation that 'It may be said that here, in free America, he founded an empire of love.'[27] This empire, according to Woodbury, encompassed all races and all creeds. Thomas Wentworth Higginson saw a similar destiny in O'Reilly. According to Higginson, O'Reilly had a mission to unify American society:

> He knew that American civilization was a failure, if it was only large enough to furnish a safe and convenient shelter for the descendants of Puritans and Anglo-Saxons, leaving Irishmen and Catholics outside. In doing that work he became our teacher. Himself a self-liberated convict, he set us free. Himself a faithful advocate of a great and powerful religion, he taught a standard of religious toleration such as many a Protestant has yet to learn.[28]

Higginson's sentiments have been echoed by many students of O'Reilly's life. From this viewpoint O'Reilly had a historical mission to bring America's Catholics and Protestants together. Much has been made of the fact that Boston's Brahmins chose O'Reilly to compose a poem at the dedication of the 'national monument to the Pilgrim Fathers' in 1889.[29] This was a genuine attempt among some of Boston's Protestant community to reach out to the Irish community and a man who had spent twenty years denouncing sectarianism, no matter its origin.

Throughout his career in the United States O'Reilly had worked hard to create common ground between native Protestant and newly arrived Irish but late-nineteenth-century Boston was a city in which religious animosities continually bubbled beneath the surface.[30] The year 1884 saw the election of the first Irish Catholic mayor of Boston and a concerted bid by the Republican Party to steal the Irish vote from the Democrats. It was inevitable that the growing visibility and political power of Catholics would result in a backlash. Over the following six years of O'Reilly's life Evangelical Protestants and Catholics fought legislative and newspaper battles over public school funding and police recruitment among other issues. As one of the city's most famous Catholics O'Reilly became a target for religious bigots. One letter is suggestive of the general tone: 'John Boyle O'Reilly: – The following is a sentence that is as true as you are a mick: Rum, Romanism and Rebellion. Eat it, swallow it, but it is going to live. Hoping the day is not far off when you and your broilers will be boiled in hell. Hurrah for the Queen. Damn the Irish.'[31]

O'Reilly's Catholicism was an uncomfortable fact for at least some of his American friends and in parts of his life O'Reilly straddled two worlds. George Noble Plunkett, recalling some time he spent with O'Reilly at the Papyrus Club, highlighted these tensions:

He was a founder of the Papyrus Club, the Bohemian Academy of Boston, and to the last it obeyed his welcome sway. I well remember one pleasant evening I spent there by his invitation, in company with many kindly workers in the arts and sciences. I believe a few creeds and nationalities were represented; I fear we two were the only Irish, and the only Catholics there.[32]

Walt Whitman, after O'Reilly's death, claimed, 'But O'Reilly was no Catholic! – it was not in him. I know that he was in the formal sense – it was the thing to be, he was born to it – was in fact a Catholic as he was a Democrat, for reasons that did not run to the deep.'[33] O'Reilly had doubtlessly heard similar comments from his Boston Brahmin friends. He replied to one correspondent, named only as 'J', with the condescending tone of someone who is tired of explaining themselves:

And yet your letter makes me smile. Puritan you, with your condemnation of the great old art-loving, human, music-breathing, color-raising, spiritual, mystical, symbolical Catholic Church! A great, loving, generous heart will never find peace and comfort and field of labor except within her unstatistical, sun-like, benevolent motherhood. J . . . I am a Catholic just as I am a dweller on the planet, and a lover of yellow sunlight, and flowers in the grass, and the sound of birds. Man never made anything so like God's work as the magnificent, sacrificial, devotional faith of the hoary but young Catholic Church. There is no other church; they are all just way stations.[34]

O'Reilly expressed this tension in an 1878 letter to his Protestant friend and fellow member of the Papyrus Club, Edwin P. Whipple: 'Truly, if I were not editor of The Pilot . . . you would never think me such a terrific Papist and paddy.'[35] The comment seems to have been meant as a joke but the tension was evidently a factor in some of O'Reilly's relationships with his Protestant friends and colleagues. O'Reilly, in return, was sometimes scornful of his Protestant neighbours who worshipped 'with the intellect at so many dollars an hour, in an economical church, a hand-organ in the gallery, and a careful committee to keep down the expenses.'[36]

The challenge of religious intolerance was one issue that O'Reilly confronted as an immigrant leader. O'Reilly was keenly aware of his role as a leader of the Irish immigrant community and it was through The Pilot that he sought to encourage Irish assimilation into the United States. O'Reilly may have been forcibly removed from Ireland but the American years of his life are effectively an emigrant's story, albeit an uncharacteristic one. It has long been Ireland's tragedy that people as talented as O'Reilly have been forced to leave the country, whether this was a result of poverty, British misrule of the island or, since independence, the cynical policy common to nearly all governments of the Irish state, which sees emigration as a safety valve by which to maintain social cohesion and keep down unemployment figures. We have seen how Irish emigration to the United States had grown massively during the nineteenth century and O'Reilly spoke to a huge immigrant community in the United States. What it is hard to judge is how successful O'Reilly was in influencing his readers. Could his success be quantified through using the circulation figures of The Pilot? Unfortunately, newspaper circulation figures for the time come with the caveat that there was no independent means of verifying a newspaper's sales.

The Pilot, in its own pages, often claimed a circulation of around 100,000 copies but this should probably be considered a form of self-advertising rather than an accurate sales figure. The newspaper industry did have an annual newspaper directory, which published circulation figures as supplied by individual papers. Through this directory we can see that The Pilot claimed a circulation of 55,000 copies in 1872, O'Reilly's first full year as editor.[37] This rose to 60,000 copies in 1880 and 72,000 copies in 1889, O'Reilly's last full year as editor. This is, admittedly, a limited means by which to assess O'Reilly influence and ultimately it tells us little. It does, at least, suggest that the paper, under O'Reilly's editorship, had performed well in a crowded market and that by 1889 it had increased its 1872 circulation by nearly one third. However, the reasons why *The Pilot*'s readers bought the paper are less tangible. One reason for the paper's popularity was undoubtedly O'Reilly's personal success. He had achieved a prestige that they craved yet he remained recognisably Irish. In fact, he scorned the 'Oirish' persona, that some of his countrymen developed.[38] Yet O'Reilly did not pander to his readers' prejudices or portray himself as a man of the people. Father William Byrne, a long-time friend, said of O'Reilly, 'He would no more deign to flatter the populace than to cringe to power'.[39] The editor of *The Pilot* had a number of core issues to which he returned again and again: civil rights; Home Rule for Ireland; workers' rights; the necessity of breaking up monopolies; the protection of democracy against the threats posed by financial and political elites; and the role of the Irish in the United States.[40]

The editorial line pursued by O'Reilly in regard to these topics did not alienate his readers, even if they sometimes disagreed with what he wrote. Perhaps it was O'Reilly's personal style that made his paper popular. O'Reilly was never a mere controversialist and he edited *The Pilot* with a grace that can make his paper seem staid when viewed from the perspective of the noisy culture we inhabit today. Although he was not shy of indulging in editorial feuding with other journalists, he had a facility to hear and respect the arguments of others. In 1871 he had started his journey as editor with a statement of intent:

> We [*The Pilot*] don't believe in that ignorant old prejudice that sneers at every man who changes his opinions. There is much of Ireland's bane in the habit. The man who has the courage to honestly change his opinions is the best man. If convinced that we were pursuing a wrong course, or that a better one was open, we would change every day in the year . . . It is better to be Right than Stubborn.[41]

This approach was obvious in his paper and in his life. As regards race relations he was a radical and far ahead of the society in which he lived. When it came to workers' rights, O'Reilly was a reformer although he found it far easier to highlight injustices than to offer solutions. On Ireland he was, at first, a revolutionary but when he participated in the Land

League and the National League he was numbered among the conservatives. O'Reilly would probably have rejected that last label. He would have contended that he was acting to secure the best available opportunities for Ireland while also maintaining unity of spirit among the Irish in America. From 1871 until his death he had carried on the mission of *The Pilot* to make the Irish a self-respecting and integral part of the American citizenry. He never failed to offer his critique of things Irish but he had the ability to differentiate between criticism and cynicism. When O'Reilly urged the assimilation of the Irish into American society he did not advocate that they repress or divest themselves of their past or their heritage, but he was certain that the best way for them to progress was via participation in one of the two great American political parties. That was why he argued against any specifically Catholic or Irish parties.[42] Similarly, he urged black Americans to maintain their sense of identity and to vote for either the Democrats or Republicans as means to an end. O'Reilly regarded the United States as the inevitable outcome of history's march and the way forward for humanity. As he saw it, if all citizens of the country, no matter what race or creed, could be provided with equal economic and political opportunity then they would amalgamate their qualities to form 'the best of all races'.[43]

Before we leave this study of O'Reilly's life, let us take one last glance at the character of the man. He was a carer to an ill wife and a devoted father to four daughters. To his wife he left his share in *The Pilot*. The O'Reilly family had their struggles with illness and worry but what little knowledge we have of their life together tells us that there was love and happiness also.[44] At a remove of well over 100 years the true quality of the person can never be reawakened but, in the reactions of others, we can get a sense of O'Reilly's charisma and his loving nature. An extraordinary outpouring of grief followed in the wake of his death and the published condolences could fill a volume on their own. Maybe Michael Davitt, writing in 1904 and long after he and O'Reilly had taken separate political paths, best encapsulated the reasons why so many people were enraptured by the man from Dowth:

He was probably as lovable a character as nature in her happiest moods ever moulded out of Celtic materials: handsome and brave, gifted in rarest qualities of mind and heart, broad-minded and intensely sympathetic, progressive and independent in thought, with an enlightened and tolerant disposition, in religion and politics, more in keeping with a poetic soul than with an ordinary human temperament. He was a personification of all the manly virtues. No one could know him without becoming his friend, and it was impossible to be his enemy once you experienced the spell of his affectionate personality.[45]

O'Reilly worked towards achieving many goals: racial harmony; an America where equality of opportunity was afforded to all citizens; a free, happy and democratic Ireland; a peaceful and mutually prosperous relationship between Ireland and England; an America where the economic exploitation of workers was penalised rather than rewarded.[46] That these hopes were unfulfilled at his death should not diminish the importance of O'Reilly. As Patrick Collins said of his friend in Tremont Temple: 'He was Irish and American – intensely both, but more than both. The world was his country, and mankind was his kin.'[47] He sought to make the world a fairer and gentler place and for many people he became a beacon of hope. He was no pacifist and he believed that there were times when peoples and countries had no other option than to fight in their own defence against unwarranted aggression. Yet he had an abiding confidence in the power of the written word, in clear and honest journalism and in public debate as the engines of social progress. Underpinning O'Reilly's journalism and poetry, his exertions on behalf of the Irish Land League and the Irish National League and his unrelenting commitment to civil rights, there was an idealistic belief in human dignity and the democratic process. Those ideals were, are, and will always be, worth striving for. John Boyle O'Reilly's greatest and most enduring legacy is his example.

Notes

Chapter 1

1   Address by the President of the United States of America, John Fitzgerald Kennedy: Dáil Éireann Debates, vol. 203 (28 June 1963). The quotation used by Kennedy is a couplet called 'Distance' from O'Reilly's 1886 collection, *In Bohemia*.

2   Mary Boyle O'Reilly to J. McCarthy, 10 February 1924: Mary Boyle O'Reilly Papers, John J. Burn's Library, Boston College. See also Roche, James Jeffrey, *Life of John Boyle O'Reilly: Together with his Complete Poems and Speeches* (Philadelphia, John J. McVey, 1891), pp 1–12.

3   *Ibid.*; he had five sisters and two brothers.

4   Estimates for the attendance at this event range from 750,000 up to 1 million people.

5   Roche, *Life*, p. 4.

6   Information and comments relating to William O'Reilly's teaching career taken from National School Registers ED/2: 1832–1963, National Archives of Ireland.

7   Kenneally, Ian, *Courage and Conflict: Forgotten Stories of the Irish at War* (Cork, The Collins Press, 2009); see pp 164–5 for Holland's childhood during the Famine.

8   Stout, Geraldine, *Newgrange and the Bend of the Boyne* (Cork, Cork University Press, 2002), p. 161.

9   Roche, *Life*, pp 4–5.

10 *Ibid.*, p.4. See also O'Higgins, Brian, 'John Boyle O'Reilly – Glimpses of his Boyhood', *Donahoe's Magazine*, LIV (August 1905), pp 162–8.

11 Roche, *Life*, p. 375.

12 From a short article about O'Reilly and his literary influences in the *Boston Daily Globe*, 14 September 1890.

13 O'Higgins, 'Glimpses of his Boyhood', pp 162–8.

14 Roche, *Life*, p. 384.

15 *Ibid.*, p. 5.

16 *Ibid.*, pp 5–6, for details of his apprenticeship.

17 For history of Preston during that time, see University of Central Lancashire website, 'A History of Preston', at http://www.uclan.ac.uk/schools/education_social_sciences/history/potted_history.php.

18   Roche, *Life*, p. 7.
19   *Ibid.*
20   Bull, Stephen, *Volunteer! The Lancashire Rifle Volunteers, 1859–1885* (Lancashire County Museums Service, 1993), p. 8.
21   Roche, *Life*, pp 7–8.
22   *Ibid.*, p. 7.
23   *Ibid.*, p. 8.
24   Devoy, John, *Recollections of an Irish Rebel* (New York, Chase D. Young, 1929; facs. edn, Shannon, Irish University Press, 1969), p. 152. Devoy would have a long connection with O'Reilly and a chapter of his memoir was devoted to the Meath man.
25   Roche, *Life*, p. 27.
26   Devoy, *Recollections*, p. 154.
27   Roche, *Life*, pp 11–12.
28   *Ibid.*

Chapter 2

1   Comerford, R. V., *The Fenians in Context: Irish Politics and Society 1848–82* (Dublin, Wolfhound Press, 1998), p. 39.
2   Mitchel, John, *Jail Journal; or Five Years in British Prisons* (Dublin, J. Corrigan, 1864), pp 28–29.
3   O'Leary, John, *The Writings of James Fintan Lalor* (Dublin, T. G. O'Donoghue, 1895), p. 82.
4   Editorial on the role of IRB in Irish history, *Irish Freedom*, November 1910.
5   Ryan, Desmond, *The Fenian Chief: a Biography of James Stephens* (Dublin, Gill & Son, 1967), p. 91.
6   Lee, J. J., *The Modernisation of Irish Society: 1848–1918* (Dublin, Gill & Macmillan, 2008), p. 56.
7   The American Civil War had started earlier that year and in November the Union warship *San Jacinto* intercepted the British mail ship *Trent*. The British ship, although neutral, was carrying two Confederate diplomats, John Slidell and James Mason, to Europe. These were arrested by the crew of the *San Jacinto*, leading to a diplomatic battle between the Union government of Abraham Lincoln and Lord Palmerston's British government, the British arguing that the Union navy had no right to board one of its ships. This row rumbled on for weeks before Lincoln relented and ordered the release of the two diplomats.
8   *Irish People*, 17 September 1864.
9   Strathnairn memo to Cabinet, June 1867, cited in McConville, Seán, *Irish Political Prisoners, 1848–1922: Theatres of War* (London, Routledge, 2003), p. 119. Lord Strathnairn had briefed the British Cabinet on the state of Ireland and the rise of Fenianism over the previous decade.
10   Comerford, *Fenians in Context*, p. 109.
11   See, for example, *Nation*, 24 October 1863.

12   Kee, Robert, *The Green Flag, The Bold Fenian Men*, vol. 2 (London, Penguin Books, 1989), p. 20.

13   McGee, Owen, *The IRB: the Irish Republican Brotherhood from the Land League to Sinn Féin* (Dublin, Four Courts Press, 2005), p. 28.

14   *Ibid.*

15   *Ibid.*

16   Strathnairn memo to Cabinet, June 1867, cited in McConville, *Irish Political Prisoners*, p. 108.

17   McConville, *Irish Political Prisoners*, p. 145.

18   The letter, sent by James Stephens to Fenian 'captains', was read out in the Commons by Sir George Grey: Hansard, HC (series 3) vol. 181, cols 669–72 (16 Feb. 1866).

19   John Devoy's account of his life can be found in Devoy, *Recollections*. See also the modern biographies of Devoy: Dooley, Terence, *'The Greatest of the Fenians': John Devoy and Ireland* (Dublin, Wolfhound Press, 2003); and Golway, Terry, *Irish Rebel: John Devoy and America's Fight for Irish Freedom* (New York, St Martin's Press, 1998).

20   Devoy, *Recollections*, pp 145–6.

21   *Ibid.*, pp 145–53.

22   *Ibid.*, p. 153.

23   Roche, *Life*, p. 16.

24   Devoy, *Recollections*, p. 153.

25   *Ibid.*

26   *Ibid.*, p. 154.

27   *Ibid.*, pp 152–3.

28   Another possible version of the oath that O'Reilly may have taken could be: 'I John Boyle O'Reilly, do solemnly swear in the presence of Almighty God, that I will do my utmost, at every risk, while life last, to make Ireland an independent democratic republic; that I will yield implicit obedience in all things not contrary to the law of God, to the commands of all my superior officers, and that I shall preserve inviolable secrecy regarding all transactions of this secret society that may be confided to me. So help me God! Amen.

29   Devoy, *Recollections*, p. 152.

30   Comerford, *Fenians in Context*, p. 111.

31   Devoy, *Recollections*, p. 155.

32   *Ibid.*, p. 156.

33   *Ibid.*, pp 148–50. Curry, whom Devoy described as 'The most useful and efficient man I had assisting me', was later arrested, sentenced to two years imprisonment and fifty lashes.

34   *Ibid.*, p. 155.

35   Letter from Wodehouse to Earl of Clarendon, cited in Ó Broin, Leon, *Fenian Fever: an Anglo-American Dilemma* (London, Chatto & Windus Ltd., 1971), p. 28.

36   McGee, *IRB*, p. 32.

37   Lee, *Modernisation of Irish Society*, p. 55.

38   Devoy, *Recollections*, p. 156. The commanding officer, Valentine Baker, would become an infamous figure in late-nineteenth-century Britain. Baker, a veteran of the Crimean War, was dismissed from the British army in 1876 and became an officer in the Ottoman army. He then found himself in Egypt where, in 1884 at the Battle of El Teb, he led an Egyptian paramilitary force to a disastrous defeat by their Sudanese opponents.

39   Roche, *Life*, p. 19.

40   Devoy, *Recollections*, p. 155.

41   Facsimile of O'Reilly's letter from prison, reprinted in Roche, *Life*, pp 64–5.

42   *Ibid.*, p. 20 and p. 22: Murphy was charged with being a deserter from the British army. This charge would later be shown to be false and Murphy would be released.

43   Facsmile of O'Reilly's letter: *ibid.*, pp 376–77.

44   *Ibid.*, p. 19. See also O'Reilly, John Boyle, 'The Old School Clock', in *Songs from the Southern Seas and Other Poems* (Boston, Roberts Brothers, 1873).

45   *Ibid.*, p. 26. O'Reilly left the following note with Murphy: 'MY DEAR OLD FELLOW: I have a good many more bits of poetry of my own manufacture, but they are of a nature which would not serve you were they discovered going to you. I also was cautioned about this courier, but I think he is true. If you get this, and can depend on any one to call, I'll give you a long letter and more poems. I wrote "The Old Clock" to-day. If you can possibly give a copy of it to my father, do. He or my brother will tell you all about the "Old Clock", etc. I was reminded of it by looking at the prison clock this morning.'

46   It is not clear how or when they were discovered but these documents found their way into the hands of Vere Foster, the celebrated educator and first president of the Irish National Teachers' Organisation. Foster would later travel to America and return the manuscript to O'Reilly.

47   Roche, *Life*, p. 376.

Chapter 3

1   Roche, *Life*, p. 22. Roche's biography of O'Reilly contains a transcript of the trial, from which many of the quotations that follow have been taken.

2   Murphy would be acquitted. As noted in chapter 2, he had been wrongly arrested due to a case of mistaken identity.

3   Perhaps this 'O'Loughlen' was a member of the famous legal family from Clare. Sir Michael O'Loghlen (1789–1842) had been Solicitor General for Ireland, while his son Colman O'Loghlen (1819–1877) would become Judge Advocate General in 1868. Other family members were also part of the legal profession.

4   Devoy, *Recollections*, p. 161. Devoy used Roche's court transcript to give an account of O'Reilly's trial but also added some notes of his own.

5   *Ibid.*, p. 162.

6   *Ibid.*

7   *Ibid.*

8   *Ibid.*, p. 163.

9   Roche, *Life*, p. 25.

10   *Ibid.*, pp 25–6.

11   *Ibid.*, p. 27.

12   *Ibid.*

13   *Ibid.*, pp 28–9.

14   *Ibid.*, p. 30.

15   Devoy, *Recollections*, p. 172.

16   Roche, *Life*, p. 35.

17   *Ibid.*, p. 38.

18   *Ibid.*, p. 40.

19   Devoy, *Recollections*, p. 184. Devoy claimed that a police inspector told him that: 'Foley was the man who had given us away.' Foley had also been a key witness in the prosecution of Thomas Chambers, a soldier who was later incarcerated with O'Reilly in various English prisons.

20   Roche, *Life*, p. 39.

21   *Ibid.*, p. 40.

22   *Ibid.*, p. 43. Devoy claimed that Roche misspelled Meara's name and that he was actually called Maher. Whichever version is correct, this soldier had also been a key witness in the prosecution of Thomas Chambers.

23   *Ibid.*, p. 43.

24   *Ibid.*, p. 42.

25   *Ibid.*, p. 43.

26   Devoy, *Recollections*, pp 155–6.

27   Roche, *Life*, p. 44.

28   *Ibid.*

29   Devoy, *Recollections*, pp 160.

30   Roche, *Life*, p. 36

31   *Ibid.*, pp 46–7.

32   *Ibid.*, p. 47.

33   *Ibid.*, p. 48.

Chapter 4

1   Mayhew, Henry and Binny, John, *The Criminal Prisons of London and Scenes of Prison Life* (London, Griffin, Bohn & Co., 1862), p. 116. Mayhew was a co-founder of *Punch* magazine and a noted journalist of the time. Much of his early journalistic work involved investigations into the life of London's working class and the city's destitute. In the 1850s and 1860s he and Binny investigated the conditions within London's prisons.

2   Archer, Thomas, *The Pauper, the Thief and the Convict: Sketches of some of their Homes, Haunts and Habitats* (London, Groombridge & Sons, 1865), p. 193.

3   Archer, *The Pauper*, pp 193–4.

4   Mayhew & Binny, *Criminal Prisons*, p. 239.

5   *Ibid.*, pp 239–40. The statistics for illness and death that Mayhew used were from the 1850s although his book suggests that illness, especially respiratory disease, was still a problem for Millbank's convicts into the 1860s.

6   Archer, *The Pauper*, p. 203.

7   Roche, *Life*, p. 53. See also Archer, *The Pauper*, p. 205.

8   Archer, *The Pauper*, p. 197.

9   *Ibid.*, p. 205.

10 Cashman, Denis B., *The Life of Michael Davitt* (Boston, Murphy & McCarthy, 1881), p. 27. See also Moody, T. W., *Davitt and the Irish Revolution, 1846–1882* (Oxford, Clarendon Press, 1981), p. 149.

11 Roche, *Life*, p. 52.

12 *Ibid.*, p. 54. Roche included a short document written by O'Reilly four years after he left Millbank, in which O'Reilly confirmed, 'I was in separate confinement in Millbank.'

13 Mayhew & Binny, *Criminal Prisons*, p. 102. In some prisons inmates were even masked while on exercise, although this does not seem to have occurred at Millbank while O'Reilly was there.

14 *Ibid.*

15 *Ibid.*, pp 100–7. Although the silent system was not standardised until 1865, it had been in operation in some English prisons before that date. See also Archer, *The Pauper*, pp 199–200, for an account of the system's application in Millbank.

16 Cashman, *Davitt*, p. 26.

17 Roth, Mitchel P., *Prisons and Prison Systems: a Global Encyclopedia* (Santa Barbara, Greenwood Press, 2006), pp 86–7.

18 Archer, *The Pauper*, p. 199.

19 Mayhew, *Criminal Prisons*, p. 271. Prison authorities across England, however, still considered dark cells to be an integral part of prison life. When Mayhew toured Millbank, one of the prison warders proudly informed him that Millbank's dark cells were 'the best dark cells in all England'.

20 Archer, *The Pauper*, p. 202.

21 *Ibid.*, p. 201. This was the menu for 1865 but the amount of food given to prisoners during O'Reilly's stay at Millbank may have been a little smaller. This resulted from the harsher regulation produced by 1865 Prison Act. That year Thomas Archer noted in his book that 'a slight reduction in the quantity of food is to be tried as an experiment.' O'Reilly did not complain about the food at Millbank although Roche, based on conversations with his friend, described it as 'sufficient to sustain life, but nothing more.' See also Roche, *Life*, p. 52.

22 Roche, *Life*, p. 54.

23 Mayhew, *Criminal Prisons*, p. 239.

24 *Ibid.*, p. 312. Mayhew does not mention a specific figure for Millbank but, in other prisons, 2 lb of picking was the regular daily quota for male prisoners, such as O'Reilly, not engaged in hard labour.

25   *Ibid.*
26   O'Reilly, John Boyle, *Moondyne* (facs. edn, Gloucester, Dodo Press, 2006), p. 93.
27   Cashman, *Davitt*, p. 23.
28   Roche, *Life*, pp 54–5.
29   *Ibid.*
30   *Ibid.*
31   *Ibid.*
32   Cashman, *Davitt*, pp 31–2. See also McConville, *Irish Political Prisoners*, pp 280–93, for an excellent analysis of Michael Davitt's long incarceration in Dartmoor.
33   Roche, *Life*, p. 56.
34   *Ibid.*, p. 63. See also *Boston Daily Globe*, 28 December 1890, for an obituary of Michael Lavin, a fellow inmate of O'Reilly, who moved to Massachusetts after his release from prison (around 1870). He described himself and O'Reilly as also being involved in hauling stones and manure. Lavin died on 27 December 1890.
35   *Ibid.* The only sources for information on these escape attempts are James Jeffrey Roche's biography and the Lavin obituary in the *Boston Daily Globe*. However, there is little reason to doubt that O'Reilly made those efforts to escape. Roche learned of the incidents from O'Reilly. He also obtained some extra information on the Dartmoor escape from Lavin. There is no indication that Lavin fabricated or embellished his account of O'Reilly's escape. Nor are Roche's accounts of the escapes implausible. They fit with the sometimes impetuous nature of O'Reilly and they form a pattern that would culminate in his remarkable escape from Western Australia. Also, at Chatham, Portsmouth and Dartmoor, O'Reilly spent most of his day working in the open air and this afforded him opportunities to abscond that were not available in Millbank. For Lavin's brief account of his time in Dartmoor with O'Reilly see *Boston Daily Globe*, 28 December 1890. The obituary contains quotes from Lavin, which confirm that O'Reilly made an escape and remained free for two days.
36   *Ibid.*
37   *Ibid.*, p. 64.
38   *Ibid.*, pp 64–5.
39   *Ibid.*
40   *Ibid.*

Chapter 5
1   Five of these were sentenced to execution during a trial that took place in October. Three of the condemned were publicly hanged in Manchester the following month. See chapter 6.
2   Roche, *Life*, p. 176–7. McCarthy died within a few days of his release. Before their eventual release from prison both men would become the focus of

public campaigns for clemency. There was much public debate as to whether the men had been mistreated in prison. See McConville, *Irish Political Prisoners*, pp 293–7 & pp 307–11.

3   Roche, *Life*, p. 65.

4   *Ibid.*

5   *Ibid.*

6   Sullivan III, C. W., *Fenian Diary: Denis Cashman on Board the* Hougoumont (Dublin, Wolfhound Press, 2001). Sullivan's book includes Cashman's diary and also includes many poems written by the Fenians while aboard the ship as well as a short notebook kept by John Flood.

7   Cusack, M. K. (ed.), *John Sarsfield Casey: Journal of a Voyage from Portland to Fremantle on Board the Convict Ship* Hougoumont (Pittsburgh, Dorrance Publishing Co., 1988). Casey was ill for much of the voyage and his diary is a less detailed account of events than Cashman's, concentrating more on his personal discomfort rather than the wider situation aboard the ship.

8   Fennell's diary, despite its relative limitations as a source for the voyage, is still of much use and benefits from an excellent annotated edition. See Fennell, Philip and King, Marie (eds), *Voyage of the* Hougoumont *and Life at Fremantle: the Story of an Irish Rebel* (Bloomington, Indiana, Xlibris, 2000).

9   Sullivan, *Denis Cashman*, pp 54–5; 15 October 1867.

10   Roche, *Life*, p. 65.

11   *Ibid.*, p. 66.

12   *Ibid.*

13   *Ibid.*

14   *Ibid.*, p. 67.

15   O'Reilly, *Moondyne*, p. 213. In the novel O'Reilly calls the ship the *Houguemont*.

16   *Ibid.*, p. 214.

17   Carroll, Martin C., *Behind the Lighthouse: the Australian Sojourn of John Boyle O'Reilly* (University of Iowa, unpublished PhD thesis, 1955), p. 285. Delany would serve as chaplain to the town of Fremantle from 1869 to 1878. Carroll was an American Fulbright scholar who, in the 1950s, spent time in Western Australia researching O'Reilly's convict experiences. He was the first person to utilise sources such as Denis Cashman's diary and he collected evidence of the oral tradition through which O'Reilly's story was remembered in Western Australia. His work is a vital resource in the study of O'Reilly's Australian life.

18   *Ibid.*, p. 518.

19   *Ibid.*, pp 101–2.

20   *Ibid.*, p. 105.

21   *Ibid.*, pp 102–3.

22   Sullivan, *Denis Cashman*, pp 136–7. Cashman added two pages of appendix at the end of his diary, which contained extra details on the voyage, although there is no indication when these were added.

23   R16: Register of the *Hougoumont* convicts, Battye Library, Perth.

24   *Ibid.*

25   Sullivan, *Denis Cashman*, p. 137, appendix.

26   *Ibid.*, p. 64; 24 October 1867.

27   *Ibid.*, p. 137, appendix.

28   *Ibid.*, p. 68; 29 October 1867.

29   *Boston Herald*, 24 August 1890. Cashman provided the paper with an obituary on O'Reilly, in which he detailed the circumstances surrounding their proposed takeover of the *Hougoumont*. While aboard the ship Cashman could not have risked writing anything about the plot, although his diary for 29 October contains a reference to a two-hour meeting below deck, which he calls 'school', perhaps a code for a discussion of the plot. See Sullivan, *Denis Cashman*, p. 66–7.

30   *Ibid.* Cashman's account suggests that it was the presence of the criminal convicts that convinced many of the Fenians any attempt to take the ship would end in disaster. Those Fenians who had left families behind were especially nervous about the idea of a mutiny.

31   Sullivan, *Denis Cashman*, p. 71; 5 November 1867.

32   *Ibid.*

33   Fennell & King, *Voyage of the* Hougoumont, p. 115.

34   *Ibid.*

35   Sullivan, *Denis Cashman*, p. 73; 8 November 1867. Apart from the oppressive heat the journey continued to be a welcome break from prison life in England and Ireland. The region they were passing through was rich with marine life and the diaries of Cashman and the others note regular distractions caused by sightings of sharks, pods of dolphin and flying fish.

36   *The Wild Goose*, 1.

37   Sullivan, *Denis Cashman*, p. 77; 13 November 1867.

38   *Ibid.*, p. 132; 3 January 1868.

39   Cusack, *John Sarsfield Casey*, p. 20.

40   Rats aboard ship are mentioned several times in the diaries of Casey, Cashman and Fennell.

41   Sullivan, *Denis Cashman*, p. 92; 2 December 1867.

42   *Ibid.*, p. 98; 8 December 1867.

43   *Ibid.*, p. 108; 16 December 1867.

44   Fennell & King, *Voyage of the* Hougoumont, pp 153–4.

45   Cusack, *John Sarsfield Casey*, p. 27.

46   Sullivan, *Denis Cashman*, p. 107; 22 December 1867.

47   *Ibid.*, p. 108; 25 December 1867.

48   *The Wild Goose*, 7.

49   Sullivan, *Denis Cashman*, p. 108; 25 December 1867.

50   *Ibid.*, p. 132; 3 January 1868.

51   *Ibid.*, pp 140–1.

Chapter 6

1   Carroll, *Lighthouse*, p. 157.

2   *Ibid.*, p. 161.

3   *Ibid.*

4   Hughes, Robert, *The Fatal Shore: a History of the Transportation of Convicts to Australia, 1787–1868* (London, Collins Harvill, 1987), p. 1.

5   Shaw, A. G. L., *Convicts and the Colonies* (Dublin, The Irish Historical Press, 1998), p. 353.

6   This order for the 'Act for the Transportation of Offenders from Great Britain' read: 'Her Majesty, by and with the advice of Her Privy Council, doth order and it is hereby ordered, that upon and from the first day of June in this present year, Her Majesty's settlements in Western Australia shall be places to which felons and other offenders in the United Kingdom then being or thereafter to be under sentence or order of transportation or banishment shall be conveyed under provisions of the said recited Act.'

7   Crowley, Francis Keble and De Garis, Brian K., *A Short History of Western Australia* (South Yarra, Victoria, Macmillan Company of Australia, 1969), p. 21.

8   Amos, Keith, *The Fenians in Australia: 1865–1880* (Sydney, New South Wales University Press, 1988), p. 123. This important survey of the Fenians in Australia has much information on the attitudes of Australians towards the Fenians as well as on the convicts who served time on the continent.

9   *The Irishman*, 26 April 1868.

10   Carroll, *Lighthouse*, p. 100.

11   *Fremantle Herald*, 28 December 1867.

12   Reilly, J. T., *Reminiscences of Fifty Years in Western Australia* (Melbourne, Sands & McDougall, 1903), pp 84–5.

13   *Ibid.*, p. 99; quoted in *Perth Inquirer*, 12 February 1868.

14   *Fremantle Herald*, 21 December 1867.

15   Quotations from a letter from Manning to Crampton, 2 December 1867, cited in Amos, *Fenians*, pp 94–5.

16   Carroll, *Lighthouse*, p. 218.

17   Letter from Hampton to Buckingham, 29 January 1868: *ibid.*, p. 220.

18   *Fremantle Herald*, 11 January 1868.

19   *Ibid.*

20   *Ibid.*, 25 January 1868.

21   *Ibid.*, 11 April 1868. Cozens had maintained this argument from the day his ship arrived at Fremantle.

22   Although the general atmosphere, to judge from the tone of the *Fremantle Herald*, had calmed, there was evidently lingering nervousness among the colonists. In late February the gunboat *Brisk* fired a few practice rounds during night manoeuvres. The noise caused some Fremantle residents to believe that a Fenian ship had attacked the town and they 'rushed all but naked into the streets'. See *Fremantle Herald*, 29 February 1868.

23   O'Reilly, *Moondyne*, pp 270–1. O'Reilly heard the name 'Moondyne' while in Western Australia; a local bushranger named Joseph Bolitho Johns was popularly known as 'Moondyne Joe'. Johns is a legendary figure in Western Australian history but O'Reilly's Moondyne bears very little resemblance to the bushranger's life-story. For a history of Joseph Bolitho Johns, see Elliot, Ian, *Moondyne Joe: the Man and the Myth* (Perth, Hesperian Press, 1998).

24   Davidson, Ron, *Fremantle Impressions* (Fremantle, Fremantle Press, 2008), pp 199–200.

25   Fremantle Prison, *Building the Convict Establishment*, 2009, p. 5.

26   Fremantle Prison, *Convict Daily Life*, 2009, p. 2.

27   *Ibid.*, p. 1.

28   *Ibid.*, p. 4.

29   Cell description was noted on author's visit to prison. Fremantle Prison has been a working museum since 1992.

30   Fremantle Prison, *Convict Daily Life*, p. 1.

31   Roche, *Life*, p. 70.

32   Carroll, *Lighthouse*, pp 235–6.

33   *Ibid.*, p. 289.

34   Amos, *Fenians*, p. 125.

35   McConville, *Irish Political Prisoners*, pp 132–3.

36   Evans, A. G., *Fanatic Heart: a Life of John Boyle O'Reilly 1844–1890* (Perth, University of Western Australia Press, 1997), pp 102–3. The full poem is printed in Sullivan, *Denis Cashman*, pp 148–9.

37   *Boston Herald*, 24 August 1890.

38   Carroll, *Lighthouse*, pp 234–6.

39   *Ibid.*, p. 236.

40   *Ibid.*, p. 239.

41   *The Irishman*, 26 April 1868.

42   *Ibid.*, 11 April 1868.

43   Roche, *Life*, p. 70.

44   O'Reilly, *Moondyne*, p. 5.

45   Roche, *Life*, p. 70. See also Carroll, *Lighthouse*, p. 293.

46   *Ibid.*, p. 71. See also the letter from E. H. Withers on 'O'Reilly's escape from Bunbury', *Western Mail*, 2 March 1939. Withers also claimed that O'Reilly was a convict constable. He was a child when O'Reilly was in Western Australia. Nearly every morning, while herding his father's cattle, he met O'Reilly as the convict 'took messages between the camp and the head depot in town'.

47   Carroll, *Lighthouse*, pp 295–7.

48   Roche, *Life*, p. 72.

49   *Ibid.*

50   *Ibid.*, p. 73.

51   Carroll, *Lighthouse*, pp 297–300.

52   Roche, *Life*, p. 71.

53   Carroll, *Lighthouse*, pp 246–7.

54   For a study of the English newspaper coverage of the Fenians at this time, see De Nie, Michael, '"A Medley Mob of Irish-American Plotters and Irish Dupes": the British Press and Transatlantic Fenianism', *Journal of British Studies*, 40, 2 (April 2001).

55   Carroll, *Lighthouse*, p. 181.

56   *Ibid.*, p. 184.

57   Roche, *Life*, p. 76.

58   Article by O'Reilly entitled 'After Ten Years', *Boston Daily Globe*, 24 July 1879. This offered some detail on his life as an Australian convict; see also n. 80 below.

59   Keneally, Thomas, *The Great Shame: a Story of the Irish in the Old World and the New* (London, Chatto & Windus, 1998), p. 501.

60   Hovey, William A., *Selected Poems of John Boyle O'Reilly* (San Francisco, Paul Elder & Co., 1904), pp vi–vii.

61   Carroll, *Lighthouse*, p. 300.

62   *Fremantle Herald*, 10 October 1868. These prisoners were also given a special uniform to distinguish them from regular convicts. See also Fremantle Prison, *Convict Daily Life*, p. 1.

63   Fremantle Prison, *Convict Daily Life*, p. 4.

64   Fennell & King, *Voyage of the* Hougoumont, p. 226–7.

65   Fremantle Prison, *Convict Daily Life*, p. 4.

66   Millett, Mrs Edward, *An Australian Parsonage: or, the Settler and the Savage in Western Australia* (London, E. Stanford, 1872), p. 242.

67   Carroll, *Lighthouse*, p. 303.

68   *Fremantle Herald*, 23 November 1867. This practice of firing the guns was ended because, as often as not, it terrified the inhabitants of Fremantle.

69   Carroll, *Lighthouse*, p. 304.

70   *Ibid.*, pp 305–6.

71   *Accounts and Papers of the House of Commons, 1862* (crime, prisons and police), p. 35.

72   O'Reilly, *Moondyne*, p. 73.

73   Carroll, *Lighthouse*, p. 315. For more detail on Maguire, see Waters, Ormonde D. P., 'John Boyle O'Reilly', *Seanchas Ardmhacha: Journal of the Armagh Diocesan Historical Society*, 13, 1 (1988), pp 178–9.

74   *Boston Daily Globe*, 24 July 1879.

75   *Ibid.*

76   Carroll, *Lighthouse*, pp 311–12.

77   Roche, *Life*, p. 77.

78   *Ibid.*, p. 294.

79   *Ibid.*

80   *Philadelphia Times*, 25 June 1881, and *Boston Daily Globe*, 24 July 1879. Young, born in Boston, was a historian who worked for a time on the *Boston Daily Globe*. In 1879 O'Reilly contributed a short article (approximately 1,500 words) to that newspaper on the subject of his escape, in which he gave a self-censored version of his time in Australia, making no mention of Jessie

Woodman. Most of the detail of the article concerned the actual escape and it is clear that this formed the basis for Young's later article. Young's version of the escape was more detailed than O'Reilly's had been (approximately 4,500 words) and it seems that he had obtained the extra information in conversations with O'Reilly. By 1881 both men had been friends for the best part of a decade through their mutual membership of the Papyrus Club.

81   Davitt, Michael, *Life and Progress in Australasia* (London, Methuen & Co., 1898), p. 458.

82   *Ibid.*, p. 456.

83   *The West Australian*, 20 December 1952. The paper contains an article by Martin Carroll called 'The Mark of Boyle O'Reilly's escape', in which he describes his interview with Anne Stokes.

84   Carroll, *Lighthouse*, p. 324.

85   See MN1344, 'Original Transcript of Journalist Stenography on Cover of John Boyle O'Reilly's Notebook Containing Poems', transcript by Gillian O'Mara, Battye Library, Perth (1992). I am grateful to Mrs O'Mara for taking time to answer some of my queries on this document. The Battye Library also holds a copy of O'Reilly's notebook: see MN1221, Papers of John Boyle O'Reilly, ACC 3708A. Ormonde Waters was one historian who doubted that the affair had happened, calling the idea 'preposterous'. See Waters, Ormonde D. P., 'John Boyle O'Reilly and the *Catalpa* Ballad', *Records of Meath Archaeological and Historical Society*, 4, 5 (1971).

86   MN1344, O'Mara transcript, Battye Library, Perth.

87   MN1221, Papers of John Boyle O'Reilly, ACC 3708A, Battye Library, Perth.

88   Amos, *Fenians*, p. 155.

89   *Ibid.* See also Keneally, *Great Shame*, p. 501.

90   O'Reilly, *Moondyne*, pp 130–1.

91   Amos, *Fenians*, p. 155, and Carroll, *Lighthouse*, p. 326.

92   Carroll, *Lighthouse*, p. 326.

93   O'Reilly, John Boyle, *The Statues in the Block and Other Poems* (Boston, Roberts Brothers, 1884).

94   MN1221, Papers of John Boyle O'Reilly, ACC 3708A, Battye Library, Perth.

95   Amos, *Fenians*, p. 154. The spelling of O'Reilly as Riley was a mistake although it has led one historian, Rica Erickson, to claim that Timperley was referring to a person other than John Boyle O'Reilly. However, the evidence all points to Riley being O'Reilly and the only similarly named Fenian convict was James Reilly who was stationed at the West Guildford convict station, 120 miles away.

96   Davitt, *Australasia*, p. 458.

97   Evans, *Fanatic Heart*, p. 130. It is unclear whether Dr Lovegrove was affiliated with the police or the prison service but it seems that he did not inform any officials of O'Reilly's attempted suicide.

98   Carroll's article, *The West Australian*, 20 December 1952.

99   Devoy, John, *Devoy's Post Bag*, vol. II (Dublin, C. J. Fallon, 1948), p. 563.

100　Details below from the *Boston Daily Globe*, 24 July 1879.

101　*Philadelphia Times*, 25 June 1881. See also Amos, *Fenians*, p. 157, who notes that only probationary convicts such as O'Reilly and not ticket-of-leave convicts were required to wear the special convict boots.

102　Amos, *Fenians*, p. 159.

103　Carroll, *Lighthouse*, p. 305.

104　*Philadelphia Times*, 25 June 1881. Presumably he later gave the letter to Maguire to post to his father.

105　*Boston Daily Globe*, 24 July 1879.

106　*Ibid.*

Chapter 7

1　*Boston Daily Globe*, 24 July 1879. O'Reilly wrote that, because the policy of transportation had now ended, he felt more able to announce publicly the names of those who had helped him escape from Western Australia. 'In the following account', he wrote, 'I have suppressed only the names of those still connected with the government of the colony.' One of his helpers, Thomas Milligan, did not want his name to be publicly known and so is referred to as 'M'. Key figures such as Patrick McCabe and James Maguire are named. Alexander Young, in his *Philadelphia Times* article, also referred to Milligan as 'M'.

2　*Ibid.*

3　*Philadelphia Times*, 25 June 1881. See also Carroll, *Lighthouse*, p. 336. The identity of Maguire's two cousins remains a mystery, although one local tradition uncovered by Carroll stated that a former Fenian named Owen Shanahan obtained the civilian boots that Maguire later gave to O'Reilly and that he also participated in the escape. This claim was disputed by Maguire's descendants.

4　*Ibid.*

5　Carroll, *Lighthouse*, p. 334.

6　The other man in the boat was either Mark Lyons or John McKree, both Irishmen who had assisted in the planning and execution of the escape. See *Western Mail*, 19 January 1939 and 2 March 1939.

7　*Boston Daily Globe*, 24 July 1879. In his article O'Reilly stressed that he understood Milligan's decision and stated that 'He was a brave man.'

8　*Philadelphia Times*, 25 July 1881.

9　*Ibid.*

10　*Ibid.*

11　Carroll, *Lighthouse*, p. 343. Young's account referred to Jackson as 'Johnson'. O'Reilly's article also referred to Jackson as 'Johnson'. If this was an attempt to disguise Jackson's name it was not a very good one.

12　*Ibid.*

13　Amos, *Fenians*, p. 166.

14　Carroll, *Lighthouse*, p. 339.

15   Ibid., p. 338.
16   Ibid., p. 340.
17   Ibid., p. 341.
18   Philadelphia Times, 25 June 1881.
19   Ibid.
20   Ibid.
21   Ibid.
22   Ibid.
23   Carroll, Lighthouse, p. 354.
24   Philadelphia Times, 25 June 1881.
25   Boston Daily Globe, 24 July 1879.
26   Ibid.
27   Davitt, Australasia, pp 460–1.
28   Philadelphia Times, 25 June 1881.
29   Carroll, Lighthouse, pp 341–2.
30   Ibid., p. 350.
31   Ibid., p. 352.
32   Amos, Fenians, p. 166.
33   Evans, Fanatic Heart, p. 147.
34   Amos, Fenians, p. 155.
35   Philadelphia Times, 25 June 1881.
36   Ibid.
37   Erickson, Rica and O'Mara, Gillian, Convicts in Western Australia 1850–
      1887, Dictionary of Western Australians, vol. IX (Perth, University of
      Western Australia Press 1994).
38   Boston Daily Globe, 24 July 1879.
39   O'Reilly, Moondyne, p. 12.
40   Boston Daily Globe, 24 July 1879.
41   Western Mail, 19 January 1939.
42   Philadelphia Times, 25 June 1881.
43   Ibid. See also The West Australian, 20 December 1952. Maguire would 'live
      until his 83rd year', survived by nine children and a successful farm.
      O'Reilly, for the rest of his own life, kept in contact with Maguire and sent
      him every copy of The Pilot until his death in 1890. Regrettably, following
      Maguire's death, his contacts with O'Reilly and documents relating to the
      escape 'were destroyed by some relatives'; see Carroll, Lighthouse, p. 308.
44   Carroll, Lighthouse, p. 352.
45   Roche, Life, p. 83.
46   Letter sent to the police superintendent of Western Australia, M. S. Smith,
      reprinted in Carroll, Lighthouse, pp 468–9.

Chapter 8

1   Creighton, Margaret S., Rites & Passages: the Experience of American
      Whaling, 1830–1870 (Cambridge, Cambridge University Press, 1995), p. 6.

2   *Ibid.*, pp 23–4.

3   The whaling industry was further disadvantaged by the fact that declining whale populations had forced the ships into longer and more expensive expeditions, thus pushing up their prices even further.

4   Hohman, Elmo Paul, *The American Whaleman: a Study of Life and Labor in the Whaling Industry* (New York, Longmans, Green & Co., 1928), p. 302. Hohman goes into great detail about life aboard a whaling ship but his work is also an analytical study of the rise and subsequent decline of the industry.

5   *Ibid.*, pp 302–8.

6   Evans, *Fanatic Heart*, p. 158.

7   *Boston Daily Globe*, 24 July 1879.

8   Hohman, *American Whaleman*, pp 14–15.

9   *Ibid.*, p. 13.

10   Evans, *Fanatic Heart*, p. 160.

11   Roche, *Life*, p. 91.

12   *Ibid.*

13   Hohman, *American Whaleman*, pp 155–156.

14   *Ibid.*, p. 156.

15   *Ibid.*, p. 159.

16   *Ibid.*, p. 160.

17   Letter from Henry Hathaway in which he described the whale hunt, reproduced in *Boston Daily Globe*, 3 February 1886. This book's version of the hunt is based on Hathaway's account. See also Roche, *Life*, pp 84–5. In his biography of O'Reilly, Roche printed a copy of this letter. According to Roche, O'Reilly had previously confirmed to him that Hathaway's version was an accurate retelling of what happened that day.

18   'The Amber Whale', in O'Reilly, John Boyle, *Songs, Legends and Ballads* (Jackson, Massachusetts, The Pilot Publishing Company, 1882).

19   Roche, *Life*, pp 98–9; taken by Roche from a personal log kept by Hathaway.

20   Evans, *Fanatic Heart*, p. 165.

21   Carroll, *Lighthouse*, p. 497.

22   *Ibid.*, p. 360. There is some uncertainty as to the history of these men. Both of them had escaped from Bunbury earlier in 1869. It is possible that they had stowed away aboard the *Gazelle*, as suggested by Carroll, but neither man is mentioned in the accounts of O'Reilly, Roche or Hathaway. It seems more likely that they took advantage of the carnival atmosphere in Bunbury during February to sneak aboard a whaling ship. The authorities in Western Australia would send a police sergeant to escort both men back to Fremantle. Remarkably, McGuiness would escape from Mauritius before this happened and he disappears from the records. After returning to Western Australia Connor was given three years' hard labour on top of his original sentence. He died in Perth in 1888. For the records of each man see Erickson & O'Mara, *Convicts in Western Australia*.

23   Account of the magistrate's inspection aboard the *Gazelle* from Roche, *Life*,
      p. 86. See also a letter written by O'Reilly to Dublin's *Nation* newspaper on
      9 October 1869, printed in *Nation*, 30 October 1869.

24   Quotation is from an unnumbered document in the John Boyle O'Reilly
      papers in Boston College's John J. Burns Library. It contains Hathaway's
      version of what happened when the magistrate came aboard ship. It is very
      similar to the account of the magistrate's inspection in Roche's biography of
      O'Reilly and probably served as a source for that book. Roche included
      Hathaway's statement that O'Reilly had tried to kill himself in Australia
      without comment. Roche may have learned about the suicide attempt from
      Hathaway but there remains no indication that he knew the full story
      behind what had happened.

25   See the case of Captain Anthony of the *Catalpa* rescue in chapter 12.
      Anthony effectively ended his career as a whale ship captain as a result of
      aiding escaped convicts.

26   Roche, *Life*, p. 87.

27   *Ibid.*, p. 88.

28   *Nation*, 30 October 1869.

29   *Ibid.*

30   Roche, *Life*, p. 88.

31   *Nation*, 30 October 1869.

32   Carroll, *Lighthouse*, p. 498. Bowman, in his own way, was almost as
      indefatigable as O'Reilly. After serving six months in solitary confinement he
      began a concerted letter-writing campaign to the governor and Comptroller-
      General of the state. By 1873 he had received a conditional pardon.

33   Roche, *Life*, p. 88.

34   *Ibid.*, p. 89.

35   *Ibid.*

36   *Ibid.*

37   *Ibid.*

38   *Ibid.* By 1886 Hathaway had settled in New Bedford and this afforded
      Roche an opportunity to interview the sailor about O'Reilly's life aboard
      ship. Hathaway gave Roche access to a diary he kept on board the *Gazelle*,
      and which contained some jottings by O'Reilly.

39   *Ibid.*, p. 90

40   *Ibid.*, p. 91.

41   *Ibid.*, p. 99.

42   *Ibid.*

43   *Ibid.*

44   *Ibid.*

45   *Nation*, 30 October 1869.

46   *The Pilot*, 8 January 1870 and 12 February 1870. See also Roche, *Life*, p. 99–
      100.

Chapter 9

1   Interview with Mary Boyle O'Reilly (O'Reilly's daughter), *The West Australian*, 14 December 1935.

2   Roche, *Life*, p. 100. Roche stated that O'Reilly arrived on 23 November 1869 but Francis McManamin, a Jesuit who wrote a study of O'Reilly's life in the 1970s, demonstrated that the *Bombay* had arrived the previous day. Roche had obtained the date from O'Reilly and it shows that O'Reilly often erred when giving dates for events. It was a characteristic that Roche was aware of, writing that 'his memory was unreliable in the matter of the dates'. See McManamin, Francis G., *The American Years of John Boyle O'Reilly, 1870–1890* (New York, Arno Press, 1976), p. 38.

3   *Nation*, 30 October 1869. For the letter to *The Irishman*, see Roche, *Life*, pp 255–6; it differs little from the letter to the *Nation*.

4   Roche, *Life*, p. 101.

5   *The Pilot*, 8 January 1869. See also reports of 12 February and 29 October 1870 for more examples of O'Reilly's lectures.

6   Kenneally, *Conflict*, p. 141.

7   Roche, *Life*, p. 105. O'Mahony had collected some money for O'Reilly. Roche includes a letter, written to O'Mahony from Boston on 23 February 1870: 'Dear Sir, I am sorry that your letter has remained unanswered until now. I was absent from Boston and did not receive it. Will you, in returning this check for ten pounds to the Ladies' Committee in Ireland, express my deep gratitude for their thoughtful kindness Of course, I cannot accept it. There are many in Ireland – many who suffer from the loss of their bread-winners in the old cause – they want it; let them have it. It is enough – more than enough – for me to know that I have been remembered in Ireland, and that still, in the old land, the spirit of our cause and the energies of our people are living and acting. I remain, dear Colonel, Very truly yours, J. Boyle O'Reilly.'

8   In 1867 John Savage had been elected as leader of the 'O'Mahony Wing' of the Fenians.

9   Devoy, *Recollections*, p. 159.

10   *The Pilot*, 2 April 1869.

11   Roche, *Life*, p. 103

12   *Ibid.*, and career details that follow.

13   *Ibid.*

14   Evans, *Fanatic Heart*, p. 178.

15   In an interview with the *Boston Daily Globe*, 11 August 1890, Donahoe described how he brought O'Reilly into *The Pilot*.

16   For Donahoe's career, see Frawley, Sister Mary Alphonsine, *Patrick Donahoe* (Washington, DC, The Catholic University of America Press, 1946).

17   *Ibid.*, p. 14.

18   *The Pilot*, 22 December 1838.

19   Donahoe, Patrick, 'Reminiscences of An Old Time Journalist: a Letter to Martin J. Griffin', *Records of the American Catholic Historical Society*, xv (1904), pp 314–17.

20   Editorial written by Thomas D'Arcy McGee, *The Pilot*, 8 June 1844.

21   Walsh, Francis Robert, 'The Boston Pilot: a Newspaper for the Irish Immigrant', 1829–1908 (Boston University, unpublished PhD thesis, 1968), p. vii.

22   *Ibid.*, p. 58.

23   Donahoe's Emigrant Savings Bank was a very successful business but it had competitors within the Irish community. See *The Pilot*, 30 April 1870, for a news item on the New York-based bank, Irish Emigrant Society.

24   *New York Times*, 6 April 1876. According to the paper, his annual profit from all his business may have been $100,000 per annum.

25   Frawley, *Donahoe*, p. 210.

26   Copy of letter to Crissy Watkinson, cited in Roche, *Life*, pp 105–6.

27   Steward, Patrick, 'Erin's Hope: Fenianism in the North Atlantic, 1858–1876' (University of Missouri, unpublished PhD thesis, 2003), pp 205–14. This is the most detailed account of the planning and execution of the Ridgeway battle. See also Hernon, Ian, *Britain's Forgotten Wars: Colonial Campaigns of the 19th Century* (Stroud, Sutton Publishing, 2006), which includes a chapter on the Fenian invasion of Canada.

28   Ellis, William Hodgson, 'The Adventures of a Prisoner of War', *The Canadian Magazine of Politics, Science, Art and Literature*, 13, 3 (July 1899), p. 202.

29   Steward, *Erin's Hope*, p. 13

30   *Ibid.*, see pp 284–314 for the decline of Fenian membership within the United States and the continual divisions within the movement from 1867 to 1870.

31   McManamin, *American Years*, p. 44.

32   *The Pilot*, 4 June 1870.

33   Henri Le Caron would remain a trusted member of Clan na Gael into the 1880s. Le Caron testified to the Parnell Commission of 1888–89 and thus exposed his double life. See Caron's memoir: Le Caron, Henri, *Twenty-Five Years in the Secret Service: Recollections of a Spy* (London, William Heinemann, 1892).

34   Steward, *Erin's Hope*, p. 318.

35   *The Pilot*, 4 June 1870.

36   Roche, *Life*, pp 110–11. Roche included a copy of O'Reilly's original report from the front, which was subsequently edited before inclusion in *The Pilot*; see the edition of 4 June 1870.

37   See *The Pilot*, 4 June 1870, for a copy of Grant's proclamation.

38   *Ibid.* After the retreat from Eccles Hill, O'Neill admonished his men and declared: 'I now leave you now in command of Boyle O'Reilly.'

39   Le Caron, *Secret Service*, p. 88.

40   *Ibid.*, p. 89.

41   Steward, *Erin's Hope*, p. 321 and *New York Times*, 30 July 1870. Despite the failure of the invasion and his arrest, O'Neill was not yet finished with Canada. The country had become his white whale. In 1871 he launched a third expedition into Canadian territory, this time into the Red River area

of Manitoba, scene of a Métis rebellion in 1869 against the Canadian confederation. O'Neill commanded a grand total of forty-one men and sought to form an alliance with the Métis. He ended up behind bars. Again, his incarceration was brief and he was soon back on US soil; see Steward, *Erin's Hope*, pp 328–31.

42 Roche, *Life*, p. 111.

43 *The Pilot*, 4 June 1870. See also Steward, *Erin's Hope*, p. 320–2, for accounts of the skirmishing that took place along the border over the following days.

44 *The Pilot*, 4 June 1870.

45 *Ibid.*, 11 June 1870.

46 John Boyle O'Reilly to 'The Officers and Members of the Fenian Brotherhood of Boston', 31 July 1870: John Boyle O'Reilly Papers, John J. Burn's Library, Boston College.

47 Devoy, *Recollections*, p. 159.

48 Ibson, John Duffy, *Will The World Break Your Heart? Dimensions and Consequences of Irish-American Assimilation* (New York, Garland Publishing, 1990), p. 67. Ibson devotes eight pages of his study to O'Reilly.

49 For an account of McGee's death see Keneally, *Great Shame*, pp 495–6.

50 For example, see *Nation*, 11 June 1870.

51 *The Pilot*, 23 July 1870.

52 *Ibid.*, 29 July 1871.

53 Ibson, *Will The World Break Your Heart?*, p. 67.

54 *Ibid.*

55 *Ibid.*

56 Mitchell, Edward Page, *Memoirs of an Editor: Fifty Years of American Journalism* (New York, C. Scribner's Sons, 1924), p. 94. Mitchell had met O'Reilly though a friend who had a room in the same lodging house as the Irishman. Of O'Reilly, he said, 'no man had ever impressed me more strongly with the vividness of an amiable personality.'

57 Denieffe, Joseph, *A Personal Narrative of the Irish Revolutionary Brotherhood* (New York, The Gael Publishing Company, 1906), pp 290–1. A copy of this letter, dated 14 September 1871, was included in the appendices of Denieffe's memoir.

58 Circulation figures from this time are often impossible to gauge accurately. In its own columns *The Pilot* regularly claimed its circulation to be around 100,000 copies but the *American Newspaper Directory* for 1872 described the paper as claiming to have a circulation of 55,000. See *American Newspaper Directory* (New York, George P. Rowell & Co., 1872), p. 78.

59 Roche, *Life*, p. 126.

60 *Ibid.* See also Frawley, *Donahoe*, pp 81–2.

61 Evans, *Fanatic Heart*, p. 175.

62 Roche, *Life*, p. 130.

63 *The Pilot*, 28 May 1870. It is the poem that was related to his suicide attempt in Australia, which begins with the lines: 'Have I no future left to me / Is

there no struggling way'. It seems certain that O'Reilly did not tell Roche about Jessie Woodman nor did he ever tell his friend of the suicide attempt. Roche wrote of the poem that 'It is interesting for its hopeful spirit'; see Roche, *Life*, p. 107.

64   Denieffe, *Personal Narrative*, pp 201–2. The quote is from an O'Reilly letter, dated 27 September 1871, to O'Donovan Rossa. See also Roche, *Life*, pp 132–3.

65   Roche, *Life*, p. 133.

66   For a contemporary history of the Boston fire, see Conwell, Russell, *A Great Fire in Boston* (Boston, B. B. Russell, 1873). See also the modern account of Sammarco, Anthony Mitchell, *The Great Fire of 1872* (Mount Pleasant, SC, Arcadia Publishing, 1997). Sammarco's book serves as a photographic record of the devastation wrought by the fire.

67   For *The Pilot*'s account of the fire, see the editions of 23 November and 30 November 1872.

68   Letter to John Lothrop Motley, 16 November 1872, cited in Morse, John Torrey, *Life and Letters of Oliver Wendell Holmes*, vol. II (Boston, Houghton Mifflin & Co., 1896), pp 197–8.

69   *The Pilot*, 23 November 1872,

70   *Ibid.*, for details of financial loss and comment on the fire.

71   *Ibid.*, 30 November 1872.

72   *Ibid.* See also *The Pilot*, 7 December 1872.

73   Conwell, *Great Fire*, pp 250–1. The piece, whether written by Conwell or not, was originally in the *Boston Daily Globe*. According to Conwell's account, many other newspaper offices were damaged by the fire, although only a few to the same level as *The Pilot*.

74   Details and comments below from the account of that fire in *The Pilot*, 14 June 1873.

75   Roche, *Life*, p. 133.

76   *Ibid.*

77   'To Captain David R. Gifford, of the whaling bark Gazelle, of New Bedford, I dedicate this book': O'Reilly, *Songs from the Southern Seas*.

78   Roche, *Life*, p. 206.

79   Letter from O'Reilly to Crissy Watkinson, 7 September 1874: *Ibid.*, pp 133–4.

80   Frawley, *Donahoe*, p. 217.

81   *Ibid.*, p. 215.

82   *Ibid.*, p. 159.

83   *Ibid.*

84   *Ibid.*, pp 228–30. See also *New York Times*, 8 April 1876, in which Donahoe blamed his decision to endorse loans valued at a total of over $200,000 as the cause of his demise. Finotti, an importer of Italian produce, was the brother of Reverend Joseph M. Finotti, a literary editor of *The Pilot* from 1854–1868.

85   *New York Times*, 4 April 1876.

86   Frawley, *Donahoe*, p. 297. The exact sum, as defined by his creditors, was $569,051.31.

87   Throughout February 1876 *The Pilot* had covered the demise of Donahoe's business; see editions of 5, 12, 1 and 26 February. See also Frawley, *Donahoe*, pp 219–21, for detail on these negotiations.

88   Frawley, *Donahoe*, p. 242. Frawley wrote that there was no evidence that this bank was ever legally constituted.

89   *Ibid.* See also *New York Times*, 6 April 1876, which named some of the smaller investors such as one Patrick Murphy who had invested $50 with Donahoe. The sums invested were mostly in the range of a few tens to a few hundred dollars per person. The largest deposit seems to have been around $2,000. Apart from individual investors, a number of charities had also deposited funds with Donahoe and they seem to have been responsible for the larger investments. According to the paper's 'Special Correspondent', Donahoe had started his private bank in 1874.

90   *Ibid.* See also *The Pilot*, 19 February 1876, in which the paper carried messages of support for Donahoe that had appeared in other newspapers.

91   *Ibid.*

92   O'Reilly letter to Charles Hurd, 27 January 1876: John Boyle O'Reilly Papers, Boston Public Library.

93   Frawley, *Donahoe*, p. 222. See also *Boston Daily Globe*, 17 April 1876.

94   Letter by Donahoe, dated 18 April, 'To the patrons of the Pilot', in the *Boston Daily Globe*, 19 April 1876.

95   *The Pilot*, 29 April 1876.

96   Stoddard, Richard Henry and Gilman, Arthur, *Poets' Homes: Pen and Pencil Sketches of American Poets and their Homes* (Boston, D. Lothrop Company, 1879), p. 214.

97   *The Pilot*, 29 April 1876.

98   'Labor Force, series D 1–682', *Historical Statistics of the United States, Colonial times to 1970*, vol. 1 (United States Bureau of the Census, 1975).

Chapter 10

1   Roche, *Life*, pp 194–5.

2   Shankman, Arnold, 'Black on Green: Afro-American Editors on Irish Independence', 1840–1921, *Phylon*, 41, 3 (1980), p. 285

3   Lee, J. J, and Casey, Marion R. (eds), *Making the Irish American: History and Heritage of the Irish in the United States* (New York, New York University Press, 2006), p. 669.

4   England, Bishop John and Read, George William, *Letters of the Late Bishop England to the Hon John Forsyth* (Baltimore, J. Murphy & Co., 1844). Bishop England's first two letters, out of a total of eighteen, were devoted to explaining the Vatican's condemnation of the international slave trade and also to explaining why that condemnation was not directed at 'domestic slavery' within the United States. The Pope, England explained, had only

condemned the forcible capture of free people and the subsequent trading of such individuals as slaves, not the legal position within many American states whereby individuals were born into slavery. The rest of the letters were devoted to a history of slavery within the context of Christianity. England may have been trying to overwhelm Forsyth with detail. By 'Letter VIII', he had only reached the mid-fifth century and St Patrick's mission to Ireland.

5   Letter XVI, *ibid.*, p. 134.

6   O'Connell, Daniel and Mathew, Theobald, *Address of the People of Ireland to their Countrymen and Countrywomen in America*, 1847.

7   *Ibid.*

8   *The Pilot*, 19 March 1842. Hughes soon admitted that the document was real but urged Catholics to ignore its contents since it emanated from a 'foreign' source.

9   England & Read, *Letters of Bishop England*, p. 19.

10   Shankman, 'Black on Green', p. 288

11   England & Read, *Letters of Bishop England*, introductory note by Read.

12   *The Pilot*, 3 March 1855.

13   *Ibid.*, 31 December 1859.

14   For the Irish involvement in the Civil War, see Kenneally, *Conflict*, pp 107–163. See also Bruce, Susannah Ural, *The Harp and the Eagle: Irish-American Volunteers and the Union Army, 1861–1865* (New York, New York University Press, 2006).

15   Shankman, 'Black on Green', p. 286.

16   For an account of the riots see Kenneally, *Conflict*, pp 136–8.

17   *The Pilot*, 7 April, 22 September and 1 December 1866.

18   *Ibid.*, 10 February 1866.

19   Trexler, Sister Margaret Ellen, 'American Catholics and Negroes', *Phylon*, 30, 4, (1969), pp 355–6.

20   *Proceedings of the California State Convention of Colored Citizens Held in Sacramento on the 25th, 26th, 27th, and 28th of October 1865* (San Francisco, 1969), p. 95; see pp 83–4 for the debate that led to this resolution. The names of Robert Emmet and Daniel O'Connell figured prominently and one delegate, W. Yates, proposed an extraordinary resolution that offered support for the 'Fenian movement to liberate Ireland from the yoke of British bondage'. He then declared that, once black Americans had achieved full civil rights in the US, 40,000 coloured troops could be raised to assist the Irish against the 'hypocritical English bull'. This resolution was voted down. There was some opposition to a resolution in favour of Irish independence with one delegate claiming that 'the Irishman was the most deceitful of all nations'.

21   Ferreira, Patricia J., 'Frederick Douglass in Ireland: the Dublin Edition of his Narrative', *New Hibernia Review*, 5, 1 (Spring 2001), p. 54.

22   Shankman, 'Black on Green', p. 290.

23   *Ibid.*

24   *Ibid.*, p. 294.

25   *The Pilot*, 7 February 1874.
26   *Ibid.*, 5 May 1877. O'Reilly's original article on the Typographical Society had been published three months earlier and, since then, he had engaged a few letter writers on the topic. His May editorial is a good example of his approach to black civil rights over the previous three years.
27   *Ibid.*
28   *New York Times*, 14 April 1873.
29   *The Pilot*, 26 April 1873.
30   *Ibid.*, 15 July 1876.
31   *New York Herald*, 7 July 1876. For an account of the battle, specifically the involvement of Irish-born troops, see Kenneally, *Conflict*, pp 191–234.
32   *The Pilot*, 15 July 1876.
33   *Ibid.*
34   The act, which was opposed by most Native American representatives, allowed the United States government to break up reservation land. The reservations had heretofore been commonly owned by the tribe but after the act the land was divided into small allotments and put under the ownership of individual Native Americans.
35   Roche, *Life*, pp 342–3.
36   *Ibid.*, p. 343.
37   *The Pilot*, 1 February 1890.
38   Bruce was the first African American to serve a full term in the United States Senate, sitting from 1875–1881 as senator for Mississippi.
39   Report of a speech that O'Reilly delivered to a meeting of the Massachusetts Colored League on 7 December 1885, *Boston Daily Globe*, 8 December 1885.
40   *Ibid.* See also the report on O'Reilly's Boston speech in *New York Freeman*, 26 December 1885. The *New York Freeman* was a short-lived African-American paper that ran from 1884 to 1887 before it was transformed into the *New York Age*. See also Roche, Life, pp 738–42 for the complete version of the speech.
41   *The Pilot*, 19 June 1886.
42   For an account of the massacre see *New York Times*, 19 March 1886. The paper reported: 'Negroes shot down like dogs' by 'about 100 well armed men'. Many more people were wounded during the attack and died in the days after, although the exact number of deaths is uncertain.
43   Roche, *Life*, pp 288–90. See also *The Pilot*, 17 April 1886.
44   Roche, *Life*,, p. 742.
45   *Boston Daily Globe*, 19 December 1888. O'Reilly would also, in a manner similar to the way in which he covered the achievements of Irish people, print stories on the lives of individual African Americans who had achieved success in various fields; see, for example, *The Pilot*, 13 April 1889, for the long obituary given to Lewis Hayden, a former slave who escaped from the South and became a wealthy Boston businessman.
46   Kenneally, James J., 'Catholicism and Women Suffrage in Massachusetts', *The Catholic Historical Review*, 53, 1 (April 1967), p. 43.

47   *Ibid.*, p. 44.

48   *The Pilot*, 24 February 1883.

49   Conway, Katherine E. and Cameron, Mabel Ward, *Charles Francis Donnelly: a Memoir* (New York, James T. White & Co., 1909), pp 30–1.

50   Diner, Hasia, *Erin's Daughters in America: Irish Immigrant Women in the Nineteenth Century* (Baltimore, John Hopkins University Press, 1983), pp 139–53.

51   Frothingham, Rev. O. B., O'Reilly, John Boyle *et al.*, *Woman Suffrage, Unnatural and Inexpedient*, 1886. O'Reilly's contribution to the pamphlet was dated 11 February 1886.

52   O'Reilly, John Boyle, 'What has Ireland Gained by Agitation?', *American Catholic Quarterly Review*, 8 (October 1883), p. 715.

53   *The Pilot*, 18 April 1885.

54   *Ibid.*

55   *Ibid.*

56   *Ibid.*, 6 July 1876.

57   Roche, *Life*, p. 382. See also Ryan, Dennis P., *Beyond the Ballot Box: a Social History of the Boston Irish, 1845–1917* (Amherst, MA, University of Massachusetts Press, 1989), p. 73. Elmhurst was the favoured school for the children of rich Irish Catholics in the Boston area. The children of Patrick Collins similarly attended the school.

58   Mary Boyle O'Reilly papers, Boston Public Library. Included with the papers is a biographical note of Mary, which details her education. She wrote for several periodicals including *Harper's Weekly* and the *Boston Daily Globe*. She was also a foreign correspondent who reported from Russia and Mexico. During the First World War she entered Belgium and witnessed the German army's destruction of Louvain. Amid her many charitable and social works she sat on the board of directors for the Women's Educational Union. She died in 1937. See also her interview with *The West Australian*, 14 December 1935.

59   Conway became a staff member of *The Pilot* in 1883. In 1905 she became editor of the paper. For a study of Conway's career see Kane, Paula M., 'The Pulpit of the Hearthstone: Katherine Conway and Boston Catholic Women, 1900–1920', *US Catholic Historian*, 5 (1986).

60   Lyons, Louis Martin, *Newspaper Story: One Hundred Years of the Boston Globe* (Cambridge, Belknap Press, 1971), p. 10.

61   *Ibid.*

62   From a speech given by O'Reilly on the first ladies' night of the Papyrus Club, 22 February 1879, cited in Roche, *Life*, p. 193.

63   Speech by Higginson at the official city memorial service for O'Reilly: City Council of Boston, *A Memorial of John Boyle O'Reilly, from the City of Boston* (Boston, 1891), p. 43.

64   *The Pilot*, 18 April 1885.

65   Roche, *Life*, p. 227.

66   *The Pilot*, 1 June 1872.

67   *Ibid.*, 25 March 1871.

68   *Ibid.*, 15 March 1873.

69   *Ibid.*, 25 August 1877.

70   *Ibid.*, 29 April 1876; and for quotations and details of the strike in this paragraph.

71   Although O'Reilly never dwelt in any great detail on the issue of Chinese immigration to the United States, he did oppose their use as imported labour and strike-breakers. He also criticised the Chinese for not assimilating into the wider society. He did, however, state that if Chinese immigrants settled in the United States then they should be treated the same as any other group; see *The Pilot*, 24 June 1876, 4 January 1879, 26 September 1885 and 19 April 1890.

72   *Ibid.*, 17 June 1876.

73   See Kenny, Kevin, *Making Sense of the Molly Maguires* (Oxford, Oxford University Press, 1998), p. 127–9.

74   Kenny, a historian who has written the most detailed account of the group, has shown that 'the trade union and the Molly Maguires were clearly very different modes of labor organization.' See Kenny, *Molly Maguires*, p. 286.

75   *The Pilot*, 28 July 1877; see also 25 August 1877.

76   Kenny, *Molly Maguires*, p. 265.

77   *Ibid.*, p. 240.

78   *The Pilot*, 28 July 1877.

79   *Ibid.*, 12 November 1887.

80   *Ibid.*, 7 January 1878.

81   *Ibid.*, 28 February 1880.

82   *Ibid.*, 2 October 1886.

83   *Ibid.*

84   *Ibid.*, 10 August, 1878.

85   *Ibid.*, 18 January 1879.

86   *Ibid.*, 28 January 1888.

87   See, for example, *The Pilot*, 15 January 1881.

88   Mann, Arthur, *Yankee Reformers in the Urban Age* (Chicago, University of Chicago Press, 1974), p. 35.

89   McManamin, *American Years*, pp 202–3.

90   *The Pilot*, 24 March 1883.

91   *Ibid.*, 20 January 1883.

92   *Ibid.*, 24 March 1883.

93   *Ibid.*

94   *Ibid.*, 15 December 1883.

95   *Ibid.*, 10 May 1873.

96   Leiken, Steven Bernard, *The Practical Utopians: American Workers and the Cooperative movement in the Gilded Age* (Detroit, Wayne State University Press, 2005), p. 54.

97   *Ibid.*, p. 55.

98   *The Pilot*, 4 August 1877.

99   *Ibid.*, 2 January 1875.

100   *Ibid.*, 27 April 1878. See also 17 April 1880. O'Reilly had been interested in this idea since at least 1876 when, on 7 October, he advised prospective Irish farmers: 'Don't buy farms in New England.' Instead, he counselled, they should go west or south.

101   See Curran, R. Emmett, '"The Social Question": American Catholic Thought and the Socio-Economic Order in the Nineteenth Century', *US Catholic Historian*, 5, 2 (1986), p. 172.

102   Shannon, James P., *Catholic Colonization on the Western Frontier* (New Haven, Yale University Press, 1957), p. 75. There were a few smaller and more localised Irish-Catholic groups at this time that had similar aims: see Moynihan, James H., *The Life of Archbishop John Ireland* (New York, Arno Press, 1976), pp 20–32.

103   Spalding, John Lancaster, *The Religious Mission of the Irish* (Manchester, NH, Ayer Publishing, 1978), p. 147.

104   Shannon, *Catholic Colonization*, pp 264–7. Although Shannon credits Bishop Ireland with making Minnesota 'a center of Catholic culture', he admits that the colonisation 'failed to bring enough tenants out of the East to relieve noticeably the social tensions in that area.'

105   *The Pilot*, 23 June 1883.

106   'From The Earth, A Cry', O'Reilly, *The Statues in the Block*.

107   The novel began its serialisation on 30 November 1878 under the title of *Moondyne Joe*, but this was soon shortened to *Moondyne*. The book had reached its twelfth edition by 1891.

108   O'Reilly, *Moondyne*, p. 122.

109   *Ibid.*

110   *Ibid.*, p. 123.

111   *Ibid.*, p. 124.

112   *Ibid.*, p. 124

113   *Ibid.*

114   Mann, *Yankee Reformers*, p. 50.

115   *The Pilot*, 22 January 1887.

116   Letter by Lathrop to the editor, 11 August 1890, *The Critic*, 16 August 1890.

117   Foner, Eric, *Politics and Ideology in the Age of Civil War* (Oxford, Oxford University Press, 1980), pp 162–3.

118   *Ibid.*, p. 160.

119   *Ibid.*, p. 162.

120   Curran, 'American Catholic Thought', p. 183.

121   *Ibid.*, p. 186.

122   Gibbons similarly respected O'Reilly and, in 1891, provided the preface to Roche's biography.

123   Kerby Miller has written that by the mid-1880s 'Irish-American churchmen' had divided into three groups: radicals, liberals and conservatives. Cardinal Gibbons and Bishop Ireland were among the leaders of the liberal group. See Miller, Kerby, *Emigrants and Exiles: Ireland and the Irish Exodus to North America* (Oxford, Oxford University Press, 1985), p. 528.

124   See, for example, *The Pilot*, 25 February 1885, in which O'Reilly ridiculed the idea of the survival of the fittest.

125   *Ibid.*, 26 July 1879.

126   Brown, Thomas, N., 'The Origins and Character of Irish-American Nationalism', *The Review of Politics*, 18, 3 (July 1956), p. 350.

127   *Ibid.*, pp 350–1.

128   *Ibid.*, p. 351.

129   Speech to the Grand Army of the Republic, 31 May 1886, cited in Roche, *Life*, p. 721.

130   *The Pilot*, 31 May 1890.

Chapter 11

1   For the background to the various amnesty campaigns see McConville, *Irish Political Prisoners*, pp 214–75.

2   Letter of 19 January 1871, reprinted in Devoy, *Post Bag*, vol. I, p. 9.

3   Letter from O'Reilly to Devoy, 26 May 1871: *ibid.*, p. 41.

4   Devoy, *Recollections*, p. 252. There has been a long-standing tendency amongst historians to portray O'Reilly as the orchestrator of what would later be called the *Catalpa* rescue; for example, see Laubenstein, William J., *The Emerald Whaler* (London, André Deutsch, 1961). However, Devoy was the initiator and mastermind of the rescue.

5   A good primer on the *Catalpa* rescue is Fennell, Philip A., 'History into Myth: The *Catalpa*'s Long Voyage', *New Hibernia Review*, 9, 1 (Spring 2005). See also Fennell, Philip and King, Marie (eds), *John Devoy's* Catalpa *Expedition* (New York, New York University Press, 2006). A near-contemporary account is by Pease, Zephania W., *The* Catalpa *Expedition* (New Bedford, MA, G. S. Anthony, 1897). Pease's account is based heavily on newspaper reports and on his conversation with George Anthony, of whom he was a longstanding friend. It provided much information on the actual voyage of the *Catalpa*.

6   Devoy was part of a ten-man Clan na Gael rescue committee. Although he was assisted by other Clan members, such as James Reynolds and Dr William Carroll, Devoy masterminded the planning of the rescue. The committee also ran a successful fund-raising campaign to pay for the mission.

7   Moody, *Davitt*, p. 136.

8   Devoy, *Recollections*, p. 253.

9   Fennel & King, *John Devoy's* Catalpa *Expedition*, pp 44–5. Devoy was later 'reproached' by a member of the Boston branch for 'keeping the members in ignorance of my mission while I told John Boyle O'Reilly all about it.'

10   Letter from O'Reilly to Devoy, 4 December 1874, reprinted in Devoy, *Post Bag*, vol. I, p. 86.

11   Devoy, *Recollections*, p. 254.

12   *Boston Daily Globe*, 12 October 1902. In an article called 'Saved O'Reilly's Life' the paper gave an outline of Hathaway's career. By 1902 he had progressed up the ranks to become a shipping commissioner.

13   *Gaelic American*, 23 July 1904. From July to October of that year Devoy published a series of articles about the *Catalpa* rescue.

14   Devoy, *Post Bag*, vol. I, p. 91.

15   Devoy, *Recollections*, p. 254. For a brief background to Anthony's life see Fennell, 'History into Myth', p. 84. See also Pease, Catalpa *Expedition*, p. 76.

16   *Ibid.*

17   Devoy, *Post Bag*, vol. I, p. 98.

18   Fennell & King, *John Devoy's* Catalpa *Expedition*, p. 60.

19   Devoy, *Recollections*, p. 255. The two men first arrived in Sydney on 15 October, reaching Fremantle on 16 November.

20   *Gaelic American*, 27 August 1904.

21   Amos, *Fenians*, p. 206.

22   Carroll, *Lighthouse*, pp 453–4.

23   Letter from Robinson to Carnarvon, 13 April 1876, cited in McConville, *Irish Political Prisoners*, p. 210.

24   The plan had suffered from late complications such as the unexpected arrival of a third Clan na Gael agent, Thomas Brennan, in Australia. Breslin and Desmond had also been shocked to find that two Irish Fenians, Denis McCarthy and John Walsh, had been sent from the UK to make a rescue attempt. Breslin and Desmond overcame these problems and incorporated the two Fenians into the Clan operation. See, Amos, *Fenians*, pp 221–2.

25   Amos, *Fenians*, p. 234.

26   *The Pilot*, 29 July 1876. See also *Boston Daily Globe*, 9 August 1876, for a slightly different wording of the confrontation.

27   Fennell & King, *John Devoy's* Catalpa *Expedition*, p. 104.

28   Pease, Catalpa *Expedition*, p. 170.

29   *Ibid.*, p. 171, and for the quotations that follow in this paragraph.

30   *The Pilot*, 2 September 1876.

31   *Ibid.*

32   *Ibid.*

33   *The Times*, 26 June 1876 and *Western Australian Times*, 25 August 1876.

34   See, for example, *The Pilot*, 2 September 1876.

35   Roche, *Life*, p. 133.

36   Gilman, *Poets' Homes*, p. 202.

37   *Ibid.*, p. 205.

38   *Ibid.*, p. 209

39   *Ibid.*

40   See Roche, *Life*, p. 354, where he describes Mary Boyle O'Reilly as having 'been an invalid for years'. In a memorial speech for O'Reilly in 1890 Thomas Wentworth Higginson also spoke of Mary being an 'invalid'; see City Council of Boston, *Memorial*, p. 43. Mary Boyle O'Reilly died in 1897.

41   Evans, *Fanatic Heart*, p. 200.

42   Roche, *Life*, p. 133.

43   Blanid's ill health crops up occasionally in O'Reilly's writing. See the letter to Edward Moseley, 27 June 1888, in Roche, *Life*, p. 317, in which O'Reilly describes her suffering from a prolonged fever.

44   De Tocqueville, Alexis, *Democracy in America*, vol. II (Cambridge, MA, Sever & Francis, 1863), p. 133.

45   Roche, *Life*, p. 136.

46   *Ibid.*, pp 138–9.

47   *Ibid.*, p. 199.

48   *Ibid.*

49   Traubel, Horace, *With Walt Whitman in Camden*, vol. 2 (New York, The Century Company, 1906), p. 37. See also Krieg, Joann P., *Whitman and the Irish* (Iowa City, University of Iowa Press, 2000), p. 139.

50   O'Reilly, John Boyle (ed.), *The Poetry and Song of Ireland* (New York, Gay Brothers & Co., 1887)

51   *The Pilot*, 19 February 1876.

52   Letter from Wilde to O'Reilly, 16 December 1876, cited in Hart-Davis, Rupert, *The Letters of Oscar Wilde* (New York, Harcourt Brace, 1962), pp 26–7.

53   Letter from Wilde to O'Reilly, 27 September 1882, cited in Hart-Davis, Rupert, *More Letters of Oscar Wilde* (New York, Vanguard Press, 1985), p. 48. They may have met again when Wilde passed through Boston during September of that year. While in the city he called on O'Reilly, only to find that the perpetually busy editor was out of the office. He gently chided O'Reilly, 'If I knew your hours I would come and see you, but I can't if you insist on taking dinner at the wrong time.'

54   *Ibid.*

55   Roche, *Life*, p, 241. For a detailed analysis of the novel see chapter 2 of Susanna Margaret Ashton's *In Partnership: Collaborating to Construct American Authorship, 1870–1920* (University of Iowa, unpublished PhD thesis, 1998).

56   For example, see *Boston Daily Globe*, 27 July 1884. Each excerpt from *The King's Men* printed in the paper carried the heading 'Copyrighted by Robert Grant, May 1884'.

57   Ashton, *Partnership*, p. 37.

58   *Ibid.*, p. 37.

59   Fanning, Charles, *The Irish Voice in America: 250 Years of Irish-American Fiction* (Lexington, KY, University Press of Kentucky, 2000), p. 164.

60   Grant, Robert, O'Reilly, John Boyle, Stimson, Frederic Jesup and Wheelright, John Tyler, *The King's Men: a Tale of Tomorrow* (New York, Charles Scribner's Sons, 1884), p. 16.

61   Ashton, *Partnership*, p. 38.

62   *New York Times*, 17 August 1884.

63   Roche, *Life*, p. 241.

64   *Ibid.*

65   Ashton, *Partnership*, p. 39.

Chapter 12

1   U2, *Rattle and Hum* (Island Records, 1988).

2   See Hoagland, Kathleen, *One Thousand Years of Irish Poetry* (Devin-Adair, New York, 1947).

3   'A White Rose', O'Reilly, John Boyle, *In Bohemia* (New York, Cashman, Keating & Co., 1886).

4   Evans, *Fanatic Heart*, p. 222.

5   Undated letter from *Literary Life* to O'Reilly, reprinted in Roche, *Life*, p. 295.

6   *Ibid.*, p. 296.

7   Undated letter from O'Reilly to *Literary Life*, reprinted Roche, *Life*, p. 296.

8   *Ibid.*

9   Roche, *Life*, p. 333. See also *New York Times*, 20 January 1884.

10   Letter from O'Reilly to the poet Julia Dorr, 28 January 1885, cited in McManamin, *American Years*, p. 237.

11   An undated review in *Literary World*, found in a personal scrapbook containing reviews and other items: John Boyle O'Reilly Papers, John J. Burn's Library, Boston College.

12   Letter from O'Reilly to Julia Dorr, 16 March 1878, cited in McManamin, *American Years*, p. 237.

13   See, for example, the critical review of *The Statues in the Block* in the *Atlantic Monthly*, June 1881.

14   *Ibid.*

15   Roche, *Life*, p. 334.

16   Carroll, *Lighthouse*, p. 141.

17   O'Higgins, Brian, 'John Boyle O'Reilly – Glimpses of his Boyhood', *Donahoe's Magazine*, LIV (August 1905), p. 165.

18   Carroll, *Lighthouse*, p. 24.

19   From a log that O'Reilly kept during a speaking tour in March 1890, cited in Evans, *Fanatic Heart*, p. 242.

20   Grant, Robert, *Fourscore: an Autobiography* (Boston, Houghton Mifflin & Co., 1934), p. 170.

21   *Boston Transcript*, 28 February 1888.

22   All poems in this paragraph from O'Reilly, *Songs, Legends and Ballads*.

23   See, for example, the article 'Carlyle on the Atheistic Darwins' in *The Pilot*, 2 December 1876. In this article O'Reilly gave prominence to Thomas Carlyle's denunciation of Darwin, the scientist's father and grandfather, and then *The Origin of Species*. See also *Boston Daily Globe*, 14 September 1890, in which O'Reilly stated his admiration for Carlyle.

24   O'Reilly had used *The Pilot* to advocate his ideas on education from his early days on the paper. See editions of 24 January 1874, 31 March 1877, 23 June 1877, and 3 March 1883.

25   'Star-Gazing', O'Reilly, *Songs, Legends and Ballads*.

26   Connolly, Daniel, 'Irish-American Poets', *The Irish Monthly*, 14, 154 (April 1886), p. 198.

27   'The City Streets', O'Reilly, *In Bohemia*.

28   'The Three Queens', *ibid.*

29   *The Pilot*, 19 June 1886. See also Conway, Katherine E., *Watchwords from John Boyle O'Reilly* (Boston, Joseph George Cupples, 1892), p. 39.

30   'Crispus Attucks', reprinted in Roche, *Life*, pp 408–13. Roche's biography included many O'Reilly poems that were not in the official collections or were written after O'Reilly's last volume, *In Bohemia*.

31   'Wendell Phillips', O'Reilly, *In Bohemia*.

32   Unnamed couplet appearing before the poem 'The Well's Secret', O'Reilly, *The Statues in the Block*.

33   'Her Refrain', *ibid.* See also Conway, *Watchwords*, p. 15.

34   See the poems 'The Statues in the Block' or the 'Night Thoughts', both written in Western Australia.

35   'A Disappointment', O'Reilly, *In Bohemia*.

36   O'Reilly, *Moondyne*, p. 128.

37   'Jacqueminots', O'Reilly, *The Statues in the Block*.

38   'The Patriot's Grave', O'Reilly, *Songs, Legends and Ballads*.

39   From a eulogy that O'Reilly delivered on 23 November 1885 at the funeral of former *Hougoumont* Fenian Edward Kelly, cited in Roche, *Life*, p. 737.

40   'John Mitchel', O'Reilly, *Songs, Legends and Ballads*.

41   'A Song for the Soldiers', O'Reilly, *The Statues in the Block*.

42   'Dolores', O'Reilly, *Songs, Legends and Ballads*.

43   'Prometheus-Christ', O'Reilly, *The Statues in the Block*.

44   From Whitman's preface to the 1855 edition of *Leaves of Grass*, cited in Kummings, Donald D., *A Companion to Walt Whitman* (Malden, MA, Wiley-Blackwell, 2009), p. 356.

45   'America', O'Reilly, *In Bohemia*.

46   'Liberty Lighting the World', reprinted in Roche, *Life*, pp 420–2.

47   'The Pilgrim Fathers', *ibid.*, pp 397–404.

48   'My Native Land', O'Reilly, *Songs, Legends and Ballads*.

49   'The Priests of Ireland', *ibid.*

50   'The Statues in the Block', O'Reilly, *The Statues in the Block*.

51   'The Patriot's Grave', O'Reilly, *Songs, Legends and Ballads*.

52   'Ireland 1882', O'Reilly, *In Bohemia*.

53   'Erin', *ibid.*

54   Connolly, Daniel, 'Two Irish-American Poets', *The Irish Monthly*, 15, 164 (February 1887), p. 87.

55   Roche, *Life*, p. 381. See also *Boston Daily Globe*, 14 September 1890, for a piece in which O'Reilly discusses his childhood love of Shakespeare.

56   Fanning, *Irish Voice*, pp 162–3.

57   *New York Herald*, 24 March 1889.

58   Conway, *Watchwords*, p. xxxv.

59   Connolly, 'Two Irish-American Poets', p. 87.

60   Simonds, Arthur Beaman, *American Song* (Charleston, BiblioBazaar, 2008), p. 267.

61   McManamin, *American Years*, p. 239.
62   *New York Times*, 16 April 1881.

Chapter 13

1   O'Connor, Thomas H., *The Boston Irish: a Political History* (Old Saybrook, CT, Konecky & Konecky, 1995), pp xv–xvi.
2   According to Roger Daniels, the entire Catholic population of the United States in 1790 stood at around 25,000 people; see Daniels, Roger, *Coming to America: a History of Immigration and Ethnicity in American Life* (Princeton, Harper Collins, 2002), p. 138.
3   Handlin, Oscar, *Boston's Immigrants: a Study in Acculturation* (New York, Atheneum, 1969), p. 243.
4   *Irish World*, 25 September 1886.
5   *Ibid.*
6   For a social history of the Irish in Boston see Ryan, *Ballot Box*.
7   *The Pilot*, 1 May 1875.
8   *Ibid.*, 24 January 1874. The Catholic Church regularly urged its congregations to build parish schools; see Ryan, *Ballot Box*, pp 61–3.
9   McManamin, *American Years*, p. 164.
10   See *The Pilot*, 21 December 1889 and 18 January 1890.
11   *Ibid.*, 19 September 1885.
12   *Ibid.*, 4 November 1871.
13   For a detailed study of *The Pilot*'s coverage of education under O'Reilly's editorship see McManamin, *American Years*, pp 157–76.
14   *The Pilot*, 17 February 1877.
15   Walsh, *Boston Pilot*, pp 220–1.
16   *The Pilot*, 9 December 1874.
17   *Ibid.*, 17 February 1877.
18   *Ibid.*, 28 August 1880.
19   O'Connor, *Boston Irish*, p. 141.
20   *The Pilot*, 20 October 1877.
21   Speech by O'Reilly reported in the *Boston Daily Globe*, 30 October 1884.
22   Miller, *Exiles*, p. 329.
23   *The Pilot*, 24 February 1876.
24   *Ibid.*, 14 June 1884.
25   Speech by O'Reilly reported in the *Boston Daily Globe*, 30 October 1884.
26   For Ford's support of Blaine, see Rodechko, James Paul, *Patrick Ford and his Search for America: a Case Study of Irish-American Journalism, 1870–1913* (New York, Ayer Publishing, 1976), pp 140–2. For Devoy's support of Blaine, see Golway, *Irish Rebel*, pp 151–2.
27   Boller, Paul F., *Presidential Campaigns* (Oxford, Oxford University Press, 1985), pp 149–50. Burchard made his bigoted comment while denouncing Republicans who had crossed party lines to support Cleveland, the so-called 'Mugwumps'.

28 *The Pilot*, 21 September, 28 September and 5 October 1878. Butler publicly declared his support for 'Greenback' policies. The Greenbacks were an American political movement that opposed monopolies and argued for the retention as currency of paper money, which had first been issued during the Civil War.

29 *Ibid.*, 13 December 1873.

30 *Ibid.*, 24 June 1876.

31 *Ibid.*, 8 September 1877.

32 Moody, *Davitt*, pp 8–9.

33 For the amnesty campaign that led to Davitt's release, see McConville, *Irish Political Prisoners*, pp 308–12.

34 Moody, *Davitt*, p. 225.

35 *Ibid.*, pp 231–2.

36 Davitt's speech reported in the *Irish World*, 26 October 1878.

37 Letter from Devoy to Dublin's *Freeman's Journal*, 11 December 1878, explaining the New Departure: reprinted in Cashman, *Davitt*, p. 98.

38 Speech by Devoy reported in the *Irish World*, 26 October 1878.

39 *New York Herald*, 25 October 1878. See also *The Pilot*, 2 November 1878.

40 *Ibid.*, 27 October 1878.

41 *The Pilot*, 2 November 1878.

42 From Davitt's diary, 7 December 1878, cited in Moody, *Davitt*, p. 260. The 'state treasurership' that Davitt mentioned was the position of State Auditor for Massachusetts. In 1878 the Democrats wanted to nominate O'Reilly for this position. Although O'Reilly expressed 'profound gratitude to the Democratic people of Massachusetts', he refused the offer, saying that a political job would damage his independence as an editor; see the letter from O'Reilly to the Democratic Party in the *Boston Daily Globe*, 21 September 1878.

43 Davitt, Michael, *The Fall of Feudalism in Ireland* (Shannon, Irish University Press, 1970), p. 130.

44 *Ibid.*, pp 130–1.

45 *Ibid.*, p. 129.

46 *Ibid.*, p. 130. Davitt wrote this book in 1904 so it is doubtful if he reported the exact words of O'Reilly. However, the speech fully matches O'Reilly's opinions as expressed in *The Pilot* and elsewhere.

47 *The Pilot*, 21 December 1878.

48 *Ibid.*

49 *Ibid.*

50 Moody, *Davitt*, pp 297–8. Devoy claimed that Parnell agreed to a four-point programme whereby: Parnell would never say or do anything to discredit the idea of complete Irish independence; nothing short of a national parliament that held power over all vital national interests was acceptable to Ireland; the land question would be settled on the basis of a peasant proprietorship and compulsory purchase; and that Irish members of the British parliament who

were elected through the support of the Land League or other nationalist bodies would comprise an independent Irish party.

51   The general consensus among historians is that Devoy overstated what was agreed at these meetings. Paul Bew, as one example, wrote that any agreement 'can only have been highly notional'; see Bew, Paul, *Charles Stewart Parnell* (Dublin, Gill & Macmillan, 1991), p. 28.

52   Davitt, *Feudalism*, p. 147.

53   *Ibid*: p. 151. Davitt noted that under the terms of the Land Act of 1881 the tenants on the Bourke Estate had their rents reduced by a further 40 per cent.

54   Lyons, F. S. L., *Charles Stewart Parnell* (London, Fontana Press, 1991), p. 92.

55   *Ibid.*

56   Moody, *Davitt*, p. 306.

57   Davitt to O'Reilly, 22 October 1879, cited in Devoy, *Post Bag*, vol. I, p. 457.

58   *The Pilot*, 15 November 1879

59   O'Reilly to Devoy, 15 November 1879, cited in Devoy, *Post Bag*, vol. I, p. 462.

60   *The Pilot*, 10 January 1880.

61   Davitt, *Feudalism*, p. 196.

62   *Ibid.*, p. 128.

63   McManamin, *American Years*, p. 111.

64   Foner, *Ideology*, p. 156. Once O'Reilly had refused the presidency, McCafferty seems to have been chosen as a compromise candidate.

65   McManamin, *American Years*, p. 85. See also Dooley, *Greatest of the Fenians*, pp 123–4. The decision to start an American version of the Land League upset Clan na Gael leaders such as William Carroll since they feared interference from powerful Irish figures like Parnell would damage their aim to be the dominant force in Irish-American nationalism. Devoy was adamant that a strong central leadership body was needed for the American Land League because he hoped it might be infiltrated by Clan na Gael, who could then control the whole organisation.

66   O'Reilly's speech to the convention, reported in Cashman, *Davitt*, pp 223–3.

67   O'Reilly to Devoy, 26 March 1880, cited in Devoy, *Post Bag*, vol. I, p. 510.

68   Green, James J., 'American Catholics and the Irish Land League, 1879–1882', *The Catholic Historical Review*, 35, 1 (April 1849), p. 30

69   For an account of Davitt's time in Portland, see Moody, *Davitt*, pp 466–533.

70   Davitt, *Feudalism*, p. 339.

71   Moody, *Davitt*, p. 495. See also *The Freeman's Journal*, 19 October 1881.

72   Foner, *Ideology*, pp 160–1. Although Ford was distrusted by conservatives his fund-raising made him 'embarrassingly indispensible' to the League; see Miller, *Exiles*, p. 540.

73   Lee, *Modernisation of Irish Society*, p. 96. Lee writes that the paper 'touched a weekly circulation of 20,000 in Ireland during 1880'. See also Rodechko, *Patrick Ford*, p. 186. According to Rodechko the Spread the Light Fund sent 450,000 copies of the *Irish World* to Ireland during the years 1879–1882.

74   *The Pilot*, 5 November 1881. See also Bagenal, Philip H., *The American Irish and their Influence upon Irish Politics* (Boston, Roberts Brothers, 1882), pp 217–19.

75   Brown, Thomas N., *Irish-American Nationalism, 1870–1890* (Philadelphia and New York, J. B. Lippincott Company, 1966), p. 121.

76   Green, 'American Catholics', p. 38.

77   *Ibid*. Gilmour had long been nervous about the League and in 1879 had tried to prevent the sale of copies of the *Irish World* in his diocese.

78   O'Reilly, 'Ireland's Opportunity – Will it be Lost?', *American Catholic Quarterly Review*, 7 (January 1882), p.114

79   *Ibid.*, p. 115.

80   *Ibid.*, p. 116.

81   *Ibid.*

82   *Ibid.*, p. 118.

83   *Ibid.*, p.120

84   *The Pilot*, 25 March 1882.

85   *Irish World*, 3 December 1881.

86   McManamin, *American Years*, p. 95.

87   Davitt, *Feudalism*, p. 359. See also Curran, M. P., *Life of Patrick A. Collins: with Some of his Most Notable Public Addresses* (Norwood, MA, The Norwood Press, 1906), pp 65–7.

88   Roche, *Life*, p. 218. The telegram read: To Charles Stewart Parnell, House of Commons, London: A reward of $5000 (£1000) is hereby offered by the Irishmen of Boston for the apprehension of the murderers, or any of them, of Lord Cavendish and Mr Burke, on Saturday, May 6. On behalf of the Irishmen of Boston, John Boyle O'Reilly, Patrick A. Collins.

89   O'Reilly, 'What has Ireland Gained?', p. 711.

90   Roche, *Life*, pp 224–5.

91   See McManamin, *American Years*, p. 67.

92   For example, see *The Pilot*, 1 June 1878.

93   Speech by O'Reilly on the 'Irish National Cause' in Boston, 20 October 1885, cited in Roche, *Life*, p. 263.

94   Moody, *Davitt*, p. 534.

95   Davitt, *Feudalism*, pp 377–8.

96   George, Henry, *Progress and Poverty* (Elibro, 1955), p. 263.

97   Moody, Davitt, p. 519. See also Brown, *Nationalism*, pp 125–6.

98   *The Pilot*, 1 July 1882. During 1886 O'Reilly briefly supported Henry George's unsuccessful bid to win New York's mayoral election; see *The Pilot*, 9 October 1886 and 22 January 1887.

99   McManamin, *American Years*, p. 100.

100   Letter from O'Reilly to the Democratic Party, printed in the *Boston Daily Globe*, 21 September 1878.

101   Speech given by O'Reilly to the meeting, cited in Roche, *Life*, pp 231–2.

102   For an analysis of the *Irish World*'s involvement in the Skirmishing Fund and its coverage of the subsequent bombings, see Whelehan, Niall, 'Skirmishing, the

Irish World and Empire, 1876–1886', Éire-Ireland, 42, 1&2 (Spring/Summer 2007). See also Rodechko, Patrick Ford, pp 185–6 and 192–5.

103   For an account of Holland's life and work on submarines, see Kenneally, Conflict, pp 164–190.

104   For a detailed study of the dynamite campaigns, see McConville, Irish Political Prisoners, pp 326–60.

105   McGee, IRB, p.82.

106   Whelehan, 'Skirmishing', pp 190–200. See also Rodechko, Patrick Ford, pp 192–5. In 1915, two years after Ford's death, the Irish World printed a book of letters that Ford had written in 1881 to British Prime Minister William Gladstone; see Ford, Patrick, The Criminal History of the British Empire (New York, The Irish World, 1915).

107   Devoy had been dismissed from the New York Herald after falling out with its owner James Gordon Bennett Jr. The Herald had been an outspoken critic of Parnell during his tour of the United States in 1880, a policy which had caused Devoy much personal embarrassment. See Golway, Irish Rebel, p. 131.

108   Devoy, Post Bag, vol. II, p. 233.

109   For example, see The Pilot, 24 January 1881.

110   New York Times, 5 January 1885.

111   Ibid., 3 February 1885. Understandably, O'Donovan Rossa claimed that Dudley was a British agent. However, she seems to have acted entirely of her own accord, motivated by newspaper condemnations of Rossa and her personal anger at his role in funding and organising bombings in England.

112   Ibid., 4 February 1885.

113   The Pilot, 14 February 1885.

114   Ibid., 28 February 1885.

115   Ibid., 11 April 1885. See the edition of 16 September 1876 for similar sentiments.

116   Speech by O'Reilly on the 'Irish National Cause' in Boston, 20 October 1885, cited in Roche, Life, p. 263.

117   Ibid., p. 247.

118   Ibid.

119   See interview with O'Reilly in Boston Daily Globe, 15 February 1885.

120   For exchange that follows, see Hansard, HC (series 3) vol. 296, cols 1131–8 (31 March 1885).

121   Ibid. After O'Reilly's death, Harcourt claimed that O'Reilly had escaped from Western Australia while on parole and this was why the Irishman's request to visit Canada had been rejected. Harcourt was either mistaken or disingenuous, since O'Reilly had never been given parole while in Australia; see Roche, Life, pp 254–5.

122   McManamin, American Years, pp 101–2.

123   O'Reilly, John Boyle, 'At Last', North American Review, 142, 350 (January 1886), p. 109.

124   Ibid., p. 110.

125   O'Reilly to Devoy, 3 May 1886, in Devoy, Post Bag, vol. II, p. 280.

126 *Ibid.*

127 *The Pilot*, 17 April 1886. O'Reilly was particularly dismissive of the veto powers enshrined in the bill, which allowed the first order to block legislation of the second.

Chapter 14

1   Letter from O'Reilly to Stoddard, 21 June 1882, cited in Roche, *Life*, p. 292. The title of this chapter comes from *In Bohemia*'s 'The Word and the Deed': 'The Word must be sown in the heart like seed / Men's hands must tend it, their lives defend it / Till it burst into flower as a deathless Deed'.

2   Gilman, *Poets' Homes*, pp 209–10.

3   *Ibid.*

4   *Ibid.*

5   Roche, *Life*, p. 290. The period of vertigo mentioned by Roche happened during June 1886.

6   *Ibid.*, p. 137

7   *Ibid.*

8   Morgan, James, *The Life Work of Edward A. Moseley in the Service of Humanity* (Read Books, 2009), pp 265–6.

9   *Ibid.*, p. 265.

10   *Ibid.*, p. 264.

11   *Ibid.* Moseley recalled what was perhaps the last occasion on which O'Reilly donned boxing gloves (Moseley did not give the date for this sparring session but it seems to have been during 1888 or 1889). One afternoon he called into *The Pilot* office. On seeing his friend, O'Reilly said to Moseley, 'Dear Old man, I have been working so hard! Let us go down to the club and I will throw some of the blood out of my brain into my arms and fists.' They fought a tough contest until it became apparent that 'one of the other of us must go down'. Another club member jumped into the ring to separate the two pugilists.

12   Moseley, Edward A., 'John Boyle O'Reilly, The Man', *Donahoe's Magazine*, 30, 3 (September 1893), p. 247.

13   Darby, Paul, 'Gaelic Sport and the Irish Diaspora in Boston, 1870–90', *Irish Historical Studies*, 33, 132 (November 2003), p. 397. O'Reilly acted as a judge at each annual athletics meet until his death.

14   *Ibid.*

15   *Ibid.*

16   *The Pilot*, 15 May 1886.

17   Frawley, *Donahoe*, pp 245–55.

18   *The Pilot*, 29 April 1876.

19   McManamin, *American Years*, p. 135.

20   Letter from O'Reilly to Williams, 12 May, 1886: *Ibid.*, p. 136.

21   Letter from O'Reilly to Williams, 31 August, 1886: *Ibid.*

22   *The Pilot*, 15 May 1886.

23   *Ibid.*

24   17 June 1886, in Roche, *Life*, p. 293.

25   21 June 1886, *ibid*. That night O'Reilly was joined by Father Teeling and a couple of the priest's acquaintances for a celebratory dinner. He received twenty roses – 'one for each year of the sentence' – from his guests. The former convict spent the next few days canoeing before returning to Boston on 24 June, seemingly refreshed by his holiday: 'God bless dear Domus Tranquilla and its occupants! May they all enjoy as charming and invigorating a stay in it as mine has been!'

26   Roche also makes note of this discrepancy; see Roche, *Life*, p. 294.

27   O'Reilly, *In Bohemia*, from the poem of the same name.

28   *The Pilot*, 19 January 1885.

29   Unpublished account of a dinner that O'Reilly attended in March 1890, recounted in Evans, *Fanatic Heart*, p. 242.

30   For a history of the Charity Organization Society in the United States, see Herrick, John Middlemist and Stuart, Paul H., *Encyclopedia of Social Welfare History in North America* (Thousand Oaks, CA, Sage, 2005), pp 49–51. See also O'Reilly, *Moondyne*, p. 122, for similar sentiments on wealth and charity.

31   O'Reilly, *In Bohemia*, from the poem of the same name.

32   'The Cry of the Dreamer', *ibid*.

33   Letter from O'Reilly to Devoy, 24 July 1886, in Devoy, *Post Bag*, vol. II, p. 286.

34   Plunkett, George Noble, 'Recollections of John Boyle O'Reilly', *The Irish Monthly*, 19, 211 (January 1891), p. 23.

35   *Boston Daily Globe*, 21 July 1882.

36   See O'Reilly, John Boyle, *Ethics of Boxing and Manly Sport* (Boston, Tickner & Co., 1888), pp 5–6.

37   *Ibid.*, p. vii.

38   *Ibid.*, p. xi.

39   *Ibid*; pp vii–viii.

40   Ryan, *Ballot Box*, pp 115–16.

41   Isenberg, Michael T., *John L. Sullivan and His America* (Urbana, University of Illinois Press, 1994), p. 79.

42   *Ibid.*

43   See, for example, *New York Times*, 29 May, 1888; this positive review praised O'Reilly's 'breezy individual style which holds the reader throughout.' The paper agreed with O'Reilly's declaration that 'we must save athletics from the professional athlete.'

44   Roche, *Life*, p. 314.

45   The house had been damaged by a storm in November 1888 but refurbished during the following year. Today, the building houses the Hull Public Library.

46   Letter to Moseley, 27 June 1888, cited in Roche, *Life*, p. 314.

47   *Ibid.*, p. 430.

48   See the speech by Higginson, in City Council of Boston, *Memorial*, p. 43.

49 'Wendell Phillips', O'Reilly, *In Bohemia*.

50 For a study of Grady's career and the development of his New South ideology see Harold D. Mixon's 'Henry Grady as a Persuasive Strategist', in Waldo W. Braden, (ed.), *Oratory in the New South* (Baton Rouge, Louisiana State University Press, 1979). Grady had been unwell at the time of his Boston speech and his condition became suddenly worse a few days later. He died of pneumonia on 23 December 1889.

51 Grant, Donald Lee & Grant, Jonathan, *The Way it Was: the Black Experience in Georgia* (Athens, GA, University of Georgia Press, 2001), p. 186. See also *Boston Daily Globe*, 13 December 1889, for a report on the speech.

52 For the reaction to the speech, see Mixon, 'Henry Grady', pp 106–109. Apart from *The Pilot*, there was little critical commentary within the Boston press, although the *Boston Daily Globe*, 23 December 1889, printed an interview with a former southern resident, Reverend Joshua A. Brockett, which rejected the veracity of Grady's version of life in the South.

53 *The Pilot*, 21 December 1889.

54 *Ibid.*, 18 January 1890.

56 *Ibid.*, 28 June 1890.

57 Letter from O'Reilly to Harson, 25 September 1889, cited in Roche, *Life*, p. 338.

58 *Ibid.*, p. 340.

59 Morgan, *Edward A. Moseley*, p. 268.

60 Undated letter from O'Reilly to Moseley, cited in Roche, *Life*, p. 339.

61 Evans, *Fanatic Heart*, p. 243.

62 Roche, *Life*, p. 340.

63 *Boston Daily Globe*, 11 August 1890. One of the paper's reporters had spent some time with O'Reilly the previous Wednesday.

64 The account of O'Reilly's final day is based on reports from the *Boston Daily Globe*, 11 August 1890, and *The Pilot*, 16 August 1890, as well as Roche, *Life*, pp 352–6. The *Globe*'s version included a short interview with Dr Litchfield.

65 *Boston Daily Globe*, 11 August 1890.

66 *Ibid.*, for interview with Dr Litchfield and details that follow.

67 Roche, *Life*, p. 355.

69 *The Pilot*, 16 August 1890.

70 Interview with Dr Litchfield, *Boston Daily Globe*, 11 August 1890.

71 Roche, *Life*, p. 355.

72 *The Pilot*, 16 August 1890.

Epilogue

1 'A Passage', O'Reilly, *In Bohemia*.

2 Roche, *Life*, pp 355–6.

3   Report on Tyndall's death, *New York Times*, 25 December 1893.

4   Francis R. Walsh, 'John Boyle O'Reilly, The Boston Pilot, and Irish-American Assimilation, 1870–1890', in Jack Tager and John W. Ifkovic (eds), *Massachusetts in the Gilded Age: Selected Essays* (Amherst, MA, University of Massachusetts Press, 1985), p. 159.

5   I am grateful to Dr Michael Curran for providing his expertise on O'Reilly's medical history.

6   Roche, *Life*, pp 359–60.

7   *Ibid.*, p. 360.

8   Plunkett, 'Recollections', p. 25.

9   *Ibid.*, p. 26.

10   For Walker's words at the memorial service, see City Council of Boston, *Memorial*, pp. 51–3.

11   Bledsoe, Thomas, 'John Boyle O'Reilly: Poet-Prophet of Democracy', *The Crisis* (January 1945), p. 18.

12   City Council of Boston, *Memorial*, p. 42.

13   Quotations in the paragraphs that follow from Ibson, *Will The World Break Your Heart?*, pp. 68–72.

14   Walsh, 'John Boyle O'Reilly', p. 150.

15   Miller, *Exiles*, pp 498–9 and pp 546–7.

16   *Ibid.*, p. 499.

17   Ibson, *Will The World Break Your Heart?*, p. 71.

18   Roche, *Life*, p. 137.

19   Plunkett, 'Recollections', p. 21.

20   Traubel, *With Walt Whitman*, p. 8.

21   Roche, *Life*, p. 73.

22   Plunkett, 'Recollections', p. 20.

23   Roche, *Life*, p. 47.

24   *Ibid.* Roche did not name the soldier but John Devoy stated that it was Patrick Foley; see Devoy, *Recollections*, p. 157.

25   For example, see Evans, *Fanatic Heart*, p. 257. It was inevitable, amid twenty years of journalism and the political climate of the time, that some of O'Reilly's comments would be critical of English people. See for example Roche, *Life*, p. 278, where O'Reilly, during 1886, accused the English 'masses' of being 'deficient in the spirit of liberty, in the dignity of humanity'. Such hyperbolic attacks were atypical.

26   Roche, *Life*, pp 306–8.

27   City Council of Boston, *Memorial*, p. 20.

28   *Ibid.*, p. 40.

29   Roche, *Life*, pp 335–7.

30   For example see Bendroth, Margaret, 'Rum, Romanism, and Evangelism: Protestants and Catholics in Late-Nineteenth-Century Boston', *Church History*, 68, 3, (September 1999).

31   Mann, *Yankee Reformers*, p. 42.

32   Plunkett, 'Recollections', p. 20.

33	Traubel, *With Walt Whitman*, p. 68.
34	Roche, *Life*, p. 377.
35	O'Reilly to Whipple, 20 March 1878: John Boyle O'Reilly Papers, Boston Public Library.
36	Speech to a predominantly black audience following the Carrollton Massacre of 1886, cited in Roche, *Life*, pp 289–90.
37	See *American Newspaper Directory* (New York, George P. Rowell & Co., 1872) and *American Newspaper Annual 1880* (Philadelphia, N. W. Ayer & Sons, 1880) and *American Newspaper Annual 1889* (Philadelphia, N. W. Ayer & Sons, 1889).
38	Roche, *Life*, p. 388. Roche wrote that O'Reilly hated 'the recounting of so-called "Irish" stories and all imitations of "the brogue".'
39	City Council of Boston, *Memorial*, p. 22.
40	Roche mentions that O'Reilly had been working on a book called *The Country with A Roof*. Roche described it as an 'allegorical satire on the existing social condition'. It is not clear how close to completion this book was at the time of O'Reilly's death. The whereabouts of this manuscript are unknown; see Roche, *Life*, p. 385.
41	*The Pilot*, 12 August 1871.
42	See, for example, *The Pilot*, 21 January 1876.
43	*Ibid.*, 28 August 1880.
44	Mary Boyle O'Reilly sold her share of the paper to Archbishop Williams who sold the whole paper 'at a price much below value' on 20 November 1890. The new proprietor was the paper's original owner, Patrick Donahoe; see *Frawley*, Donahoe, p. 256.
45	Davitt, *Feudalism*, p. 129.
46	See also Doyle, David, 'John Boyle O'Reilly and the Irish Adjustment in America', *Journal of the Old Drogheda Society*, 10 (1996), pp 19–20. Doyle writes that 'it is strange that some brand him a conservative'.
47	City Council of Boston, *Memorial*, p. 55.

Bibliography

PRIMARY SOURCES

Archives
Battye Library, Perth
MN1221, Papers of John Boyle O'Reilly, ACC 3708A
MN1344, 'Original Transcript of Journalist Stenography on Cover of John Boyle O'Reilly's Notebook Containing Poems', transcript by Gillian O'Mara (1992)
Newspaper collection
R16: Register of the *Hougoumont* convicts

Boole Library, University College, Cork
The Pilot, 1829–1938

Boston Public Library
John Boyle O'Reilly papers
Mary Boyle O'Reilly papers
Newspaper collection

James Hardiman Library, National University of Ireland, Galway
Newspaper collection

John J. Burns Library, Boston College
John Boyle O' Reilly papers
Mary Boyle O'Reilly papers

National Archives of Ireland, Dublin
National Schools Register ED/2

National Archives, Kew, United Kingdom
Newspaper collection

National Library of Ireland, Dublin
John Devoy papers
Larcom papers

Newspaper collection

New York Public Library
Photographic collection
Microfilm collection: *The Wild Goose*

United States Library of Congress, Washington, DC
Photographic collection

Parliamentary Debates
Dáil Éireann debates
Hansard, House of Commons debates

Official Reports
Accounts and Papers of the House of Commons, 1862 (crime, prisons and police)
American Newspaper Annual, 1880 & 1889 (Philadelphia, N. W. Ayer & Sons)
American Newspaper Directory (New York, George P. Rowell & Co., 1872)
'Labor Force, series D 1–682', *Historical Statistics of the United States, Colonial
    Times to 1970*, vol. 1 (United States Bureau of the Census, 1975)
*Proceedings of the California State Convention of Colored Citizens Held in Sacramento
    on the 25th, 26th, 27th, and 28th of October 1865* (San Francisco, 1969)

Pamphlets
Fremantle Prison, *Building the Convict Establishment*, 2009
Fremantle Prison, *Convict Biographies*, 2009
Fremantle Prison, *Convict Daily Life*, 2009
Frothingham, Rev. O. B., O'Reilly, John Boyle *et al.*, *Woman Suffrage, Unnatural
    and Inexpedient*, 1886
Nadanasabapathy, Visualingam, *John Boyle O'Reilly: a Bibliography*, 1976
O'Connell, Daniel and Mathew, Theobald, *Address of the People of Ireland to
    their Countrymen and Countrywomen in America*, 1847

Newspapers
Atlantic Monthly
Boston Daily Globe
Boston Herald
Boston Transcript
Brisbane Courier
Drogheda Argus
Fremantle Herald
Gaelic American

Irish Freedom
Irish People
Irish World
Nation (Dublin)
New York Freeman
New York Herald
New York Times
New Zealand Tablet
Perth Gazette
Philadelphia Times
Preston Guardian
The Critic
The Freeman's Journal (Dublin)
The Irishman
The Pilot
The Times
The *West Australian (Western Australian Times* pre-1879*)*
The Wild Goose
Western Mail

BOOKS AND ARTICLES

Amos, Keith, *The Fenians in Australia: 1865–1880* (Sydney, New South Wales University Press, 1988)

Archer, Thomas, *The Pauper, the Thief and the Convict: Sketches of some of their Homes, Haunts and Habitats* (London, Groombridge & Sons, 1865)

Ashley, Clifford Warren, *The Yankee Whaler* (New York, Courier Dover Publications, 1991)

Ashton, Susanna, 'John Boyle O'Reilly and Moondyne', *History Ireland*, 10, 1 (2002)

— , *In Partnership: Collaborating to Construct American Authorship, 1870–1920* (University of Iowa, unpublished PhD thesis, 1998)

Bagenal, Philip H., *The American Irish and their Influence upon Irish Politics* (Boston, Roberts Brothers, 1882)

Barry, Liam, *Western Australia's Great Escape* (Australind, Western Australia, CFN Publications, 1992)

Bayor, Ronald H. & Meagher, Timothy J., *The New York Irish* (Baltimore, John Hopkins University Press, 1996)

Bendroth, Margaret, 'Rum, Romanism, and Evangelism: Protestants and Catholics in Late-Nineteenth-Century Boston', *Church History*, 68, 3 (September 1999)

Betts, John R., 'The Negro and the New England Conscience in the Days of

John Boyle O'Reilly', *The Journal of Negro History*, 51, 4 (October 1966)

Bew, Paul, *Charles Stewart Parnell* (Dublin, Gill & Macmillan, 1991)

Bledsoe, Thomas, 'John Boyle O'Reilly: Poet-Prophet of Democracy', *The Crisis* (January 1945)

Boller, Paul F., *Presidential Campaigns* (Oxford, Oxford University Press, 1985)

Boyce, D. G., *Nineteenth Century Ireland: the Search for Stability* (Dublin, Gill & Macmillan, 2005)

— and O'Day, Alan (eds), *Parnell in Perspective* (London, Taylor & Francis, 1991)

Braden, Waldo W. (ed.), *Oratory in the New South* (Baton Rouge, Louisiana State University Press, 1979)

Brendon, Piers, *The Decline and Fall of the British Empire, 1781–1997* (London, Vintage, 2008)

Brown, Thomas N., *Irish-American Nationalism, 1870–1890* (Philadelphia and New York, J. B. Lippincott Company, 1966)

— 'The Origins and Character of Irish-American Nationalism', *The Review of Politics*, 18, 3 (July 1956)

Bruce, Susannah Ural, *The Harp and the Eagle: Irish-American Volunteers and the Union Army, 1861–1865* (New York, New York University Press, 2006)

Bull, Philip, *Land, Politics & Nationalism: a Study of the Irish Question* (Dublin, Gill & Macmillan, 1996)

Bull, Stephen, *Volunteer! The Lancashire Rifle Volunteers, 1859–1885* (Preston, Lancs, Lancashire County Museums Service, 1993)

Campbell, Malcolm, *Ireland's New Worlds: Immigrants, Politics, and Society in the United States and Australia, 1815–1922* (Madison, University of Wisconsin Press, 2007)

Carroll, Martin, 'The Mark of Boyle O'Reilly's Escape', *West Australian*, 20 (December 1952)

— *Behind the Lighthouse: the Australian Sojourn of John Boyle O'Reilly* (University of Iowa, unpublished PhD thesis, 1955)

Casey, John Sarsfield, *The Galtee Boy: a Fenian Prison Narrative* (Dublin, University College Dublin Press, 2005)

Cashman, Denis B., *The Life of Michael Davitt* (Boston, Murphy & McCarthy, 1881)

City Council of Boston, *A Memorial of John Boyle O'Reilly, from the City of Boston* (City Council of Boston, 1891)

Comerford, R. V., *The Fenians in Context: Irish Politics and Society, 1848–82* (Dublin, Wolfhound Press, 1998)

Connolly, Daniel, 'Irish-American Poets', *The Irish Monthly*, 14, 154 (April 1886)

— 'Two Irish-American Poets', *The Irish Monthly*, 15, 164 (February 1887)

Conway, Katherine E., *Watchwords from John Boyle O'Reilly* (Boston, Joseph George Cupples, 1892)

— and Cameron, Mabel Ward, *Charles Francis Donnelly: a Memoir* (New York, James T. White & Co., 1909)

Conwell, Russell, *A Great Fire in Boston* (Boston, B. B. Russell, 1873)

Creighton, Margaret S., *Rites & Passages: the Experience of American Whaling, 1830–1870* (Cambridge, Cambridge University Press, 1995)

Crowley, Francis Keble and De Garis, Brian K., *A Short History of Western Australia* (South Yarra, Victoria, Macmillan Company of Australia, 1969)

Curran, M. P., *Life of Patrick A. Collins: with Some of his Most Notable Public Addresses* (Norwood, MA, The Norwood Press, 1906)

Curran, R. Emmett, '"The Social Question": American Catholic Thought and the Socio-Economic Order in the Nineteenth Century', *US Catholic Historian*, 5, 2 (1986)

Cusack, M. K. (ed.), *John Sarsfield Casey: Journal of a Voyage from Portland to Fremantle on Board the Convict Ship* Hougoumont (Pittsburgh, Dorrance Publishing Co., 1988)

Daniels, Roger, *Coming to America: A History of Immigration and Ethnicity in American Life* (Princeton, Harper Collins, 2002)

Darby, Paul, 'Gaelic Sport and the Irish Diaspora in Boston, 1870–90', *Irish Historical Studies*, 33, 132 (November 2003)

Davidson, Ron, *Fremantle Impressions* (Fremantle, Fremantle Press, 2008)

Davitt, Michael, *The Fall of Feudalism in Ireland* (Shannon, Irish University Press, reprint, 1970)

— *Life and Progress in Australasia* (London, Methuen & Co., 1898)

De Nie, Michael, '"A Medley Mob of Irish-American Plotters and Irish Dupes": the British Press and Transatlantic Fenianism', *Journal of British Studies*, 40, 2 (April 2001)

Denieffe, Joseph, *A Personal Narrative of the Irish Revolutionary Brotherhood* (New York, The Gael Publishing Company, 1906)

De Tocqueville, Alexis, *Democracy in America*, vol. II (Cambridge, MA, Sever & Francis, 1863)

Devoy, John, *Devoy's Post Bag*, vol. I (Dublin, C. J. Fallon, 1948)

— *Devoy's Post Bag*, vol. II (Dublin, C. J. Fallon, 1948)

— *Recollections of an Irish Rebel* (New York, Chase D. Young, 1929; facs. edn, Irish University Press, 1969)

Diner, Hasia, *Erin's Daughters in America: Irish Immigrant Women in the Nineteenth Century* (Baltimore, John Hopkins University Press, 1983)

Donahoe, Patrick, 'Reminiscences of An Old Time Journalist: a Letter to Martin J. Griffin', *Records of the American Catholic Historical Society*, xv (1904)

Dooley, Terence, 'The Greatest of the Fenians': John Devoy and Ireland (Dublin, Wolfhound Press, 2003)

Doyle, David, 'John Boyle O'Reilly and the Irish Adjustment in America', Journal of the Old Drogheda Society, 10 (1996)

Edwards, Rebecca Brooke, Angels in the Machine: Gender in American Party Politics from the Civil War to the Progressive Era (Oxford, Oxford University Press, 1997)

Eisen, George and Wiggins, David Kenneth, Ethnicity and Sport in North American History and Culture (Santa Barbara, CA, ABC-CLIO, 1994)

Elliot, Ian, Moondyne Joe: the Man and the Myth (Perth, Hesperian Press, 1998)

Ellis, William Hodgson, 'The Adventures of a Prisoner of War', The Canadian Magazine of Politics, Science, Art and Literature, 13, 3 (July 1899)

England, Bishop John and Read, George William, Letters of the Late Bishop England to the Hon. John Forsyth (Baltimore, J. Murphy & Co., 1844)

English, Richard, Irish Freedom: the History of Nationalism in Ireland (London, Macmillan, 2006)

Erickson, Rica and O'Mara, Gillian, Convicts in Western Australia 1850–1887, Dictionary of Western Australians, vol. IX (Perth, University of Western Australia Press, 1994)

Evans, A. G., Fanatic Heart: a Life of John Boyle O'Reilly, 1844–1890 (Perth, University of Western Australia Press, 1997)

Fanning, Charles, The Irish Voice in America: 250 Years of Irish-American Fiction (Lexington, KY, University Press of Kentucky, 2000)

Fennell, Philip A., 'History into Myth: The Catalpa's Long Voyage', New Hibernia Review, 9, 1 (Spring 2005)

— and King, Marie (eds), John Devoy's Catalpa Expedition (New York, New York University Press, 2006)

— and King, Marie (eds), Voyage of the Hougoumont and Life at Fremantle: the Story of an Irish Rebel (Bloomington, Indiana, Xlibris, 2000)

Ferreira, Patricia J., 'Frederick Douglass in Ireland: the Dublin Edition of his Narrative', New Hibernia Review, 5, 1 (Spring 2001)

Foner, Eric, Politics and Ideology in the Age of Civil War (Oxford, Oxford University Press, 1980)

Ford, Patrick, The Criminal History of the British Empire (New York, The Irish World, 1915)

Foster, R. F., Modern Ireland, 1600–1972 (London, Penguin Books, 1989)

— (ed.), The Oxford History of Ireland (Oxford, Oxford University Press, 1989)

Frawley, Sister Mary Alphonsine, Patrick Donahoe (Washington, DC, The Catholic University of America Press, 1946)

Galluzzo, John, The Golden Age of Hull (Stroud, The History Press, 2006)

George, Henry, Progress and Poverty (Elibro, 1955)

Golway, Terry, *Irish Rebel: John Devoy and America's Fight for Irish Freedom* (New York, St Martin's Press, 1998)

Grant, Donald Lee & Grant, Jonathan, *The Way it Was: the Black Experience in Georgia* (Athens, GA, University of Georgia Press, 2001)

Grant, Robert, *Fourscore: an Autobiography* (Boston, Houghton Mifflin & Co., 1934)

— and O'Reilly, John Boyle, Stimson, Frederic Jesup and Wheelright, John Tyler, *The King's Men: a Tale of Tomorrow* (New York, Charles Scribner's Sons, 1884)

Green, James J., 'American Catholics and the Irish Land League, 1879–1882', *The Catholic Historical Review*, 35, 1 (April 1849)

Handlin, Oscar, *Boston's Immigrants: A Study in Acculturation* (New York, Atheneum, 1969)

Hart-Davis, Rupert, *The Letters of Oscar Wilde* (New York, Harcourt Brace, 1962)

— *More Letters of Oscar Wilde* (New York, Vanguard Press, 1985)

Hernon, Ian, *Britain's Forgotten Wars: Colonial Campaigns of the 19th Century* (Stroud, Sutton Publishing, 2006)

Herrick, John Middlemist and Stuart, Paul H., *Encyclopedia of Social Welfare History in North America* (Thousand Oaks, CA, Sage, 2005)

Hoagland, Kathleen, *One Thousand Years of Irish Poetry* (New York, Devin-Adair, 1947)

Hobsbawm, Eric, *The Age of Capital: 1848–1875* (London, Abacus, 2004)

— *The Age of Empire: 1875–1914* (London, Abacus, 2004)

Hohman, Elmo Paul, *The American Whaleman: a Study of Life and Labor in the Whaling Industry* (New York, Longmans, Green & Co., 1928)

Hovey, William A., *Selected Poems of John Boyle O'Reilly* (San Francisco, Paul Elder & Co., 1904)

Hughes, Robert, *The Fatal Shore: a History of the Transportation of Convicts to Australia, 1787–1868* (London, Collins Harvill, 1987)

Ibson, John Duffy, *Will The World Break Your Heart? Dimensions and Consequences of Irish-American Assimilation* (New York, Garland Publishing, 1990)

Isenberg, Michael T., *John L. Sullivan and His America* (Urbana, University of Illinois Press, 1994)

Jacobson, Mathew Frye, *Special Sorrows: the Diasporic Imagination of Irish, Polish and Jewish Immigrants in the United States* (Berkeley, University of California Press, 2002)

Joyce, William Leonard, *Editors and Ethnicity: a History of the Irish-American Press, 1848–1883* (Arno Press, 1976)

Kane, Paula M., 'The Pulpit of the Hearthstone: Katherine Conway and Boston Catholic Women, 1900–1920', *US Catholic Historian*, 5, 3 (1986)

Kee, Robert, *The Green Flag, The Bold Fenian Men*, vol. 2 (London, Penguin Books, 1989)

Keneally, Thomas, *The Great Shame: a Story of the Irish in the Old World and the New* (London, Chatto & Windus, 1998)

Kenneally, Ian, *Courage and Conflict: Forgotten Stories of the Irish at War* (The Collins Press, 2009)

Kenneally, James J., 'Catholicism and Women Suffrage in Massachusetts', *The Catholic Historical Review*, 53, 1 (April 1967).

Kenny, Kevin, *Making Sense of the Molly Maguires* (Oxford, Oxford University Press, 1998)

Kinealy, Christine, *This Great Calamity: the Irish Famine, 1845–1852* (Dublin, Gill & McMillan, 2006)

Krieg, Joann P., *Whitman and the Irish* (Iowa City, University of Iowa Press, 2000)

Kummings, Donald D., *A Companion to Walt Whitman* (Malden, MA, Wiley-Blackwell, 2009)

Lane, Roger, 'James Jeffrey Roche and the Boston Pilot', *The New England Quarterly*, 33, 3 (September 1960)

Laubenstein, William J., *The Emerald Whaler* (London, André Deutsch, 1961)

Le Caron, Henri, *Twenty-Five Years in the Secret Service: Recollections of a Spy* (London, William Heinemann, 1892)

Lee, J. J., *The Modernisation of Irish Society: 1848–1918* (Dublin, Gill & Macmillan, 2008)

— and Casey, Marion R. (eds), *Making the Irish American: History and Heritage of the Irish in the United States* (New York, New York University Press, 2006)

Leiken, Steven Bernard, *The Practical Utopians: American Workers and the Cooperative movement in the Gilded Age* (Detroit, Wayne State University Press, 2005)

Lyons, F. S. L., *Charles Stewart Parnell* (London, Fontana Press, 1991)

Lyons, Louis Martin, *Newspaper Story: One Hundred Years of the Boston Globe* (Cambridge, Belknap Press, 1971)

Mann, Arthur, *Yankee Reformers in the Urban Age* (Chicago, University of Chicago Press, 1974)

Mayhew, Henry and Binny, John, *The Criminal Prisons of London and Scenes of Prison Life* (London, Griffin, Bohn & Co., 1862)

McConville, Seán, *Irish Political Prisoners, 1848–1922: Theatres of War* (Dublin, Routledge, 2003)

McGee, Owen, *The IRB: the Irish Republican Brotherhood from the Land League to Sinn Féin* (Dublin, Four Courts Press, 2005)

McGrath, Walter, 'Convict Ship Newspaper: *The Wild Goose* Re-discovered', *Journal of the Cork Historical and Archaeological Society*, LXXIV (1969)

McManamin, Francis G., *The American Years of John Boyle O'Reilly, 1870–1890* (New York, Arno Press, 1976)

Meagher, Timothy J., '"Irish All the Time:" Ethnic Consciousness among the Irish in Worcester, Massachusetts, 1880–1905', *Journal of Social History*, 19, 2 (Winter 1985)

Miller, Kerby, *Emigrants and Exiles: Ireland and the Irish Exodus to North America* (Oxford, Oxford University Press, 1985)

Millett, Mrs Edward, *An Australian Parsonage: or, the Settler and the Savage in Western Australia* (London, E. Stanford, 1872)

Mitchel, John, *Jail Journal; or Five years in British Prisons* (Dublin, J. Corrigan, 1864)

Mitchell, Edward Page, *Memoirs of an Editor: Fifty Years of American Journalism* (New York, C. Scribner's Sons, 1924)

Mixon, Harold D., 'Henry Grady as a Persuasive Strategist', in Waldo W. Braden, (ed.), *Oratory in the New South* (Baton Rouge, Louisiana State University Press, 1979)

Moody, T. W., *Davitt and the Irish Revolution, 1846–1882* (Oxford, Clarendon Press, 1981)

— 'Irish-American Nationalism', *Irish Historical Studies*, 15, 60 (September 1967)

— 'Michael Davitt in Penal Servitude', *An Irish Quarterly Review*, 30, 120 (December 1941)

Morgan, James, *The Life Work of Edward A. Moseley in the Service of Humanity* (Read Books, 2009)

Morse, John Torrey, *Life and Letters of Oliver Wendell Holmes*, vol. II (Boston, Houghton Mifflin & Co., 1896)

Moseley, Edward A., 'John Boyle O'Reilly, The Man', *Donahoe's Magazine*, 30, 3 (September 1893)

Moss, Kenneth, 'St. Patrick's Day Celebrations and the Formation of Irish-American Identity, 1845–1875', *Journal of Social History*, 29, 1 (Autumn 1995)

Moynihan, James H., *The Life of Archbishop John Ireland* (New York, Arno Press, 1976)

Munslow, Alun, 'The Decline of Ethnic Politics in Boston, 1882–1921', *Proceedings of the Massachusetts Historical Society*, ser. 3, 98 (1986)

Murdock, Harold, *Letters Describing the Great Fire of 1872* (Boston, Houghton Mifflin & Co., 1909)

Murray, John O'Kane, *A Popular History of the Catholic Church in the United States* (New York, D & J Sadlier & Company, 1876)

Newland, James, *Crispus Attucks: Patriot* (Los Angeles, Holloway House Publishing, 1995)

Ó Broin, Leon, *Fenian Fever: an Anglo-American Dilemma* (London, Chatto & Windus, 1971)

O'Connor, Thomas H., *The Boston Irish: A Political History* (Old Saybrook, CT, Konecky & Konecky, 1995)

O'Donnell, P. D., 'Dublin Military Barracks', *Dublin Historical Record*, 25, 4 (September 1972)

O'Grady, Joseph P., *Irish-Americans and Anglo-American Relations, 1880–1888* (Manchester, NH, Ayer Publishing, 1876)

O'Higgins, Brian, 'John Boyle O'Reilly – Glimpses of his Boyhood', *Donahoe's Magazine*, LIV (August 1905)

O'Leary, John, *The Writings of James Fintan Lalor* (Dublin, T. G. O'Donoghue, 1895)

Ó Lúing, Seán, *Fremantle Mission* (Tralee, Anvil Books, 1965)

Pease, Zephania W., *The Catalpa Expedition* (New Bedford, MA, G. S. Anthony, 1897)

O'Reilly, John Boyle, *Ethics of Boxing and Manly Sport* (Boston, Tickner & Co., 1888)

— *In Bohemia* (New York, Cashman, Keating & Co., 1886)

—*Moondyne* (facs. edn, Gloucester, Dodo Press, 2006)

— *Songs from the Southern Seas and Other Poems* (Boston, Roberts Brothers, 1873)

— *Songs, Legends and Ballads* (Jackson, Massachusetts, The Pilot Publishing Company, 1882)

— *The Statues in the Block and Other Poems* (Boston, Roberts Brothers, 1884)

— (ed.), *The Poetry and Song of Ireland* (New York, Gay Brothers & Co., 1887)

— 'At Last', *North American Review*, 142, 350 (January 1886)

— 'The Coercion Bill', *The North American Review*, 144, 366 (May 1887)

— 'Ireland's Opportunity – Will it be Lost?', *American Catholic Quarterly Review*, 7 (January 1882)

— 'What has Ireland gained by Agitation?', *American Catholic Quarterly Review*, 8 (October 1883)

Pettifer, Ernest W., *Punishments of Former Days* (Bradford, Clegg & Son, 1939)

Plunkett, George Noble, 'Recollections of John Boyle O'Reilly', *The Irish Monthly*, 19, 211 (January 1891)

Potter, Simon J. (ed.), *Newspapers and Empire in Ireland and Britain* (Dublin, Four Courts Press, 2004)

Reilly, J. T., *Reminiscences of Fifty Years in Western Australia* (Melbourne, Sands & McDougall, 1903)

Roche, James Jeffrey, *Life of John Boyle O'Reilly: Together with his Complete Poems and Speeches* (Philadelphia, John J. McVey, 1891)

Rodechko, James Paul, *Patrick Ford and his Search for America: A Case Study of Irish-American Journalism, 1870–1913* (New York, Arno Press, 1976)

Roth, Mitchel P., *Prisons and Prison Systems: a Global Encyclopedia* (Santa Barbara, Greenwood Press, 2006)

Russell, Francis, *The Knave of Boston: & other Ambiguous Massachusetts Characters* (Boston, Quinlan Press, 1987)

Rutherford, John, *The Secret History of the Fenian Conspiracy: its Origins, Objects & Ramifications* (London, C. Kegan Paul & Co., 1877)

Ryan, Dennis P., *Beyond the Ballot Box: a Social History of the Boston Irish, 1845–1917* (Amherst, MA, University of Massachusetts Press, 1989)

Ryan, Desmond, *The Fenian Chief: a Biography of James Stephens* (Dublin, Gill & Son, 1967)

Sammarco, Anthony Mitchell, *The Great Fire of 1872* (Mount Pleasant, SC, Arcadia Publishing, 1997)

Schofield, William G., *Seek for a Hero* (New York, Kenedy & Sons, 1956)

Shankman, Arnold, 'Black on Green: Afro-American Editors on Irish Independence, 1840–1921', *Phylon*, vol. 41, 3 (1980)

Shanley, Kevin T., 'John Boyle O'Reilly and Civil Rights', *Éire-Ireland*, 4, 3 (1969)

Shannon, James P., *Catholic Colonization on the Western Frontier* (New Haven, Yale University Press, 1957)

Shannon, William V., *The American Irish: a Political and Social Portrait* (Amherst, MA, University of Massachusetts Press, 1989)

Shaw, A. G. L., *Convicts and the Colonies* (Dublin, The Irish Historical Press, 1998)

Simonds, Arthur Beaman, *American Song* (Charleston, BiblioBazaar, 2008)

Spalding, John Lancaster, *The Religious Mission of the Irish* (Manchester, NH, Ayer Publishing, 1978)

Stephenson, P. J., 'Hidden and Vanishing Dublin: II – Fenian Dublin, 1865–1867', *Dublin Historical Record*, 1, 4 (March 1939)

Stevens, Peter, *The Voyage of the Catalpa* (London, Weidenfeld & Nicolson, 2003)

Steward, Patrick, *Erin's Hope: Fenianism in the North Atlantic, 1858–1876* (University of Missouri, unpublished PhD thesis, 2003)

Stoddard, Richard Henry and Gilman, Arthur, *Poets' Homes: Pen and Pencil Sketches of American Poets and their Homes* (Boston, D. Lothrop Company, 1879)

Stout, Geraldine, *Newgrange and the Bend of the Boyne* (Cork, Cork University Press, 2002)

Sullivan III, C. W., *Fenian Diary: Denis Cashman on Board the* Hougoumont (Dublin, Wolfhound Press, 2001)

Tagakami, Shin-Ichi, 'The Fenian Rising in Dublin, March 1867', *Irish Historical Studies*, 29, 115 (May 1995)

Tager, Jack and Ifkovic, John W. (eds), *Massachusetts in the Gilded Age: Selected Essays* (Amherst, MA, University of Massachusetts Press, 1985)

Thomson, Basil, *The Story of Dartmoor Prison* (London, William Heinemann, 1907)

— *The Story of Scotland Yard* (London, The Country Press, 1935)

Traubel, Horace, *With Walt Whitman in Camden*, vol. 1 (New York, The Century Company, 1906)

— *With Walt Whitman in Camden*, vol. 2 (New York, The Century Company, 1908)

— *With Walt Whitman in Camden*, vol. 7 (Carbondale, IL, Southern Illinois University Press, 1992)

Travers, Pauric, *Settlements and Divisions: Ireland 1870–1922* (Dublin, Helicon, 1988)

Trexler, Sister Margaret Ellen, 'American Catholics and Negroes', *Phylon*, 30, 4 (1969)

Walsh, Francis Robert, *The Boston Pilot: A Newspaper for the Irish Immigrant, 1829–1908* (Boston University, unpublished PhD thesis, 1968)

— 'John Boyle O'Reilly, The Boston Pilot, and Irish-American Assimilation, 1870–1890', in Jack Tager and John W. Ifkovic, *Massachusetts in the Gilded Age: Selected Essays* (Amherst, MA, University of Massachusetts Press, 1985)

Waters, Ormonde D. P., 'John Boyle O'Reilly', *Seanchas Ardmhacha: Journal of the Armagh Diocesan Historical Society*, 13, 1 (1988)

— 'John Boyle O'Reilly and the Catalpa Ballad', *Records of Meath Archaeological and Historical Society*, 4, 5 (1971)

Whelehan, Niall, 'Skirmishing, The Irish World and Empire, 1876–1886', *Éire-Ireland*, 42, 1 & 2 (Spring/Summer 2007)

Williams, Alexander Whiteside, *A Social History of the Greater Boston Clubs* (Barre, MA, Barre Publishers, 1970)

Index